DRAWING PEOPLE

Paul Hogarth

DRAWING PEOPLE

WATSON-GUPTILL PUBLICATIONS / NEW YORK

"Fear is the greatest friend an artist has; without it, you get careless. You can't be creative unless you're afraid."

Anthony Quinn,
interviewed by Mary Simons
in Look, *April, 1969*

Published 1971 in New York by Watson-Guptill Publications,
a division of Billboard Publications, Inc.,
165 West 46th Street, New York, N.Y.

International Standard Book Number 0-8230-1425-8
Library of Congress Catalog Card Number: 73-125850

Acknowledgments

This book grew out of Watson-Guptill editor Donald Holden's firm conviction that my best drawings are of people; and as I did not contradict him, I have only myself to blame, as I find myself writing about how I draw them! Once again, special thanks are due to his continuing confidence in my ability to write about my work and about the various problems I come up against.

I should also like to thank the following publishers and editors, whose courteous cooperation has made this book a reality: the editors of *Lithopinion* and Local One, Amalgamated Lithographers of America, New York; the editors of *Boy's Life* magazine, New York; Cassell and Co., London; Dennis Dobson Ltd., London; Doubleday and Co., New York; the editors of *Daily Telegraph Magazine,* London; Bernard Geis Associates, London; Hill & Wang, Inc., New York; The Hutchinson Publishing Group, London; Lawrence and Wishart, London; Thomas Nelson and Co., New York; Penguin Books, London; the editors of *Fortune, Sports Illustrated, Life,* and Time-Life Books, New York; The Shelbourne Hotel, Dublin; Studio Vista Ltd., London; the editors of *The Lamp* and the Standard Oil Company, New Jersey; the Strathmore Paper Company, West Springfield, Massachusetts, the editors of *Psychiatric Reporter*; Smith, Kline and French Laboratories, Philadelphia; and Wydawnictwo Artystczno-Graficzne, Warsaw; all of whom have generously allowed the publisher to include drawings of mine which they either own or have publication rights to.

For friendly assistance in the loan of photographs, proofs, or originals, I should like to personally thank the following: John Anstey, editor of *Daily Telegraph Magazine,* London; Walter Allner, art director of *Fortune*; Dr. Louis Castor, Philadelphia; Harry Diamond, art director of *The Lamp;* Desmond Flower, literary director, Cassell and Co.; Germano Facetti, art director, Penguin Books and consultant art director, British Publishing Corporation; Richard Gangel, art director, *Sports Illustrated*; Robert Hallock, art director, *Lithopinion*; Diana Klemin, art editor, Doubleday and Co.; Mill Roseman, the Lampert Agency, New York; and my good friend the artist, William A. Smith, Pineville, Pennsylvania, for his impressive photograph of myself.

I would also like to gratefully acknowledge permission of the owners to reproduce copyrighted works not in my possession, or works not in the possession of the publisher or of a magazine.

Paul Hogarth
Cambridge, England
February, 1970

OTHER BOOKS BY PAUL HOGARTH

Artist as Reporter

Brendan Behan's Island: An Irish Sketchbook (with Brendan Behan)

Brendan Behan's New York (with Brendan Behan)

Creative Ink Drawing

Creative Pencil Drawing

Defiant People

Drawings from Poland

London à la Mode (with Malcolm Muggeridge)

Looking at China

Majorca Observed (with Robert Graves)

Paul Hogarth's American Album (soon to be released)

A Russian Journey: from Suzdal to Samarkand (with Alaric Jacob)

Sons of Adam: A South African Sketchbook (known in Great Britain as *People Like Us*)

Contents

Introduction

MUCH OF MY interest in drawing springs from a strong desire to communicate—that is, from a compelling need to comment on human beings in all their strengths and frailties. The richness and variety of the subject make people the most rewarding sphere of drawing; the artist has an immediate audience. Who can resist the fascination of seeing himself emblemized as a solid citizen, pilloried as an enemy of the people, or included as a passing figure in a hasty sketch?

Drawing people is also the most challenging sphere in which to work. Whether your feeling about your subject is positive or negative, drawing people does demand that the artist make a greater effort. To express any superior understanding he may have of human nature in tangible, pictorial terms, the artist must come out of his shell. And he must work without necessarily complying with requests for faithful and literal representation.

Some artists acquire this facility remarkably early, but I would be the first to admit that it came rather late to me. As an art student, I was not overly involved with other people. Instead, I was obsessed with the spell of great literature and a commitment to philosophical and political ideas. After reading Donne, Thoreau, Dickens, Dostoevsky, and Poe, I would gaze out on a world that, by comparison, seemed composed of ciphers and spirits, rather than living flesh and blood creatures. Yet my attraction to these writers and their innate humanism itself indicated my own interest in people, even though I as yet lacked any real awareness or understanding of others.

As I gained this awareness and understanding, I began to feel that no artist could or should neglect the study of the human form. But the musty atmosphere and frustrating conventions of academic life drawing classes conspired over and over again to destroy my enthusiasm. Only when I left art school days behind did my attitude begin to change. Then, direct involvement with the human experience—whether congenial or repellent—revived my latent desire to observe people and to express those observations in a way that would be uniquely my own.

This interest in people, however, preceded any definite idea of how I would actually draw them, how I would achieve this vehicle for expression. It took a great deal of time, wandering, and self-study before I could draw people the way I wanted to. One satisfaction kept me going: the more I worked at the problem of drawing people, the more vital and rich my attitude toward drawing became. I discovered, too, that drawing people—whatever their shape, color, or size—required a resourceful repertoire of techniques. And so I began a series of explorations into the potentials of different media to enable me to build up this repertoire through the filter of my restless and changing personality.

Though the ability to draw people did not come easily to me, with constant and continual observation it did come. Appreciation was immediate. The capacity to draw people, which is really a sophisticated form of understanding human nature, is a highly regarded talent. Once you acquire this facility, you will be sought after by art directors of magazines, publishing houses, and advertising agencies, as well as by private patrons.

My previous books, *Creative Pencil Drawing* and *Creative Ink Drawing,* focus on my technical explorations in those media. While specific techniques are summarized where they arise, *Drawing People* concentrates on the problems involved in tackling the specific subject of man himself.

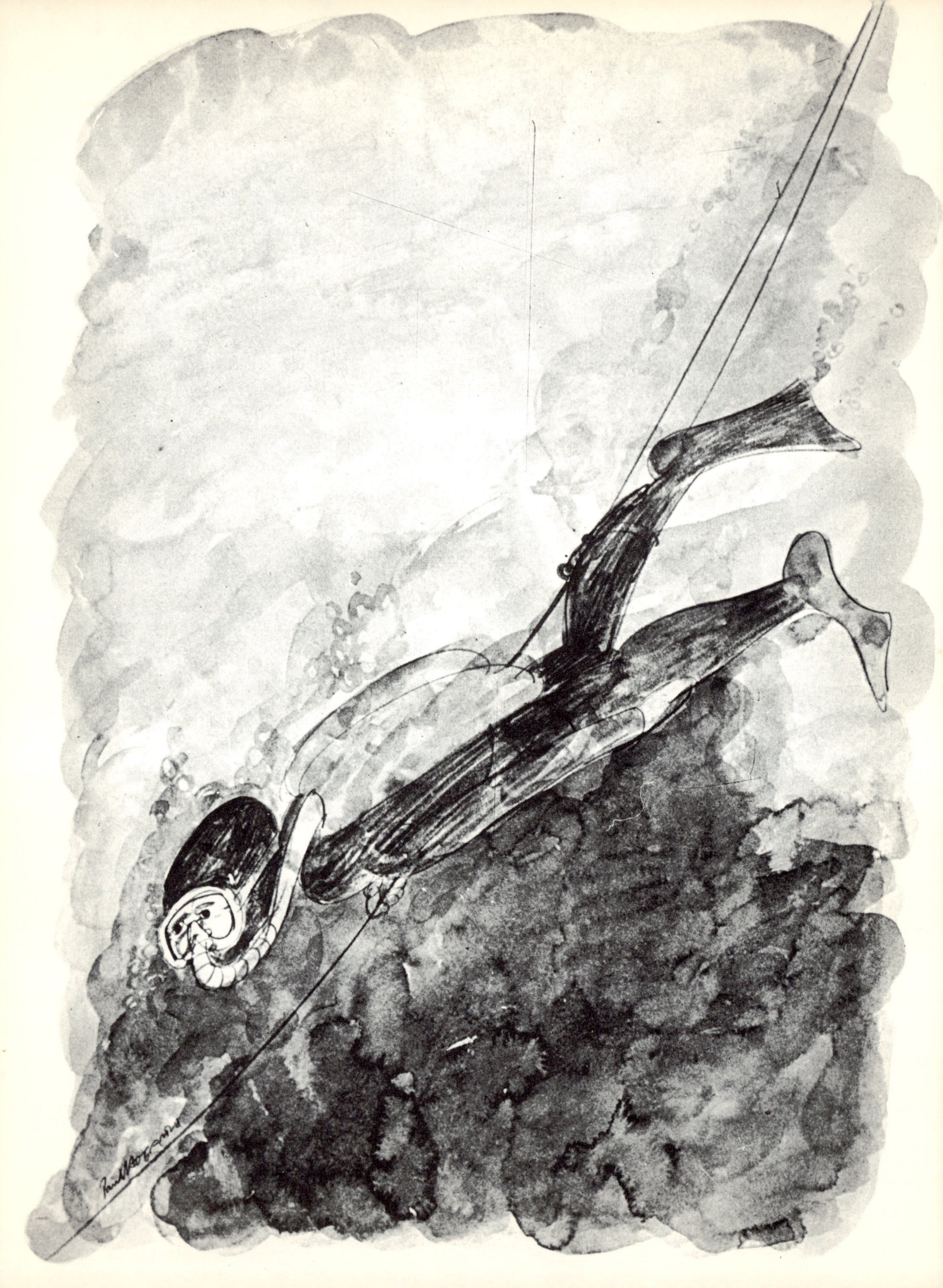

CHAPTER 1

Tools and Materials

DRAWING PEOPLE, moving or at rest, requires a variety of tools and materials. These may range from graphite pencils or charcoal leads—suitable for working in sketchbooks on location and for drawing on sheets of paper in the studio—to inks, colored markers, and watercolors, suitable for drawing on boards and papers as you work from memory or imagination for reproduction in a magazine or book. Usually, the problem of what medium to use and what equipment to carry can be resolved by considering how much time you have and where you will be working, as well as whether your drawing is for yourself, for an individual client, or for publication.

Wherever and whatever you draw, try to acquire the habit of using the right type of pencil, pen, brush, or marker for the appropriate paper. Cultivating an awareness of tools and materials, plus an appreciation of their esthetic relationship to each other, is essential to your development as an artist. However, it is not a guarantee. Despite all my experience, I occasionally run into trouble. I am sometimes tempted to try out new tools and materials at the wrong moment. This tendency can, at times, make for some painfully embarrassing interludes that I always vow not to repeat! I recall, for instance, the misery of trying to work with unsuitable tools and materials under the gaze of an important sitter! I suggest you avoid similar self-inflicted torment by confining any experiments you wish to make to life drawing class or to your studio.

Skin diver, North Sea, England, 1968
A diver goes down to check installation of the submarine pipeline through which natural gas will flow into Britain's national grid. Re-drawn (from sketches made from a floating platform) on smooth surface Hollingworth Kent Mill drawing paper. A Faber 702 sketching pencil was used to draw the figure and line. Mixtures of Grumbacher green and yellow watercolors were applied with a Japanese brush. Courtesy The Lamp. *Copyright 1968 by Standard Oil Company, New Jersey.*

The other extreme is a neurotic dependence on a trusted combination of tools and materials you know will *always* work. The danger here is that you will fall into a rut and impede the development of your drawing. You will have to take chances, but before you do, get to know your tools and materials well. Familiarize yourself with their potentials and idiosyncrasies. Stay with the tools and materials you feel comfortable with—but not for *too* long.

BEGIN SIMPLY

Postpone working with mixed media until you have gained a fair amount of practice and experience with pencil and paper. I say this because your primary concern should be to acquire the facility to draw people on a variety of occasions and under different circumstances. Therefore, you should restrict your choice of tools and materials to the simplest combination—nothing more than a sketchbook and a 6B graphite pencil or fiber tip pen—so that you can effectively concentrate on observing, and developing an acute sense of, facial expression and body movement.

PENCILS

My choice of a pencil depends as much on my state of mind as it does on the subject I propose to draw. Some days I feel like drawing with a heavy black line, other days I prefer to strive for a delicate effect. To anticipate my switches of mood, I always carry a whole batch of graphite pencils, differing widely in softness and size. This choice of pencils enables me to achieve maximum variety of line, which is particularly desirable if I do not use color. With, say, a 3B pencil, I can define my rendering much more precisely than with a 6B.

One firm favorite in the last year or so has been the German Faber 702. Outsize in diameter (Russian children call it the "big" pencil), it is almost ½" thick. Nevertheless, the 702 is a versatile and lustrously soft graphite pencil that performs superbly on almost any kind of paper. It is, however, a difficult pencil to sharpen without a good sharp-bladed knife; so always carry either a Stanley 5900 or an X-acto knife, plus a spare packet of blades.

Almost as good as the 702 is the American Veriblack 315. Among other soft black graphite pencils, I regularly use the American Venus and British Royal Sovereign pencils, 3B through 7B, in the standard size.

Conté charcoal leads and Hardtmuth charcoal crayons are also fine tools for drawing people. Both are especially suitable for figure and portrait drawing, but only if used on the right kind of paper. The Conté *Pierre Noir* leads are particularly suitable for vigorous drawing with contrast, where I need definition as much as emphasis. Hardtmuth crayons, on the other hand, are much more suitable for broader, looser drawings, and so are best when thick and soft. They are graded medium, soft, and extra soft.

It is advisable to place them in a holder, preferably the hexagonal or milled type which allows a firm, non-slip grip. They are the modern equivalent of the traditional charcoal stick, but easier and more reliable to use. The traditional stick of natural charcoal tends to break unexpectedly under the strain of vigorous or rapid drawing. The newer leads, even though almost as fragile, rarely break if used in push-action holders.

Charcoal pencils possess the same virtues as charcoal leads, but are perhaps less inhibiting to use if you prefer the feel of a pencil to that of an instrument. They are suitable for every type of figure and portrait drawing. I use them, however, mostly on location. Conté and Hardtmuth make the best charcoal pencils, but Eagle's Charco and Blaisdell's pull-thread, self-sharpening types are also highly recommended.

If you use soft graphite or charcoal pencils, you will have to spray fixative on your drawings to avoid smudging; and the sooner you do this, the better. I usually rely on Eagle or Krylon workable fixative in a spray can because they are convenient and more efficient than bottle and mouth spray fixatives.

PENS

A pen and ink drawing usually requires a little more time than a pencil drawing. Because this medium does not lend itself so easily to correction, pen and ink also obliges you to have a clear idea of what you are aiming for. I would not, for example, make a pen and ink portrait of someone whose face was totally unfamiliar to me. On the other hand, I would not hesitate to use pen and ink to draw a crowd of unfamiliar people in the foreground of a city street. Portrait drawing, always a little unnerving, encourages you to perform in a medium you feel sure of controlling.

My choice of a pen nearly always centers on a group of tough, resilient school nibs, of which the No. 5 Spencerian is, for my purpose, a good one. It usually gives me a strong basic line. If I need something extra, or more than one thickness, or a loose and spidery line, I indulge myself with fine, flexible artists' nibs like a Gillot 290 or 303, or an Esterbrook 355 or 357. Whichever I select, I make sure to place it in a good holder. A spindly penholder invariably cramps the fingers; when this happens, a line can go terribly wrong. Be sure to get a penholder that feels much the same in your hand as your favorite fountain pen or ballpoint pen.

Fountain pens are now as good for continuous drawing as they are for writing. The tough yet inexpensive Esterbrook pen stands up best of all to the vigorous pressures of my drawing; but I have also used Parker and Sheaffer fountain pens, which I also highly recommend. Before you buy a pen, try out the nib. This is the part of the pen which most often influences the way you will draw.

Ballpoints and fiber tip pens, of course, are also useful for drawing rapidly and continuously in a small sketchbook. An added advantage is that you can carry such pens in your pocket without fear of jabbing your fingers or staining your clothes. Buy the best you can afford. A good ballpoint is worth the extra cost for the fluid, expressive line it produces. I find it such a worthy tool that I often use a quality ballpoint for larger and more finished drawings, as well as for sketches.

BRUSHES

I personally prefer an Oriental brush for black and white work. Pointed Japanese or Chinese brushes are made from the hair of a wide variety of animals. They are inexpensive and stand up to a great deal of punishment from every kind of drawing ink. I can get a fine line by using the point, and a thicker one simply by increasing the downward pressure on the brush.

If I work in color, however, I use good watercolor brushes like the Winsor & Newton sables, available in many sizes, from 00 to 10. I generally use just Nos. 0, 5, and 9. Whatever brushes you prefer, look after them. Never forget to wash them out in warm, soapy water as soon as possible after use.

INKS

Most drawing inks for artists are sold in two varieties: waterproof, which (after it has completely dried) will stand up to washes of watercolor, marker strokes, or diluted washes of the same ink; and soluble, which may be washed away with water, a clean brush, and blotting paper. Both waterproof and soluble inks may be freely diluted with water. The best waterproof inks are the India inks made by Higgins, Reeves, Winsor

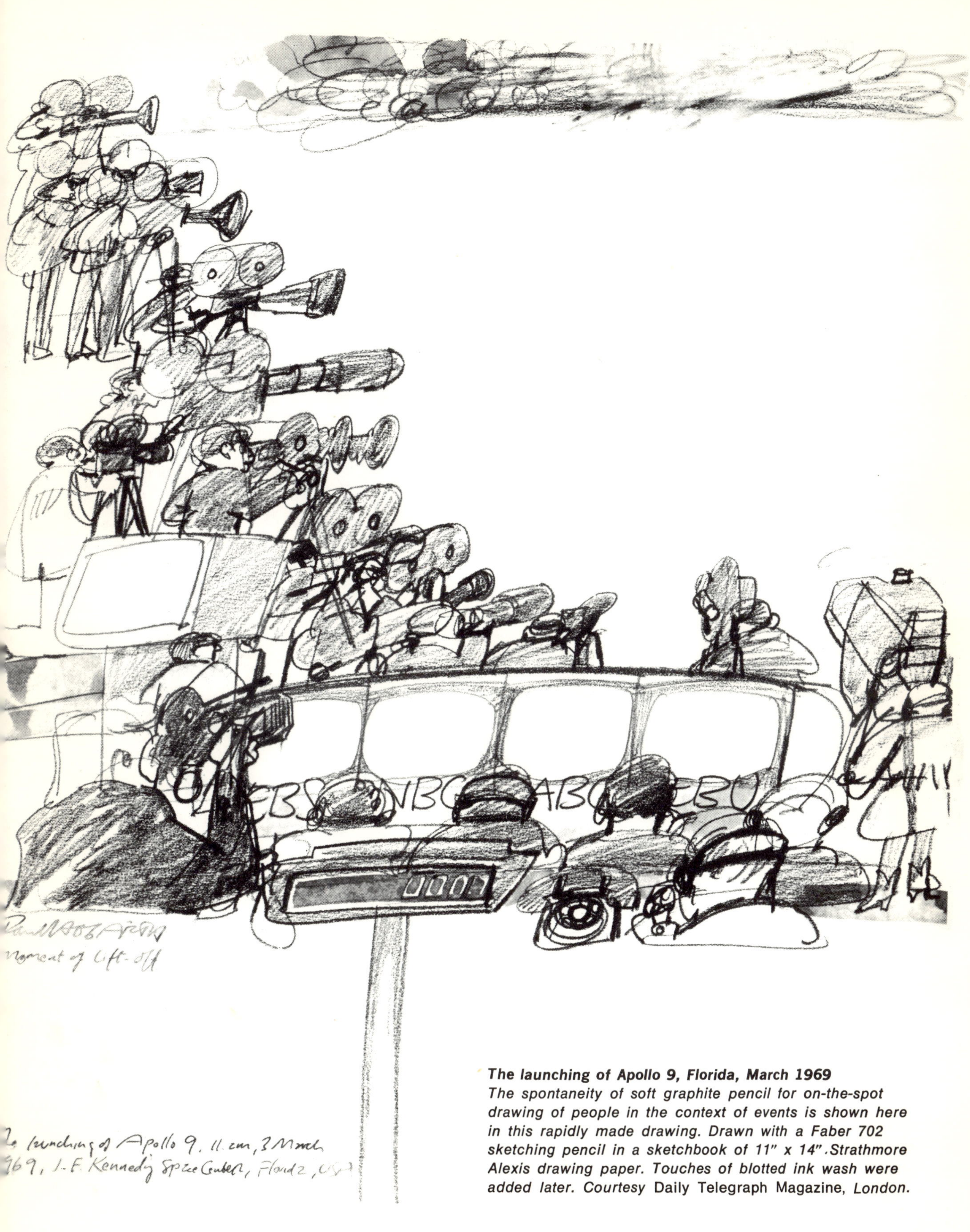

The launching of Apollo 9, Florida, March 1969
The spontaneity of soft graphite pencil for on-the-spot drawing of people in the context of events is shown here in this rapidly made drawing. Drawn with a Faber 702 sketching pencil in a sketchbook of 11" x 14" Strathmore Alexis drawing paper. Touches of blotted ink wash were added later. Courtesy Daily Telegraph Magazine, *London.*

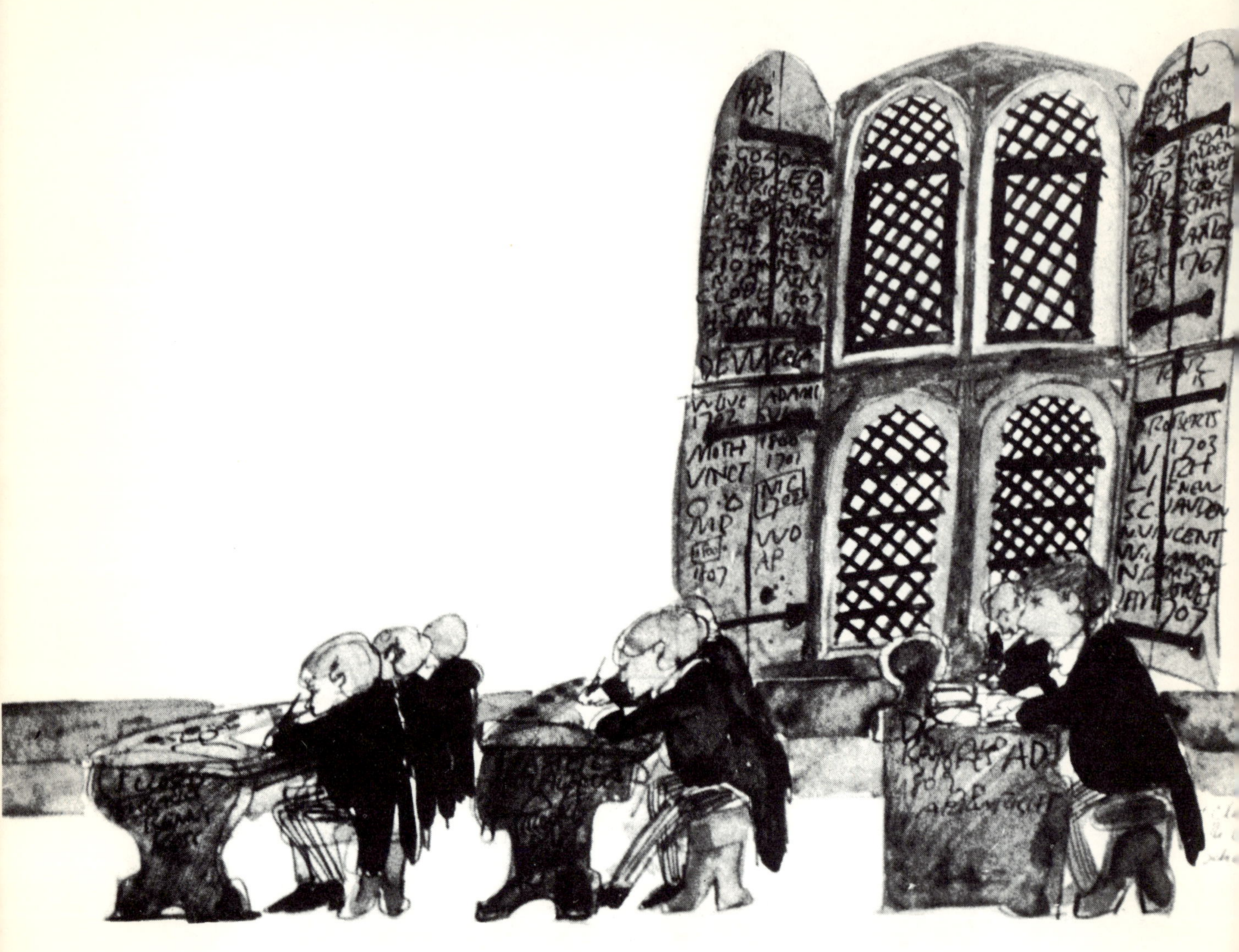

Boys at "prep," Lower School, Eton College, England, 1968
This glimpse of English private school life was made with a combination of pen, pencil, and ink wash. First, an outline drawing was made with a 6B Venus graphite pencil, then diluted washes of Higgins India ink were laid with a Japanese brush, blotted, and allowed to dry thoroughly. Details, such as the boys' clothes, were painted in with undiluted ink. Windowpanes and graffiti left by generations of boys on window shutters and desk were then drawn in with Spencerian and Gillot 303 nibs. 11" x 14" sketchbook of medium surface Strathmore drawing paper. Courtesy Boy's Life *magazine. Reproduced by special permission.*

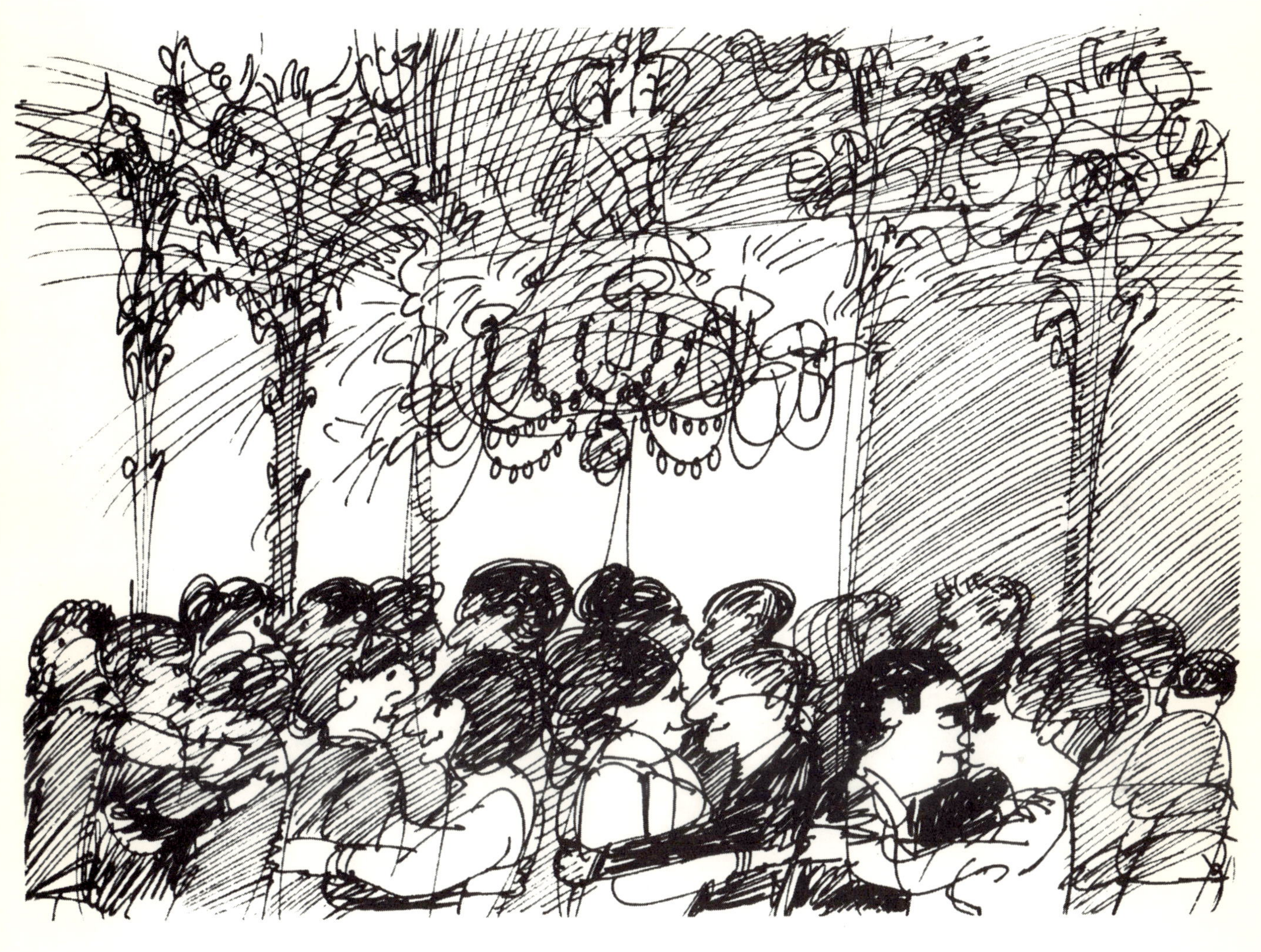

Saturday night at the Hotel Berlin, Moscow, 1967
A fountain pen and a pocket sketchbook is all I take along to make informal sketches, such as this scene of Russian nightlife. Drawn with a regular Esterbrook fountain pen in a 5" x 7" English Planet sketchbook of smooth drawing paper. From A Russian Journey: from Suzdal to Samarkand, *1969. Courtesy Cassell and Company, London; and Hill & Wang, Inc., New York.*

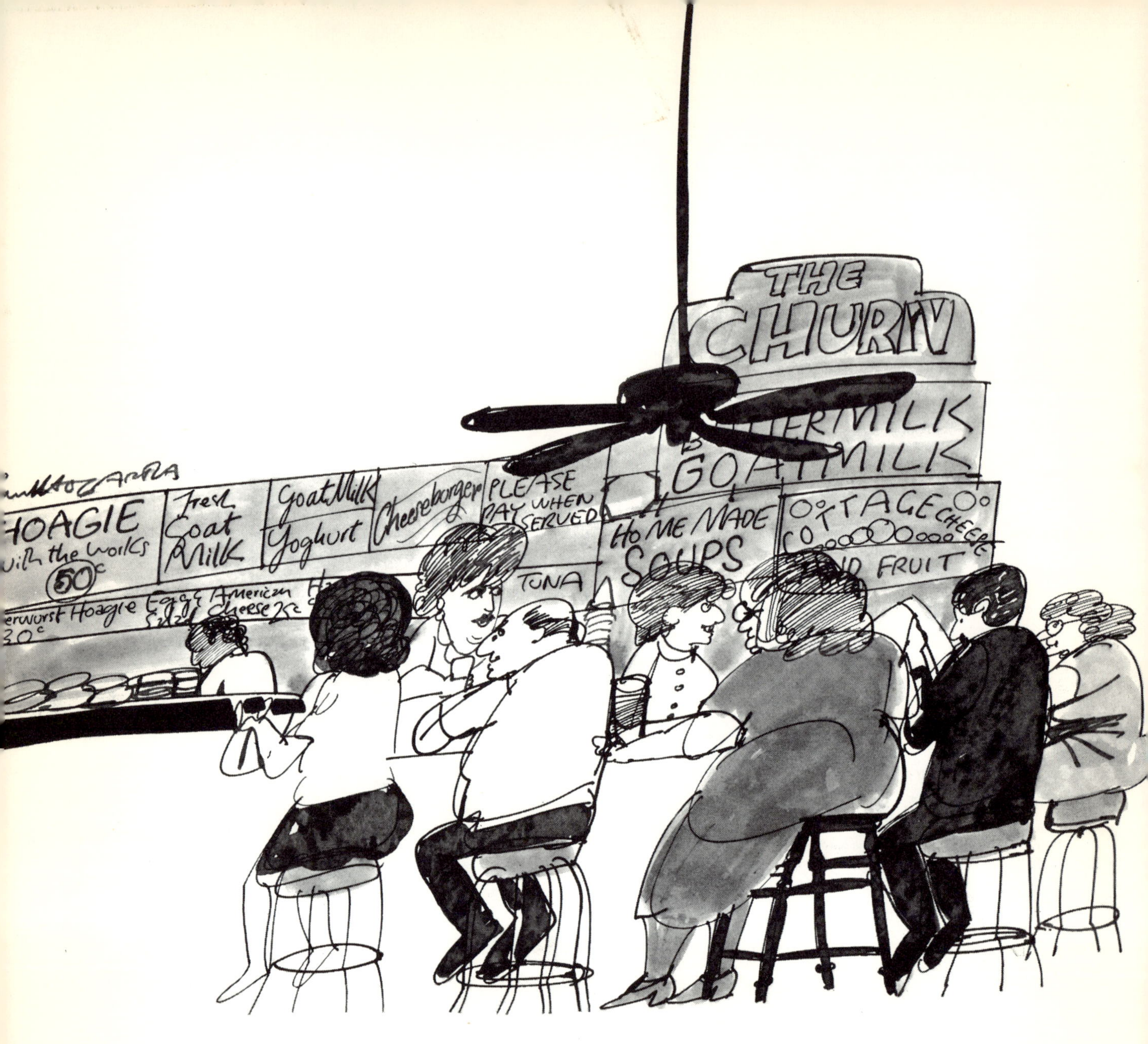

Luncheon counter at the Reading Terminal Market, Philadelphia, 1968

A pen and a brush dipped in a good fluid black ink are particularly suitable for crisp delineation of people. A smooth paper is preferable, but not essential. Here, I used one-ply, high surface Strathmore drawing paper in an 11" x 14" sketchbook. Pelikan Fount India was the ink used with an Esterbrook 357 nib and a Japanese brush.

& Newton, and Pelikan. I also recommend such excellent soluble drawing inks as Sheaffer Skrip and Higgins Eternal. Something of a cross between the two, Pelikan Fount India is a fairly waterproof ink designed for use in fountain pens.

I use the heavier waterproof inks whenever I intend to use a wash or watercolor over it, and do not want the original ink drawing to lose any of its strength or incisiveness. I use soluble inks to achieve the opposite effect. Soluble inks have an advantage over waterproof inks for painting in textural backgrounds or details of a sitter's clothes, because they can be readily diluted and reduced if the rest of the drawing needs greater emphasis. My procedure is to continually apply washes of clean, lukewarm water with a No. 10 brush, firmly blotting each application before cleaning the brush to apply the next wash.

MARKERS

During the past two years, I have become such a marker addict that I now use this tool for all kinds of assignments. An extraordinary variety of markers is now made in a wide range of permanent as well as washable colors, and with many different points and tips. With markers, it is possible to achieve the most subtle color and line combinations.

Broadly, markers come in two main types, fiber tip and felt tip, each of which is available with different points. Fiber tip markers usually have fine points and are, therefore, ideal for making incisive, detailed drawings on location. Because their colors so closely approximate artists' colors and because their tips last longer, I find the best fiber tip markers to be: the Japanese Pentel-D, available in red, blue, and black, in small and large sizes; the German Faber-Castell Presto, also available in the three basic colors; and the Esterbrook Color Pen, in eight colors.

The one that tops them all, however, is the Fine Point Studio Magic Marker Watercolor liner, which is available in three different sets of colors—twelve basic, twelve complementary, and twelve combination grays. Set 873 contains all thirty-six colors, fitted into a rotating table. Included in the package are several extra points to replace those that wear out or thicken with use.

Because I am always working against the clock, felt tip markers have revolutionized my attitude toward using color. Markers offer an extra fast way to add instant-drying color to big drawings that I would not otherwise have time to complete on the spot. I constantly use markers to fill in large areas or shapes, then immediately work over the color in graphite pencil or ink. I also combine the two different types of markers in a single drawing—for example, I use the fiber tip Fine Point Studio Magic Marker to delineate, and the large felt tip Studio Magic Marker to fill in. In fact, the more I use markers, the more ideas I develop for working with them.

Avoid the cheap markers that are made primarily for office purposes. The colors are crude and the inks penetrate almost any kind of paper. Seemingly more expensive, felt tip Studio Magic Marker liners and Faber Design Markettes are actually more economical because they are smear-proof, longer lasting, and much more reliable.

Although similar in quality, Markers and Markettes differ in appearance. The Markers, which are available in a number of colors, come in small, bottle-like containers that have a wide chisel tip. I prefer to work with the Markettes which, because of their elongated shape, can be held like a thick pen or pencil. They are available with a wide chisel tip, in seventy-two colors, or with a pointed tip, in twenty-four colors.

WATERCOLORS

Watercolors are, of course, essential in the studio; but I also slip a small box of watercolors in my bag, just in case they may be needed elsewhere. I find watercolors useful for developing an unfinished location sketch into a more elaborate drawing later, perhaps in the calm of a hotel room; or to augment my use of markers on location with a wash or two of transparent color.

These watercolors need not be expensive artists' quality. I find Grumbacher or Winsor & Newton regular quality colors entirely satisfactory. When space is really tight, I carry instead a 4″ x 6½″ aluminum box of German Marubu watercolors. These inexpensive yet brilliant colors come in circular pans of such good size that you can get a big brush into them without difficulty. The permanence of regular quality watercolors, however, cannot always be relied on. If I have an exhibit in mind which will expose my paintings to light, I use artists' quality watercolors to guarantee permanency.

PAPERS

Whether pen or pencil, all drawing media work best on the papers originally designed for them. Soft graphite pencils like the Faber 702 or the Veriblack 315 are the only exceptions to this general rule. They seem to work well on a wide range of papers which includes Bristol board, layout paper, and tracing paper. Nevertheless, they are at their best on good quality drawing paper (called "cartridge" in Great Britain) such as Strathmore or Hollingworth Kent Mill. Good quality drawing paper can readily be identified by its white color and closely grained texture. On such a paper even an HB graphite pencil or a pen will leave a lively, vigorous line. On an off-white, coarser grained drawing paper of poor quality, pen-

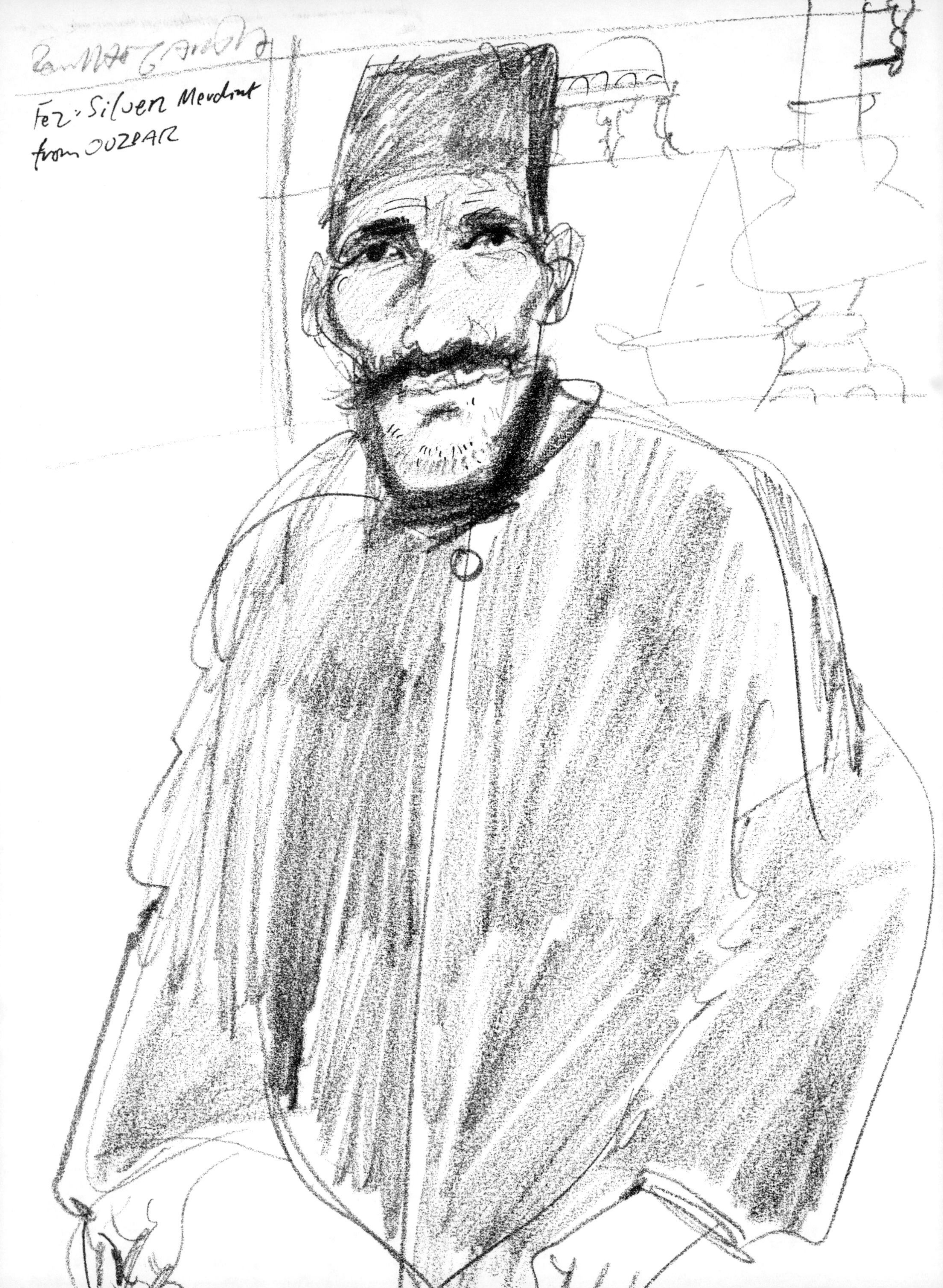
Fez: Silver Merchant
from OUZBAR

cils and pens behave unpredictably; they may sometimes be effective, but are usually not.

Charcoal pencils or Conté leads also work well on versatile Strathmore and Hollingworth Kent Mill; but they, too, are most at home on the papers made for them—the textured, laid papers, with their finely ribbed surface of parallel lines, like Strathmore Charcoal and French or Italian Ingres papers. Strathmore and Ingres papers are made in colors, and can be obtained both in single sheets and in sketchbook form.

Although inks of every kind work well on Strathmore and Hollingworth Kent Mill drawing papers, an ink line has a much more written quality on the supersmooth surface of Bristol board. Felt tip and, to a lesser extent, fiber tip pens pose a different problem. Even though they have been perfected, the chief danger to their indiscriminate use is that they will unexpectedly bleed on papers of poor quality. The only way to avoid this undesirable spreading effect is to use high quality drawing paper or Bristol board.

Watercolor by itself, or mixed media involving the use of watercolor, markers, graphite pencil, and ink, require paper of a good and reliable quality. Each medium must work satisfactorily with the other; on poor quality paper, watercolor is seldom effective over areas or shapes drawn in with markers. Watercolor dries unevenly on their weaker fibers, with the result that pencil or pen work is usually unsatisfying. Indeed, there is often the danger of breaking through the weakened fibers even when the watercolor wash has dried. Again, versatile Strathmore and Hollingworth Kent Mill drawing paper fulfill their task admirably, as does Strathmore Bristol board.

SKETCHBOOKS

When drawing people on location, I usually prefer to work in sketchbooks, because they are easily carried in hand or pocket. The size I use varies according to subject and location. For instance, when a certain amount of discretion is necessary, I work small, in a 5″ x 7″ pocket size sketchbook of good drawing paper. This size enables me to delineate the action or features of performers and spectators in burlesque shows, theaters, cabarets, and clubs without attracting undue attention. I also carry a smaller (3½″ x 5″) sketchbook of thin bank paper (a smooth, transparent, lightweight stock) on which I scribble notes, details, and ideas with a fountain, ballpoint, or fiber tip pen, or with simply a pencil.

For making either complete figures or portrait drawings in bars, on beaches, or in any public place where there is no objection to the lone artist at work, I use an 11″ x 14″ spiral-bound sketchbook. For street scenes or architectural subjects, where I really do need extra space, I use larger sketchbooks.

Silver merchant, Fez, Morocco, 1966
To avoid attracting too much attention, on-the-spot portrait sketches in the street markets of Africa and Asia are best made in a small sketchbook. This was drawn in fifteen minutes, before a crowd had time to gather, in a 7″ x 10½″ Planet sketchbook of smooth drawing paper with a Faber 702 sketching pencil. Courtesy Weekend Telegraph, *London.*

GENERAL EQUIPMENT

I thrive on a portable means of working, so my equipment is usually kept to a minimum—though there have been exceptions. I remember staggering around Russia in 1967 with an enormous postman's size bag stuffed with enough materials for a squad of artists. In addition, I carried a hefty zippered canvas portfolio heavy with sheets of paper and sketchbooks of various sizes. This unusual departure from custom was planned. I intentionally carried enough supplies to last two months because I knew that art supply stores in the Soviet Union are not as well stocked as they are in Britain and the United States. I correctly predicted that I would have to make a frequent present of an admired marker, pencil, or sketchbook.

How much and what to carry really depends on where you are traveling. Generally, my working equipment consists of single necessities which I pack with care. I carry pens, pencils, and brushes—each in separate containers—in a flat metal box (a workman's lunchbox will also do the job). Easily damaged items, such as spare nibs, are placed in plastic or aluminum boxes. I carry fixative in spray cans; and I also bring along my own water supply, held in either an artists' water container with a dipper that fits over the screw top, or (because artists' water containers rust quite easily) in a plastic army canteen with a fitted cup. A large box of cleansing tissues is also useful to have on hand.

Whether you use single sheets of paper supported by a light piece of hardboard or prefer to work with a sketchbook, you will need spring clips to hold them. And, of course, you must have a light, portable stool which folds absolutely flat and which can be stored anywhere, if necessary.

I carry small items in a satchel or shoulder bag. Large sketchbooks and sheets of paper are kept, along with a light, portable stool, in a zippered canvas, leather, or plastic carrying case, or in a portfolio. I frequently try to fit everything into one bag, as I must when traveling by air.

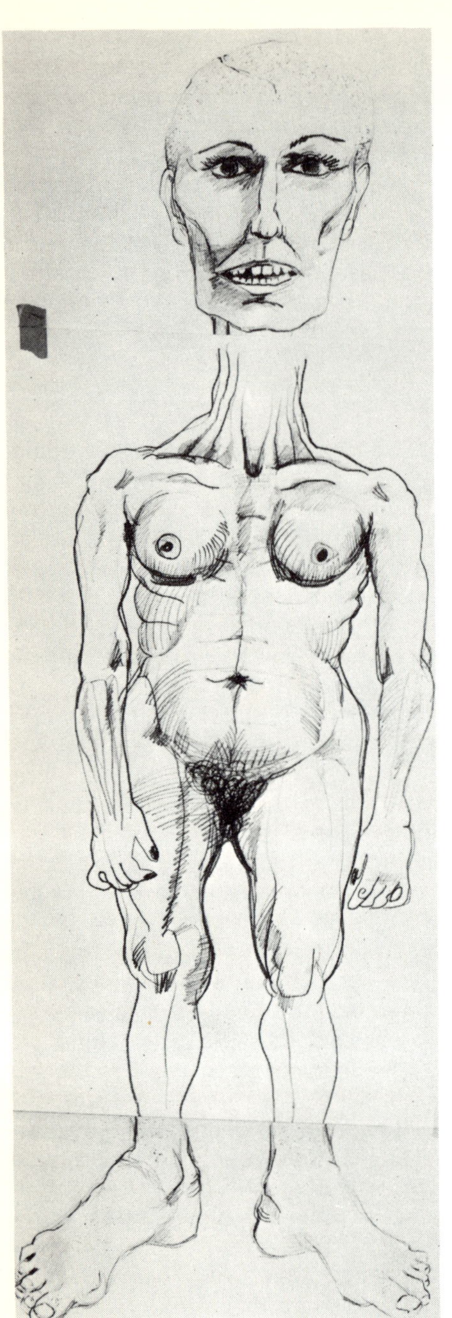

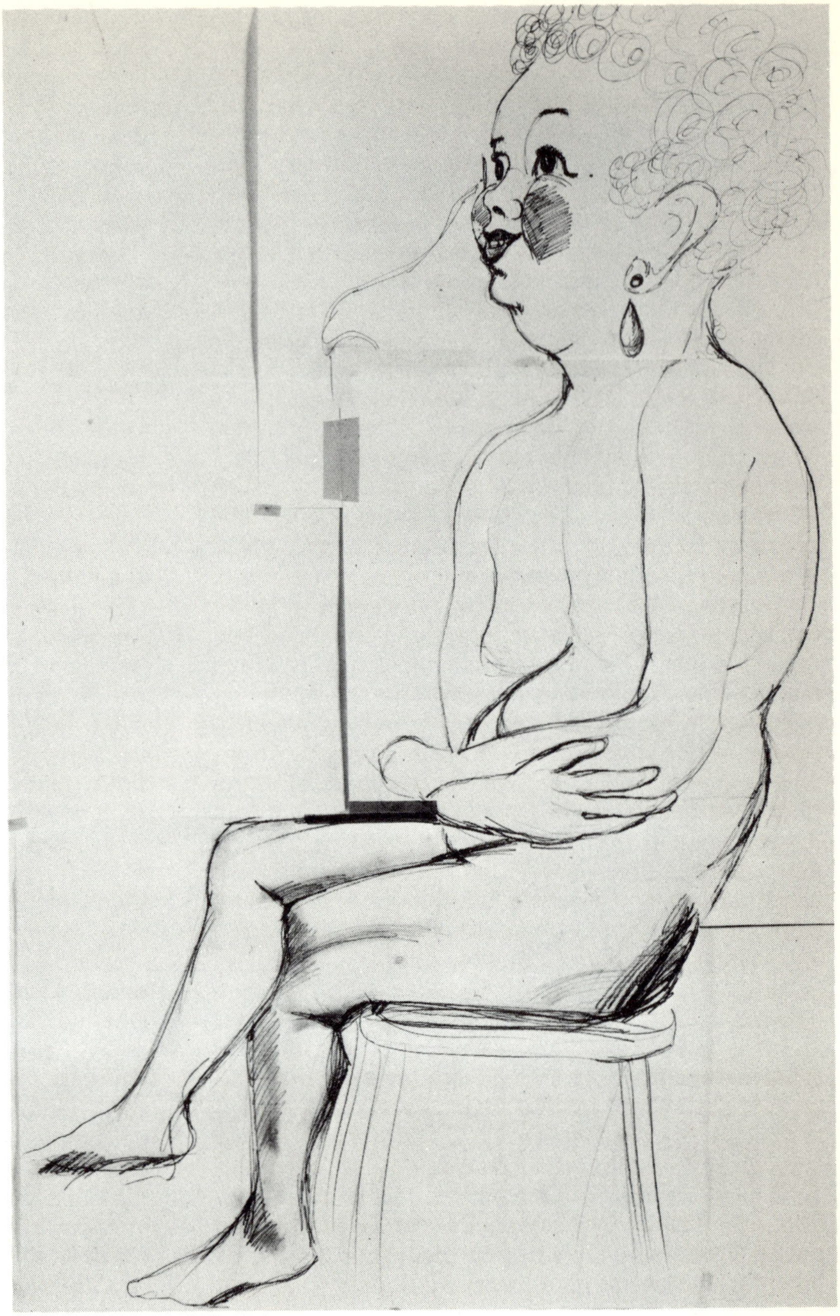

Composite figure produced by a class of my second-year illustration students at Philadelphia College of Art, 1968
Unless it can be effectively harnessed to your more inventive instincts, life drawing will inevitably bore you. This project was aimed at preventing boredom by revealing the more imaginative potentials of drawing from life—by using a regular art school model and dressing her up with a few props. Drawn and assembled collectively (each of four students drew a part and then participated in fitting them together). Four teams took part, producing a surplus of drawings for effective assembly. Materials consisted of black Pentel markers, soft Veriblack 315 sketching pencils, and 20" x 24" sheets of regular quality drawing paper. 2" Scotch tape was used to assemble each complete grotesque figure. Props consisted of a hired mardi gras *headpiece and plastic tie-on stomach.*

CHAPTER 2

A New Look at Life Drawing

BECAUSE LIFE DRAWING calls for sustained effort and concentration, you may find it difficult to learn how to draw people in the distracting, haphazard, and over-heated atmosphere of the typical life drawing class. Life classes are usually so crowded that their instructors would have to be supermen to give you the amount of personal coaching you need. Without individualized attention, a student often begins to fear that he will be left behind, and that no one gives a hoot whether or not he learns to draw.

In every life class there are two or three students who learn faster than anyone else and who are, therefore, thought to be "natural" artists. No assumption could be less true. Everyone has his own speed of working and learning. A student makes himself into an artist by his intense determination to succeed, come what may. Yet this fundamental truth often goes unrecognized. I remember feeling deeply frustrated and humiliated during my own art school days because the instructor habitually criticized me for working more slowly than others in the class.

LIFE DRAWING: VITAL YET NEGLECTED

Life drawing is a vital and basic prelude to drawing people wherever and however you want to portray them, yet it is the most neglected area of art training today.

Why this is so is a long story. Briefly, the reaction to the rigorous methods of nineteenth-century academic training, unfortunately, has been to reject much of the discipline necessary to develop competent draftsmanship. The emphasis formerly placed on subjects which train hand and eye—particularly anatomy, perspective, and drawing from life or from the antique figure—has diminished or disappeared completely. As a result, most art schools or colleges either ignore life drawing or, more commonly, approach it in a confused or placidly academic way.

Yet, paradoxically, for those who can accept it in this day and age, a truly academic training lays an excellent foundation for the development of a modern and personal style. Whatever its drawbacks, academic training is preferable to the situation in which an art school, department, or instructor is unable to devise a significant life drawing program and to recharge the subject with the enthusiasm and original thinking necessary to relate a traditional academic curriculum to contemporary needs. Under these circumstances, the average student is left to flounder alone and in frustration.

The main fault lies in the approach to the subject. Week after week, month after month, and year after year, the average art school instructor will restrict his choice of models to the one or two most readily available. Some habitually hire a well-proportioned girl, forgetting that, for the majority, such models can be despairingly impossible to draw. Other instructors, who simply could not care less, hire one limpid zombie after another, the constant sight of whom is more than enough to discourage any student from drawing people for the rest of his life.

TAKING MATTERS INTO YOUR OWN HANDS

If you are faced with the situation I have just described, you can, and you should, take matters into your own hands. First, nag your instructor to hire a variety of models—all shapes, all sizes. During the time I have been a tutor at the Royal College of Art in London, I have found alternatives to professional art school models by calling dancing schools, theatrical agencies, and homes for retired veterans, all of which have yielded a flow of dancers, midgets, actors, and Chelsea pensioners whose presence has led to lively drawing sessions. Suggest these sources (and any others you can think of) to your instructor.

If all your prodding fails, then try to work creatively with the available material. Consider the human frame as a piece of living theater which can be interpreted with imagination and fantasy. The moment you begin to harness life drawing to your inventive instincts, its tedium will disappear, and it will take an entirely new lease on life. Clap a mask (animal or human) or a wig on a model's head, dress her up in unusual gear, and immediately your contempt and boredom with the contract model will give way to renewed interest. In my own classes, I have even had students work from a moving model who danced before a large distorting mirror (the kind you see in fun houses). My students discovered that this exercise at once accelerated their speed of observation and revealed the possibilities of caricature—proving to be an excellent preparation for drawing people on location.

A SUCCESSFUL EXPERIMENT

One of the most successful life drawing experiments I ever undertook was at the Philadelphia College of Art, where I involved an entire class in a competition to produce the most grotesque life drawing. First, nude male or female models were dressed with plastic *mardi gras* headpieces and false tie-on stomachs. Then the class was divided into four groups of four to six, and every student was armed with a soft Veriblack 315 pencil or black Pentel marker and 20" x 24" sheets of drawing paper.

Facing the model, each group was given thirty minutes to draw, in his or her own way, each of the model's four parts: head, torso, hips, and feet. Group 1 was assigned to make the most of the elaborate headpiece; group 2, the torso with the false stomach; group 3, the hips and thighs; and group 4, the knees, calves, and feet. On completion, the drawings were laid out on the floor. Everyone was then encouraged to take part in relating and assembling the four different groups of drawings into single figures. This "construction" was done with masking tape. A totally unexpected and frequently hilarious figure drawing resulted. The members of the class were then asked to make a complete drawing, which would be entirely their own, from whichever figure they fancied.

Following the same procedure but using two models instead of one, the exercise subsequently evolved into a magazine assignment entitled "minus twenty-eight pounds," so called because it involved the use of two contrasting figures—one fat, and the other thin. Working collectively from these models generated intense interest and concentration; all the students were brought together and stimulated by the imaginative interpretations they had unwittingly created. By chance, a backdoor to life drawing had been discovered; and the final result—the students' redrawn version—introduced a lively and unconventional means which enabled them to see the human figure as it should be seen, in a fresh, new light.

My aim in these experiments is to free or loosen the inhibited approaches to literal representation. Any device you can think of that will heighten the feeling of the bizarre, encourage experimentation, and refresh your vision—no matter how contrived the device might seem—is well worth trying out in your life drawing class.

EXPLORING YOUR MEDIA

Whether your efforts to liven up your class succeed or fail, life drawing sessions provide you with an excellent opportunity to explore your media. Here is your chance to become thoroughly familiar with the idiosyncrasies of charcoal and graphite leads, various pens and inks, and felt or fiber tipped markers. Begin by working in the medium you find easiest. Then move from one medium to another until you discover which you prefer. Concentrate for a time on the medium of your choice. I recommend that you start with a soft (5B or 6B) or extra soft (Faber 702 or Veriblack 315) graphite pencil and work on a good drawing paper such as Strathmore Alexis, in sheets of, say, 22" x 26".

In short, take the initiative to make life drawing classes work for you. The training it offers will lay a solid foundation for the development of a modern and personal style. And, as I have suggested, you can transform a tedious ritual into an exciting series of discoveries by an imaginative use of your models.

CHAPTER 3

Drawing People in Public Places

ONCE YOU ARE familiar with the essentials of drawing the human figure, the next step is to apply what you learn in the class to the task of drawing people in public. I say *learn,* in the present tense, because drawing people as they talk, play, or relax should ideally be undertaken in conjunction with life drawing.

Drawing people on the spot may not come easily to you. When I first began to work in public, I found it difficult to persevere in what I felt to be a self-conscious and solitary activity. If you, too, experience this sense of isolation and discouragement, you can overcome it by taking a friend or fellow student along on your sketching trips or by fortifying yourself, as I did, with weekly visits to a local art museum. I recall how longingly I would gaze at the romantic drawings of the English Pre-Raphaelites and their followers John Everett Millais, Ford Madox Brown, Hughes, and Houghton—as well as the more incisive work of such moderns as Wyndham Lewis, George Grosz, and Amedeo Modigliani. How on earth, I would wonder, did they manage to inject their people with so much drama and imagination?

This constant study of past and present masters in relation to my own work helped me develop an appreciation of taste and style—that is, I learned to be self-critical. Equally important, it provided me with insight into the commonplace. For instance, the rendering of a prosaic old woman sitting in a train that I passed over one week as insignificant would unexpectedly reveal itself the following Sunday as comic or tragic. This kind of discovery never failed to refresh my vision, renew my energy, and provide the sustenance I needed to stay with the idea of being an artist. Through study and practice, I continued the never-ending process of opening my own eyes.

BE PREPARED

Begin now to acquire the habit of always carrying a small sketchbook, a pencil, and a ballpoint pen with you. Although I avoid lugging around the heavier trappings of outdoor location work, you will never catch me without my sketchbook and zippered pouch containing markers and soft pencils, a small knife, and an eraser.

SELECTING AND OBSERVING YOUR SUBJECT

I frequent bowling lanes and bars, museums and zoos, skating rinks and railroad stations—in fact, anywhere I can observe the coming and going of every human type. I take care to work where I can see most of the action without arousing too much attention. The places I have cited usually offer the kind of informal atmosphere where the presence of an artist is accepted easily enough. Surroundings such as these blunt the oddness of a drawing being made instead of a camera being clicked.

Begin by selecting people whose movements are lively and animated. Don't draw just anyone who crosses your line of vision. Instead, single out those who strike you as being interesting characters. Observe a single figure; take him or her apart mentally and imagine what kind of person he or she is. Then decide whether or not you like the look of the person. Whatever your reaction, accept it and use it as the basis of your illustration. This approach will enable you to effectively define and convey the character and personality of your subject.

CAPTURING ACTION AND CONVEYING ATMOSPHERE

Drawing people as they talk or move around in public depends not only on *how* you see them, but also on your awareness and understanding of *what is happening.* Try to develop this capacity. Once you have even a little insight, your drawing is likely to be richer. Eavesdrop on a lively conversation, if this helps, and try to illustrate what is going on. To push this approach to the limit, I often add or distort. I also like

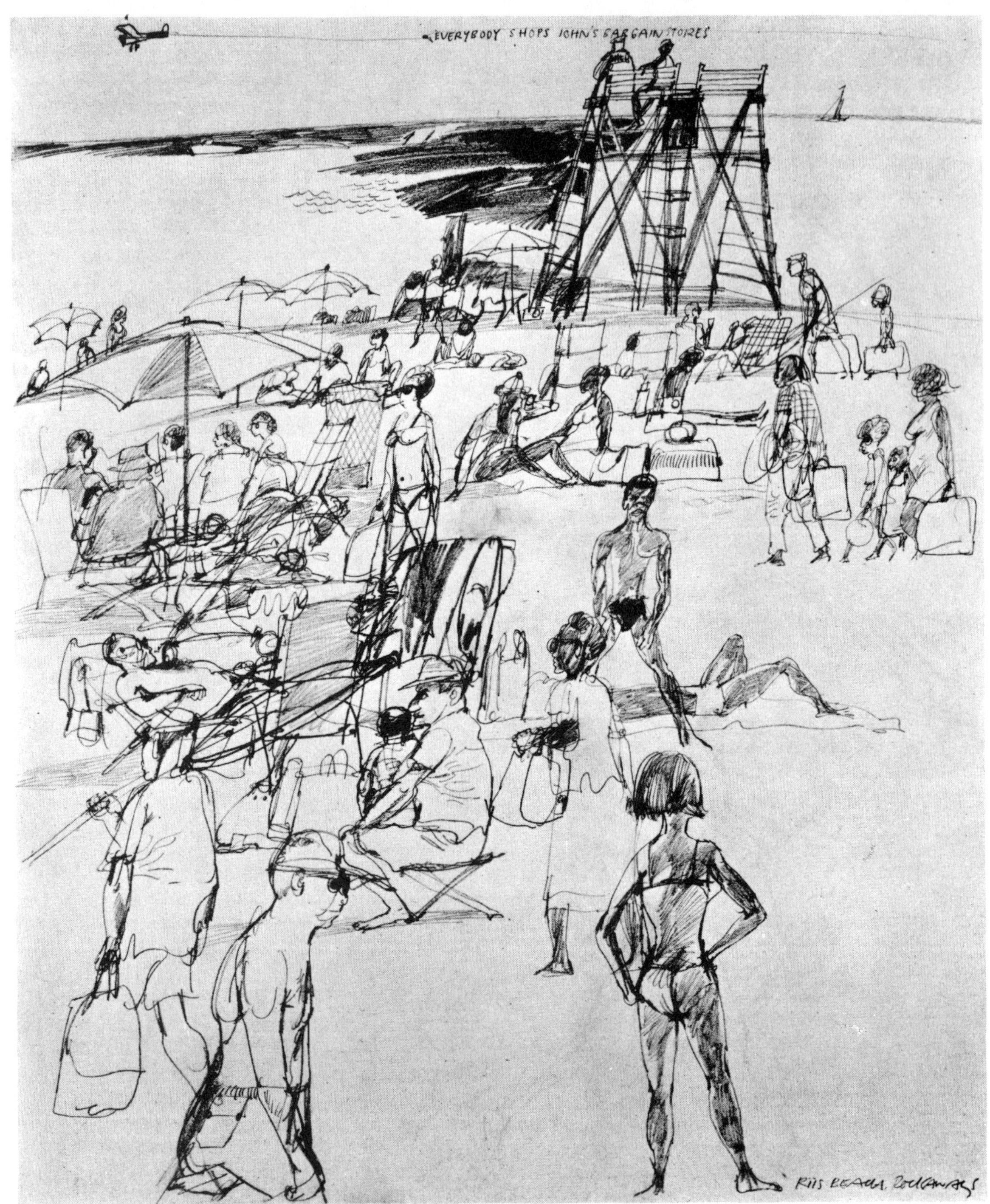

Riis Park, New York, 1963

Sometimes a street, a market, or a bar can be too friendly a place to work in. But a big, crowded beach is impersonal. No one will bother you or ask questions. And not only do people come in every size, shape, and kind, but they bathe, exercise, quarrel, and make love. This non-stop action makes a beach one of the best places to observe people and draw them. I built up this drawing from a continuous movement of people over a period of two hours, one September afternoon. Drawn with a 5B and 6B Venus graphite pencil on white Daler drawing paper. From Brendan Behan's New York, *1964. Courtesy The Hutchinson Publishing Group, London; and Bernard Geis Associates, New York.*

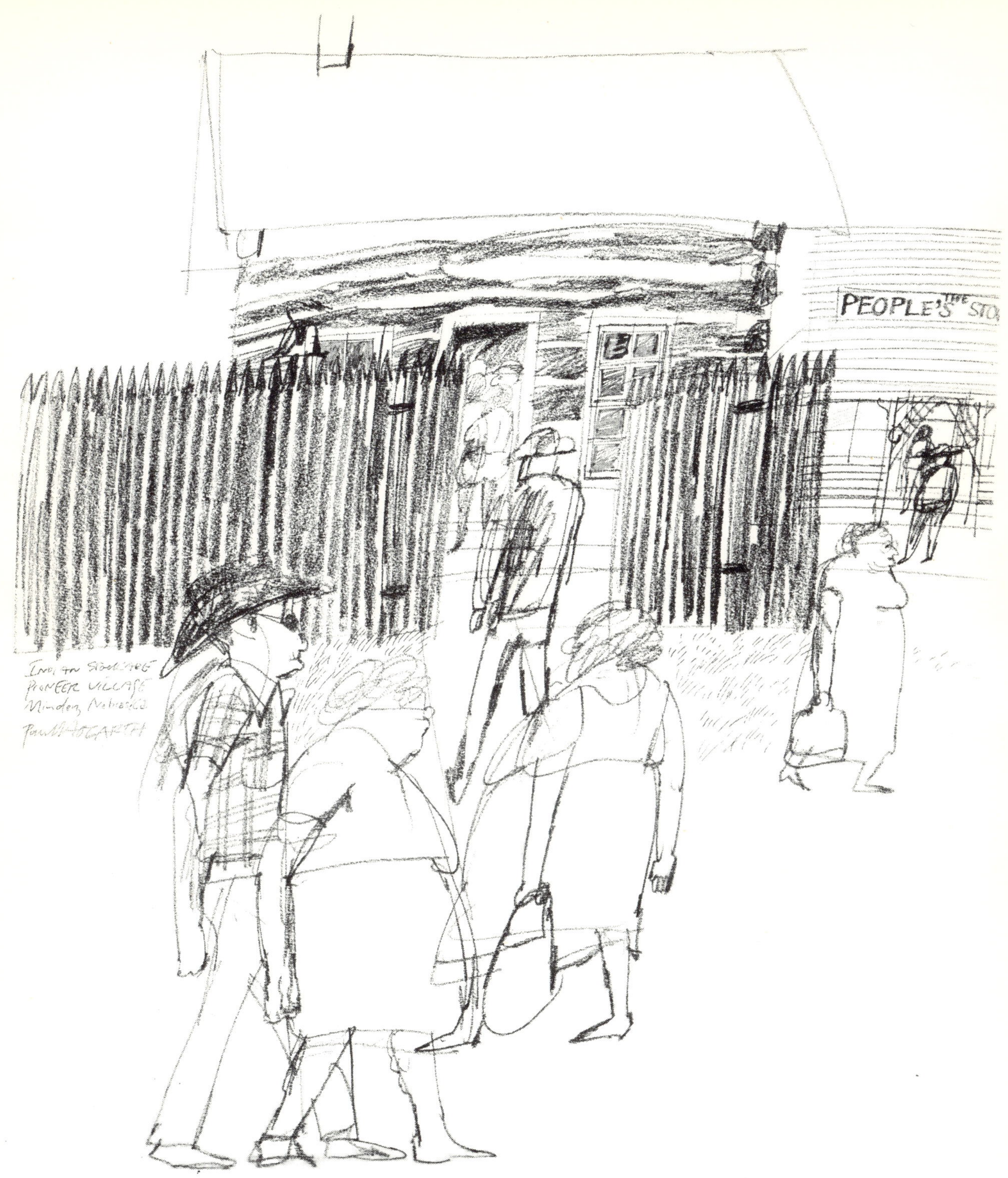

Indian stockade at Pioneer Village, Nebraska, 1965
These gaunt old farmers and their lumpy wives reminded me of my relatives back in the hills of Westmorland, England. Affinity to people often promotes a compulsion to draw them. Here, on the plains of Nebraska one Sunday afternoon, they were looking at the memorabilia of the days before washing machines and refrigerators—now housed in Harold Warp's Pioneer Museum of bygones at Minden. Drawn in an 11" x 14" sketchbook of Strathmore Alexis drawing paper with a Faber 702 sketching pencil. The hatching of the windows and the grass outside were drawn in Higgins India ink with a Spencerian school nib. Courtesy The Strathmore Paper Company, West Springfield, Mass.

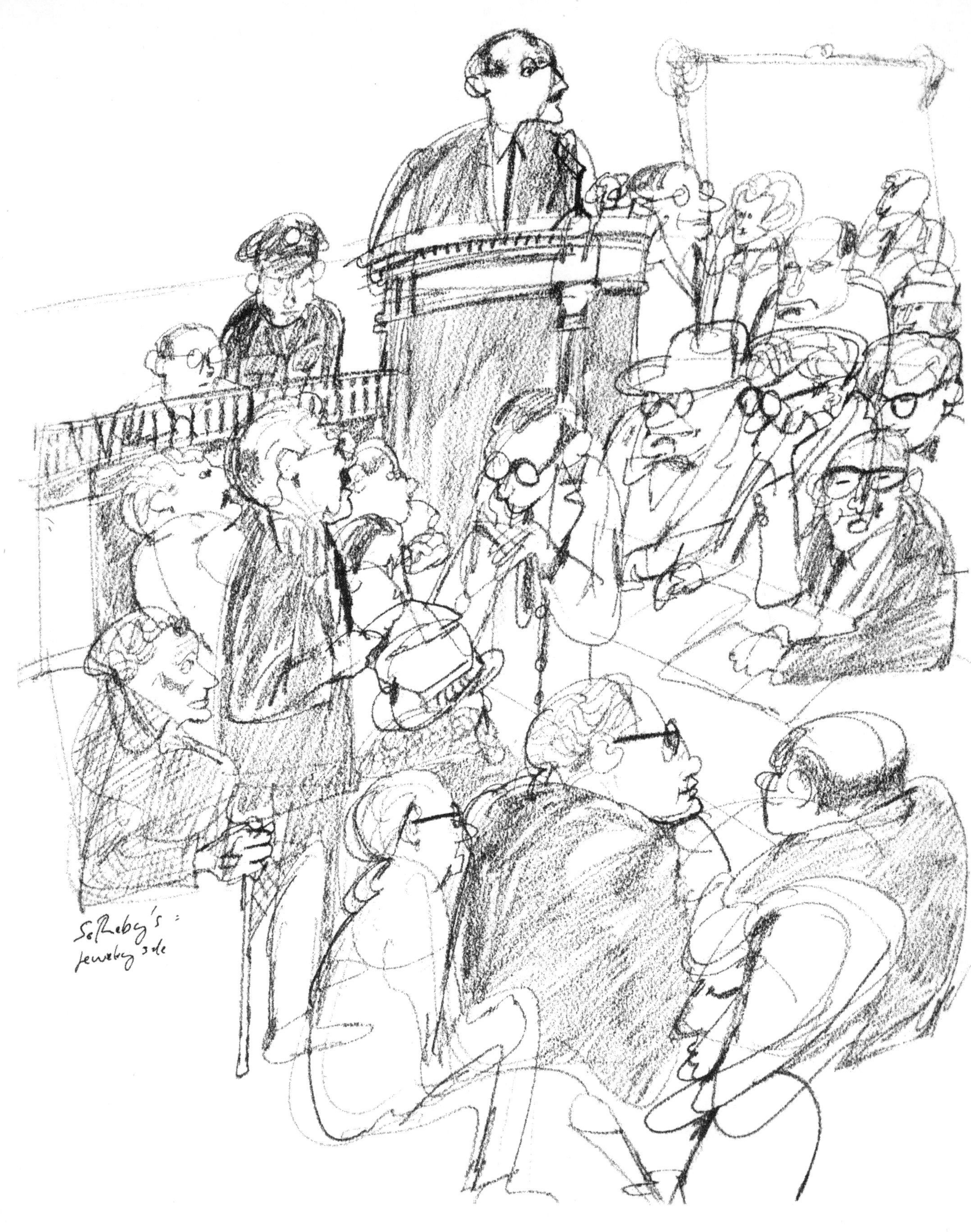
Sotheby's:
jewelry sale

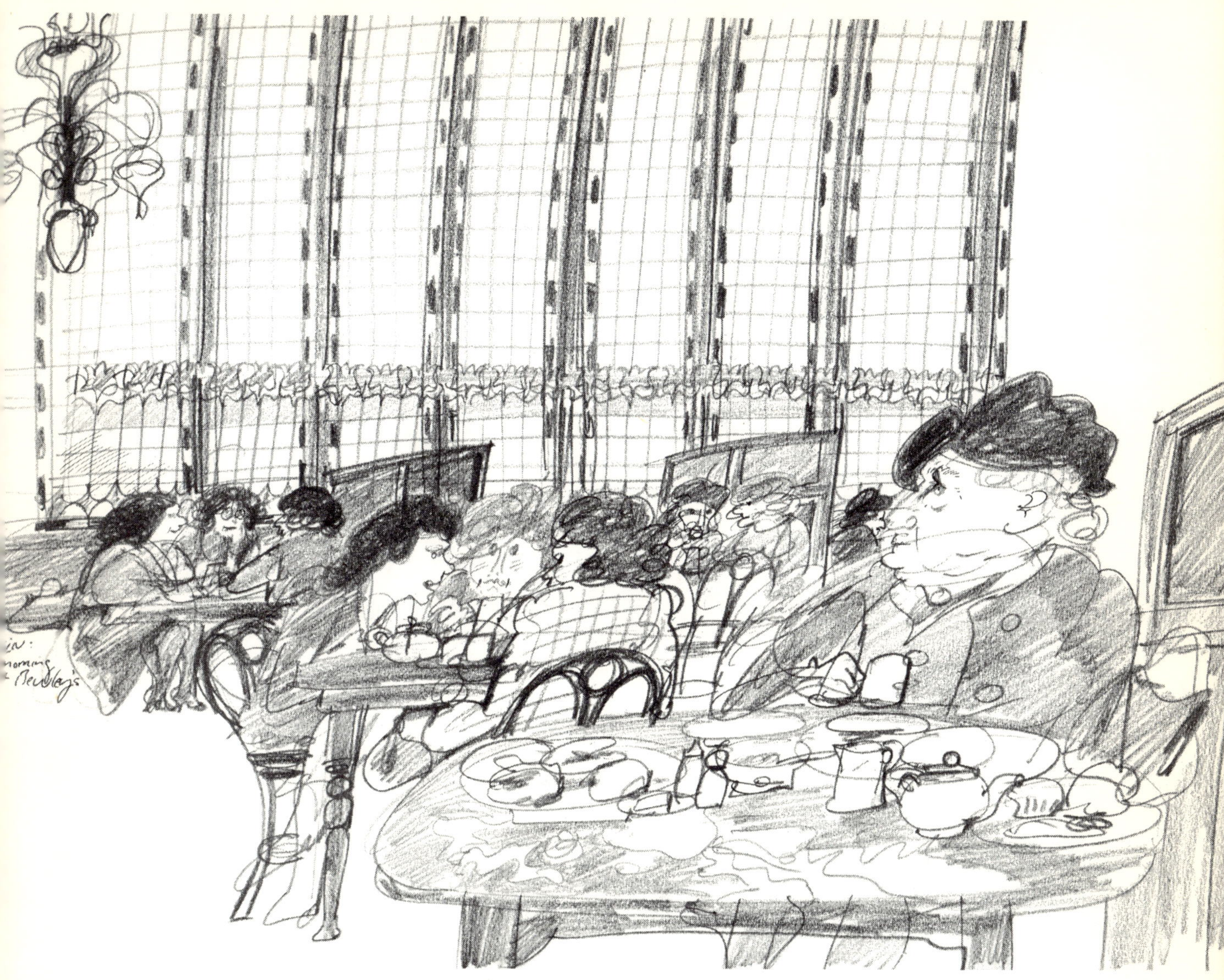

Auction at Sotheby's, London, 1966
My awareness of what was really happening makes this drawing an interpretation, as well as a drawing. What appeared to be just another auction was, in fact, a sale of family heirlooms from yet another stately country home. The owner, a frail, elderly woman (far left), was pathetically anxious to get the best price for her jewelry and objets d'art, yet she was troubled that she had to dispose of them. Antiquarians, merchants, and specialists sat around like vultures, bidding for the least possible price. The drawing took me about an hour and was made in an 11" x 14" sketchbook of Strathmore Alexis drawing paper with a Faber 702 sketching pencil. From London à la Mode, *1966. Courtesy Studio Vista Ltd., London; Hill & Wang, Inc., New York. Reproduced by permission of the owner, Miss Jean Richardson, London. (Left)*

Mid-morning tea at Bewley's, Westmorland Street, Dublin, 1969
Bewley's Oriental Cafés are a traditional Dublin meeting-place, used by all classes of Irish society—at different times of the day—from charwomen to countesses. Between ten and eleven a.m., they fill up with groups of chattering chars, who gossip amiably over wheat scones and tea before returning home. I got there before ten o'clock to choose the best vantage point opposite the marvelous art nouveau window. Drawn in about an hour in a 10¾" x 14½" Planet sketchbook of drawing paper with a Faber 702 sketching pencil. From a portfolio on Irish life and character, Courtesy Lithopinion, *Winter 1969. Copyright by Local One, Amalgamated Lithographers of America, New York. (Above)*

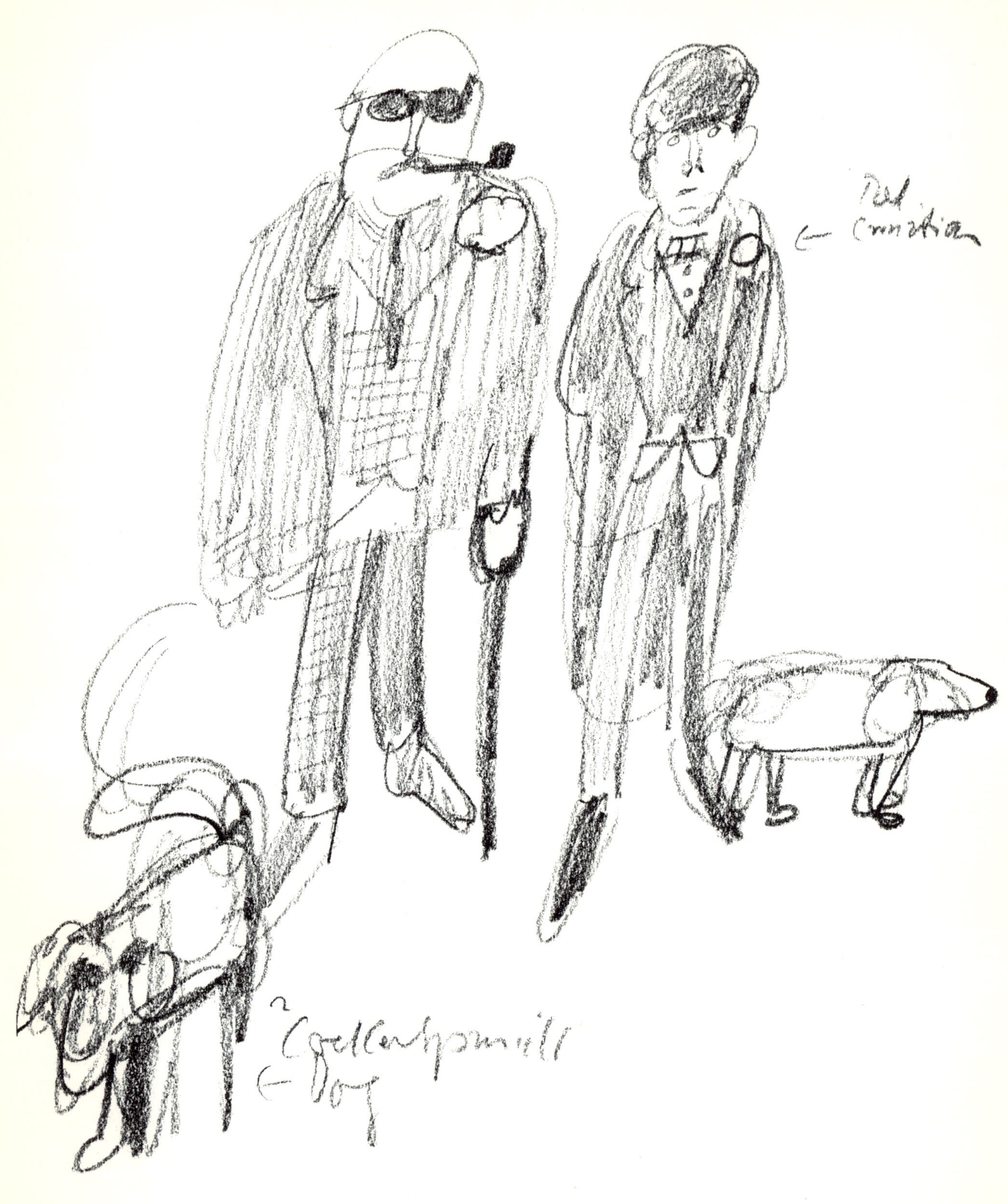

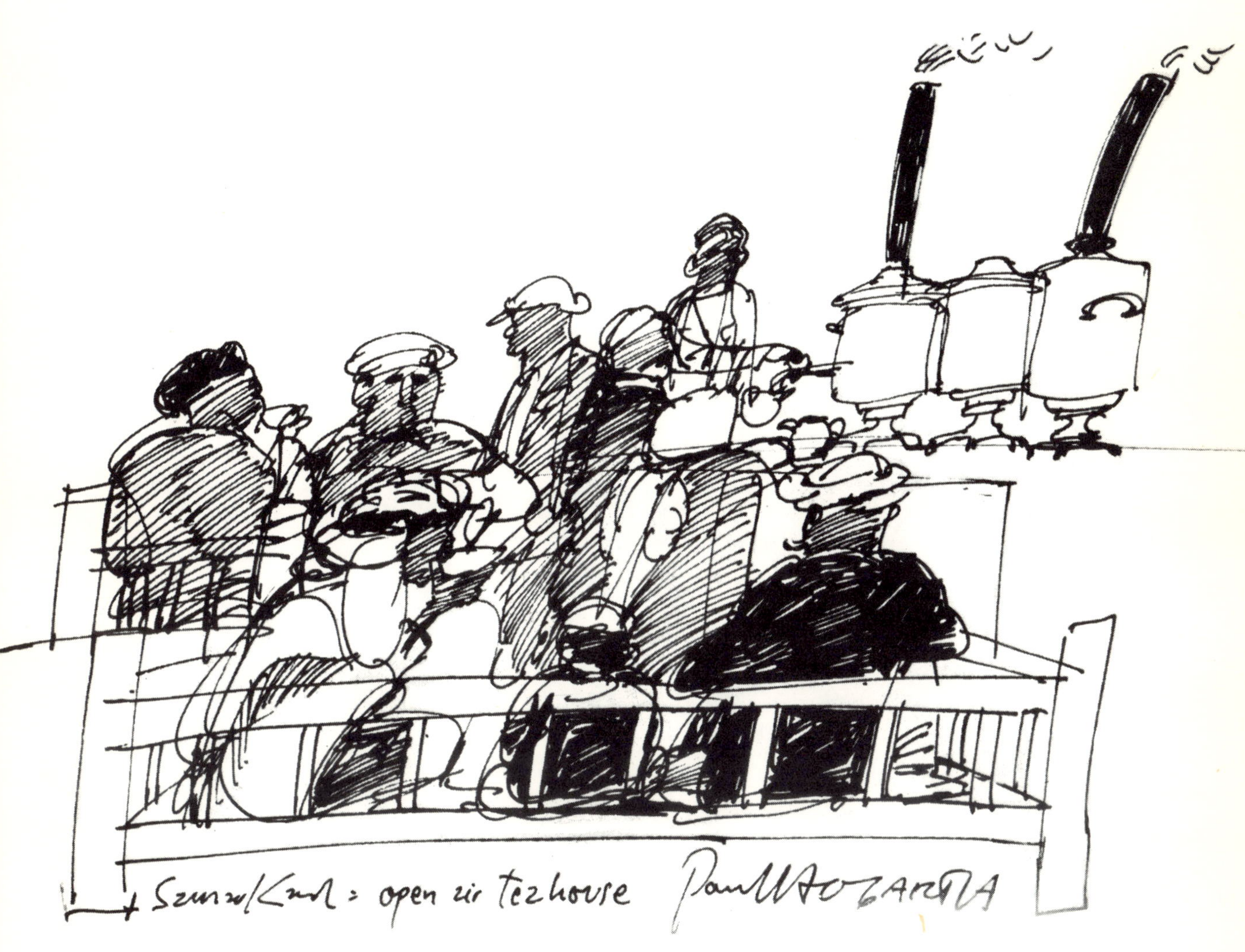

Eton sketchbook study, England, 1968
I make working studies of completely summed up characters like this one, where it just is not possible to face people and make more detailed drawings. Any significant details—such as the kind and color of the boy's buttonhole flower and the type of dog—are noted. This provides me with enough information to make more finished drawings in my studio, in this case, for a forthcoming portfolio on Eton for Boy's Life *magazine. Drawn in a 7" x 10" sketchbook of Daler drawing paper with a 7B Venus graphite pencil. (Left)*

Open-air teahouse, Samarkand, U.S.S.R., 1967
The teahouses of Asia are excellent locations for observing a wide variety of local characters. This vignette of Far Eastern Soviet life was drawn with a regular Esterbrook fountain pen in a 5" x 7" English Planet sketchbook of smooth drawing paper. From A Russian Journey: from Suzdal to Samarkand, *1969. Courtesy Cassell and Company, London; and Hill & Wang, Inc., New York. (Above)*

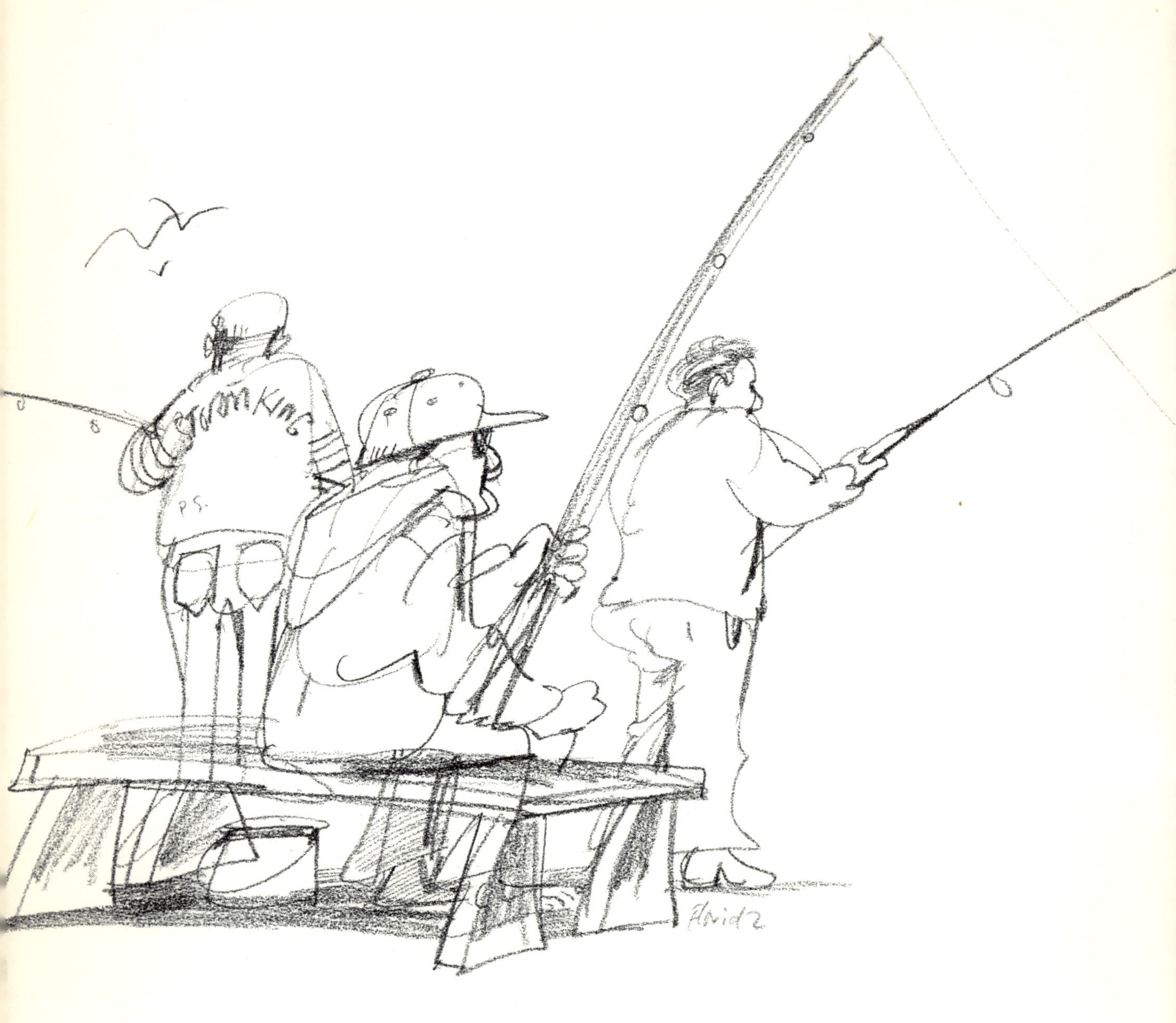

More sketchbook studies, 1967–69

These rapid character studies were made in Skopje, Yugoslavia; Fez, Morocco; and Cocoa Beach, Florida, while at work on larger drawings. They were made with a Faber 702 sketching pencil in a 5" x 7" Planet sketchbook of drawing paper.

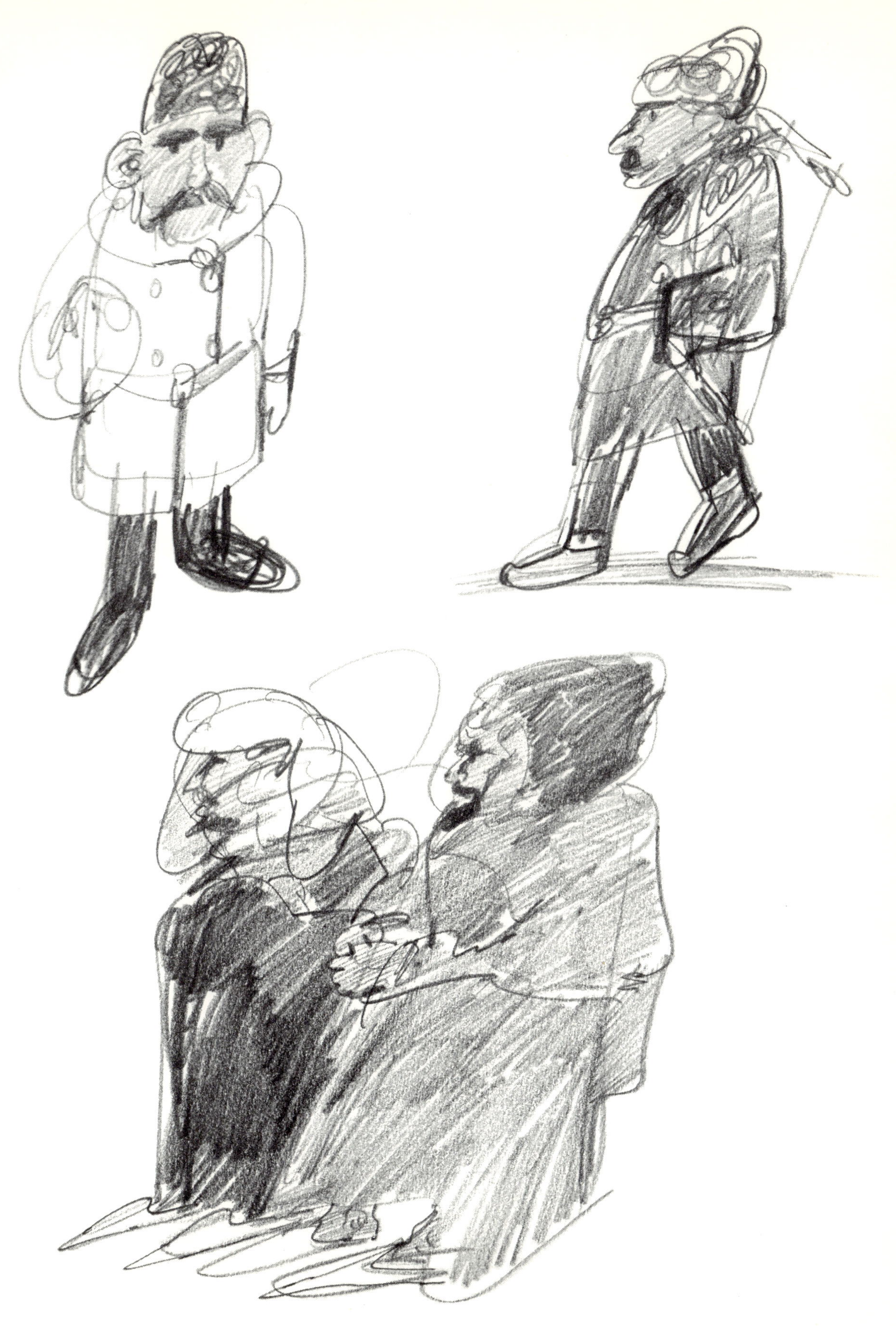

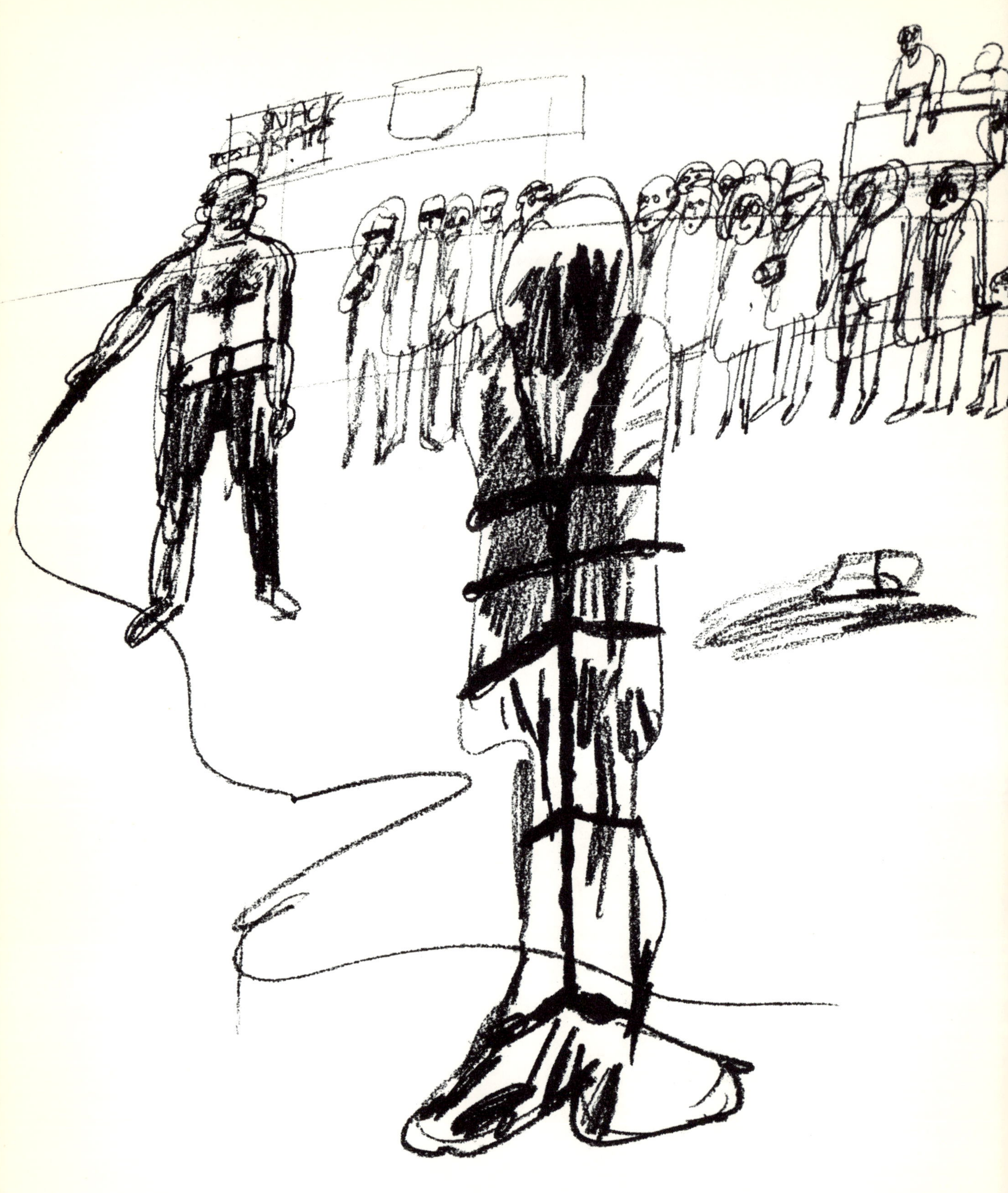

to analyze a fragment of action—like a bowling match or a baseball game—and then build up the drawing around a group involved in the activity.

Whatever your approach, incorporating your understanding of what is actually happening to a person or among several people will vitalize your work. I think my drawing, *Indian stockade at Pioneer Village, Nebraska, 1965,* was successful because I realized the significance the scene had for an older generation of local country folk, fascinated by the past they had been part of. After taking a look around the village, I found a position where I could see most of the activity. I selected a group of representative types and drew them in freely against the stockade background, which I had previously rendered much more heavily. I worked in an 11" x 14" sketchbook of Strathmore drawing paper, using a Faber 702 graphite pencil to catch the figures as they passed. In another drawing, *Bowling lane, London, 1965,* I depicted the activity of a group of bowlers by waiting for their movements to repeat themselves; at the same time, I caught the ambiance of the moment by portraying them as the closely knit circle of friends they, in fact, were.

WORKING UNDER SPECIAL CONDITIONS

Drawing people in political meetings, nightclubs, and courtrooms presents special problems to the artist. Strategic rather than esthetic, these problems should not be tackled until you have had plenty of practice drawing on location. But if you enjoy working under challenging circumstances—and I hope you do—then it is important for you to develop a sense of discretion. In such places, your wits can be just as important as your pencil. The foresight to work in a small sketchbook may make the difference between your keeping a drawing and having it whirled out of your hands by a policeman, an irate proprietor, or an overly protective custodian.

Street entertainment, Tower Hill, London, 1966
Whether they sing, dance, or juggle, itinerant street entertainers are always interesting to draw because they are such characters. Here, strong-man Bill Jones and his mate Max "work a flush," which in cockney slang means taking the tourist for a ride. Drawn in a 10¾" x 14½" English Planet sketchbook of smooth drawing paper with a Faber 702 sketching pencil. From London a la Mode, *1966. Courtesy Studio Vista Ltd., London; and Hill & Wang, Inc., New York.*

WORKING IN COURTROOMS

Courtrooms are excellent places to observe people at their very best and at their very worst. However, the courts impose restrictive rulings on artists and photographers. If you are seen drawing, you will be asked to leave. Some artists circumvent this curtailment by retiring every half-hour or so to the lavatory, where they can draw from memory in privacy and freedom. The intrepid work in minute sketchbooks secreted in their jacket pocket or concealed under a folded coat, then use these rough sketches as notes upon which to base later drawings.

WORKING IN NIGHTCLUBS

Sometime or another, you may discover a lively night spot that offers a wealth of material you absolutely must draw. You may be unable to do so because the owner objects. He may, in fact, warn you to stop on pain of being thrown out. You can sometimes avoid this embarrassing predicament by asking the owner's permission in advance, making clear that you are not a newspaperman or investigator, but simply an artist drawing purely for personal satisfaction. You may have to spend a little money to convince him, because artists, like photographers, may not be initially welcome by those anxious to avoid what they consider undesirable publicity.

If the nightclub is in your home town or any place where you are known, you may not run into difficulty. Even if you are just a visitor, everyone will feel easier if you drop by regularly while you are in town. However, if you are not a local boy, like Toulouse-Lautrec, and if you are not on an extended visit, then only one course of action is open to you: to draw as unobtrusively as possible in a pocket sketchbook or on small sheets of paper tucked into a guidebook—and then to make your get-away as quickly as possible!

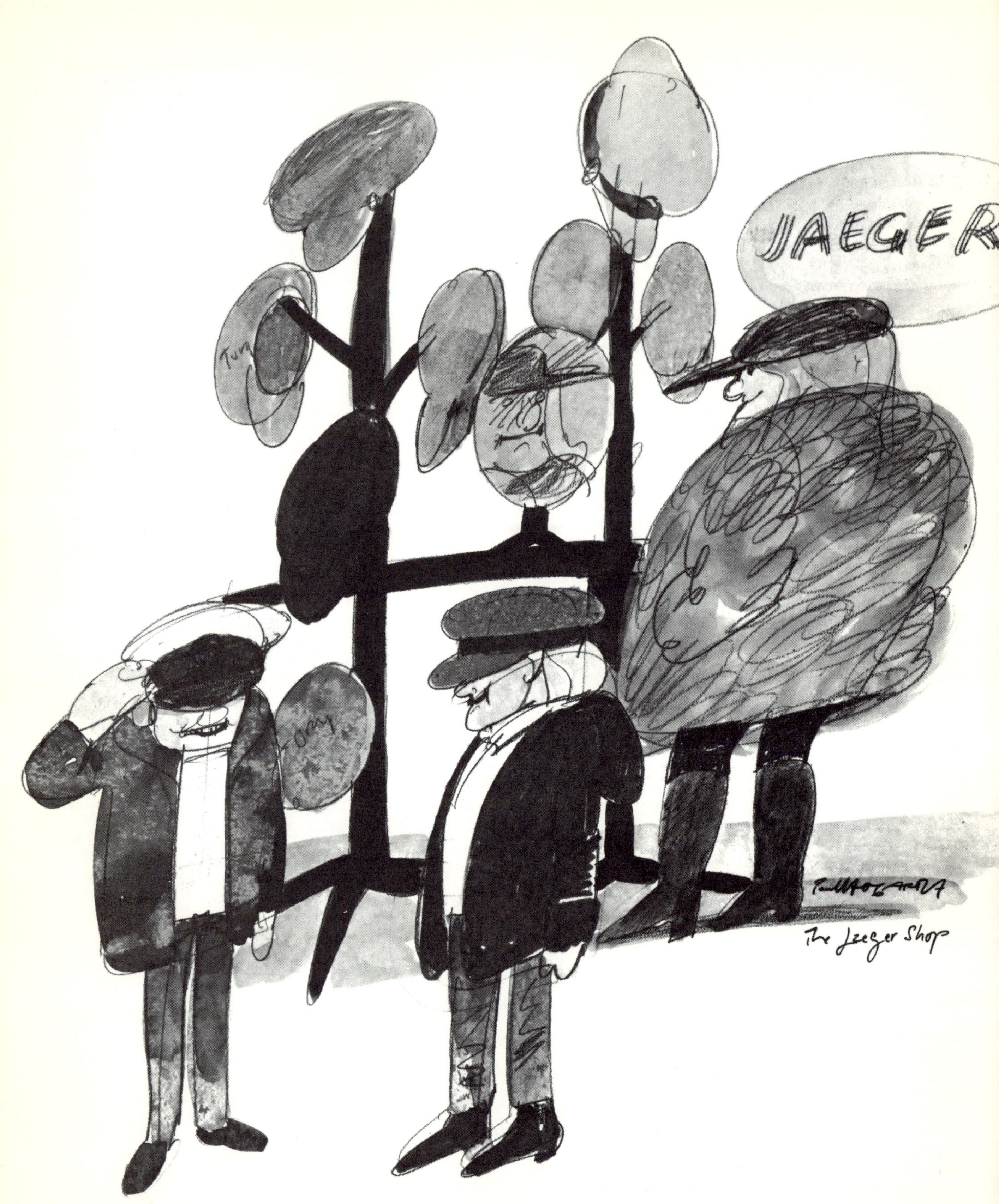
JAEGER
The Jaeger Shop

CHAPTER 4

Getting Used to Drawing People

BY ITS VERY nature, drawing people on location is a much more informal pursuit than working in a life drawing class. As part of this informal atmosphere, be prepared to put up with a certain amount of outside curiosity. More and more people are becoming genuinely interested in art and artists, are apt to show it, and will often watch the artist at work with a deep sense of humility. At times, however, the interest of the public may be a source of irritation rather than inspiration.

GRAPPLING WITH YOUR STAGE FRIGHT

Stating reasons for the public's interest in an artist's activities does not, however, make the task of drawing people any easier. My biggest problem, when confronted with the spectacle of the bustling everyday world, was to overcome a natural sense of stage fright. How, for example, does an artist approach a complete stranger who might be a possible subject for a drawing—without making a fool of himself, or of the stranger? Courage is based on a need to act; if I am motivated to draw a place or person, I can usually overcome my stage fright.

From my own experience, I have found that drawing people is best learned in easy stages. By working progressively from public locations (people in their surroundings) toward private locations (the portrait), you will gradually acquire the self-confidence to focus on the individual. Each stage orients you more to drawing people and teaches you effective ways of relaxing them *and* yourself.

Get into the habit of *looking* at people wherever you go. Build up a mental library and sketchbook of every conceivable type of human being—all shapes, types, and sizes. Socialize, if you possibly can, to help you develop an easy manner with people you meet for the first time. Try not to allow shyness to discourage you, but do not be discouraged if you remain shy. Providing you do feel a compulsion to comment on or interpret people, drawing them is simply a matter of practice and technique.

OBSERVING PEOPLE

Until you feel bold enough to venture out on location, observe people unnoticed—through a window, for example. The English illustrator Charles Keene worked in his studio, with a large mirror fixed at an angle to the street. In this way, he could see, while remaining unobserved, the colorful, changing London Strand, which he used as a basis for so many drawings of life and character for the journal *Punch.* Another famous illustrator, the Frenchman Gustave Doré, was also a shy and nervous person. Attracted to the high and low life of his day like the proverbial moth to a flame, he would either draw from behind the back of his taller friend and collaborator, the journalist Blanchard Jerrold, or he would ask for a police escort. Many of the remarkable drawings for his dramatic chronicle of Victorian life, *London: A Pilgrimage* (1870), were drawn in this way.

TIPS ABOUT WORKING ON LOCATION

When you feel ready to work on location, a good plan is to start in those places where you will be able to

Jaeger Shop, London Boat Show, Earls Court, 1968
After noticing that the place had possibilities for humorous interpretation, I sat down in the waiting area of the shop facing the sales counter. Anonymity was maintained by placing an 11" x 14" sketchbook inside a copy of Life *magazine. I missed one great drama in which a small child got himself lost but was just in time for a comedy act in which two cockney kids tried on oversized headgear while Mum fancied herself at sea in a "Francis Chichester." Drawn in twenty minutes with a Faber 702 sketching pencil in a sketchbook of three-ply, high surface Strathmore drawing paper. Courtesy* Sports Illustrated. *Copyright 1968 by Time, Inc.*

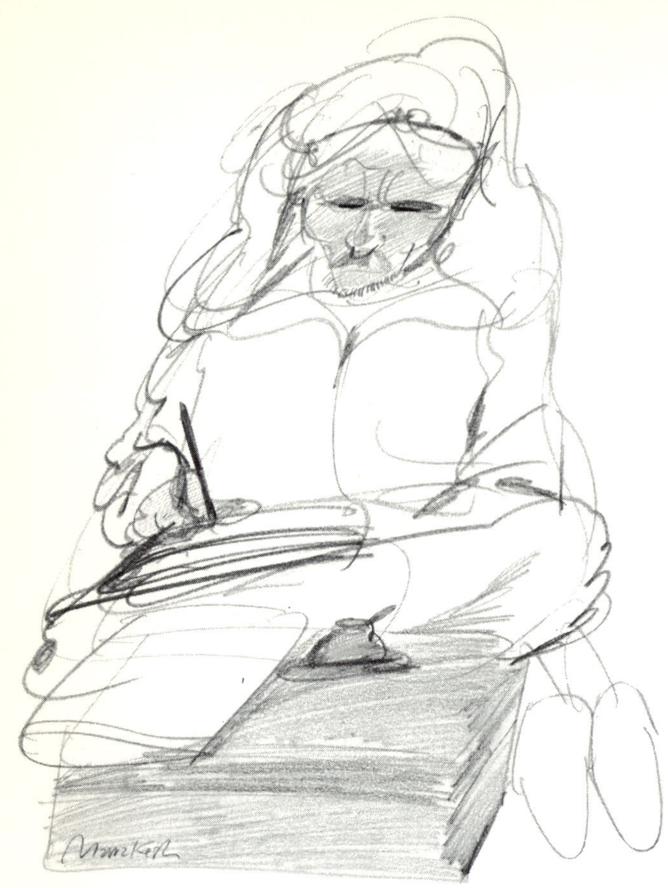

Letter-writer, Marrakesh, Morocco, 1966
Because of religious reasons, many Moslems object to being drawn or photographed. Close-up drawings are therefore sometimes difficult to obtain. Unnoticed, I got this one drawn in a few minutes by working behind the back of a water-seller. Drawn with a Faber 702 sketching pencil in a 10¾" x 14½" English Planet sketchbook of smooth drawing paper. Accents, such as the shading of the face, right hand, and inkwell, were added later with a Venus 6B graphite pencil.

work relatively undisturbed. I first began working in the waiting areas of large railroad stations (the list could also include bus terminals and airports), where a cross section of humanity remains seated for long enough periods of time to be drawn at leisure. An impersonal setting, where people are preoccupied with the problems of getting to work or returning home, enables the beginner to draw freely, without feeling eyes—which expect nothing less than a finished work of art—fastened on him.

EQUIPMENT FOR LOCATION WORK

Take along a minimum of equipment. All you need is an 11" x 14" sketchbook of drawing paper, soft graphite pencils, plus a fountain pen or thin fiber tip writing marker. A small, *light,* folding camp stool, easily carried under your arm—there is even one small enough to fit in your pocket—enables you to sit wherever and whenever you wish. Select a choice vantage point, one which is reasonably close to people (ideally, not less than ten feet away), yet far enough away to be unobtrusive. During peak travel hours, you may not be able to choose your spot. Therefore, it is worth the trouble to arrive in advance, set up, and be prepared for rush hours when the widest variety of human types and characters is to be seen.

Work from concealed or partially concealed positions to give you a sense of security and to effectively reduce unwelcome attention. To help preserve your anonymity further, place your sketchbook in a magazine or folded newspaper, as I sometimes do.

INTERPRETING THE SCENE

Before I start to work, I always take a good look around. Like a hunter, I stalk people who interest me. I think about them, imagine the sort of crazy lives they might lead, and then try to develop the drawing around these fantasies and thoughts. What I am actually doing is not so much illustrating reality as it is, but illustrating my interpretation of reality. To conform with my mental image, I often heighten the characteristics, appearance, and posture of a person, relating them in turn to the shapes of such elements as windows, lamps, and billboards. I bring in those details from anywhere, fitting them into spaces around a group or a single figure. I never add a background simply because it is there, but only when it adds considerable significance to the figure.

COPING WITH THE CURIOUS

It may not be possible to work entirely undisturbed. The difficulty with drawing on location is that people catch sight of you, and then—unable to contain their curiosity—walk over to see what you have done. They

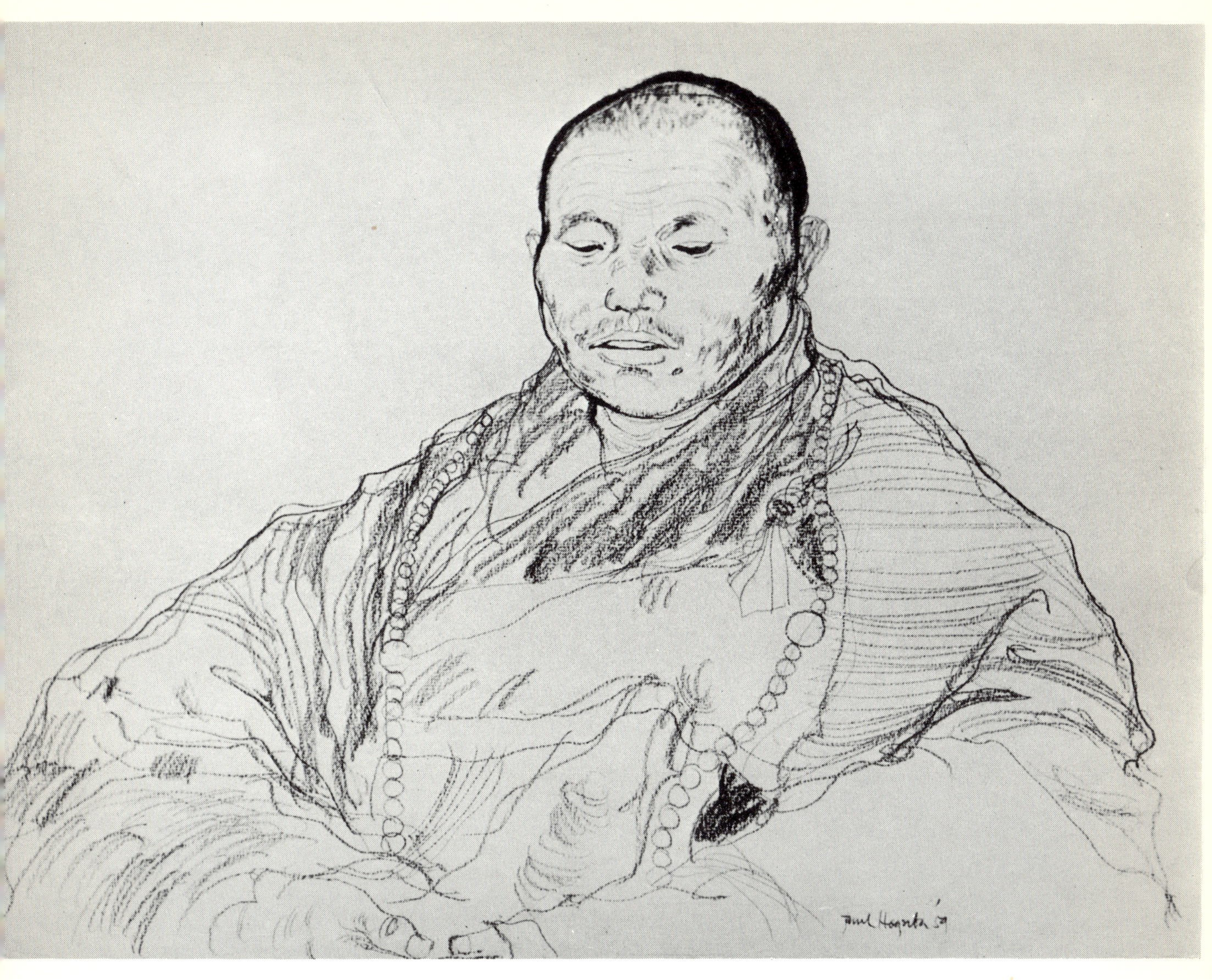

Buddhist monk, Hua Ching Chi, Sian, China, 1954
The strange exotic flavor of China motivated many of my earlier drawings of people. The totally different atmosphere emboldened me to attempt subjects I would probably not have had the courage to draw in my own country, like this gargantuan monk, who sat on a prayer-table in deep contemplation in a monastery courtyard. Drawn in an hour with a soft Hardtmuth charcoal lead on Chinese bamboo paper. From Looking at China, *1955. Courtesy Lawrence and Wishart, London. Reproduced by permission of the owner, Ronald Searle, Paris.*

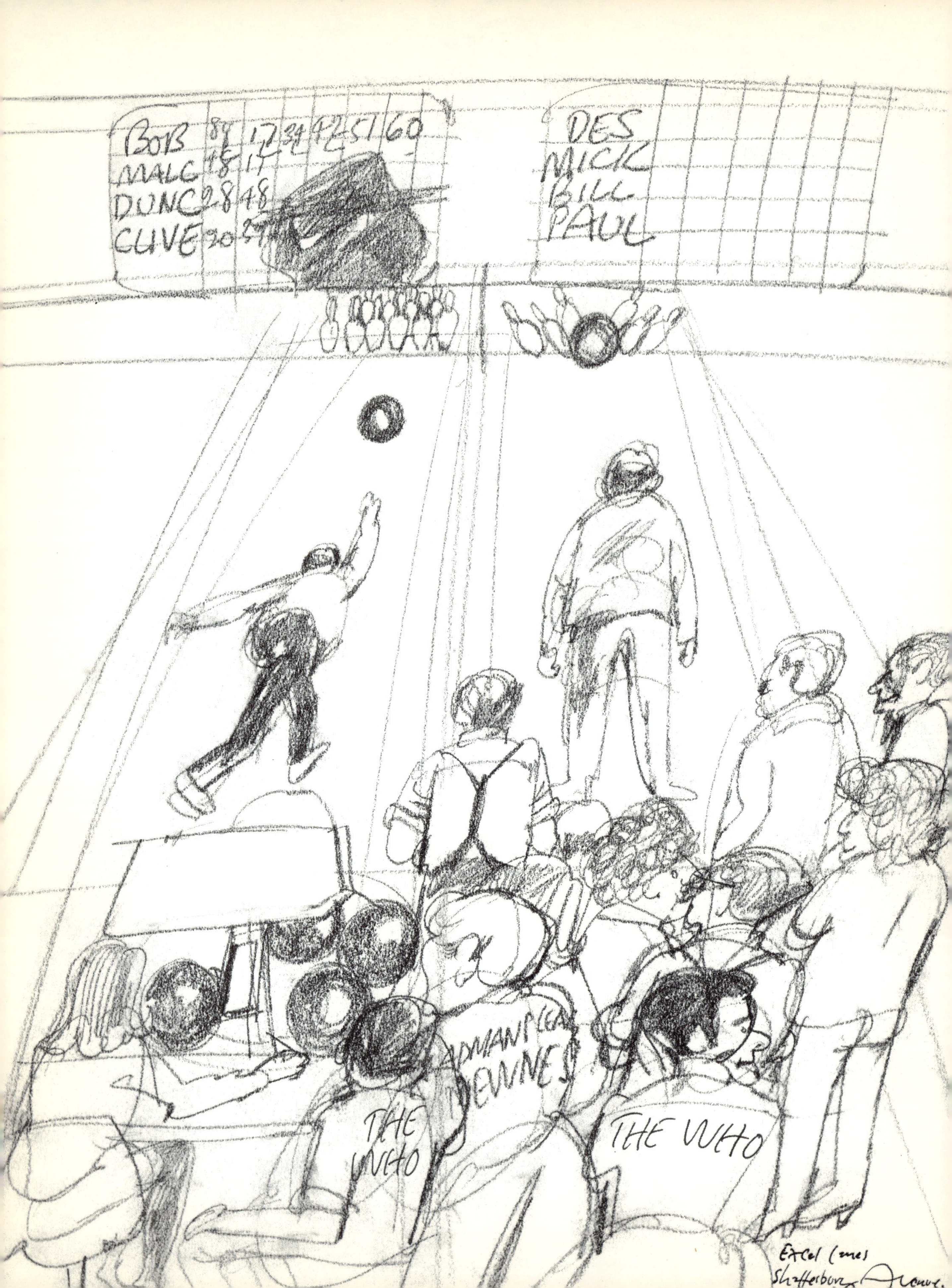
BOB
MALC
DUNC
CLIVE
DES
MICK
BILL
PAUL
THE WHO
THE WHO
Excel Lanes
Shaftesbury Avenue.

may like it or they may not. Such interest is natural enough, and one must bear it with fortitude. Sometimes I do not have this forbearance, however, and I resort to all kinds of subterfuges to avoid discovery! On these occasions, I usually pretend to be drawing something above my subjects' heads whenever they may be looking in my direction. On the other hand, you may find that some people are vain enough to freeze obligingly into complete immobility when they realize you are drawing them!

Generally, I do not actively discourage curiosity. On the contrary, it can sometimes be the means by which I can use a person or a group of people as willing models for portrait drawings. You can read more about my working in this way in the next chapter.

Personally, I found it much easier to overcome my stage fright by travel abroad. In France, Spain, and Italy, I would sit down and draw people, *and* have others watch me—without any self-consciousness. Somehow, I felt much more at ease with people I did not know. Much of one's decision to become an artist may have a great deal to do with a temporary or permanent rejection of the familiar in favor of the exotic. If this observation of mine applies to you, then working on location in a strange environment may also be a good way for you to begin. On the other hand, if you are not particularly alienated by hostile or patronizing attitudes of family, friends, and neighbors, you may find your own neighborhood or city a perfectly secure and natural context in which to work.

Wherever you choose to start drawing people, cultivate the patience and tact to recognize a stranger's interest in what you are doing. Once you have developed this perceptiveness, you will be well on your way to acquiring the ability to draw people.

Bowling lane, London, 1965
At the Excel Bowling Lanes in Shaftesbury Avenue on the fringe of Soho, the balls start rolling at five o'clock; and they keep on rolling until sunrise next day. Post Office sorting clerks, printers, and computer-operators play each other in teams with names like The Misfits, The Bookworms, *and* The Who. *"Wosn't allus like this, all 'appy like," confided a talkative attendant. "Used to get Rockers and 'ippies wontin' a cheap kip (shakedown) for the night." Drawn in ideal surroundings in about an hour with a Faber 702 sketching pencil in an 11" x 14" sketchbook of Strathmore Alexis drawing paper. From* London à la Mode, *1966. Courtesy Studio Vista Ltd., London; and Hill & Wang, Inc., New York.*

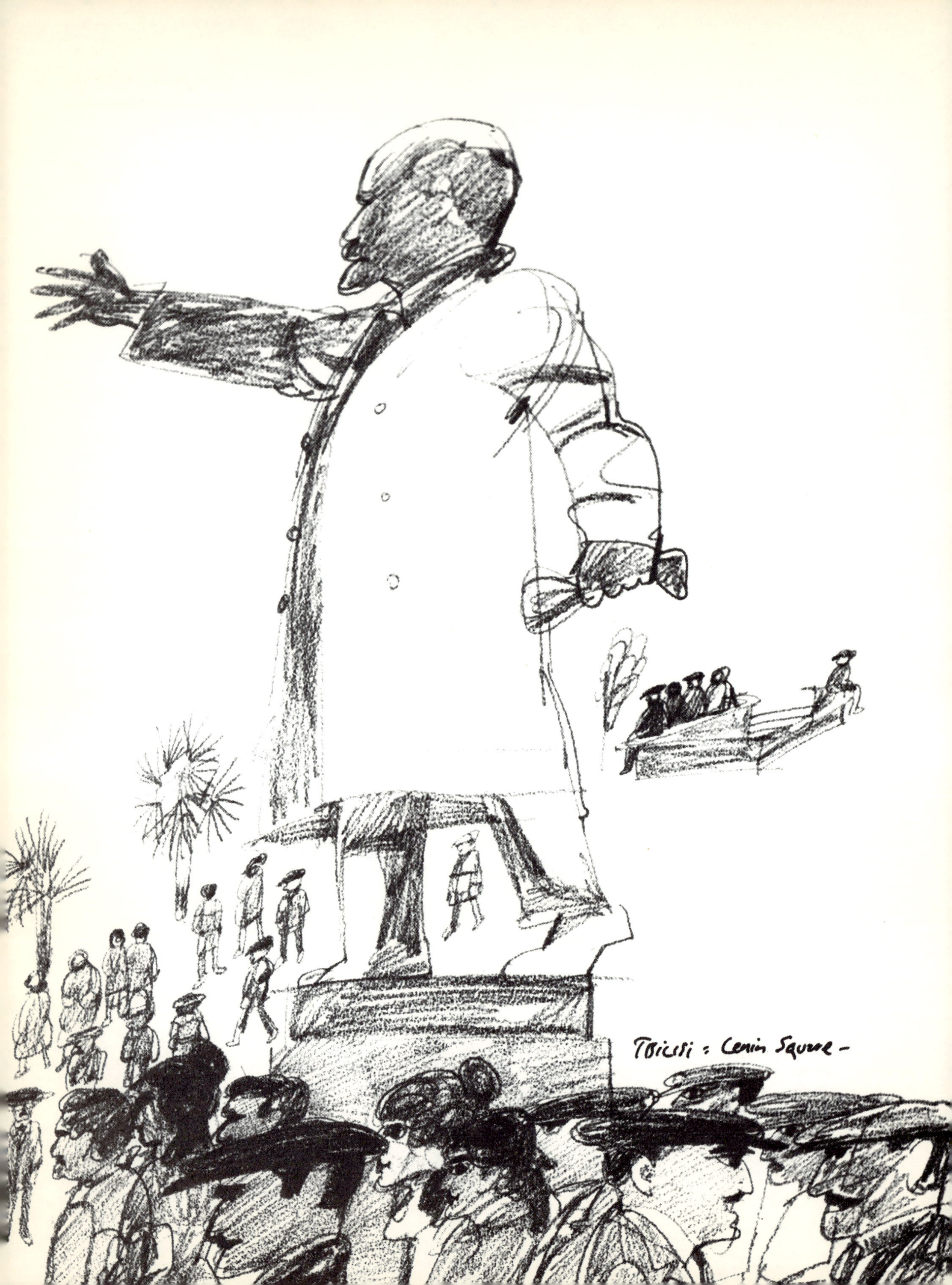
Tbilisi : Lenin Square -

CHAPTER 5

Drawing People in City Streets

CITIES, AT FIRST glance, can be frightening. Yet their complex labyrinths of stone and asphalt are immeasurably rich in humanity. This life of the streets is, in a real sense, my world. When I was a boy, streets were my playground. I am still exhilarated by the feeling that I am part of the brick and stone when I walk through the backstreets of some big city. Someone commented of the famous Swiss illustrator Steinlen that the street was his studio, because he made so many drawings of people in them. The street is also my studio.

WORKING IN ROUGH NEIGHBORHOODS

The cobbled backstreets of Dublin, the ethnic reaches of Philadelphia, and the raucous "High Streets" (Main Streets) of London are inhabited by an endless variety of ordinary people who rarely object to the chance to be portrayed by the artist.

The streets of the poor are not the only ones that move me to use them as studios. Style and elegance affect me too, and I feel almost as much at home behind a shady sycamore tree in Paris' elegant Champs Elysées as I do on New York's Lower East Side. However, I do not feel the same degree of rapport. The *Grands Boulevards* of Paris, the quiet squares of London, and New York's Fifth Avenue are, frankly, not the locales where I generally find my material for drawing what Hemingway called the "little people" (cab-drivers, shoeshine-boys, waiters, old-age pensioners, etc.).

Just as streets differ from city to city and from country to country, so do they change as they climb or descend the social scale. There are the Skid Rows and the Golden Miles, the shantytowns and the slums. Such streets, though not for the timid artist, are not as tough as they sometimes appear. I have yet to hear of any artist being beaten up or assaulted while working in a poor neighborhood. I have gone into some rough areas with my sketchbook and have been surrounded by gangs of toughs and idlers. Though their appearance may be menacing, these people watch me work with solemn and absorbed interest. The lone artist is a little like the wandering holy men of Russia, the *staretsi,* who are everywhere given shelter and are nowhere interfered with.

Ironically enough, I *have* encountered interference when working on location, but it occurred in a wealthy section, where I was the object of suspicion to a police patrol car. Anyway, the affluent are not to be seen—let alone drawn—in the streets where they live. These people and their world have to be sought elsewhere (see Chapter 9).

A SYSTEM FOR DRAWING IN THE STREET

Drawing people on location makes different demands on the artist than portrait, landscape, architectural, or any other kind of rendering does. Nevertheless, the basic problem remains essentially the same—that of organizing your reaction to a person or persons into a pictorial idea, and believing in that idea strongly enough to follow it through. Drawing people on location is essentially unpredictable and depends on the right timing, on intuition, and on luck. Hardly any drawing I make comes out quite as I anticipate, yet

Lenin Square, Tibilsi, Georgia, U.S.S.R., 1967
Wherever I worked throughout Russia, I usually had an audience. There was never any difficulty in finding me. If there was no such interest, I felt there must be something else on that day. But, curiosity, it is said, killed the cat. Like the time in Tbilisi when I had my biggest crowd yet—two hundred Georgians—watching me draw Lenin in concrete. Pressure of arms, breath, legs, and feet, however, proved too much for me, and much to everyone's disappointment (including the policeman, who looked exactly like Stalin), I had to give up! Drawn in an 11" x 14" sketchbook of Strathmore Alexis drawing paper with a Faber 702 sketching pencil. From A Russian Journey: from Suzdal to Samarkand, *1969. Courtesy Cassell and Company, London; and Hill & Wang, Inc., New York.*

on many occasions I am surprised by the batch of successful works I bring home. All you can do, therefore, is to establish a system which is flexible enough to cope with and take advantage of the unexpected.

RESEARCHING YOUR LOCATION

I have one system and it is very simple. I like to find out about a city, a district, and even a single street before I look around. I invest in a good guidebook so that I have a sound idea of the social scene and the kind of people to look for. For example, in a multiracial city like New York, where so much is happening at once, Kate Simon's excellent book, *New York: Places & Pleasures* (Meridian Paperback, $1.95), tells me *where* it all is—down to the last outdoor markets of the Lower East Side and Little Italy, and the thousand other street events like the Japanese Feast of Obon (Homage to the Dead) and the Italian *Festa* of San Gennaro.

Information can also be obtained from novels, movies, magazines, and the "What's On" column in a good local newspaper like New York's *Village Voice.* I collect all kinds of clippings, which I take along in a folder to refer to while on the road. This kind of research helps me get oriented in a city so that I can exercise my imagination much more freely when I am face to face with my subject.

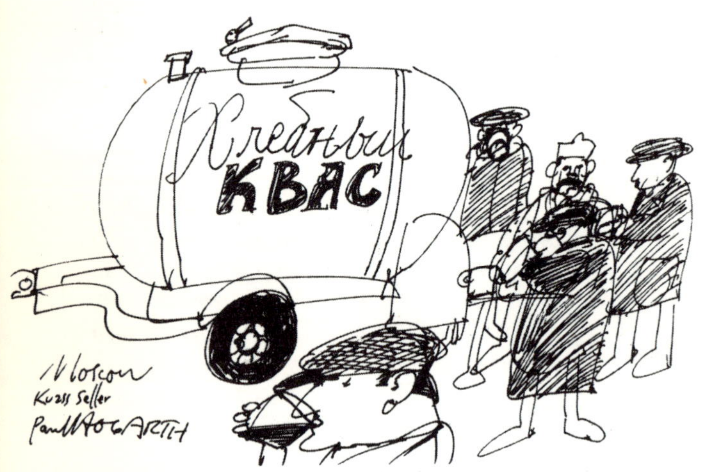

Muscovites drinking kvass in the Arbat District, Moscow, 1967
Neighborhood sights such as these, of ordinary people, invariably attract my interest. This one was made with an Esterbrook fountain pen, in a 5" x 7" English Planet sketchbook of smooth drawing paper. From A Russian Journey: from Suzdal to Samarkand, *1969. Courtesy Cassell and Company, London; and Hill & Wang, Inc., New York.*

BYSTANDERS: A HELP, NOT A HINDRANCE

I may start by drawing a street scene which involves people only as figures passing by stores or street markets. In the course of drawing such scenes, however, I move closer to people and they move closer to me; for I inevitably attract the curious, whose presence enables me to depict various characters typical of the neighborhood. To siphon off frivolous general curiosity, I choose a partially concealed position to work from. This spot may lie just off the street, in the doorway of an abandoned store, or along a side street, leaving me with a loyal core of spectators who will watch me work with particular interest for varying periods of time. If I am lucky enough to collect this captive audience, then all I have to do is take a swift look over my shoulder and pick out the face or figure my drawing needs.

SOME BASIC DECISIONS

Now I have to make a number of decisions. First, I must decide if I want any of these figures in the big street scene I'm working on. If so, should I draw them in directly now or should I note them down in a pocket sketchbook and draw them in later? These decisions largely depend on how much time I have, how much the characters interest me visually, and how long they are willing to pose.

If I am working on a busy main street full of people going about their business, I am not likely to hold an audience long enough to choose my subjects in this leisurely way. Under pressing conditions like these, I usually render the figures "on the wing" directly onto my big drawing. For more studied and detailed renderings of these busy people, I'll have to catch them in leisure moments—possibly at a bar, a theater, or a sports event. By contrast, the backstreets of a real neighborhood always provide an audience of at least one or two (depending on the time of day) who will remain with me for at least fifteen minutes. That's time enough for me to make a reasonably good study.

PUTTING YOUR SUBJECTS AT EASE

If I have a potentially cooperative audience—one that is marked by an absorbed silence, perhaps punctuated by a random compliment, and one where no one walks away, then I act. Turning over to a new page of my sketchbook, I may look up and occasionally murmur, "How about you?" I do not wait for an answer, but start drawing immediately. If I asked and then waited for permission before beginning to draw, my sitter might suddenly feel embarrassed and walk away. By continuing to draw without interruption, I am merely changing the focus of activity, while maintaining the spell I know I have established by my drawing of the street. Being asked to pose (with its risk of being made fun of) is, after all, a highly unusual request. The more friendly and easy your manner, the greater your chances for a successful drawing.

If you do not continue to relax your model by offering a certain amount of small talk, you risk dissipating the spell too quickly. To keep this from happening, I quickly get down the essential lines of my drawing and then usually ask the individuals why they are interested in drawing. If they become increasingly nervous or self-conscious, I tilt my sketchbook toward them so that they can see themselves being drawn.

If you do not care to involve yourself personally, you can find many situations to draw without directly communicating with your subject. I am thinking of lively scenes of the people who congregate in the old quarters of Asian, African, American, and European cities, where the streets are still frequented by various peddlers and itinerant entertainers. Whether they sell toys or chestnuts, water or icecream, horses or newspapers; whether they sing, dance, juggle, or recite Shakespeare, such characters are always interesting.

In such cities (particularly in Africa and Asia), there is no need to request permission to draw. Frequently, these scenes and their people become my starting point for a lively drawing of a street group which involves the most interesting character as the centerpiece. In my experience, a sort of communion is established between me and my audience, with the result that anything I draw is acceptable to them. On these occasions, the artist himself causes the wonder and awe that the antics of a wandering magician generally produce.

The streets have given me all kinds of experiences with different types of people who are sincerely absorbed in watching me work. Their intense interest, more than being a source of material, often provides the human contact I need and reassures me that, as an artist, I really have something to "say" about these people. Like an actor, I derive strength from my communication with an appreciative audience.

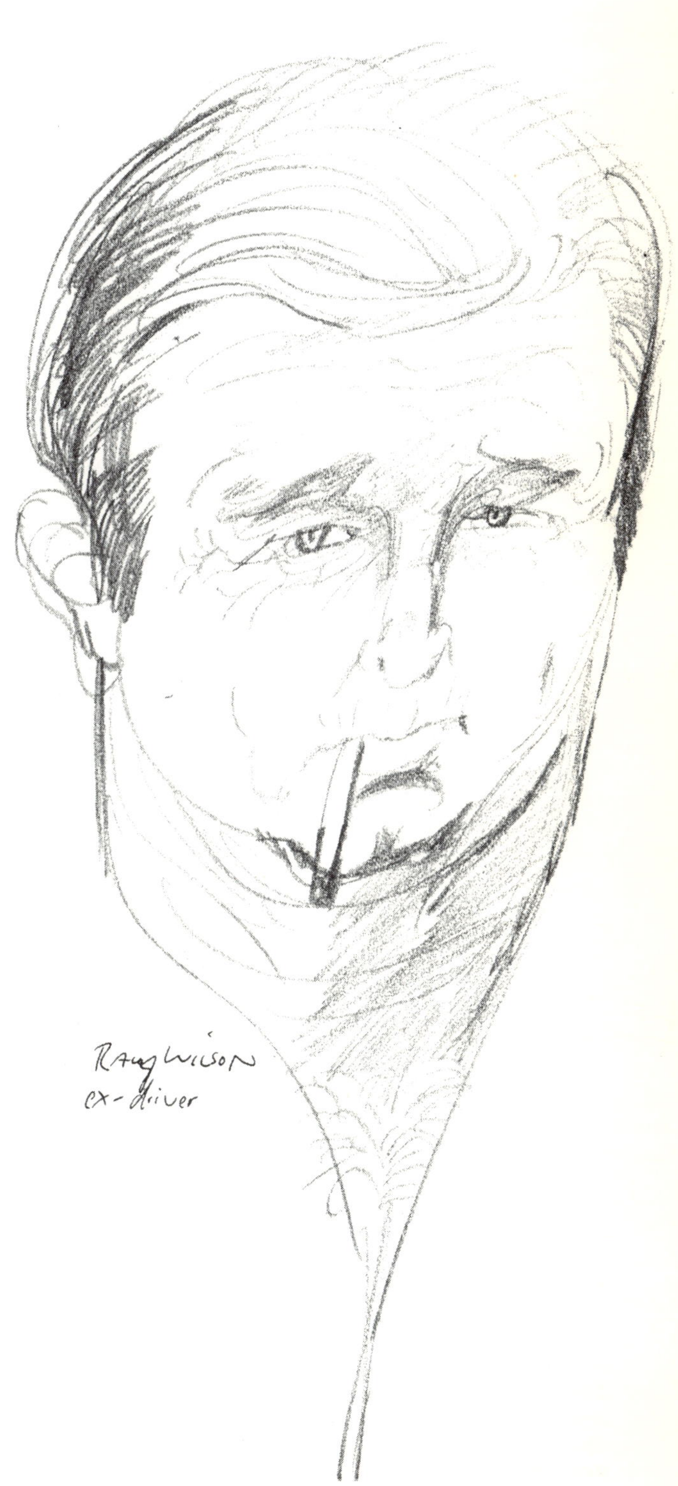

Ray Wilson, Charlotte, North Carolina, 1965
The big stock-car event, the Charlotte National 400, has as much going on behind the scenes as up front on the track where the action is. While I worked on a drawing of a pit-stop, a big rugged man watched me. Sensing his interest, and that he had something to tell me, I turned to him and drew his portrait. As I worked, he told me that he had been a driver himself, but gave up when both legs were broken in a fatal collision with Bob Myers and Curtis Carter in 1953. Now he worked with a mobile wrecking crew. "It needs," he added, "a special kind of bastard to drive those babies!" Drawn in an 11" x 14" sketchbook of Strathmore Alexis drawing paper with a Faber 702 sketching pencil. Commissioned for Sports Illustrated. *Reproduced by permission.*

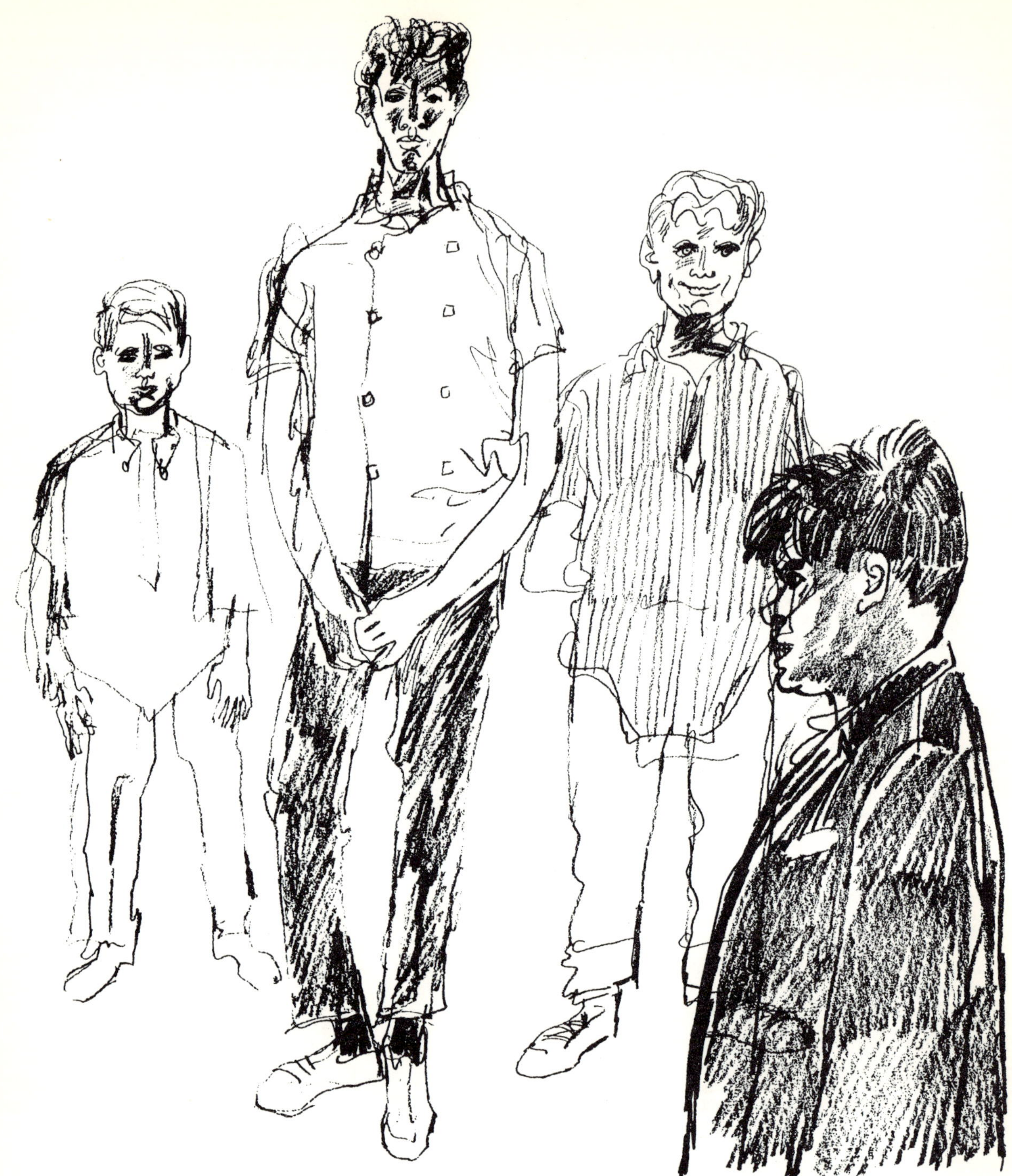

Gang boys, New York, *1962*
I was drawing Jewish and Puerto Rican stores on the Lower East Side, when "The Assassins" stopped by and watched. Sensing their interest, I started drawing them, assembling the gang around the tallest. Drawn with a 4B Venus graphite pencil on a 16" x 20½" sheet of Saunders mold-made, cream wove writing paper. From Brendan Behan's New York, *1964. Courtesy The Hutchinson Publishing Group, London, and Bernard Geis Associates, New York.*

Newspaper vendor, London, 1966

City streets are full of natural models, but this does not mean that they will always consent to being drawn. To avoid attracting their attention and the attention of others, I sometimes draw them from a concealed position. Drawn with a 7B Venus graphite pencil in a 9" x 12" sketchbook of Ingres paper. From London à la Mode, *1966. Courtesy Studio Vista Ltd., London; and Hill & Wang, Inc., New York.*

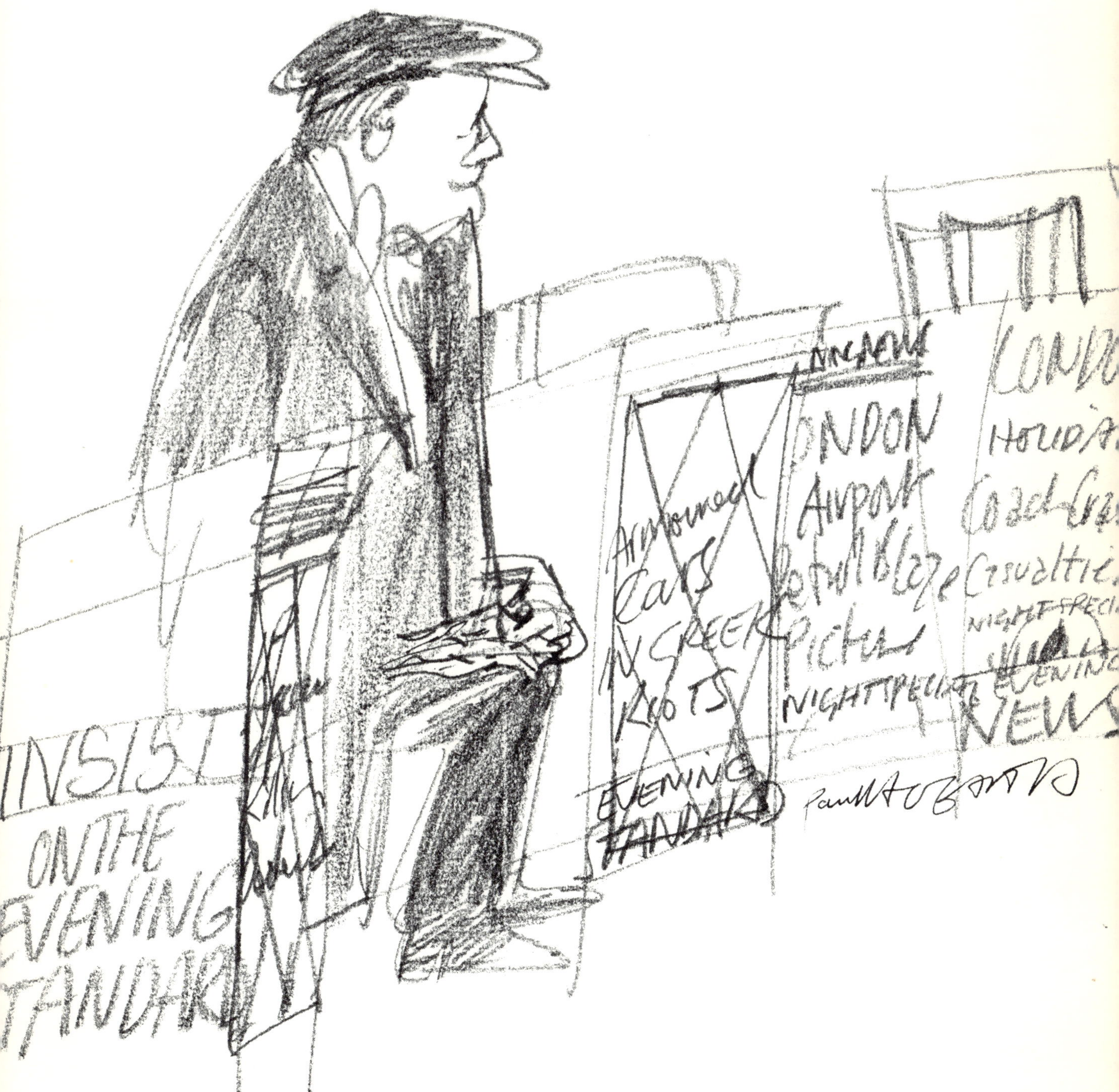

The Liverpool Cavern, England, 1965
I combined pen and pencil line for the backdrop of graffiti inscribed by the fans of this original haunt of the Beatles. The young lovers were drawn in with a Faber 702 sketching pencil in an 11" x 14" sketchbook of three-ply, high surface Strathmore drawing paper.

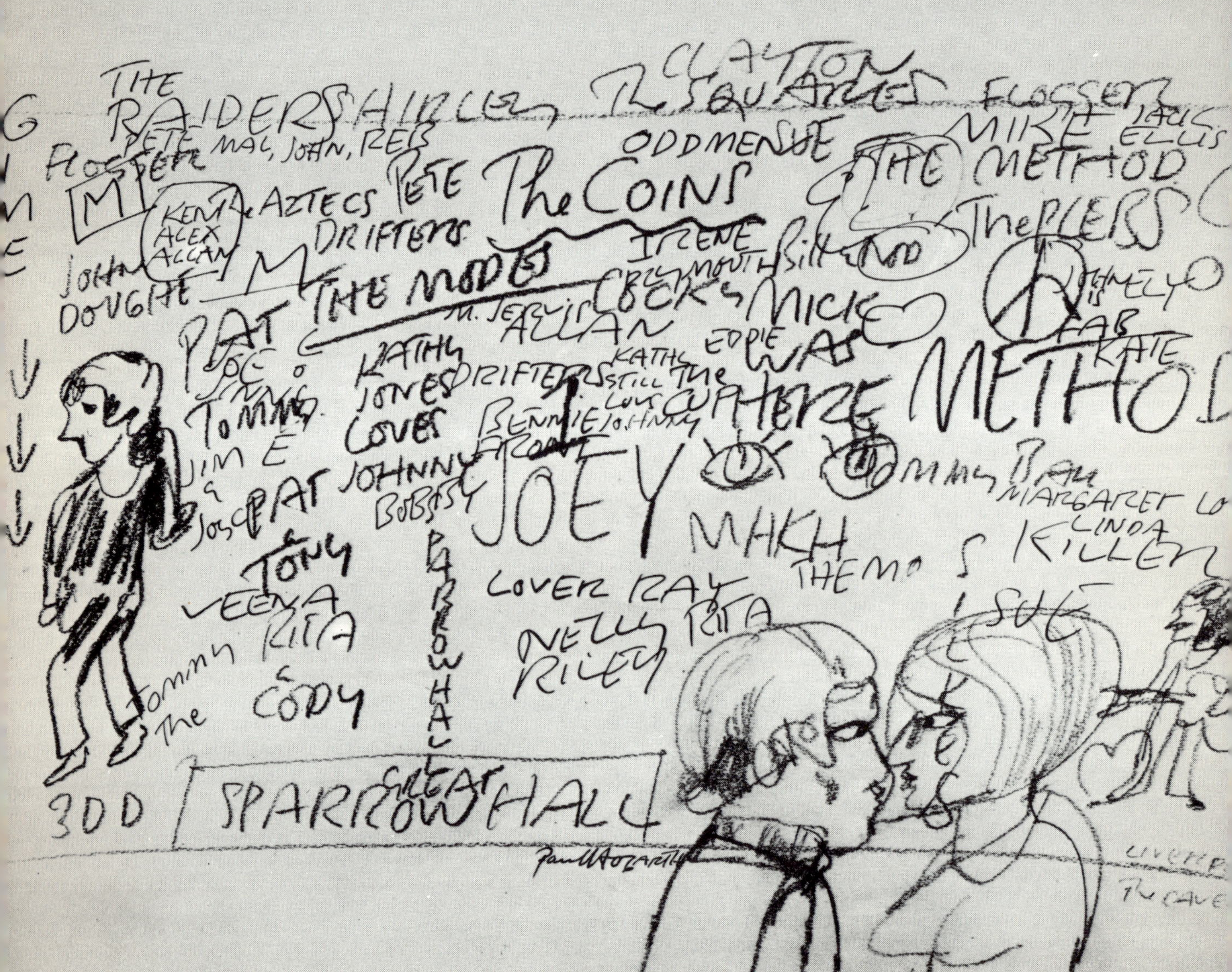

CHAPTER 6

Drawing People at Play

MY OWN ART school figure compositions, like everyone else's, were full of inhibited puppet figures dutifully shopping in markets, energetically digging up highways, or wearily going to work. Even when I was engaged in this tedium, it occurred to me that people must be much more fun to draw when they are *enjoying* themselves. But whenever I tried to draw people at play, the very sight of them having such a good time without me made me feel so desolate that I always gave up!

After these early frustrated attempts, I returned only occasionally to the subject of drawing people at play. Carried away by the spectacle of labor itself, for a long time I did little else but draw people hard at work, on farms or construction sites. My attitude began to change in 1965, when I went to the United States to report a major stock-car race, the Charlotte 400 in North Carolina, for *Sports Illustrated.* In 1961, I had tried to draw a big auto race at Le Mans, France —an effort which failed because I did not move in close enough to the people involved to draw them convincingly. Now, four years later, I had acquired confidence. New tools and materials like Faber Markettes, soft Faber 702 graphite pencils, and various Strathmore drawing papers certainly helped develop this confidence. I was also encouraged by art director Richard Gangel's quiet request that I "tell what really goes on" and by my possession of a press badge which allowed me to draw anywhere I wished. But the most important lesson I learned was that by working out an imaginative approach to an assignment or project, I was able to generate enough self-confidence to face any situation.

WORKING OUT AN APPROACH

When I returned to England with this newly won confidence, I decided to tackle a project that had long interested me, but which I had always postponed because it meant constantly observing and involving myself with people. Until I developed what I call my "approach concept," I could not imagine *how* I would draw people in the context I wished. The project long on my mind was to draw the life of London, where I had lived for many years, which I knew intimately, yet which I had hardly touched as material. Coincidentally, David Herbert, Editor of Studio Vista Ltd., proposed publishing an album of my drawings. To my delight, he supported my idea of doing a book which would illustrate London life of the 1960s.

Once we agreed on the concept of the book, all that was left to work out was the approach. London struck me as being very different from Charlotte, North Carolina. The English city teemed every single minute of the day with new, unbridled vitality. I had to devise a way to capture this action and aliveness as it occurred—and in as many different places as possible at the same time. To realize my concept, I decided to borrow the eighteenth-century printsellers' device of dividing my material into morning, noon, evening, and night subjects.

COLLECTING MATERIAL

Next, I had to discover exactly where to find the best and most lively material. I took my time with this research, building up files of notes and clippings on where and how people relaxed at various times of the day, and sometimes visiting these places for a preliminary reconnaissance. If I could not dig up the information myself, I would consult more knowledgeable friends. For example, I remember asking such a friend if English nannies could still be seen, and being advised by him to appear any morning in "The Dell" in Kensington Palace Gardens. Sure enough, the nannies—if only a few—were still there, very much the last of the old guard, and glaring suspiciously at a new generation clad in miniskirts and colored tights. As an artist, all I had to do was pin down this nostalgic and humorous scene in a 5" x 7" sketchbook, which I did from the vantage point of a park bench.

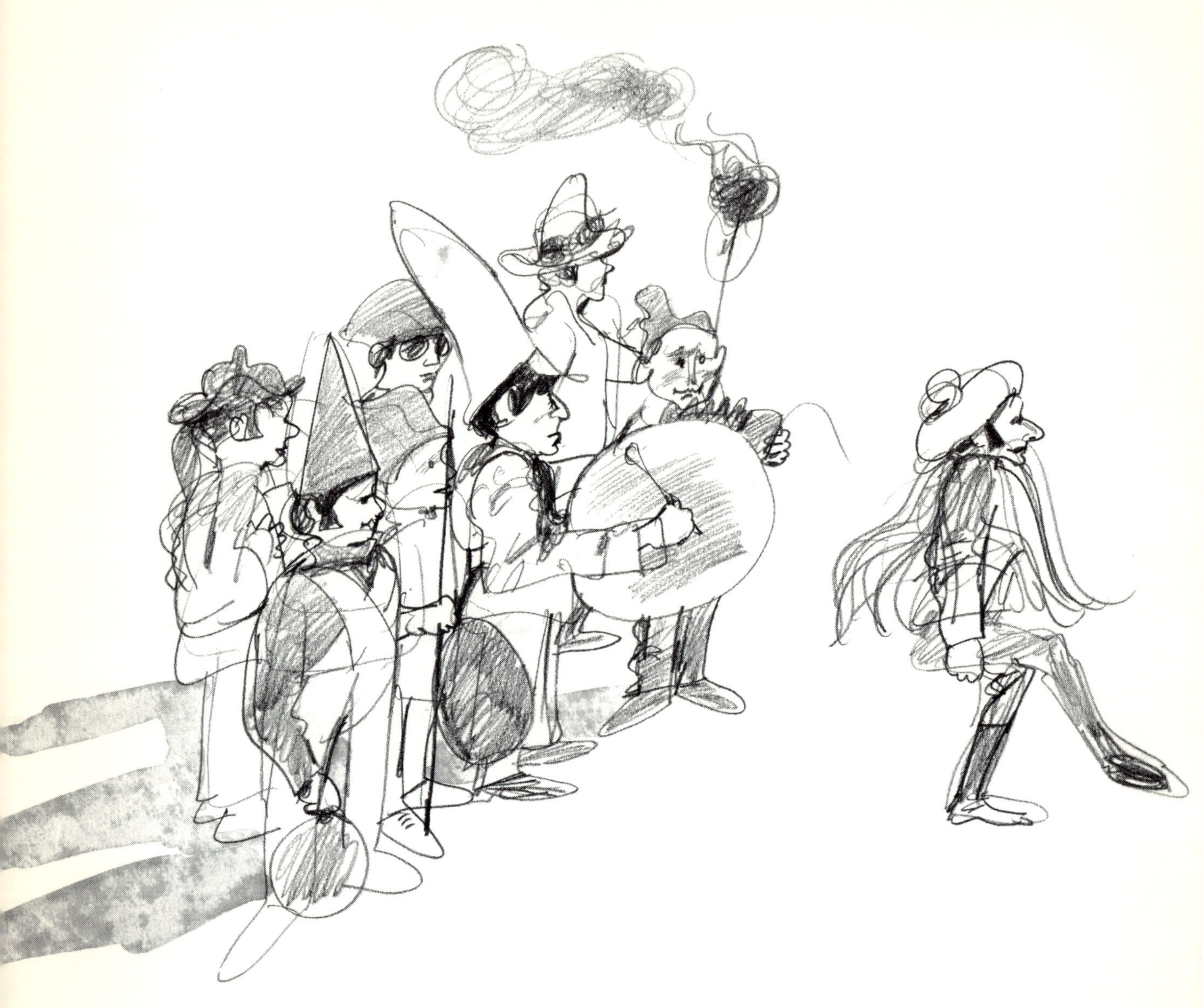

Young "Wren Boys" dancing the jig, Listowel, Ireland, 1969
The pre-Christian pop groups known as the "Wren Boys" have a junior section who perform annually through September at various folk-festivals in the southwest corner of the Emerald Isle. Drawn with Faber 702 sketching and 3B Venus pencils in a 10¾" x 14½" English Planet sketchbook of smooth drawing paper. Courtesy Lithopinion, *Winter 1969. Copyright by Local One, Amalgamated Lithographers of America, New York.*

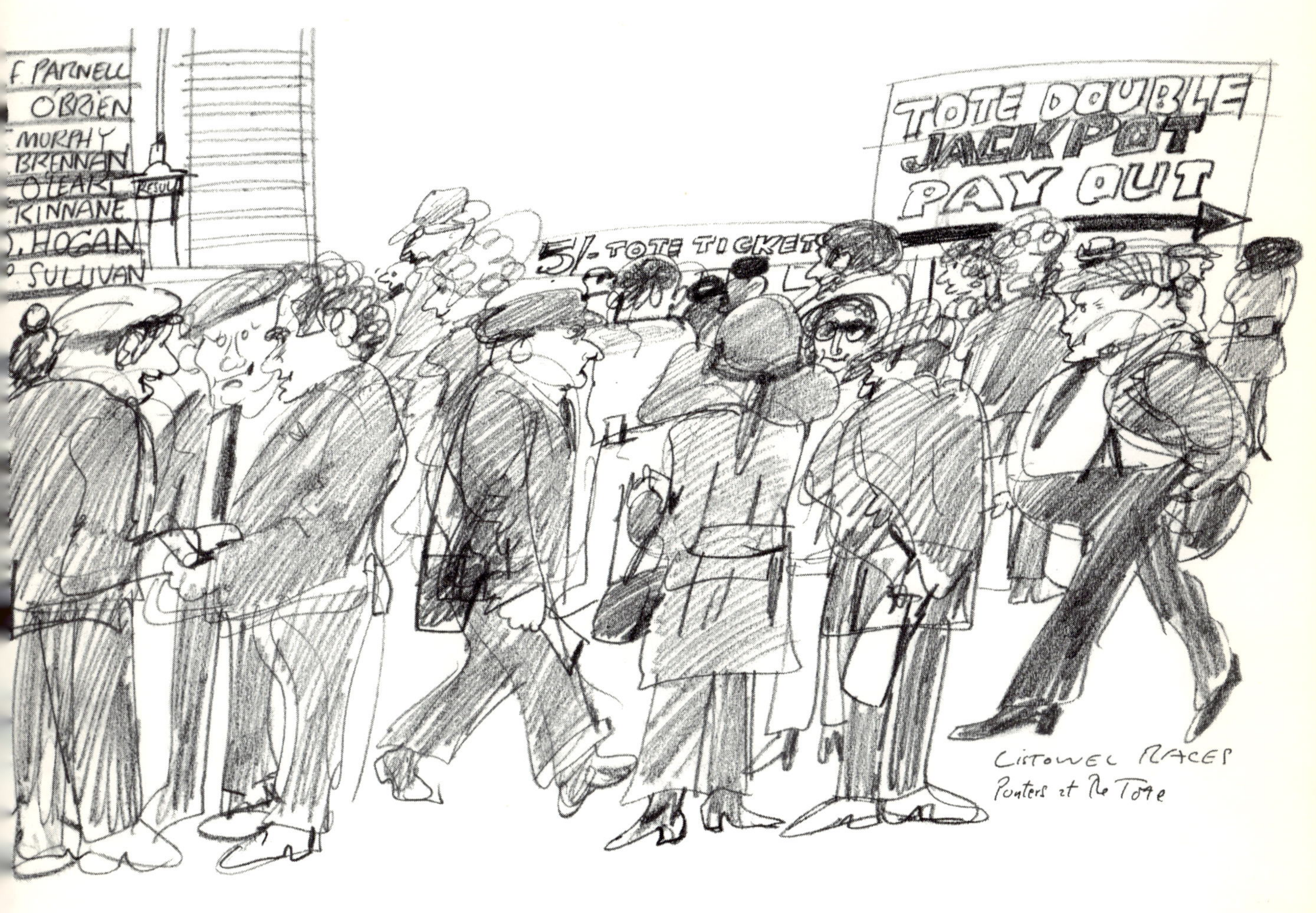

Punters at the tote, *Listowel Races, Ireland, 1969*
The gambling urge eliminates any need to conceal my activities, thus providing excellent material for character sketching. Drawn with a Faber 702 sketching pencil in a 10¾" x 14½" English Planet sketchbook of smooth drawing paper. Courtesy Lithopinion, *Winter 1969. Copyright by Local One, Amalgamated Lithographers of America, New York.*

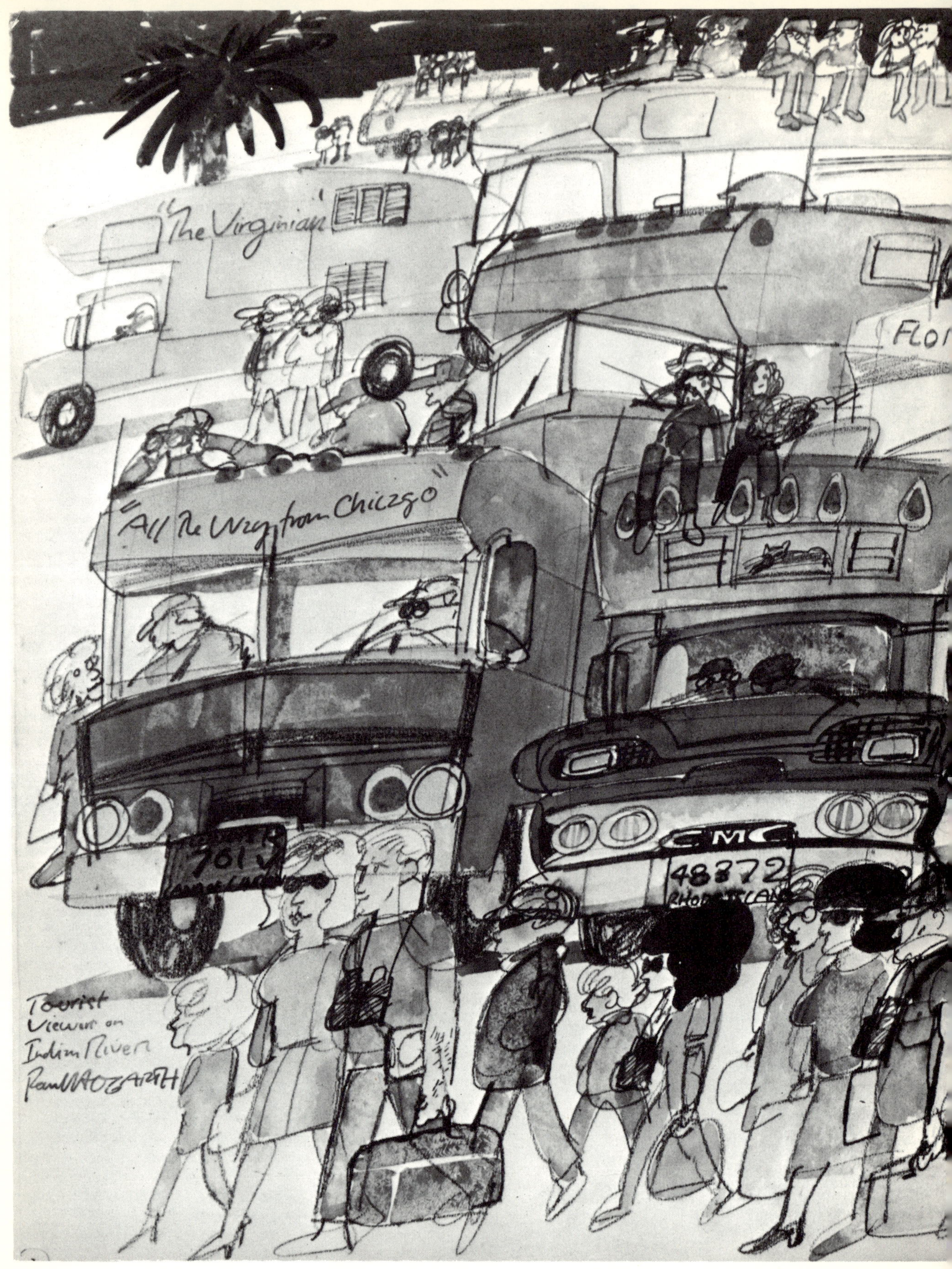
"The Virginian"
"All The Way from Chicago"
Flo
GMC
48372
Tourist
Viewers on
Indian River
Paul MOZARTH

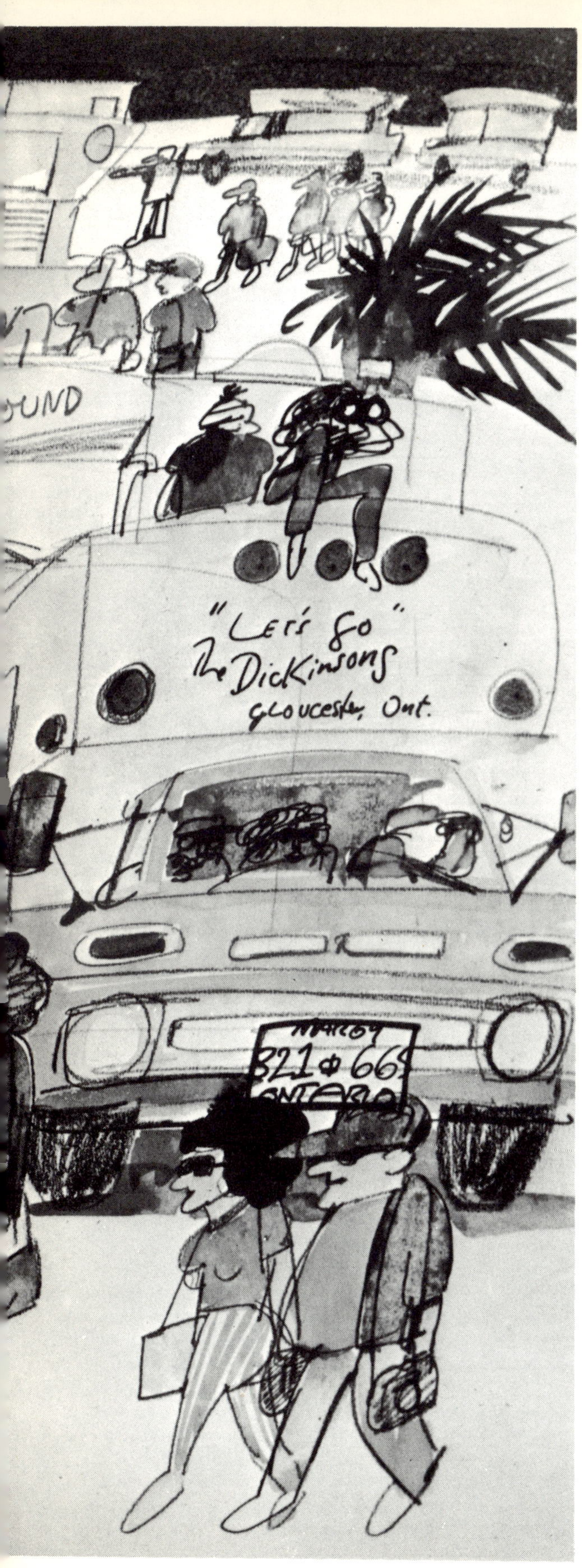

The Launching of Apollo 9, Florida, March 1969—viewers on Indian River

The best viewing area is the Indian River shoreline north of the NASA Causeway to Cape Kennedy. Many have made the trip from as far away as Canada, Chicago, Pittsburgh, and San Francisco. The best places have been filled for days; cars, campers, and mobile homes are jammed side by side. Then the great day dawns and viewers squint through telescopes and fieldglasses at Cape Kennedy, six miles distant. Drawn in an 11" x 14" sketchbook of Strathmore Alexis drawing paper with Faber Design Markettes and a Faber 702 sketching pencil. Blotted washes of Grumbacher watercolors were also used to add texture to clothing and trees; pen line was used to draw license plates and slogans on the automobiles. Courtesy Daily Telegraph Magazine, *London.*

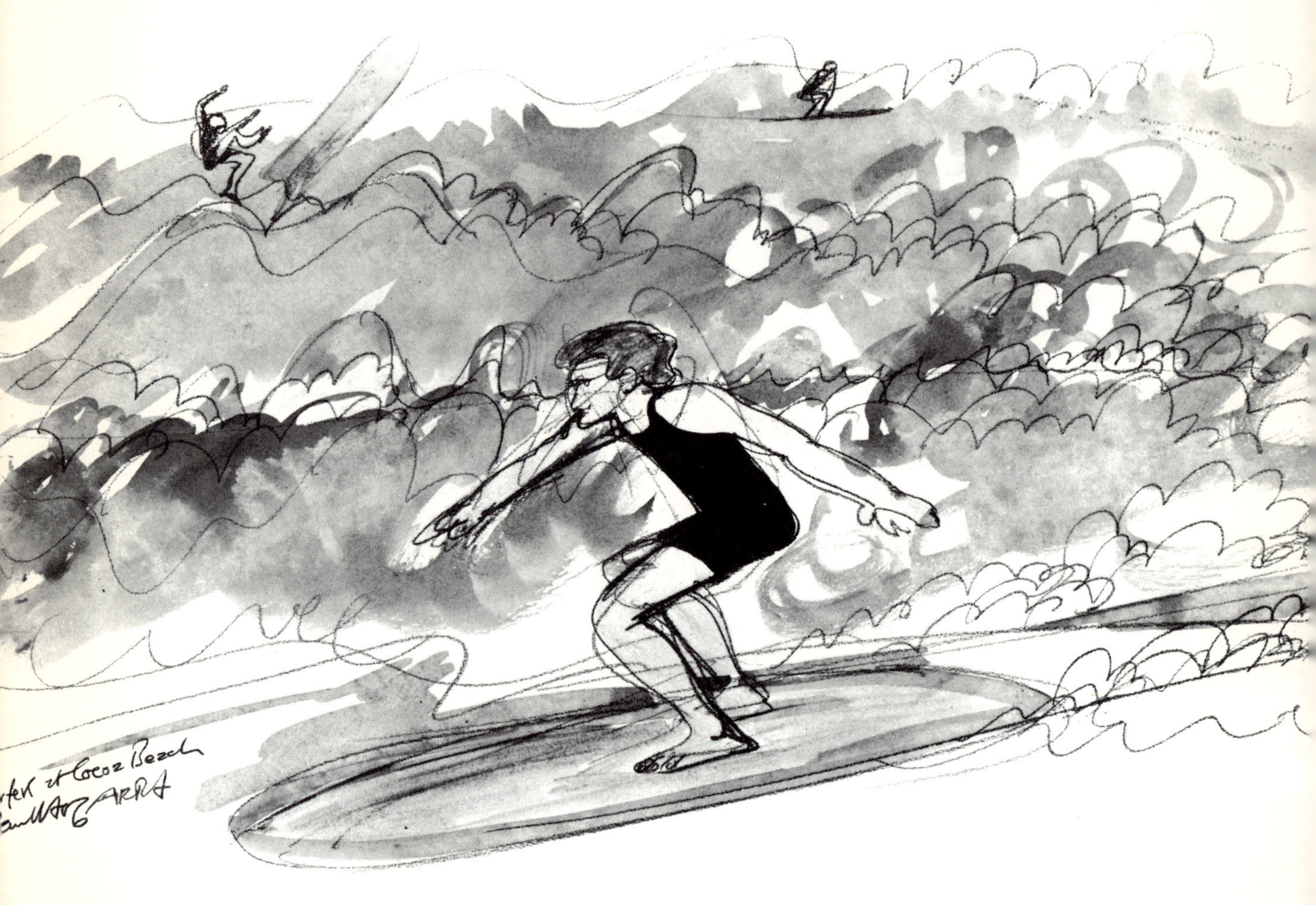

Surfers at Cocoa Beach, Florida, 1969
Rapid-action drawings of people are usually the fruit of constant analysis combined with a good sense of line and composition. More often than not, I get the one but not the other. Here, I got close to what I wanted, using a 6B Venus graphite pencil to outline the movement. Then I lightly washed in the sea with a diluted wash of veridian watercolor, bringing out the foreground figure of the boy in stronger, less diluted washes of yellow ochre and Payne's gray. Drawn in an 11" x 14" sketchbook of Strathmore Alexis drawing paper over the period of an hour. Grumbacher watercolors were applied with a Winsor & Newton No. 6 sable brush. Courtesy Daily Telegraph Magazine, *London.*

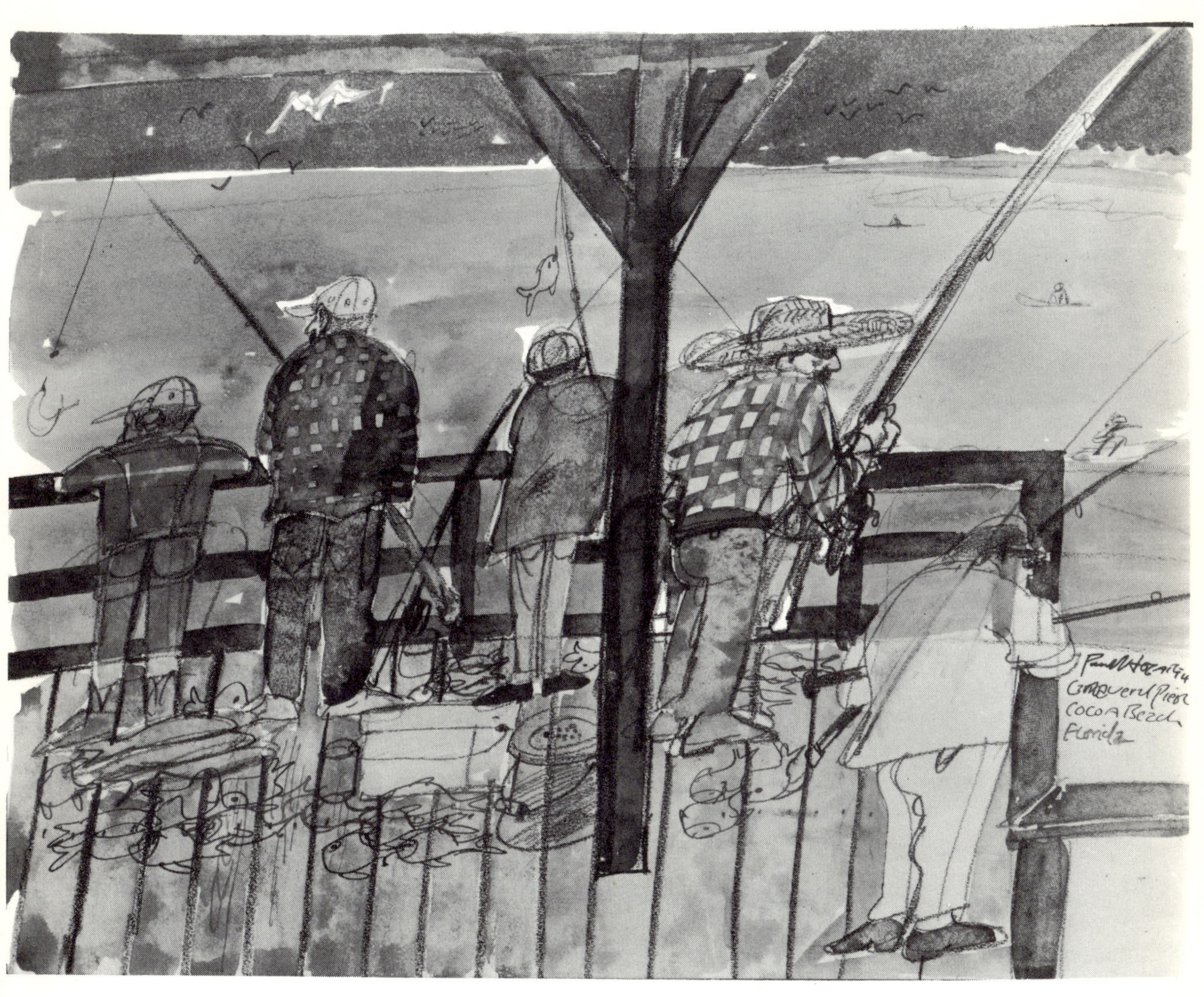

Weekend fisherman, Canaveral Pier, Florida, 1969
This Sunday morning scene in the fisherman's paradise was drawn in an 11" x 14" sketchbook of Strathmore Alexis drawing paper with a Faber 702 sketching pencil. Grumbacher watercolors were then applied with a Japanese brush to fill in the figures. When dry, diluted Pelikan Fount India ink with a Gillot 303 nib was used to draw in the wriggling forms of fish and flying birds. Courtesy Daily Telegraph Magazine, *London.*

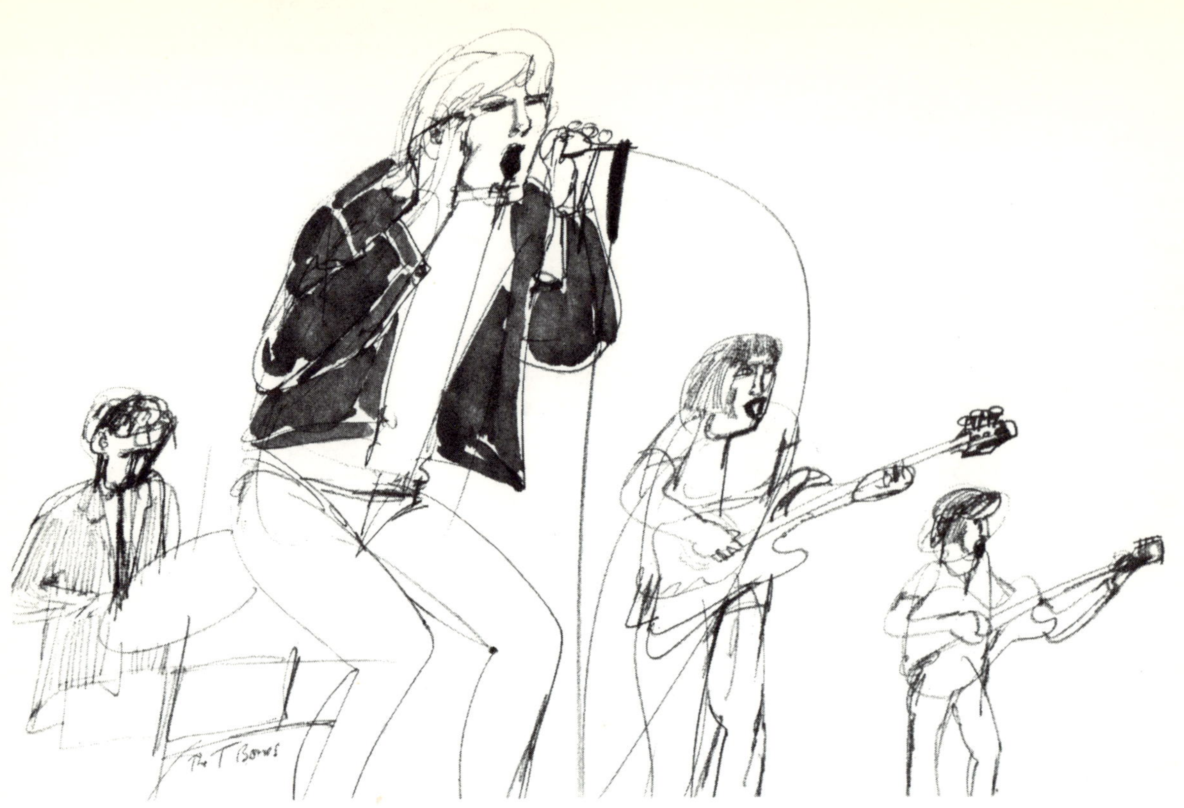

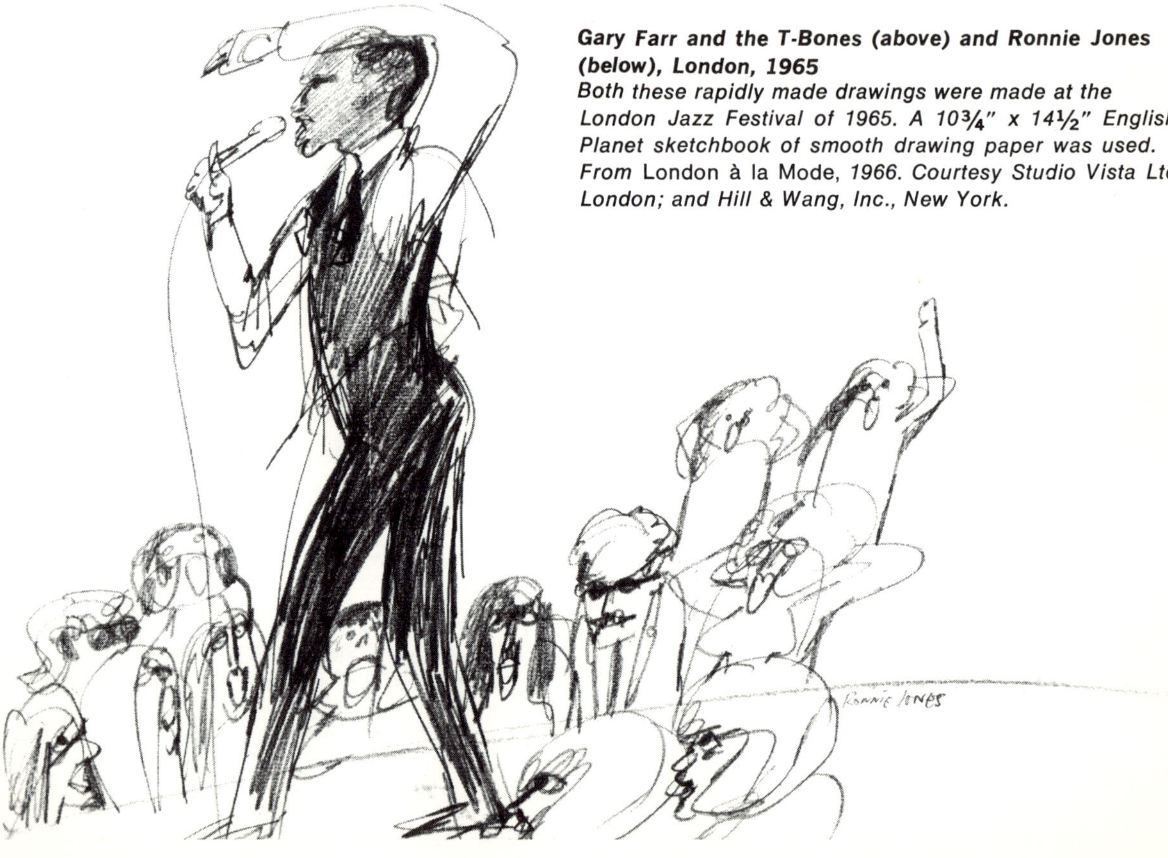

Gary Farr and the T-Bones (above) and Ronnie Jones (below), London, 1965
Both these rapidly made drawings were made at the London Jazz Festival of 1965. A 10¾" x 14½" English Planet sketchbook of smooth drawing paper was used. From London à la Mode, *1966. Courtesy Studio Vista Ltd., London; and Hill & Wang, Inc., New York.*

I can recall other such incidents, too. From a journalist friend who wrote a racing column for the London magazine *Queen,* I learned of unusual evening races at Alexandra Park, where only the very youngest and the very oldest horses run. This system of collecting information and then checking it out often saved me time and trouble. Research also shaped my feeling toward the subject and drew me closer to it.

MAKING A WORKING SCHEDULE

The next step was to make an actual working schedule from my mass of notes on places to visit and draw. So that I would not miss anything, I decided to devote one month to drawing morning scenes, one month to afternoon scenes, one month to early evening scenes, and a final month to night spots.

I usually visited places like parks, museums, and zoos in the mornings. The afternoons were spent at flower shows, circuses, and the like. In the evenings, I'd go to bowling lanes, theaters, and bingo halls. At night (which I write about more fully in the next chapter), I'd attend burlesque shows, nightclubs, and restaurants.

WORKING IN ZOOS AND MUSEUMS

To my surprise, I sometimes found that if I could successfully combine a telling image with my own sense of humor, the most stereotyped place yielded good material. In zoos, for example, the spectacle of open jaws and colorful exposures prompts either awed silence or hilarious laughter. Caged creatures frequently provoke quite unexpected dialogue from spectators. I often lounged around groups or families so that I could watch and listen. One day, in the London Zoo, I was drawing a harassed cockney mother and her four children as they silently gazed at an alligator. Soon there were whispers and chuckles from the children as the alligator stared back with what appeared to be a familiar grimace. Suddenly Mum exploded with, "If you say it looks like me agin, I'll knock yore blinkin' 'eads orf!"—a comic moment that naturally became the subject of my drawing, as I made haste to sketch her scurrying brood.

Museums, because of their atmosphere of subdued anticipation (to which my imagination immediately responds), also make good artist's haunts. Rather than draw people first and then find background objects which relate to the subject, my working procedure in museums is just the opposite. That is, I usually look for the object first, then find people that relate to it.

In the great Franklin Institute in Philadelphia, for example, I discovered the enormous seated marble figure of Benjamin Franklin which dominates a vast colonnaded court. Here, the comical efforts people make to get a good look at the statue inspired me to create a drawing in which the spectators, who have fallen flat on their backs to improve their view, happily remain on the floor because they're so tired!

WORKING IN THEATERS AND CIRCUSES

People enjoy themselves in different ways, depending on where they are, in theaters, circuses, department stores or fairs; they are moved to weep, laugh, or visibly long for the good things of life. In a theater, for example, the artist can observe in the audience a complete range of human emotions. As an artist, the best place for you to sit is on the side, about eight or nine rows back from the stage. From this spot, you can glance obliquely across a sea of faces. If the play at all reflects the human experience, the audience will soon become absorbed in the performance. This moment is the best time to work; I open a 5" x 7" sketchbook, rest it on my lap; and then, glancing up occasionally, I select the particular faces which help build in my drawing a sense of animated response to the actors' performance.

The circus, on the other hand, is itself so lively that I usually concentrate on drawing the performers, rather than the audience. Only if and when I want to capture the audience's response to a particular act, do I relate the riders, clowns, and jugglers to the spectators. At fairs, however, I like to observe the audience's facial expressions, and therefore place myself on the sidelines or behind whatever display or demonstration is taking place. At the London International Boat Show, I caught a glimpse of the crowd's wistful longing as they watched scuba divers cutting through the water with aquatic ease.

WORKING IN THE EVENING

I particularly enjoy working in the evening—from six o'clock to about nine o'clock—when innocent pleasures bring people together and when differences and arguments are few. The day's work is at last over, and the bowling lanes are crowded with clusters of laughing friends playing a game or two before they go home. A little later, the bingo halls fill up rapidly with people, old and young, who are caught up in fantasies of great expectations. Meanwhile, at the tracks (dogs in the winter, horses in the summer), the raucous cries of chain-smoking *aficionados* pierce the air, as they leave disappointments behind them and head for the nearest bar. "Bookies," gouges Morrie Levi on the slatey wall of a Victorian men's room, "are the lowest form of animal life!"

And that is only a small part of what I mean when I say that people are more fun to draw when they are enjoying themselves!

Cloisonné craftsman, China, 1954
This Peking potter is erecting an intricate framework of brass into which enamel is poured. I made the drawing in about an hour after careful analysis of the delicate movements of his hands. A medium Hardtmuth charcoal lead was used on Abbey Mill pastel paper. From Looking at China, *1955. Courtesy Lawrence and Wishart, London.*

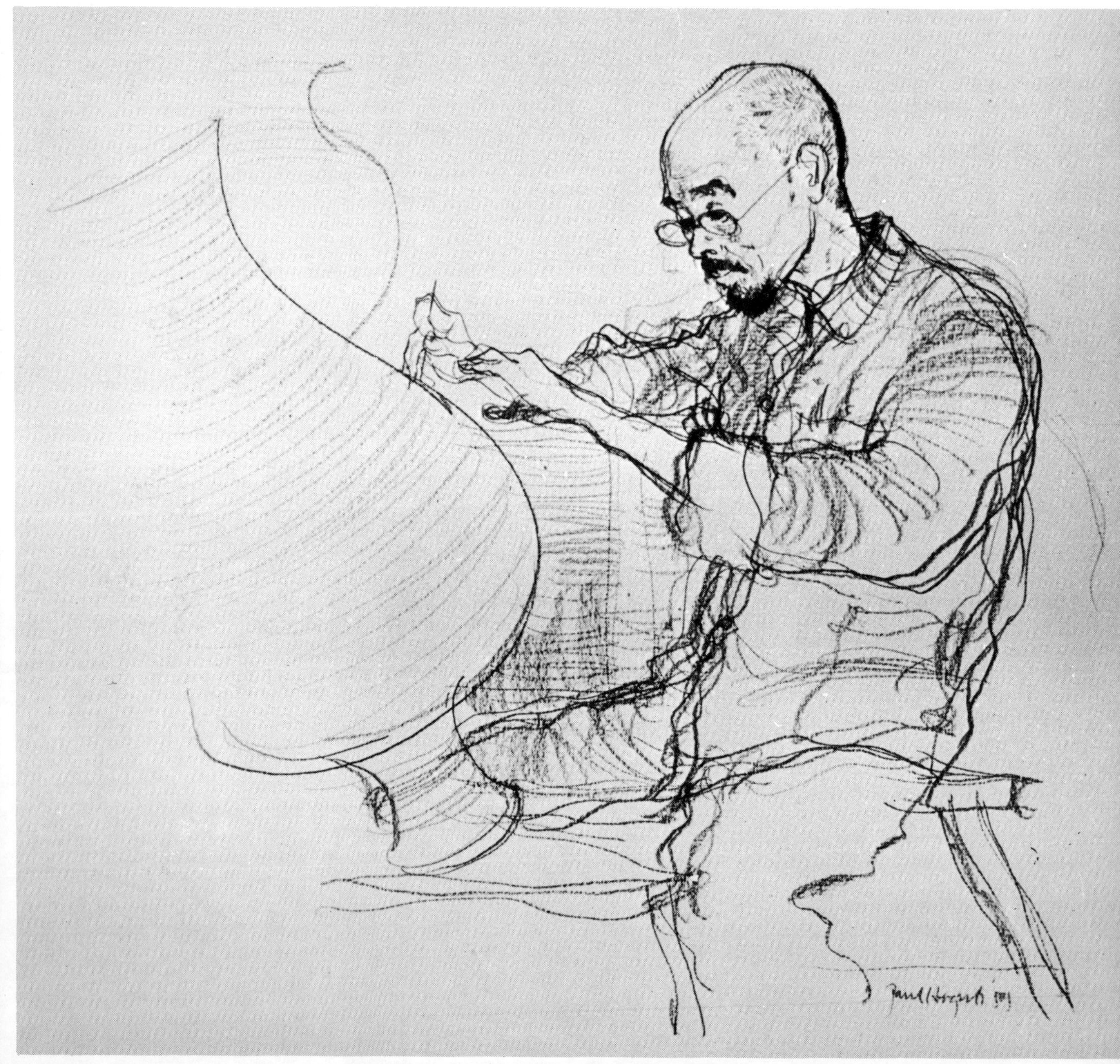

CHAPTER 7

Drawing People at Work

MAN CONSTANTLY seeks to dominate the forces of nature. He uses ever more ambitious technology, and in my observation of his struggle I have often been involved in unique and frequently adventurous spheres of activity.

WORKING IN FACTORIES

One such adventure began in the summers of 1947 and 1948, which I spent in war-ravaged Yugoslavia and Poland depicting aspects of the reconstruction of these two countries. The epic sense of collective human endeavor that was so characteristic of the post-war years throughout eastern Europe led me to focus, for the first time, on the theme of people at work. I found myself selecting and drawing groups and individuals of my own generation who seemed to symbolize the desperately heroic efforts that were being made.

It was impossible not to admire and sympathize with their efforts. The rebuilding of Warsaw, for example, made me feel that I had a strong, almost *moral,* obligation to express these feelings pictorially. This drive, in turn, gave me the necessary self-confidence to make a start on drawing people at work. Unfortunately, I found it much easier to feel than to draw, so most of these attempts never amounted to much. I had set myself the very difficult task of infusing a life class approach with the emotion of a personal eye-witness statement. In spite of the obstacles, I kept trying. Unexpectedly, encouragement came from the very people I was attempting to portray, and this was enough to keep me going!

DEPICTING INDUSTRY

I found myself recalling the past failures of my first attempts when I made a second visit to Yugoslavia in February, 1967. This time I had an assignment from *Fortune* to depict the progress of industrialization. Working alternately from a brief of suggested locales made up by Gilbert Burck (a *Fortune* contributing editor who was writing the story), and using my own initiative to find good additional material, I finally turned in a portfolio of drawings which conveyed the same spirit as my earlier work, but which was realized in a far more sophisticated manner.

I had much the same emotional reaction to the subject as before, except that now I thought about how I would make my drawing as well as of how I would dramatize a face or a figure. My brief also helped. For example, at Zagreb's Sesvete meat products complex, I realized that the most effective approach—both from my own viewpoint and that of the writer of the story—was to pictorialize the Yugoslavs operating the American-built machines used for filling cans with various kinds of food. Having made this decision, I moved on to the next step—effectively showing a worker actually *using* one of these machines. Then I noticed a former peasant woman, who, with her back to me, was operating a liver-paste filling machine. She seemed more accustomed to working on the land than in a factory, and her figure, molded by manual labor in the fields, offered a marked contrast to the smoothly functioning modern machine she controlled. This contrast was exactly the pictorial statement I wanted—a drawing not only about a worker, but also about an agricultural country rapidly industrializing itself.

GAINING ADMITTANCE TO FACTORIES

It is not as easy or as convenient to draw people at work as it is to draw them at play or in the street. Factories, farms, construction projects, and industrial plants are to be found all over the country, but the really interesting plants or exploration projects are usually not very accessible. For security reasons, they are either off-limits to the unlicensed observer or they are situated in remote places that are impossible to reach without the sponsorship of the company in question or of a magazine.

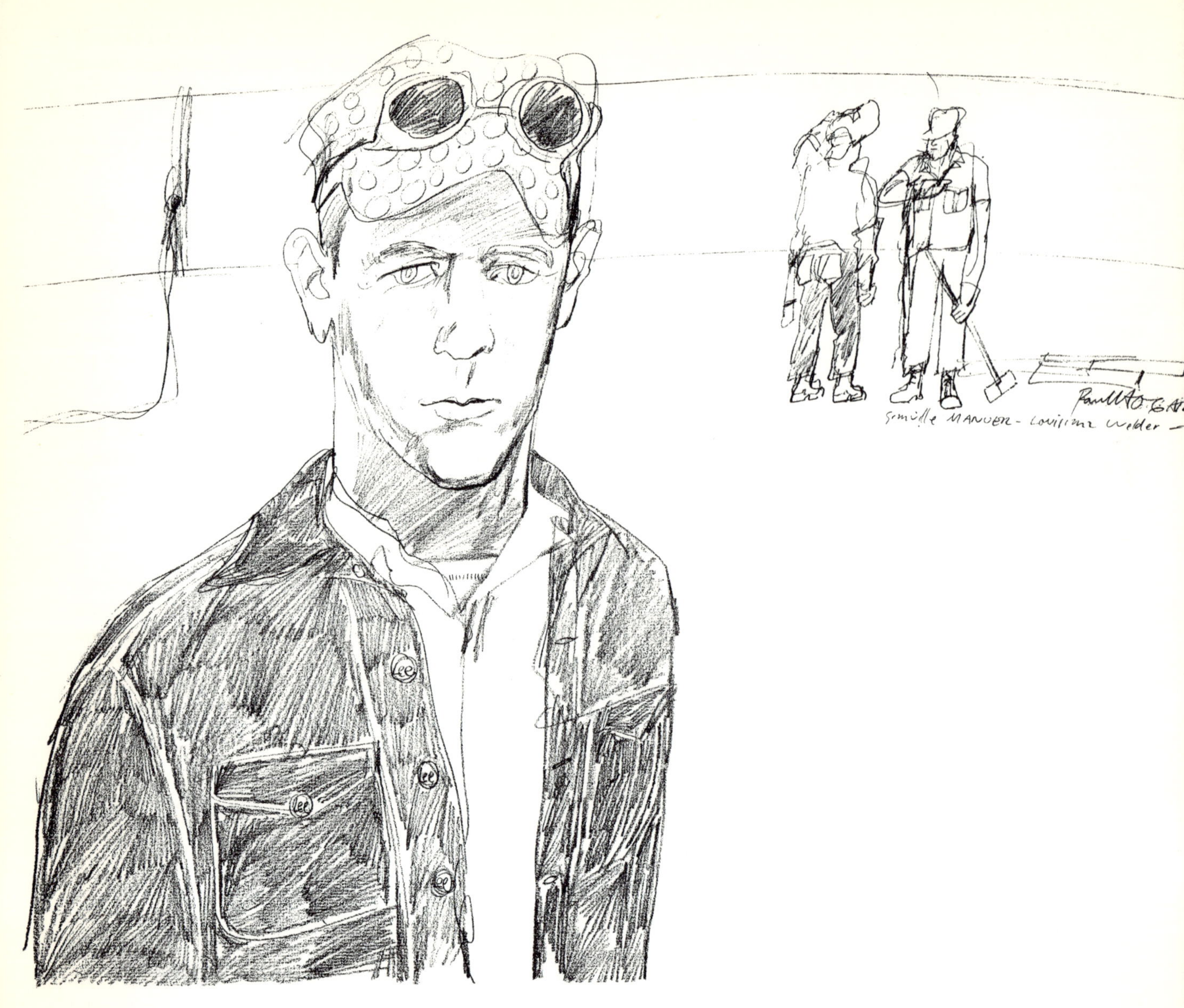

Greville Mander, Louisiana welder, 1962
One of a series of drawings reporting the construction of the Colonial Oil pipeline. Taking time off from drawing giant ditchers and pipe-bending machines, I turned to the human element, looking for a face symbolic of the pipeliners and their expertise. Drawn with 4B and 6B Eagle Charco pencils while the men took a short coffee break. On Saunders mold-made, cream wove writing paper. Courtesy Fortune *magazine. Copyright February, 1963 by Time, Inc.*

Generally, a student or artist should have little difficulty in gaining admittance to a wide range of plants, provided that he is engaged in an educational project or an actual assignment. Medium-sized firms, as well as giant corporations, are conscious enough of their public image to provide facilities to accommodate visitors. Tours and visits can usually be arranged through the firm's public relations office. Advance notice of at least two weeks is sometimes essential, and parties may be limited to a manageable size.

GENERAL PROCEDURES

Many of the problems I discussed in relation to drawing people in the street or in public places also apply to drawing them at work. How I decide to draw an individual or group depends on the time I have and on the visual interest of their work tasks. A factory, for example, may have a conveyor belt system linking different kinds of jobs. This organization of the work process may give me an idea for a drawing of a group of workers. On the other hand, I may select one man or a single machine that occupies only one figure.

Because drawing inside a plant involves you in the same bustle and confusion you find in a city street, it is advisable to use similar drawing procedures and to build up your impressions by systematically analyzing what goes on. You will find this approach a great help, enabling you to avoid confusion and to keep calm. I find that my notebook habit is a particularly helpful aid.

ENCOUNTERING FACTORY WORKERS

The experience of confronting men and women whose faces are stamped with the wearing experience of handling complicated machines can be overwhelming. Such an encounter can also embarrass the artist. Our vocation is such an exceptional one that the ordinary person seldom meets an artist—let alone understands his interests. The best way to avoid the inevitable tension of embarrassed silence is to jump right in and break the ice by expressing your natural curiosity in what the person is doing. Your drawing will then go much more easily. Confronting a worker's inevitable reactions—humorous or otherwise—in this way has invariably helped me develop a means of getting the drawing I want.

USING A GUIDE

Many larger firms have a public relations office which may offer you the services of a guide. So much the better, if that is the case. The guide may not help you make a good drawing, but his presence can serve to reassure and inspire confidence. Moreover, his way of talking, if he does his job well, can often be a useful model to follow on those occasions when you have to deal with the situation on your own.

DRAWING AN ASSEMBLY LINE

In a plant, every worker is involved in complex processes of production which seldom allow them to stop or be diverted for a single instant. Most factory work, however, is based on assembly-line procedures. Workers engaged in assembly-line work repeat their movements constantly. First, I observe the routine to get the sense of it, then I draw as much of it as I am able. When all movement has ceased, I complete the drawing from memory. Working in this way produces a much livelier drawing than if the guide were to request an employee to stop working and pose for me until I was able to "get it right."

COMPOSITION AND PERSPECTIVE

Unless it can be used to advantage, I avoid perspective. Instead, I rely on creating flat compositions in which I can develop the inherent shape of a machine or building and then exploit any fantasy their forms may suggest to me. Such an image, integrated with a figure or group of figures moving around or against it, makes a far more dynamic drawing than one which relies exclusively on perspective.

DRAWING STRENUOUS AND DANGEROUS ACTIVITIES

You will find that the reaction of people to being drawn varies a great deal. In factories, where assembly-line production creates a stoical boredom, any artist or photographer offers a welcome diversion. On the other hand, workers, miners, deep sea fishermen, and oil drilling crews, who are involved in much more strenuous activities or who may be exposed to danger, are at first much more reserved. With them, a greater degree of preliminary personal contact is necessary before you can even think of putting pencil to paper.

I had just such an experience when I spent a week in the North Sea aboard a man-made island of steel, a fixed drilling rig, where the Standard Oil Company had sent me to make drawings for their magazine *The Lamp.* From such tiny steel islands, men drill for oil and natural gas in offshore waters around the world. This particular operation took place some hundred miles off the east coast of England. Day after day, in fair weather or foul, the crews worked twelve hours on and twelve hours off for two-week periods. Each shift involved a tool-pusher (in charge of drilling tools), a driller, "roughnecks" (who wrestle with the

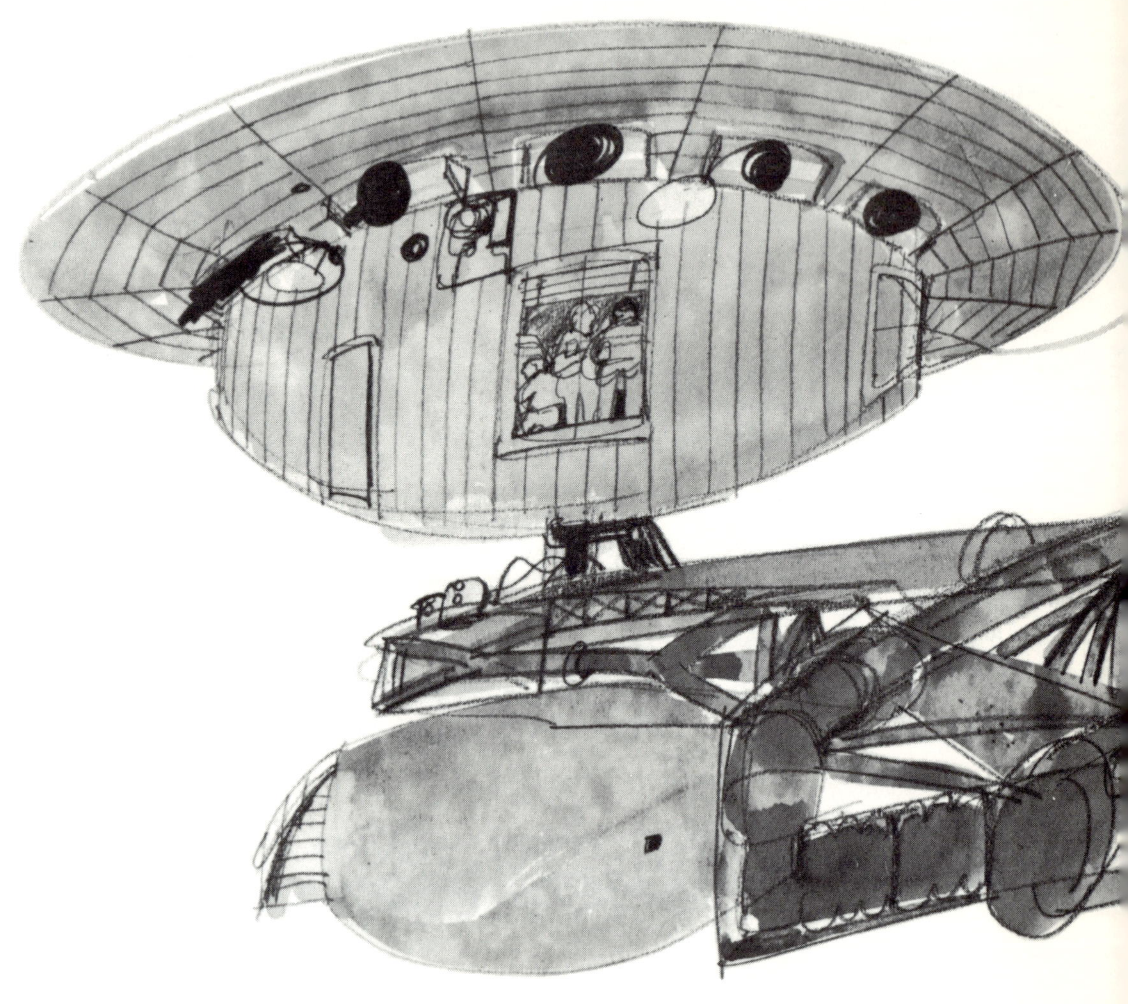

Manned Spacecraft Center, Houston, Texas, 1969
Here, a huge centrifugal machine is used to familiarize astronauts with the expected acceleration of earth orbit launch, launch-failures, and orbit re-entry, thus reproducing the actual conditions they will later encounter. I stripped off the outside of the spherical gondola so that the astronauts could be seen. Re-drawn (from on-the-spot sketches and photographs) on regular Strathmore drawing paper, with a Faber 702 sketching pencil and 3B and 6B Venus graphite pencils. Washes of Shaeffer Script ink, augmented with watercolor washes of Marabu Payne's gray were then applied with a Japanese brush. Touches of yellow and turquoise were made with Faber Design Markettes. From a portfolio on the training of astronauts commissioned by Sports Illustrated.

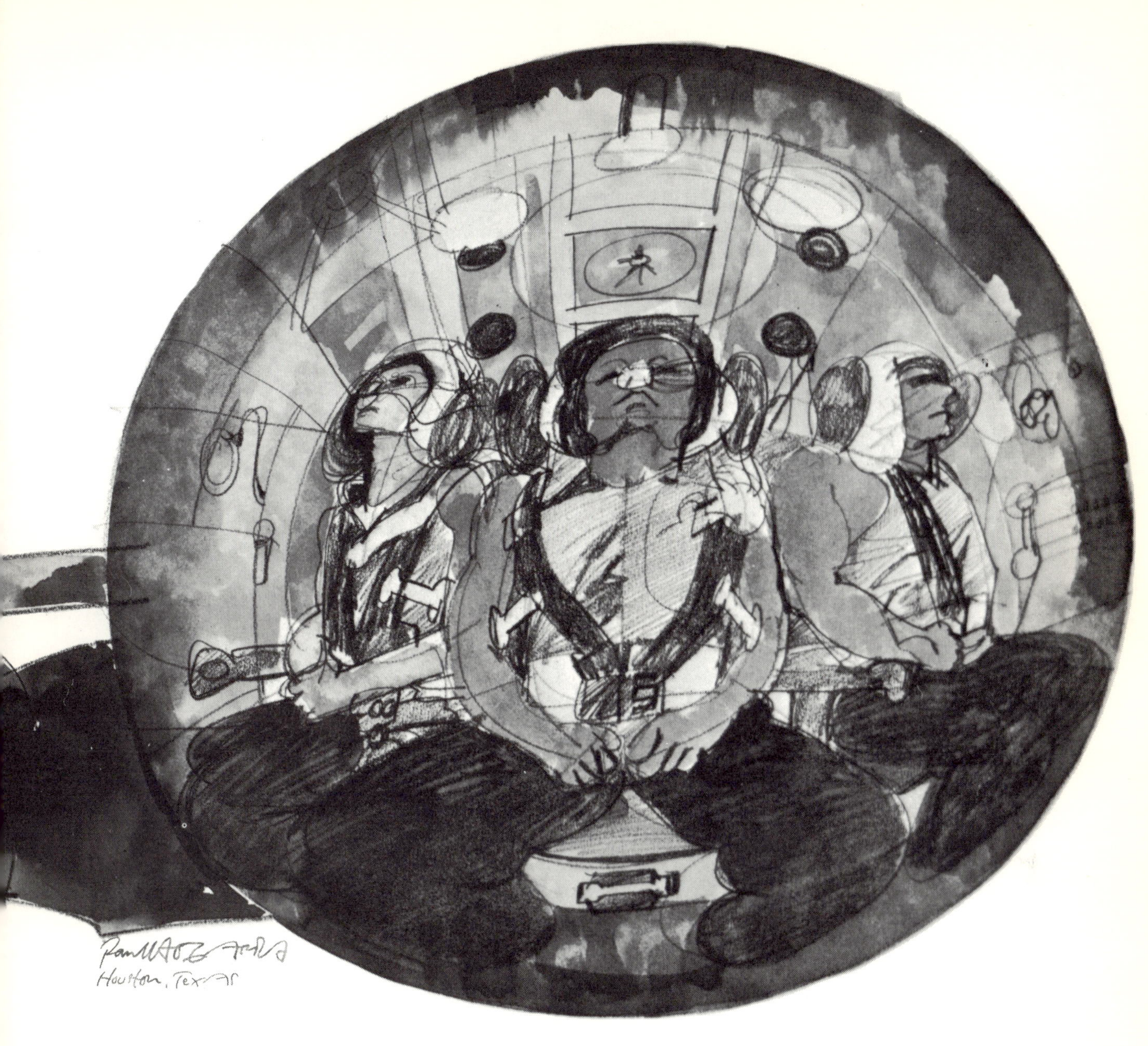

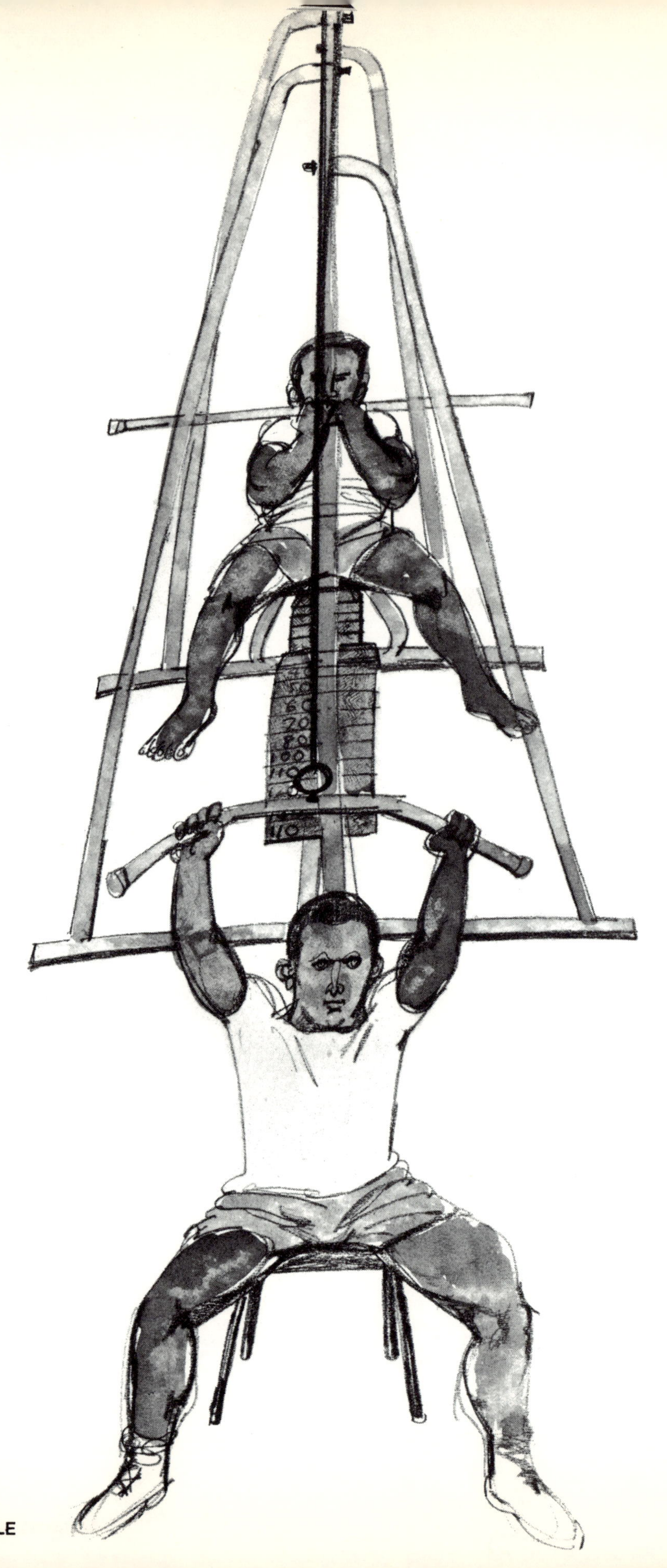

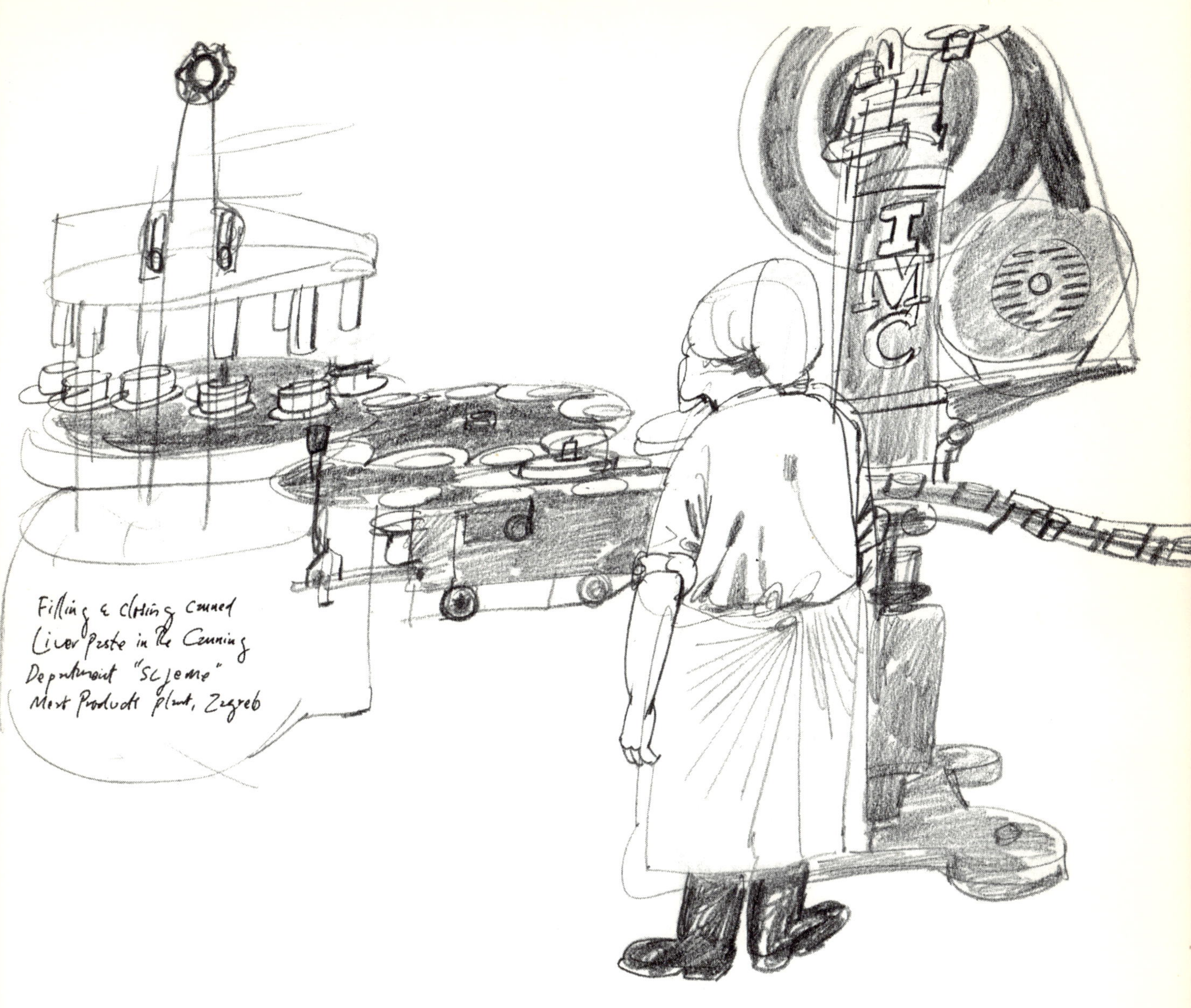

Manned Spacecraft Center, Houston, Texas, 1969
Astronauts in a physical-training workout use a weight-lifting, muscle-training device. Drawn in an 11" x 14" sketchbook of Strathmore Alexis drawing paper with Faber 702 sketching and 6B Venus graphite pencils. Washes of German Marabu watercolors were later applied with a Winsor & Newton No. 6 sable brush. Commissioned by Sports Illustrated. *(Left)*

Filling-machine in the Sljeme Meat Products Plant, Zagreb, Yugoslavia, 1967
Checked by a peasant woman, tins filled with liver paste move toward the supermarkets. One of a series of drawings for a Fortune *portfolio on the free-market economy of Yugoslavia. My choice of the peasant woman was made to show drift from land to industry in a traditionally farming country. Drawn with a Faber 702 sketching pencil in a 10¾" x 14½" English Planet sketchbook of smooth drawing paper. Courtesy* Fortune *magazine. Copyright May, 1967 by Time, Inc. (Above)*

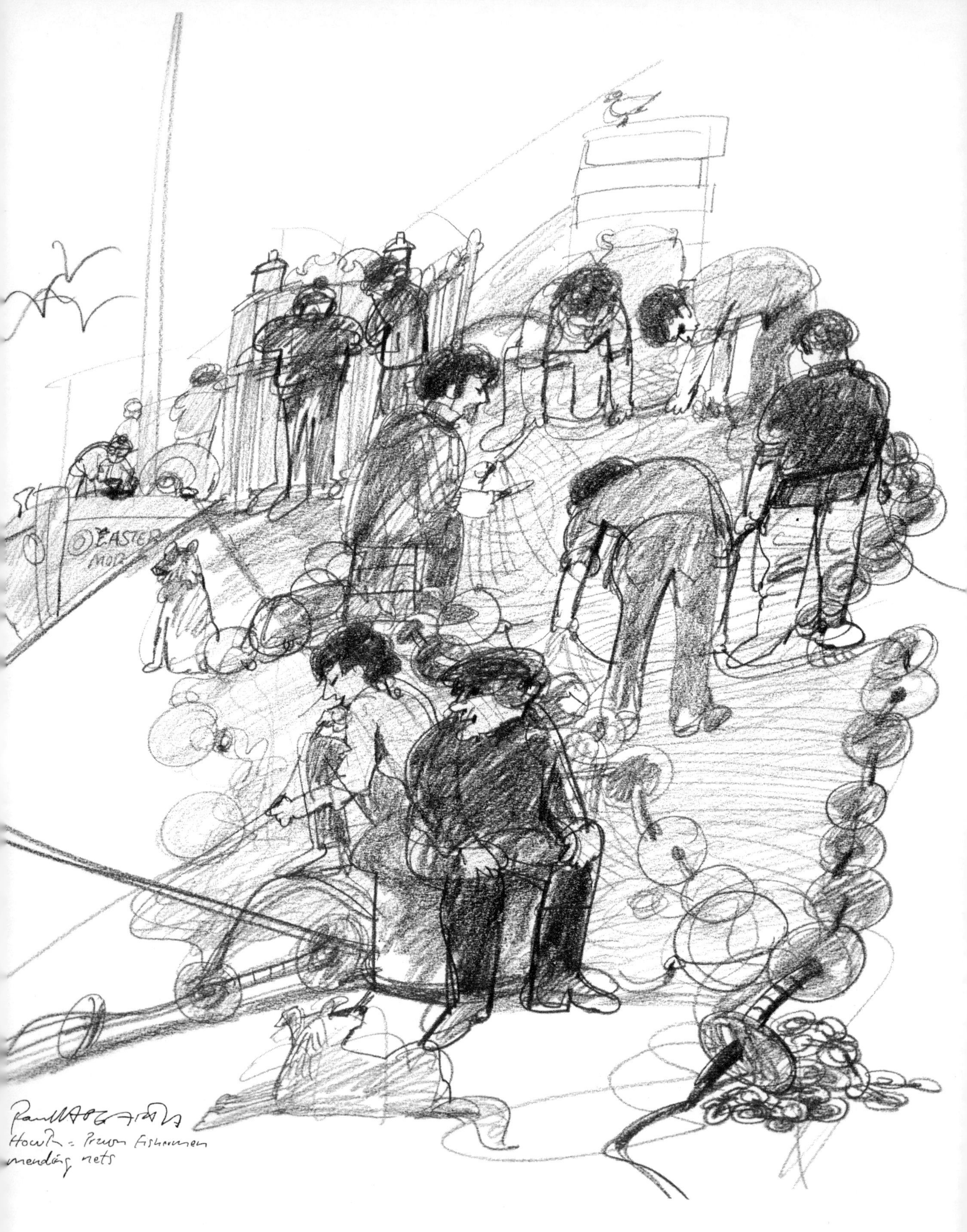
EASTER
Howth - Prawn Fishermen mending nets

heavy drill pipe), "roustabouts" (who do all the heavy, unskilled work), an engineer, skindivers, and maintenance men. All workers were under the command of a superintendent—the equivalent of the captain of a ship. Offshore drilling is dangerous, exhausting work. The North Sea is particularly prone to storms. Strong winds blow the rig in one direction while submarine currents strive to force it in another. The backwash of water piled up by severe gales creates giant waves that can sweep a rig clear from its moorings. Dense sea traffic in fog is another hazard. Mines left over from World War Two abound.

Under these arduous conditions, the men have to be approached in an easygoing manner which admits a healthy respect for their courage—without overdoing it, however. The main task is to get acquainted on an individual basis and intelligently try to discover a common interest. Esso's public relations department had forewarned me that they had little jurisdiction over the drilling crews, who are a law unto themselves. If the superintendent liked me, they predicted, he would allow me to stay for a few days. If he did not, I would find myself on the next helicopter bound for the mainland. As it turned out, things went well. I told the superintendent, a Frenchman, that I would not like *his* job, to which he replied that he would not like *mine* either! "You could easily be blown off the rig," he said. "Much too risky for me!"

Prawn fishermen, Howth, Dublin, 1969
Finding out when things happen is vital for many drawings of people at work. The famous Dublin Bay prawn fleet unloads its catch every Friday night, returning to sea on the Sunday tide. I drove down from Dublin Saturday morning to make this drawing of the men repairing their nets. Drawn in an 11" x 14" sketchbook of Strathmore Alexis drawing paper with a Faber 702 sketching pencil. Courtesy Lithopinion, *Winter 1969. Copyright by Amalgamated Lithographers of America, New York.*

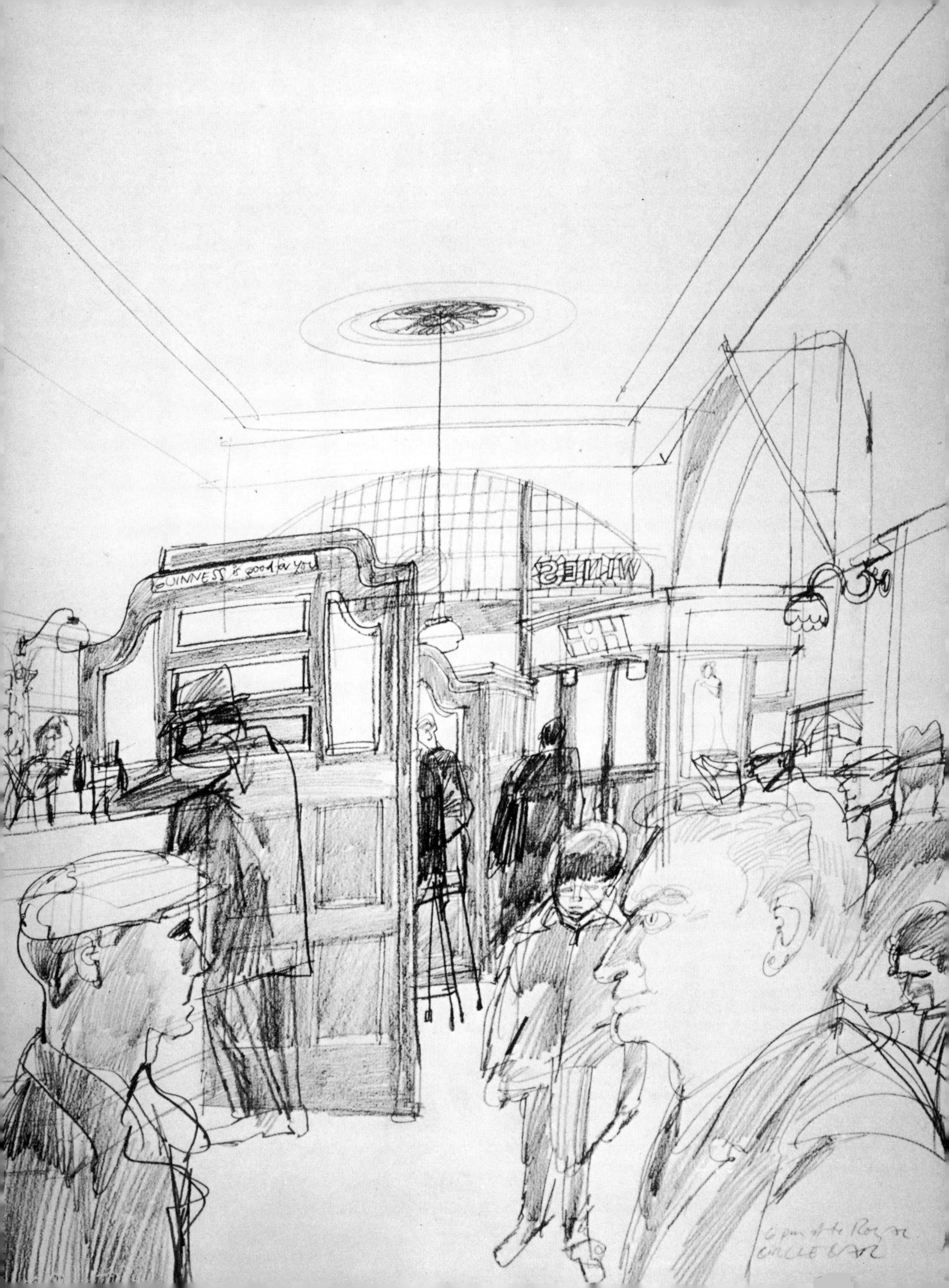
GUINNESS is good for you
WINES

CHAPTER 8

Drawing People in Bars

AN ARTIST who opens a sketchbook in a bar may arouse interest, but seldom surprise. Because people frequent bars out of a desire to communicate and be convivial, even an unusual request like being asked by an artist to pose or sit still for him is usually well taken. Therefore, bars are excellent locations to make drawings of characters—as individuals or in groups—under conditions often more favorable than those you may encounter doing portrait drawings in your own studio.

Bars, of course, come in all shapes and varieties. Wherever you find them and whatever time of day or night you enter them, bars invariably offer unrivaled opportunities to observe people—for a price less than that of a movie seat. Bars in large cities differ greatly from those in small towns and country villages. Tough or sophisticated, city bars offer all kinds of decor; town and village pubs, on the other hand, frequently provide little more than the simplicity of a family kitchen. Big-city bars include a bewildering range of haunts, each patronized by a specific group; small pubs, by contrast, are usually community clubs where plain people gather for plain talk. In any event, bars —whether city, town, or remote village—will help sharpen your eye for spotting and identifying people.

WORKING IN NEIGHBORHOOD BARS

As a first step to developing your self-confidence, get into the habit of visiting your neighborhood bar. If this local pub happens to be Irish, consider yourself fortunate. Few people equal the Irishman's natural ability to keep a good bar. Once found, an Irish saloon in any large British or American city may be long and affectionately remembered for the generally tolerant atmosphere which is as typical of it as is its company of good characters.

Take care to observe basic bar etiquette (which may or may not vary from place to place). Essentially, bar etiquette is a code of convivial conduct based on the art of getting along with other people. Once you've demonstrated your deference to the established clientele, your presence among them will be accepted.

WORKING IN UNFAMILIAR BARS

Drawing people in a bar—particularly an unfamiliar one—calls for confidence. If you (as I at times do) feel determined to go ahead, but reluctant to make a fool of yourself, by far the best course is to make the occasional *sortie* in the company of a bolder friend—one who generally knows the ropes or is acquainted with a particular bar. This approach has often enabled me to pull out a sketchbook and commence to draw all kinds of extraordinary characters that I would not otherwise have had the courage to confront.

This approach was an ideal way to work when I traveled with Brendan Behan in the remote districts of Ireland during the summer of 1960 to make drawings for our book, *Brendan Behan's Island.* I found the sudden transition from city to country difficult to accustom myself to. Night after night, I had felt at home in the bars of Dublin, where I had drawn a whole gallery of characters; but the tiny pubs of Connemara and the Isle of Aran were occupied by grave-faced fishermen who looked silently over their beers, reluctant to respond to strangers. Such men do not make friends very easily.

Brendan Behan, my bold friend on this occasion, boasted that he knew every bar in Ireland like "the

The Royal Circle Bar, Dublin, 1964
The prosperity that has hit Dublin with the force of a hurricane threatens to leave the Irish capital bereft of its fine old saloons. The Royal Circle—the bar of the Theatre Royal—has already gone to make way for a highrise office building. It was a bar rich in its associations with music hall and vaudeville. Walls were lined with showbills and photographs signed by famous artistes. Drawn with 6B and 7B Venus graphite pencils on Saunders mold-made, cream wove writing paper. Courtesy the Shelbourne Hotel, Dublin.

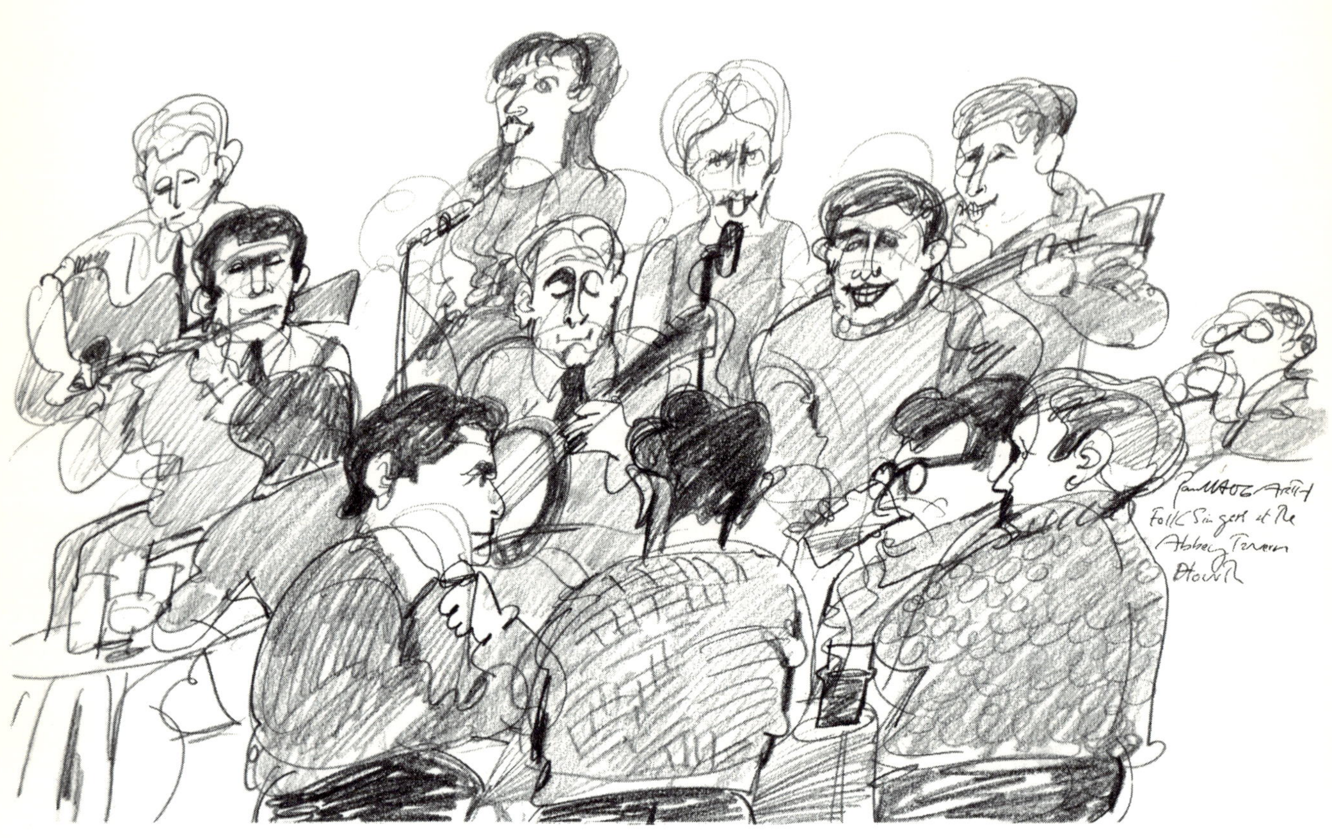

Folk singers at the Abbey Tavern, Howth, Ireland, 1969
In Ireland, at least, the common characteristic of folk-singing fans seems to be that they go in for large-knit sweaters, pipes, and beer. One such typical group was placed in the foreground against the performers. Drawn in a 10¾" x 14½" English Planet sketchbook of smooth drawing paper with a Faber 702 sketching pencil. Courtesy Lithopinion, *Winter 1969. Copyright by Amalgamated Lithographers of America, New York. (Above)*

Neary's Bar, Dublin, 1964
Neary's is a great place to draw people. It has a vaguely sinister ambiance; an entrance reminiscent of a side-door to purgatory with a fine pair of sensuous black hands grasping great lanterns aloft to illuminate the entry of the convivial. Here, the company is dominated by wealthy actors and might-as-well-spend-it types whose affluence is contemptuously commented on by the ever present, usually impoverished, fringe of literary incorrigibles. Drawn from the end of the bar before the evening rush began on Saunders mold-made, cream wove writing paper with 6B and 7B Venus graphite pencils. Courtesy the Shelbourne Hotel, Dublin. (Right)

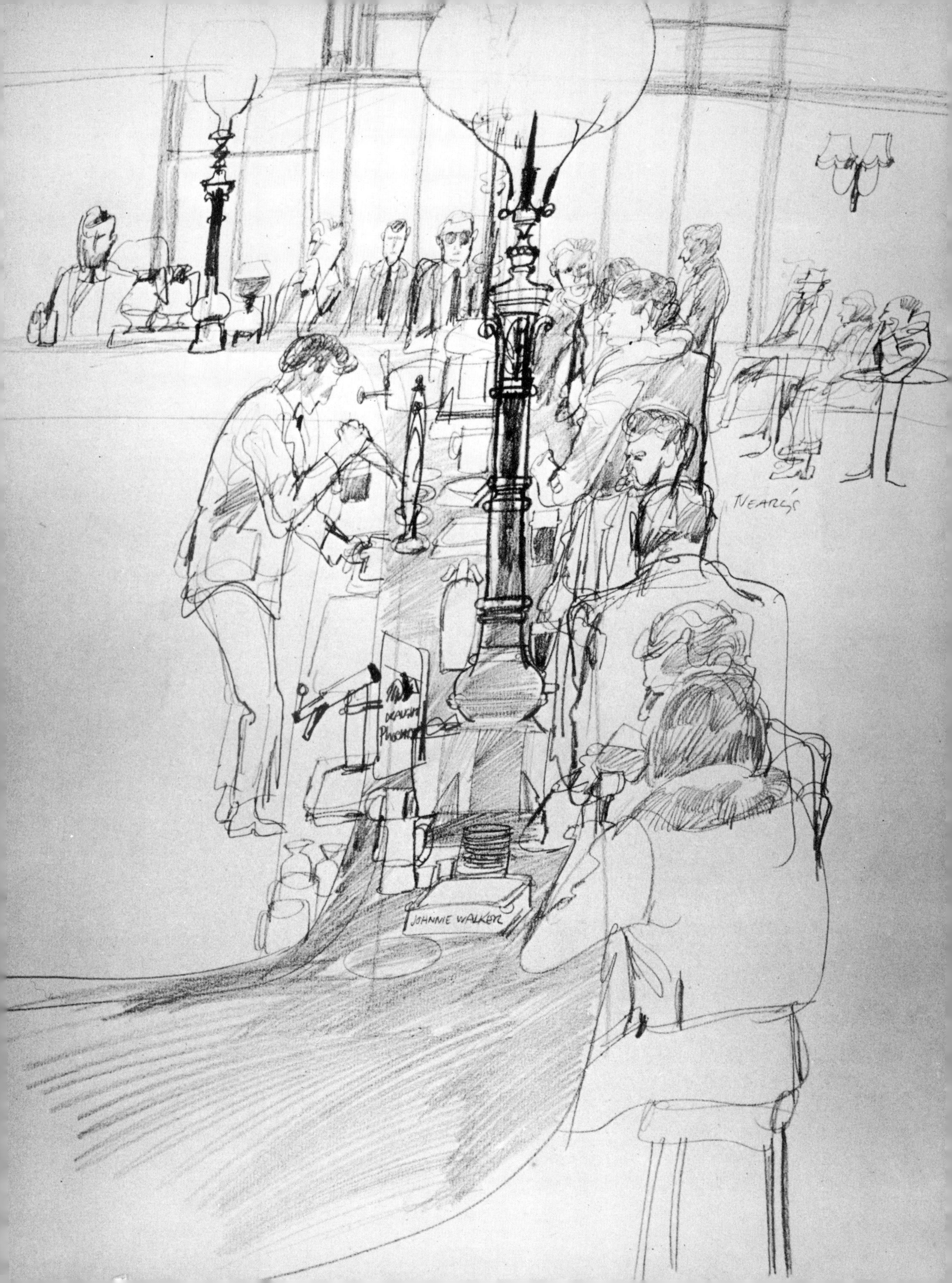
NEARY'S
JOHNNIE WALKER

Biddy Kelly in the Blue Lion, Dublin, 1959

The old Blue Lion Bar in Parnell Street is probably the nearest to the Nighttown bars described by Joyce in Ulysses. *The company includes a variety of gregarious characters from the troubled 1920s. Among them I found Biddy Kelly, a small-time moneylender to the poor. Biddy aroused reluctant admiration for her raucous ballads. Her favorite, "Friends today, Judases tomorrer," was over-intoned in a wild strident voice that had an edge like an old file. Drawn in about forty minutes on Abbey Mill pastel paper with a medium Hardtmuth charcoal lead, plus a Number 3 Conté* Pierre Noir *for finer definition of the bird-like eyes, tight mouth, and large veined hands. From* Brendan Behan's Island, *1962. Courtesy The Hutchinson Publishing Group, London; and Bernard Geis Associates, New York. Reproduced by permission of the owner, Donald Holden, Irvington, N.Y.*

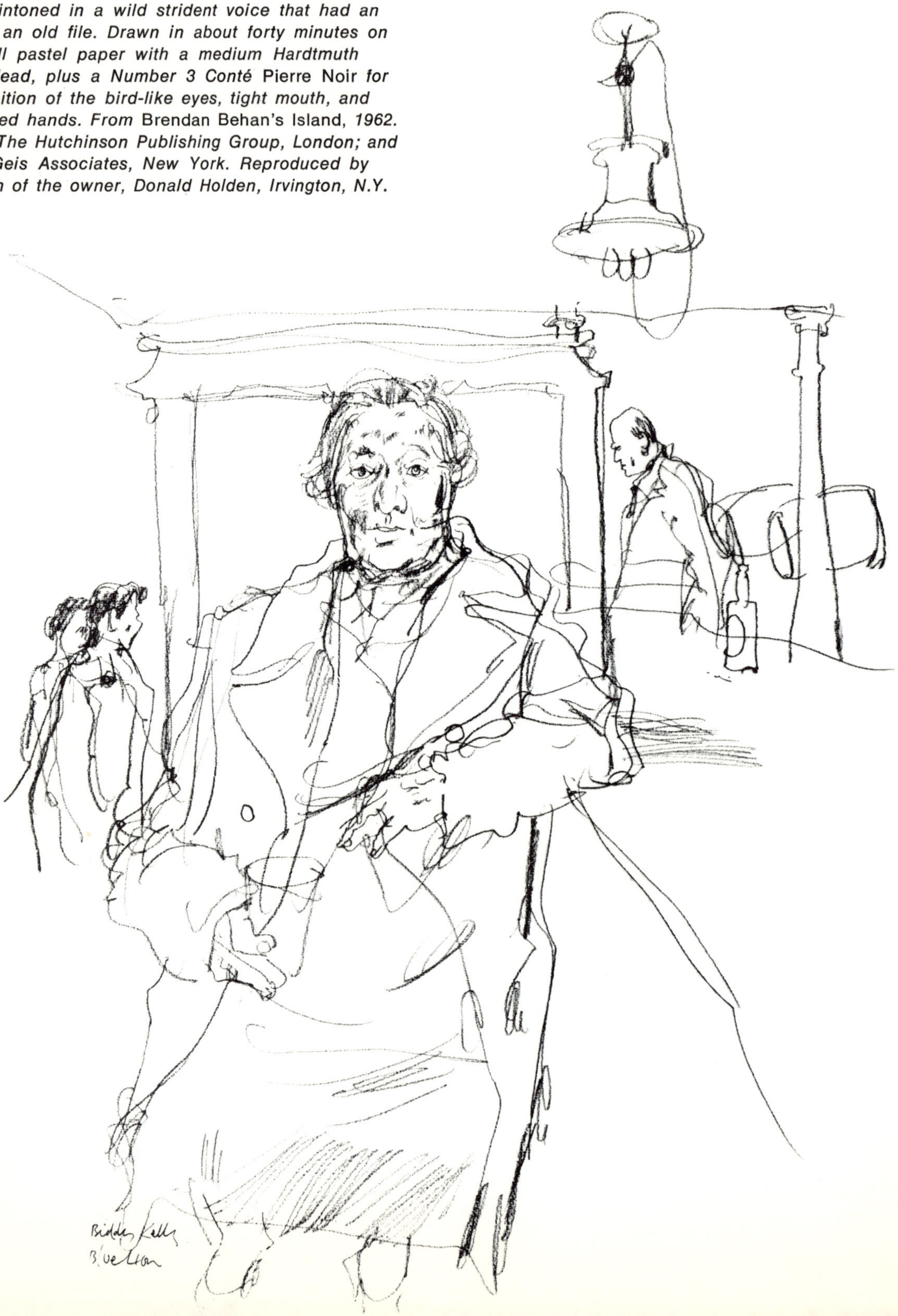

Willy Garfinkle, Oasis Bar, New York, 1963

Now and again, the "natural" portrait subject comes along, one who poses as though he's done nothing else all his life. Willy, the golden-hearted proprietor of the chromium-plated Oasis Bar on West 23rd Street, ran an honest-to-goodness place where you ate a good steak, took your liquor straight, told some good stories, and no fancy business. Drawn in about forty minutes in an 11" x 14" sketchbook of Strathmore Alexis drawing paper with a 7B Venus graphite pencil. From Brendan Behan's New York, *1964. Courtesy The Hutchinson Publishing Group, London; and Bernard Geis Associates, New York.*

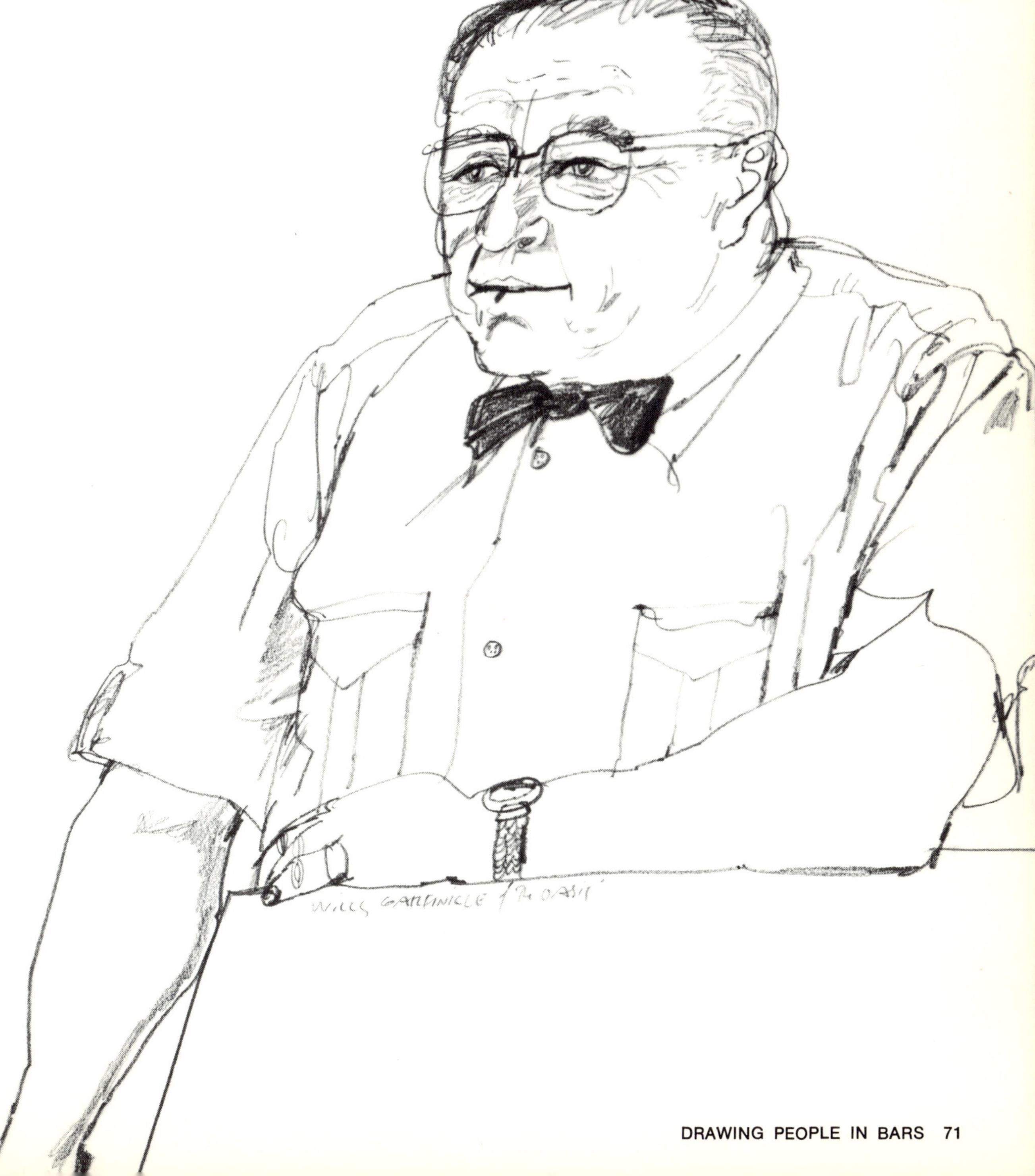

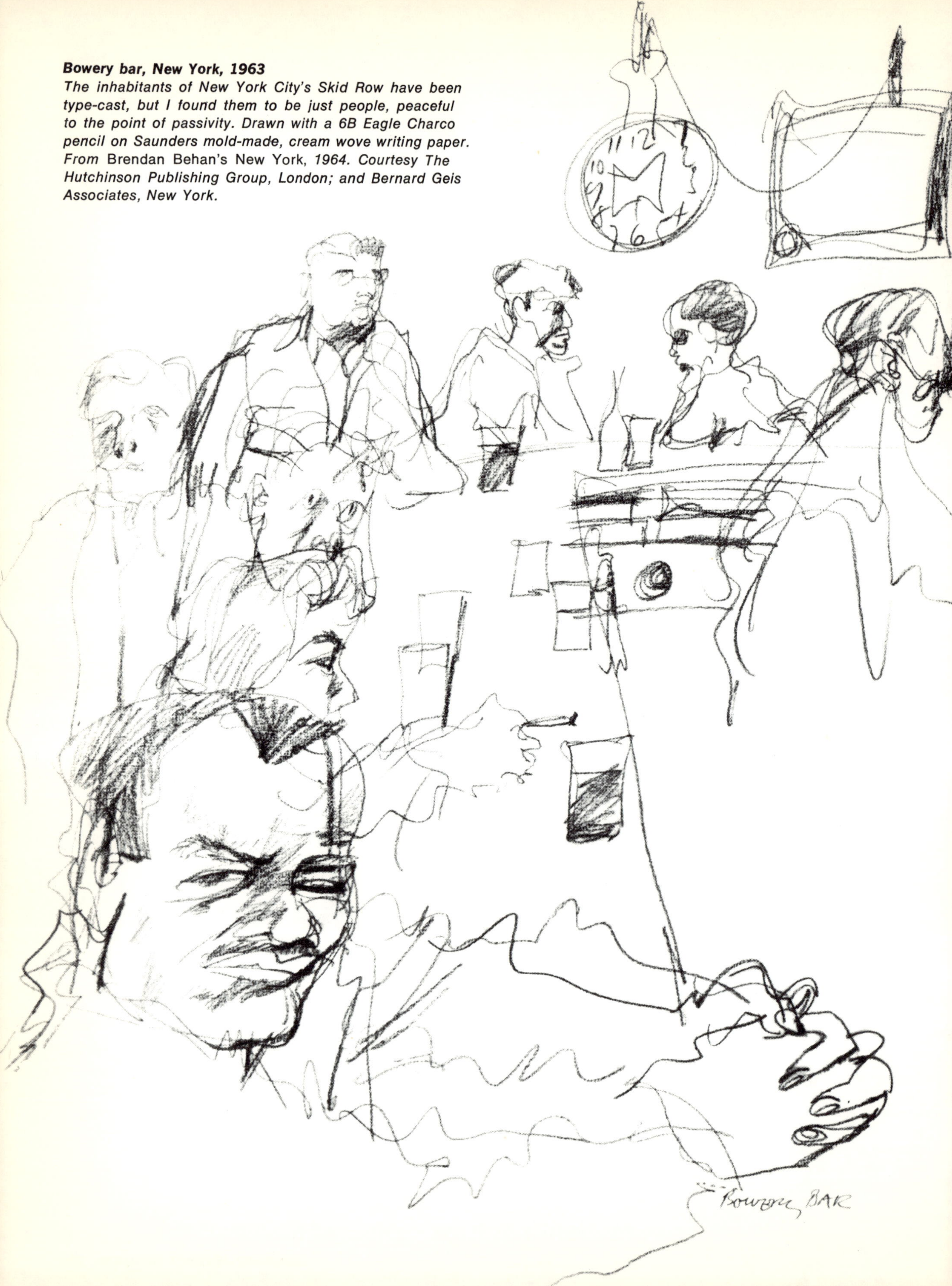

Bowery bar, New York, 1963

The inhabitants of New York City's Skid Row have been type-cast, but I found them to be just people, peaceful to the point of passivity. Drawn with a 6B Eagle Charco pencil on Saunders mold-made, cream wove writing paper. From Brendan Behan's New York, *1964. Courtesy The Hutchinson Publishing Group, London; and Bernard Geis Associates, New York.*

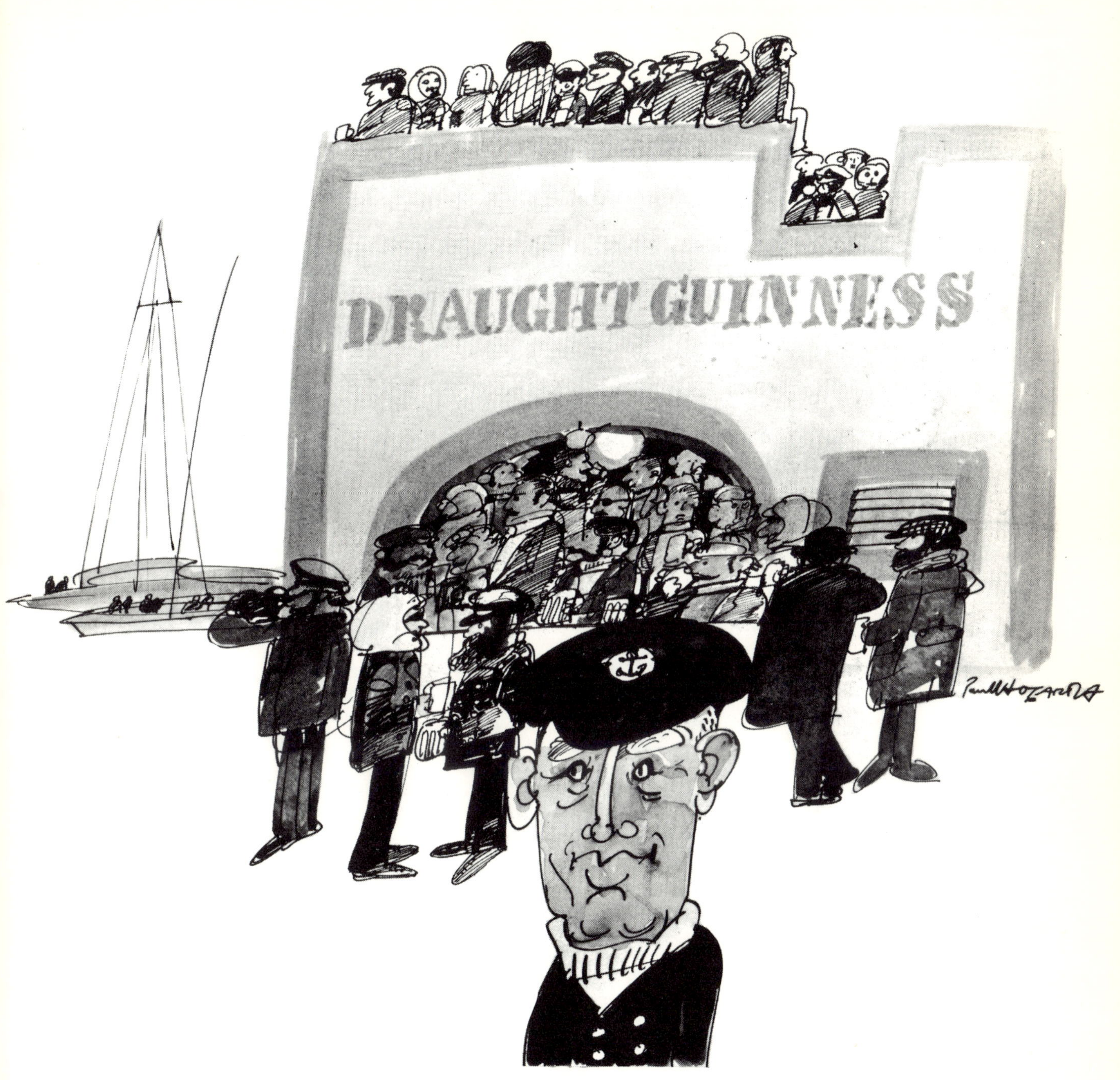

The London Boat Show, England, 1968

Overlooking the man-made Mediterranean harbor, the strategically placed Guinness bar attracted a cross section of sailors and sailing types too good to miss. The bar itself was sketched in lightly with an HB Venus pencil, then filled in with yellow and yellow-brown Faber Design Markettes. The figures were added with two weights of pen line—a Spencerian school nib for broader strokes and a Gillot 303 for the finer accents. A small Japanese brush was used for the solid areas. Drawn with Higgins India ink in an 11" x 14" sketchbook of two-ply, high surface Strathmore drawing paper. Courtesy Sports illustrated. *Copyright 1969 by Time, Inc.*

hairs on the back of me mum's ould neck." He would breeze into these remote pubs, determined to put their uncommunicative patrons through a crash course of conviviality. He seldom failed! The action would start with, "A big pint of porther for every man-jack-in-the-place!" Then Behan would startle the assembled company with a rousing rebel song, sung with operatic abandon. After a while, when the company reacted favorably and joined in the singing, he would tip me the wink which was my cue to start.

At times I had trouble finding the room to put pencil to paper. Then Behan would rush to my side, bellowing unprintable oaths and thrusting back the Philistines who were crowding me in (they would, however, be back soon after).

In spite of these raucous conditions, I turned out some of the most zestful character drawings I have ever made. After a month of such experiences, I felt cocky enough to enter *any* bar!

ESTABLISHING RAPPORT WITH BARTENDER AND CLIENTELE

As neither you nor I often have the opportunity to accompany a born showman like the late Brendan Behan, we have to content ourselves with a much less dramatic approach to drawing in bars. If I have the time, I usually start by investigating the bars that interest me *before* I actually decide to work in them. What and where these may be are sometimes common knowledge, sometimes inside information passed on by friends or noted from the pages of a good guidebook.

First, I chat with the bartender. If he is friendly, I ask if he objects to my drawing. He usually answers no, but may warn me not to get in anyone's hair. It's a good idea to ask permission, even when you don't need to. In some bars, situations can unexpectedly get out of hand—particularly late at night. Under these circumstances, a bartender can often be a useful ally.

To be caught on Skid Row, for example, without first having made contact with the bartender or chief barfly, may affront the fraternal ambiance of its male colonies of drifters, and is a blunder that may lose you interesting subjects. By "making contact," I don't mean that you must stand everyone to a drink. Contrary to popular belief, these social outcasts drink sparingly or not at all. More often than not, they crowd into bars seeking companionship and human contact. For this reason, Skid Row bars are particularly good places for drawing people. You may have to bear with the most extraordinary chronicles of suffering and misfortune, but the experience will enable you to practice your analysis of the human countenance and to make decisions on whether what you see is true or false.

You should know, too, that in some bars it is inadvisable to draw someone without first making contact with him. This kind of rapport is sometimes difficult to establish. In fact, your potential sitter may at first refuse to have anything to do with you. In such cases, you must use your wits to make your drawing. Often, the only way to do so is to develop a conversation with the person—to the point where you sense he accepts your intentions. You may have to buy him two or more drinks, but you'll get your money's worth even if the drawing does not measure up to your expectations. Developing the ability to coax someone into sitting for you and practicing your skill in putting your sitter at ease are just as important as making a good drawing.

METHODS OF WORKING

When I work in bars, tools and materials are kept to a minimum. Nevertheless, I arrive armed with two sketchbooks with which I am prepared to make several kinds of drawings (I never know what I may find). I use a 5″ x 7″ sketchbook to make thumbnail character studies when, for some reason or another, it is not convenient or wise to work larger. For rendering groups, single figures, and portraits, however, my usual standby is an 11″ x 14″ pad.

I like to arrive around six o'clock, when everyone is taking his first drink of the evening. At that hour, not many customers have come in yet, a fact that usually insures me a choice vantage point when they crowd in minutes later. The best spot to work is frequently at the far end of the bar, or facing the bar from the rear center of the room. Here I settle with my drink, scribbling down various ideas for relating a head, figure, or group of figures to some feature of the interior. I do not always carry out these ideas, but they serve to exercise my imagination, as well as my fingers. Once I have more or less decided what I want, I am prepared to draw anyone who might come along. While waiting, I sometimes draw in a background. This preparation is a useful time-saver when I have to work with one eye on the clock.

COMPOSING THE DRAWING

Having made up my mind *who* to draw, I decide whether to do a head, a three-quarter figure, or a full figure set off by smaller background figures. I may focus on a group seated around a table, drawing them close up or partially obscuring them by larger figures. If a face is striking, with great character interest, I may concentrate on the head, seeking to interpret its character. Just as often, I will use the whole figure and exploit more than facial characteristics—hands and feet, perhaps—introducing background elements as an integral part of the drawing.

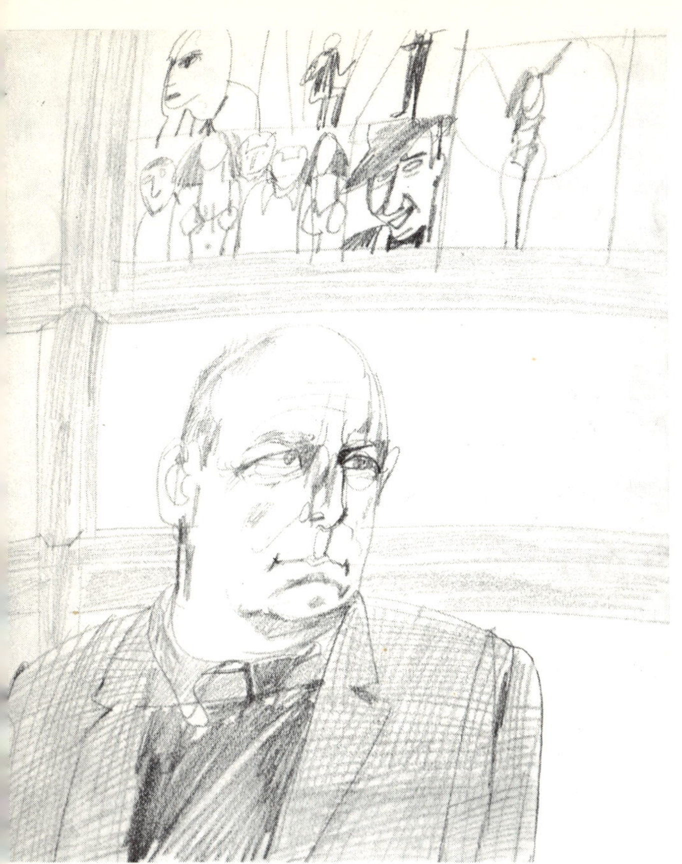

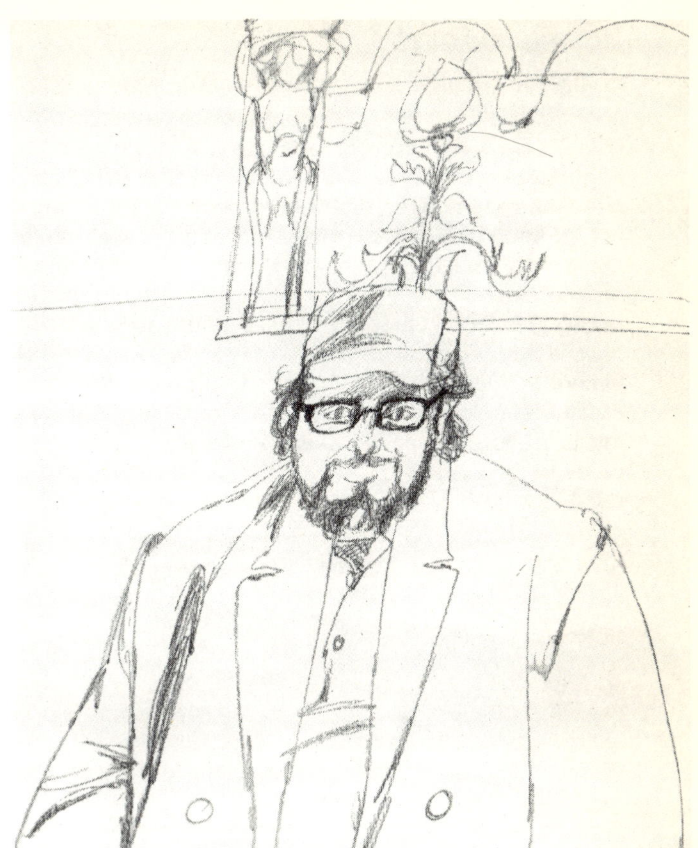

The Poet Paul Potts, London, 1966 (left) and The Poet Adrian Henri, Liverpool, 1965 (right)
Poets seem to be an intimate part of the convivial atmosphere of a well-chosen haunt, like their local bar. Both poets were drawn in about thirty-five minutes with a Faber 702 sketching pencil in an 11" x 14" sketchbook of two-ply Strathmore drawing paper. The portrait of Potts is from London à la Mode, *1966. Courtesy Studio Vista Ltd., London; and Hill & Wang, Inc., New York.*

MOVING TARGETS

The main problem in drawing people in bars is their change of movement or their sudden impatience with you. While I try to avoid engaging in prolonged or unnecessary conversation, I recognize that some verbal exchange may be required to hold a sitter's interest. In such cases, I will order him a drink and make the occasional friendly remark, but I keep my mind on the drawing. I must concentrate on making the drawing right the first time because usually I do not have a second chance. Taking my time to place the essential lines correctly, I work as surely as possible. Once these lines are down, I can then take the drawing to a more advanced stage—even if my sitter decides to leave.

A much safer bet, however, is to draw a group rather than an individual. A group tends to remain in position for longer periods of time. Even if they shift around, they generally stay inside the bar long enough for me to make a good drawing.

From some of the considerations just discussed, you can see that there is much more to drawing in bars than simply stalking interesting people and subsequently sketching them. There are no set or fixed rules to guide you. Instead, your own personality must largely determine your approach. However you respond and whatever approach you choose, you must exercise tact and initiative. Difficult as these social skills may be to develop, you will find them invaluable later on, when you handle much more difficult sitters who *ask* you to draw them!

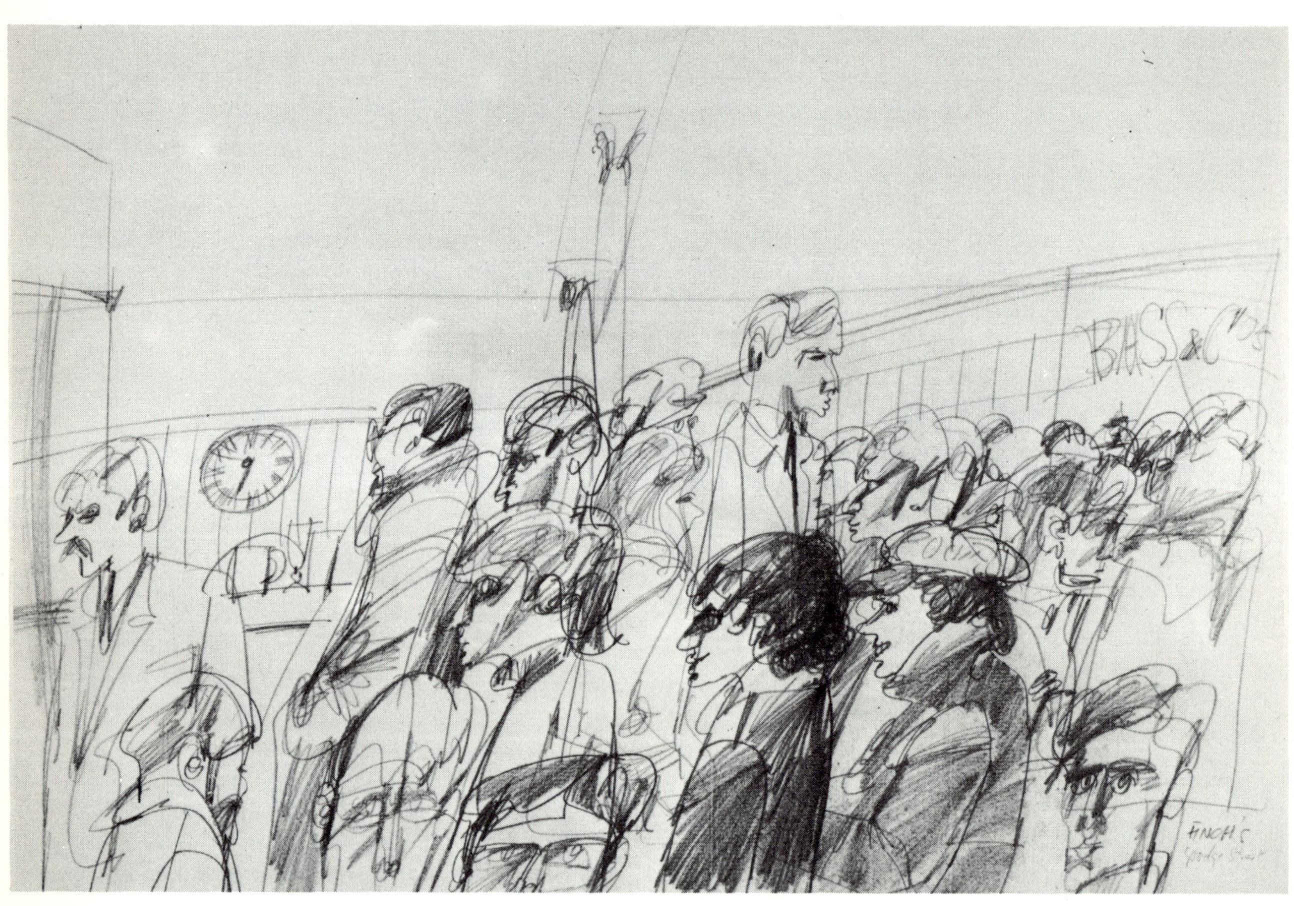

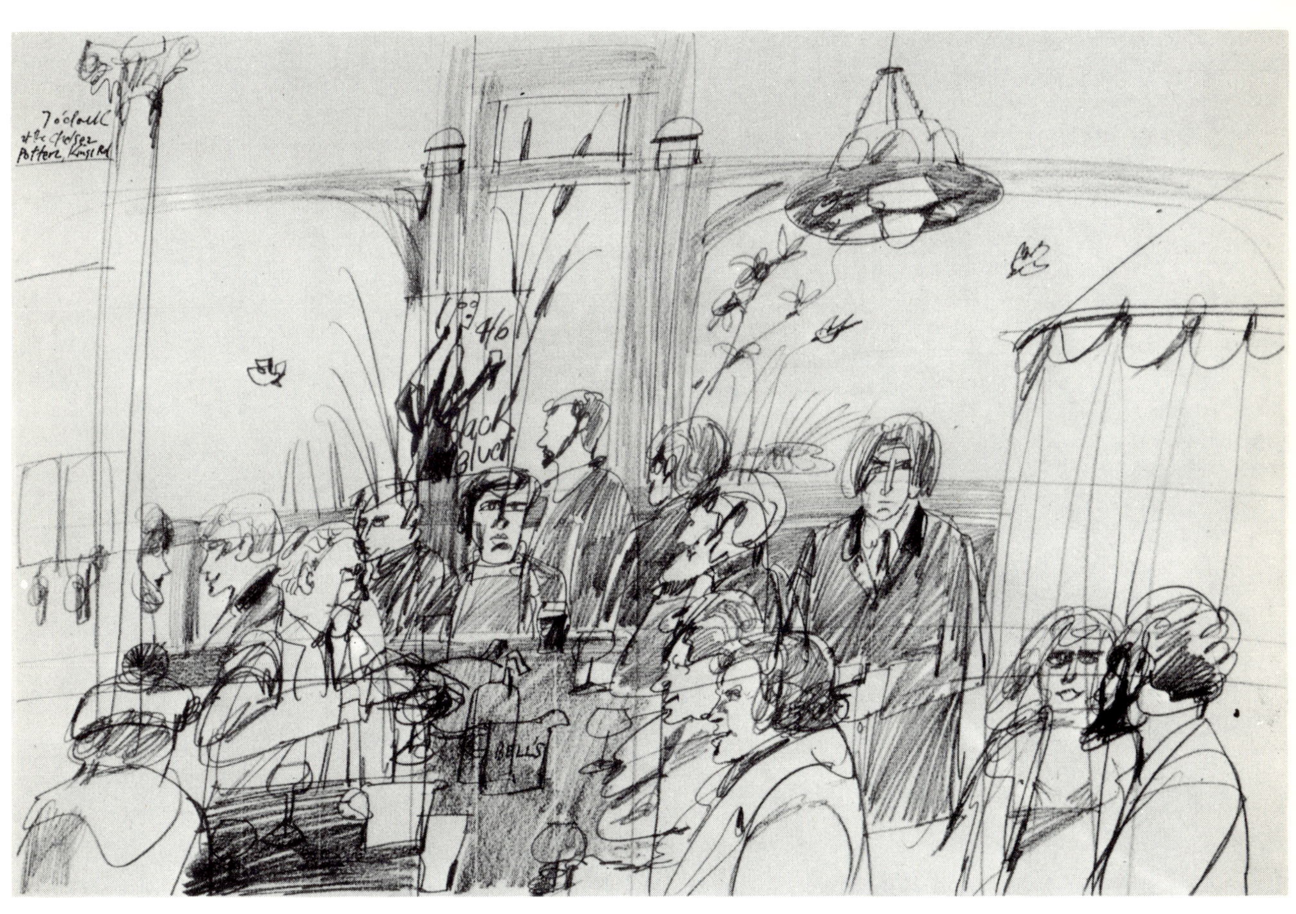

Two London bars in which both atmosphere and types are particularly stressed
Finch's, Goodge Street, 1966 *(left)—folk, country and western, on the fringe of Soho, fills up on weekends with the young on their way to listen to the big London concerts.* The Chelsea Potter, 1966 *(right)—opening time at a famous actor's bar in the King's Road, Chelsea. Both drawings were made with a Faber 702 sketching pencil in a 10¾" x 14½" English Planet sketchbook of smooth drawing paper. From* London à la Mode, *1966. Courtesy Studio Vista Ltd., London; and Hill & Wang, Inc., New York.*

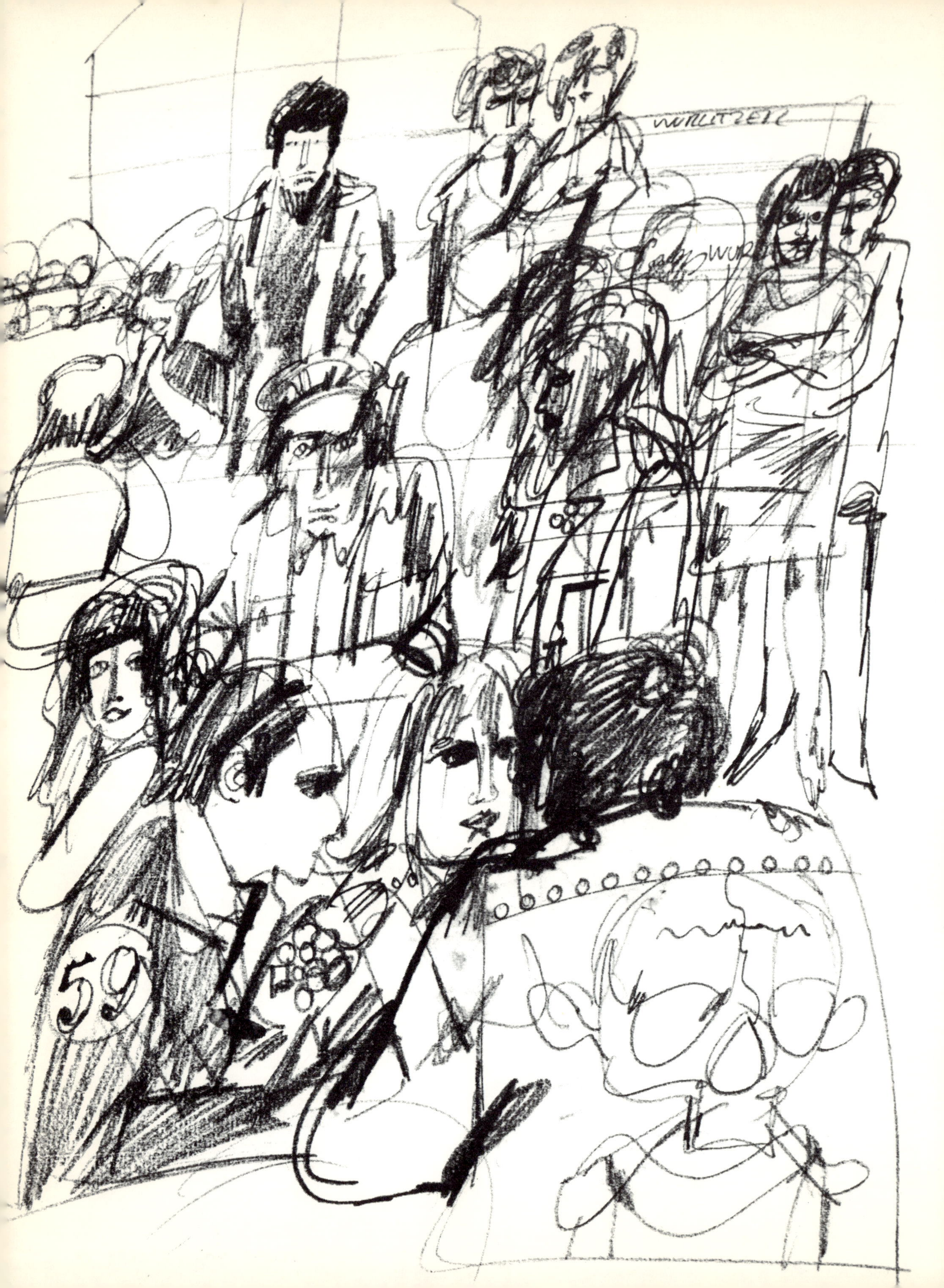
WURLITZER
59

CHAPTER 9

Drawing People in Night Spots

NIGHT SPOTS abound these days. Even the smallest city has its share of discothéques, gambling joints, strip clubs, and restaurants that are jammed with people living it up as if it were their last night on earth. There has not been anything like it since Toulouse-Lautrec rendered the rip-roaring nights of *la Belle Epoque.*

With your eye sharpened by drawing people in the streets, bars, and public places, it should not prove difficult to move on and tackle the night people in their haunts. To begin with, you will find that people in these surroundings reveal themselves quite openly, registering the gamut of human emotion and behavior much more freely than they would in the light of day. How they do so, of course, depends on whether they are dancing, eating, gambling, or watching a strip-tease show. Wherever this nightlife goes on is bound to yield dividends for adventurous pencils.

STUDY THE WORK OF YOUR PREDECESSORS

Before you set out for a night spot, however, spend a little time orienting yourself to the subject by studying the brilliant examples of night reporting which appeared in Europe and America at about the turn of the century. Between 1885 and 1910, one of the main attractions for the army of young artists who flocked to Paris, Munich, London, New York, and Berlin was the hope of publishing drawings of night-life in the host of lively and new illustrated magazines. The work of the following artists, although a random selection, is well worth looking at in this respect: Toulouse-Lautrec in *Paris Illustré* (1888), *Le Mirliton* (1887), *L'Escaramouche* (1893–1894); Miklos Vadasz in *L'Assiette au Beurre* (1906–1909); Jules Pascin in *Simplicissimus* (1905–1914); John Sloan in *Masses* (1913–1915); Kirchner, Kokoschka, and Pechstein in *Der Sturm* (1911–1917); Jacques Villon in *Frou-Frou* (1902), *Le Rire* (1903–1904), *La Vie en Rose* (1902); and George Grosz in *Die Pleite* (1919–1924), and *Der Knuppel* (1922–1928).

Illustrated ephemera of this kind is scarce—usually found only in the Library of Congress, the New York Public Library, the British Museum, or in larger university libraries. Save yourself time and trouble by first consulting the *American Union List of Serials* or the *British Union Catalogue of Periodicals* at your local library. If you find you are nowhere near such a library, the following monographs should be available from your local art school or city library: P. Huisman & M. C. Dortu, *Lautrec by Lautrec* (London and New York, 1964); William L. O'Neill, editor, *Echoes of Revolt—The Masses* (Chicago, 1966); Bittner, *George Grosz* (Boston, 1944); *Ecce Homo* (New York, 1966).

PLACES TO GO

Your local nightlife may not embrace more than a discothéque or two, a drugstore soda fountain, or a coffee shop. Nevertheless, if you tackle these subjects in the right way, they can provide ample material. The main prerequisite is to have a pictorial idea which will effectively enable you to depict a specific scene or group in the light of your own attitude toward it. This means activating your own values to interpret people at uninhibited moments as they indulge their appetites for pleasure. Your response to a situation or a scene acts as a compass, pointing your work in a particular direction. Whatever the

The Ace Café, London, 1965
This off-beat "niterie" on London's North Circular Road is packed with Rockers, or motorcycle gangs, and their girls. No one dances or stays long (maybe a fast Coke), so I had to work quickly. I got the foreground in first to key a loosely composed drawing, then added the other figures as they came and departed, roaring up and down the luridly lit highway. Drawn in a 14" x 17" Reeves sketchbook of Ingres paper with a 6B Venus graphite pencil. From London à la Mode, *1966. Courtesy Studio Vista Ltd., London; and Hill & Wang, Inc., New York.*

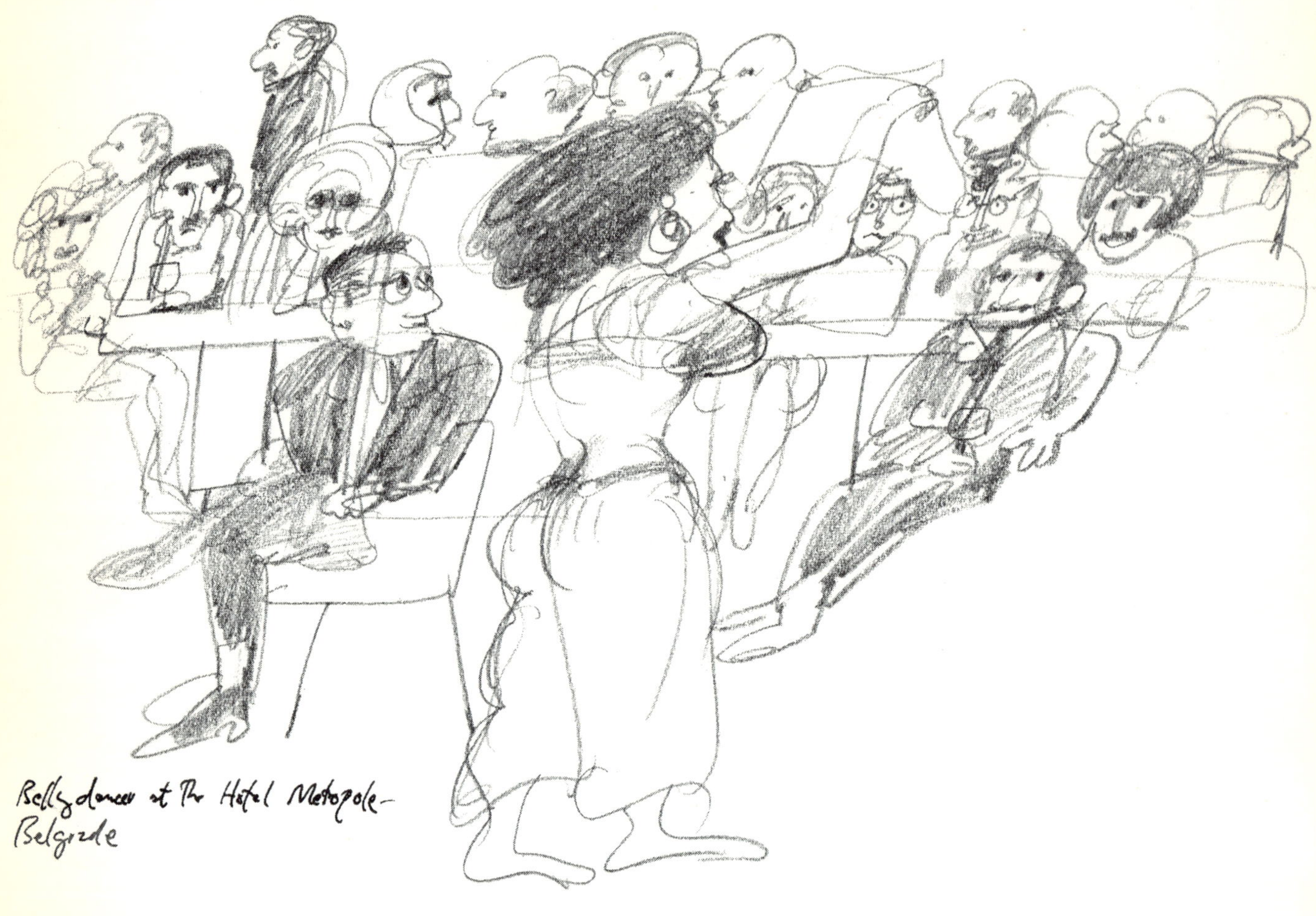

Belly dancer, Hotel Metropole, Belgrade, Yugoslavia, 1967
Here, to make a more light-hearted comment on nightlife, I used the various facial expressions of the audience. Drawn with a Faber 702 sketching pencil in a 7" x 10½" English Planet sketchbook of smooth drawing paper. Courtesy Fortune *magazine. (Above)*

Replacing a worn drilling bit, Leman natural gas field, North Sea, England, 1968
The derrick—the steel tower that is the symbol of oil or gas drilling all over the world—is a surprisingly complex structure. I decided, therefore, to select only what was essential to my drawing of a crew of "roughnecks" at work. This gave me much greater freedom to emphasize the exhausting and tedious nature of their task. Drawn in an 11" x 14" sketchbook of one-ply, medium surface Strathmore Alexis drawing paper with a Faber 702 sketching pencil and Faber Design Markettes. Washes of Grumbacher watercolor were applied later in my cabin with a Japanese brush. Courtesy, Standard Oil Company of New Jersey. Copyright The Lamp, *Winter, 1968. (Right)*

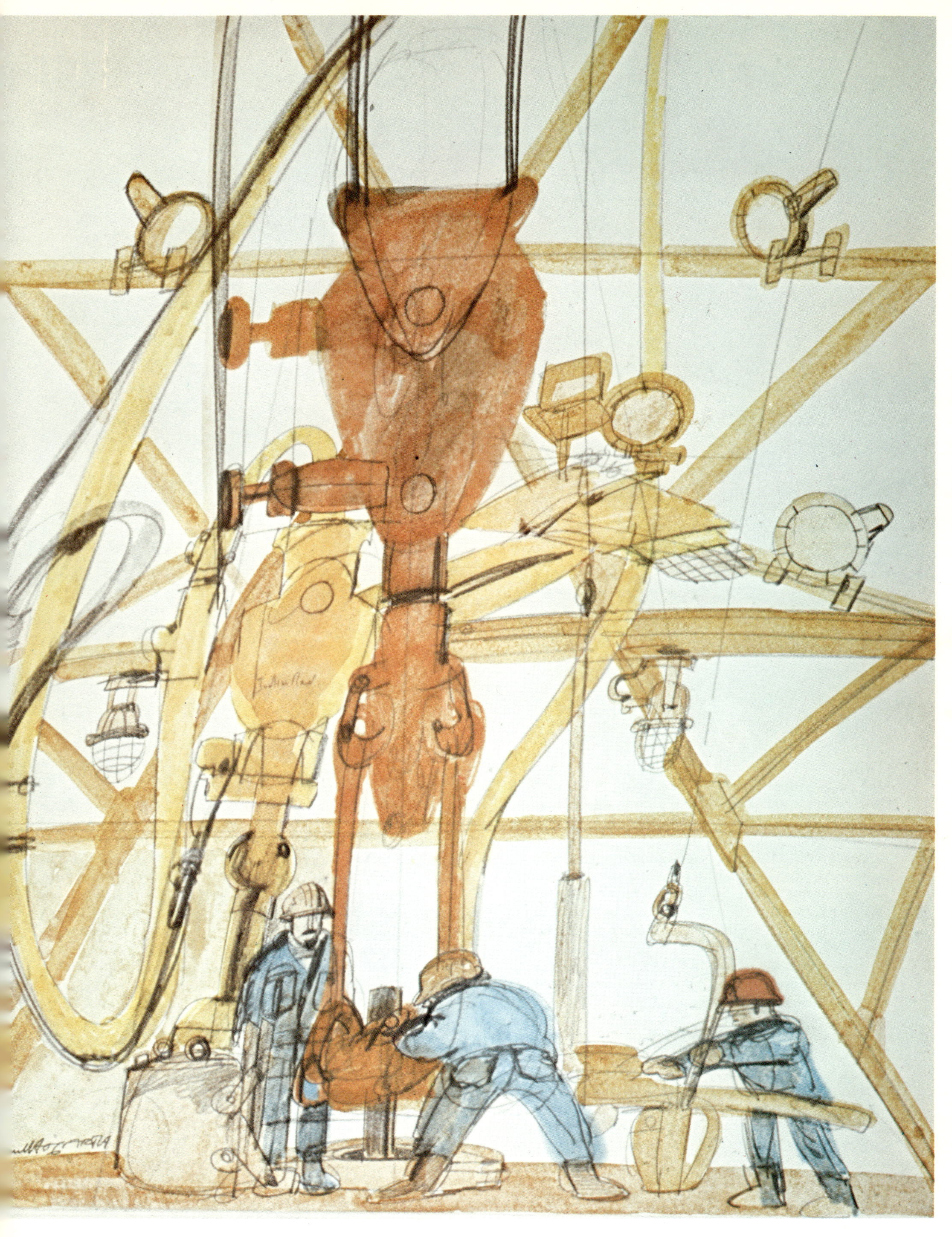

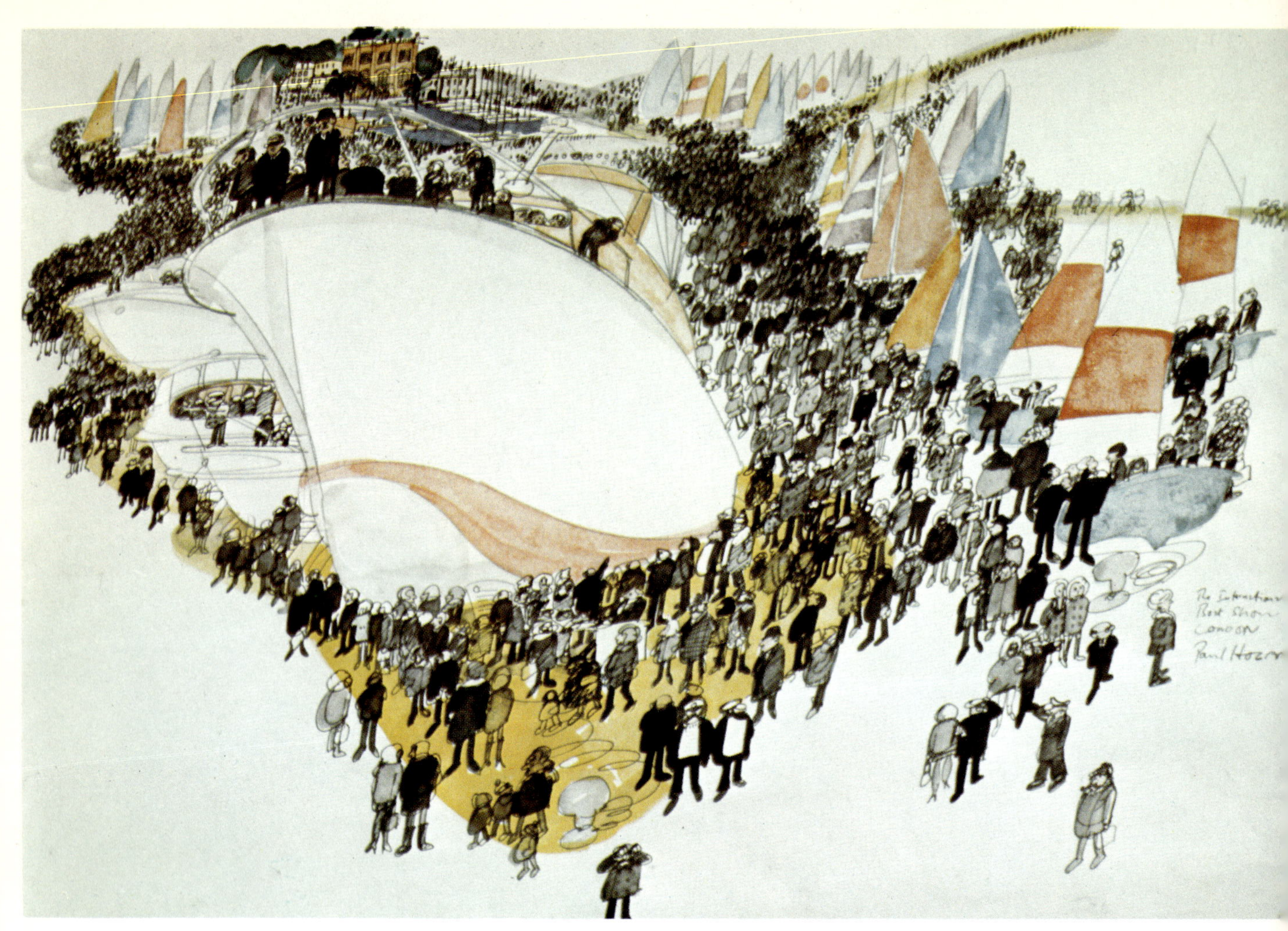

The London Boat Show, England, 1968
The annual London Boat Show is a whole eleven-acre maritime world crammed with enough boats to transport an army. During the first week of January, dense crowds of hippies, fishermen, yachtsmen of all income groups, ordinary seamen and admirals, not to mention schoolboys, inspect the latest craft. The deck of a huge luxury power boat proved to be an ideal vantage point, and an hour before the doors were officially opened found me drawing part of the vast interior with its islands of exhibits. I used a Faber 702 sketching pencil, Faber Design Markettes to quickly fill in large areas of color, and Marubu watercolors for the small areas such as sails and hulls. Then, as people began to enter, I was ready to draw them in directly with Higgins Manuscript Ink, using a Gillot 303 nib for the small figures and a stronger Spencerian school nib for the larger figures. I knew the drawing would be reduced to about half-size when reproduced, so I built up sections of the crowd by filling them in with diluted ink washes. Paper used was Hollingworth Kent Mill. From the portfolio "Afloat in the Off Season." Courtesy Sports Illustrated. *Published January 6, 1969. Copyright by Time, Inc. (Above)*

Buddy Baker, Charlotte 400, 1965
Stock-car racing depends on a tough, able elite of drivers for its thrills, and the keenly intelligent, happy-go-lucky personality of this ex-football player seemed to me to personify the courage, the guts, it takes. To emphasize this, I needed a few extra props. I asked Baker to remain seated so I could include such details as the car window, the tubular steel bracing which protects a driver from injury, the pop graffiti on the roof, and the vivid colors. Drawn in forty minutes in an 11" x 14" sketchbook of one-ply, medium surface Strathmore Alexis drawing paper with Faber Design Markettes and a Faber 702 graphite pencil. Commissioned for Sports Illustrated. *Courtesy Time, Inc. (Right)*

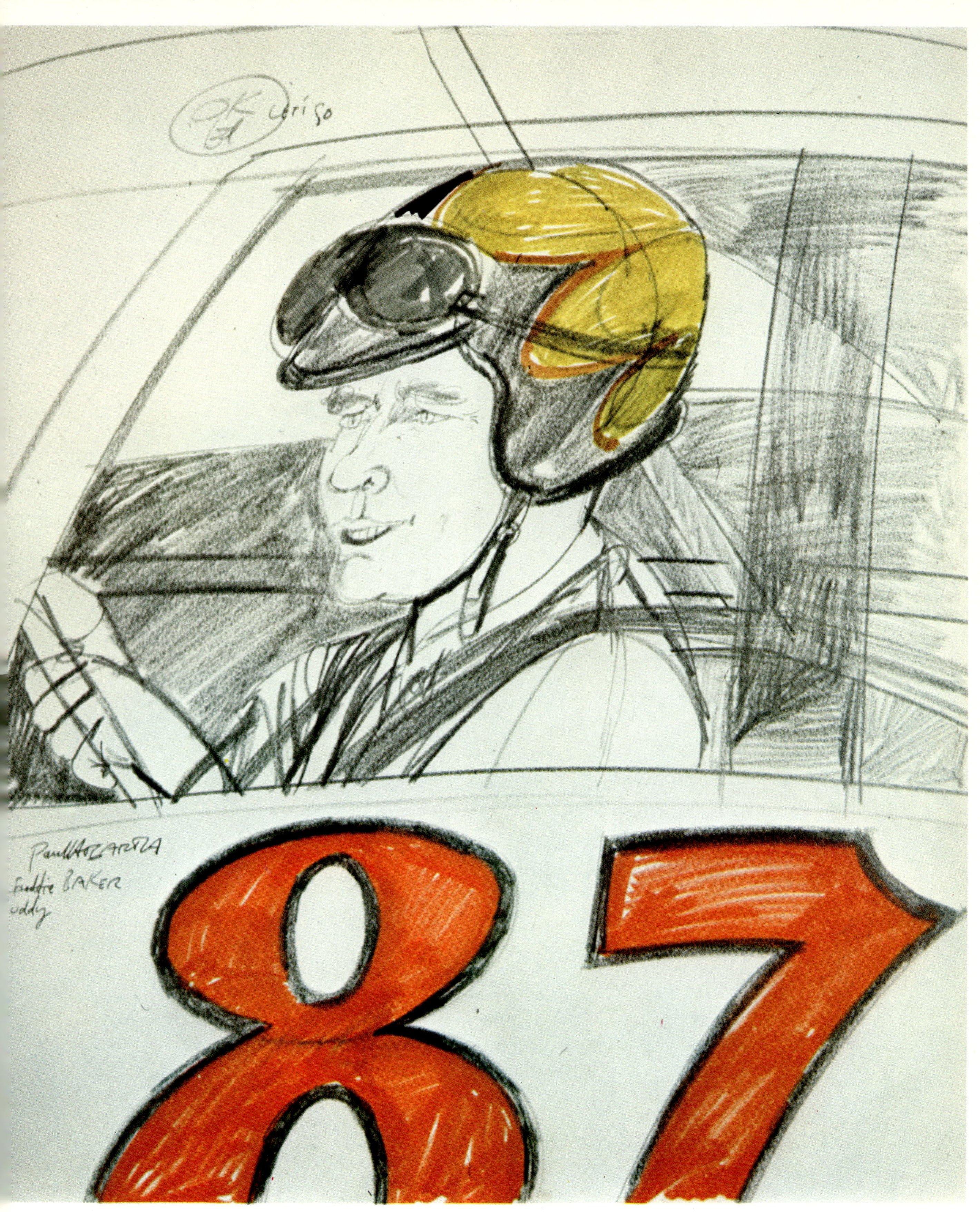
Freddie BAKER
87

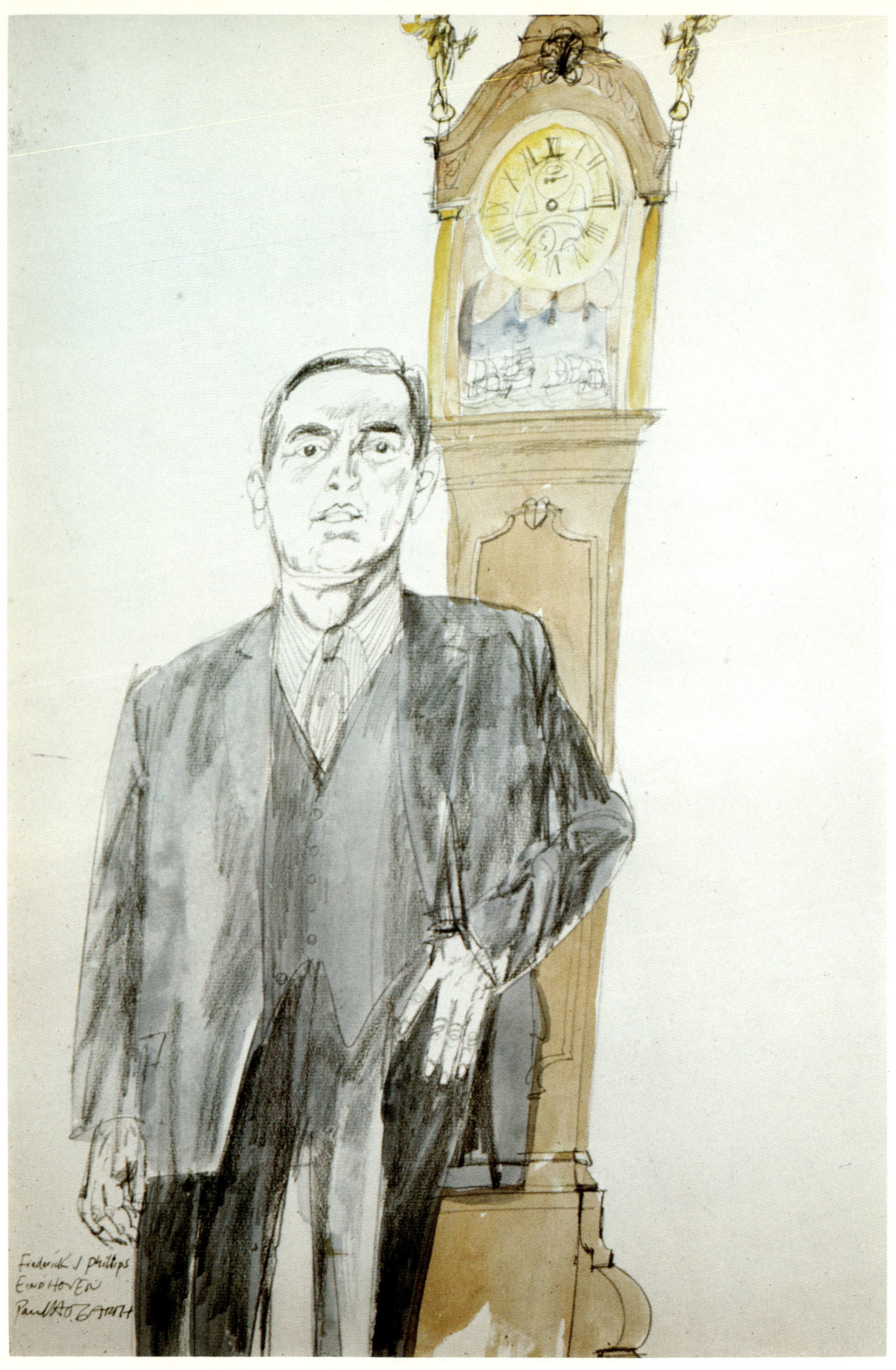
Frederick J Phillips
EINDHOVEN

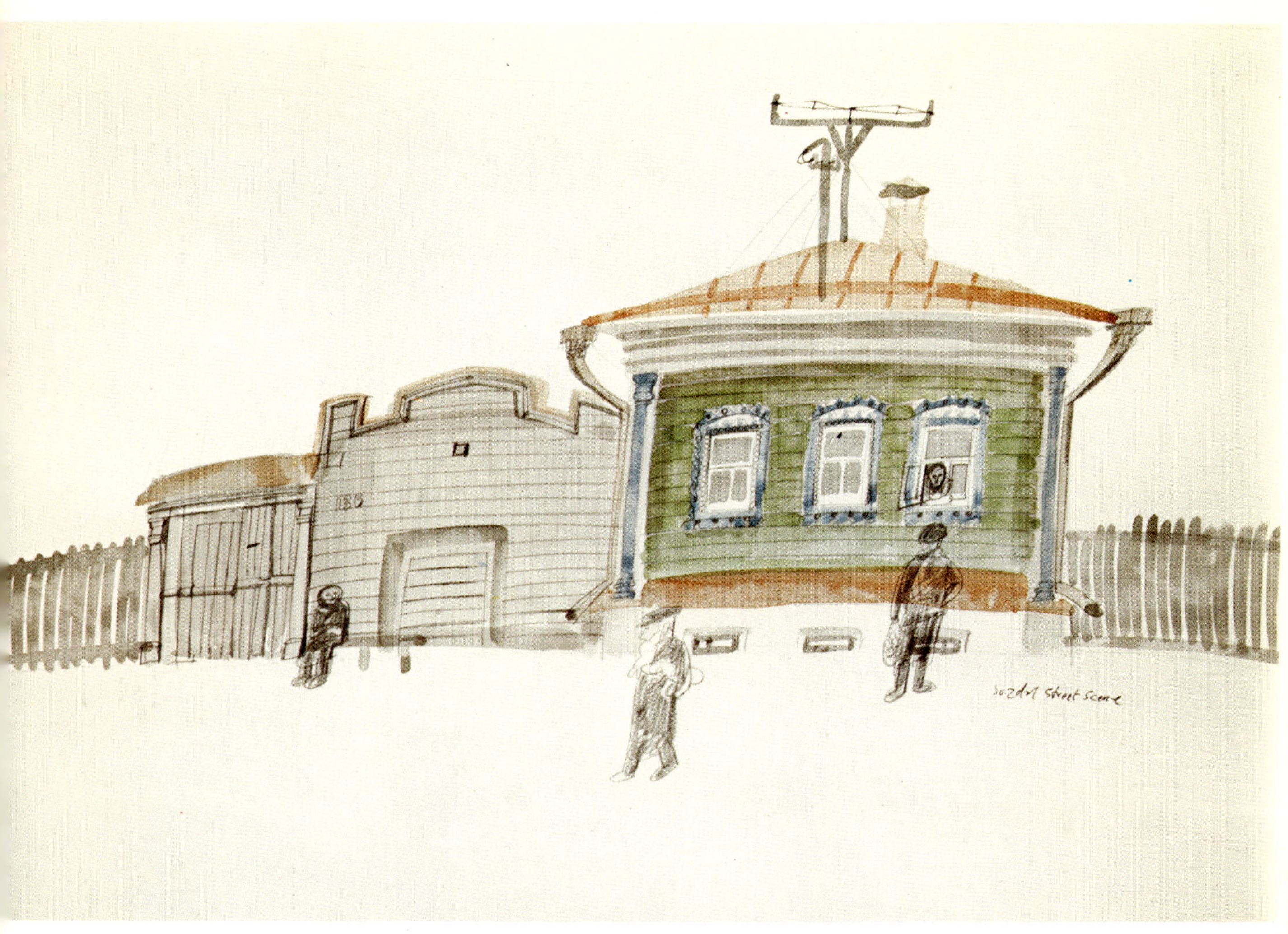

Frederick J. Phillips, Eindhoven, Holland, 1965
Europe's largest maker of electrical products, the famous tycoon Frits Phillips was almost sixty when I ascended to the twenty-fifth floor of his skyscraper apartment to draw his portrait. He looks much younger than his years even though he spent time in a Nazi prison camp during World War Two. Perhaps because of this, he is a man of great restraint and unusual sympathy who prefers to listen rather than to talk. I placed him against a fine old grandfather clock with a painted inset of a seventeenth-century Dutch merchant fleet, because he so obviously stemmed from the staunch merchant-capitalists of the period. The portrait was drawn in one hour. Another hour, however, was spent being shown the Phillips collection of Rembrandts and Delft china. Rembrandt had only himself and his patron to please; Phillips thought I had a more difficult task—to make a portrait that not only had to satisfy myself and the sitter but also the editors of Fortune! *Drawn with a 6B Venus graphite pencil on Strathmore Script paper. After notes made on the spot, washes of Grumbacher watercolor were added later with a Winsor & Newton No. 6 sable brush. Courtesy* Fortune *magazine. Copyright August 1965 by Time, Inc. (Left)*

Street scene, Suzdal, U.S.S.R., 1967
To convey the unchanged character of this old capital of Muscovy, I selected two elderly peasants from the few that passed by. Two schoolgirls, anxious to impress me with their excellent English, filled me in on both of them: the old man clutching the loaf was a carpenter and the old woman was the biggest gossip in the village. Drawn, between intervals of such talk, in a custom-made 15" x 20" sketchbook of Basingwerk Antique drawing paper with a Faber 702 sketching pencil, Faber Design Markettes, and washes of German Marubu watercolors applied with a Japanese brush. From A Russian Journey: from Suzdal to Samarkand, *1969. Courtesy Cassell and Company, London; and Hill & Wang, Inc., New York. (Above)*

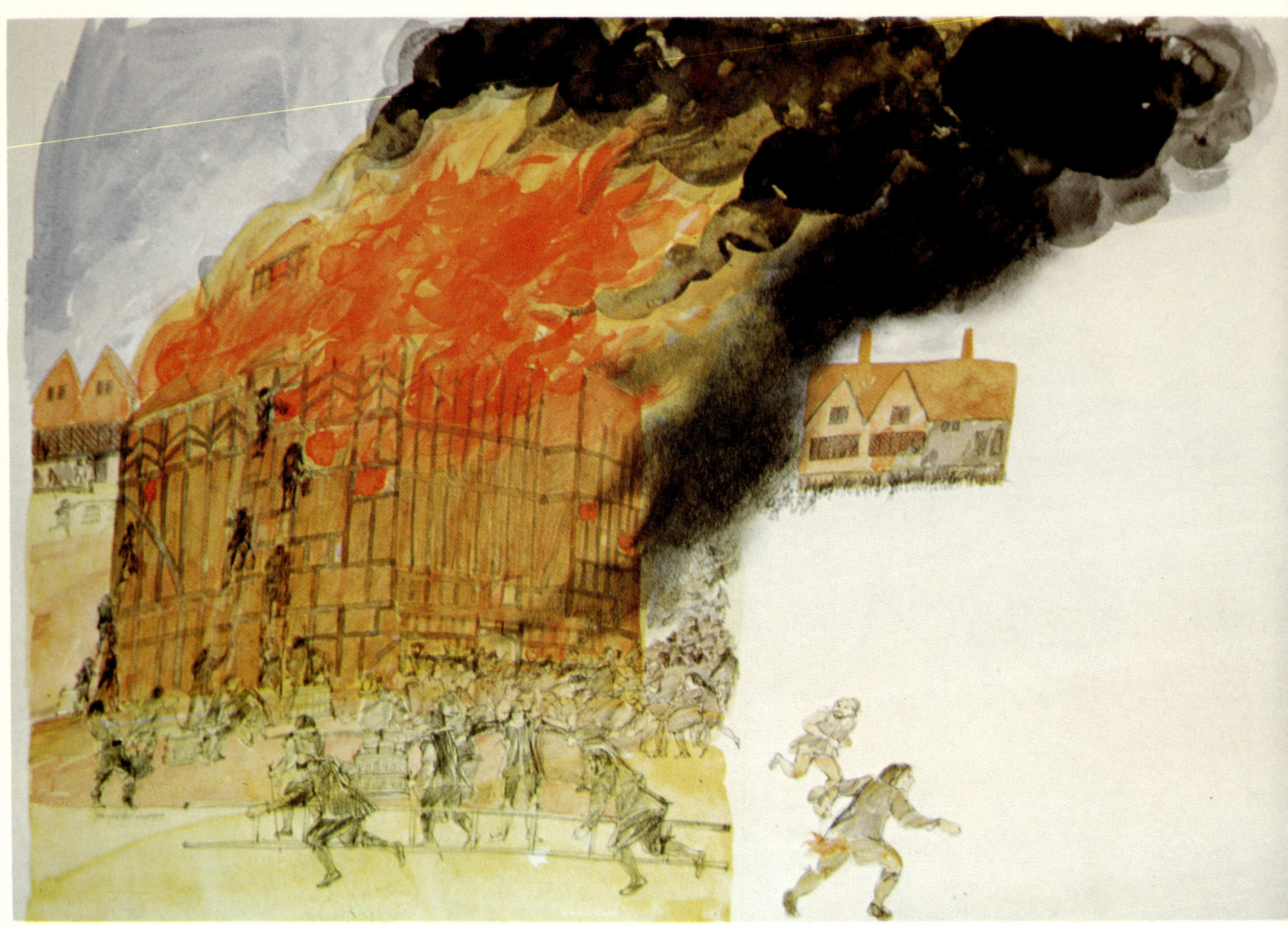

The Burning of the Globe Theatre (1613)
This illustration, one of a series made in 1964, depicts certain events of Shakespeare's lifetime, and had to be created with a great deal of emphasis on the types and characters of the period. In this particular case, I divided the Elizabethan crowd into three fields of focus: the audience rushing from the burning theatre; the firefighters running toward it; and the static throng of enthralled spectators in the distance. Although the fire is reported to have blazed wildly, everyone escaped unscathed, except one man who had to douse his burning breeches with a bottle of ale. This incident was too good to miss, so I brought the unfortunate man into the foreground at right. Drawn with Caran d'Ache charcoal lead, 4B and 6B Eagle Charco pencils, and 6B Venus graphite pencil, and augmented with passages of Winsor & Newton gouache color on Hollingworth Kent Mill paper. From the special Shakespeare number of Life, *April 23, 1964. Courtesy* Life *magazine. Copyright by Time, Inc. (Above)*

The Admiralty, Leningrad, U.S.S.R., 1967
Buildings of every type and period gain if the artist carefully selects and includes a single figure or group of figures. As this famous doorway was connected with the founding of the Russian Navy in the early years of the construction of the former capital, my Russian sailor seemed to walk by at the right moment. Drawn in a custom-made 15" x 20" sketchbook of Basingwerk Antique drawing paper with a Faber 702 sketching pencil, Faber Design Markettes, and washes of gray and ochre Grumbacher watercolor applied with a Japanese brush. From A Russian Journey: from Suzdal to Samarkand, *1969. Courtesy Cassell and Company, London; and Hill & Wang, Inc., New York. (Right)*

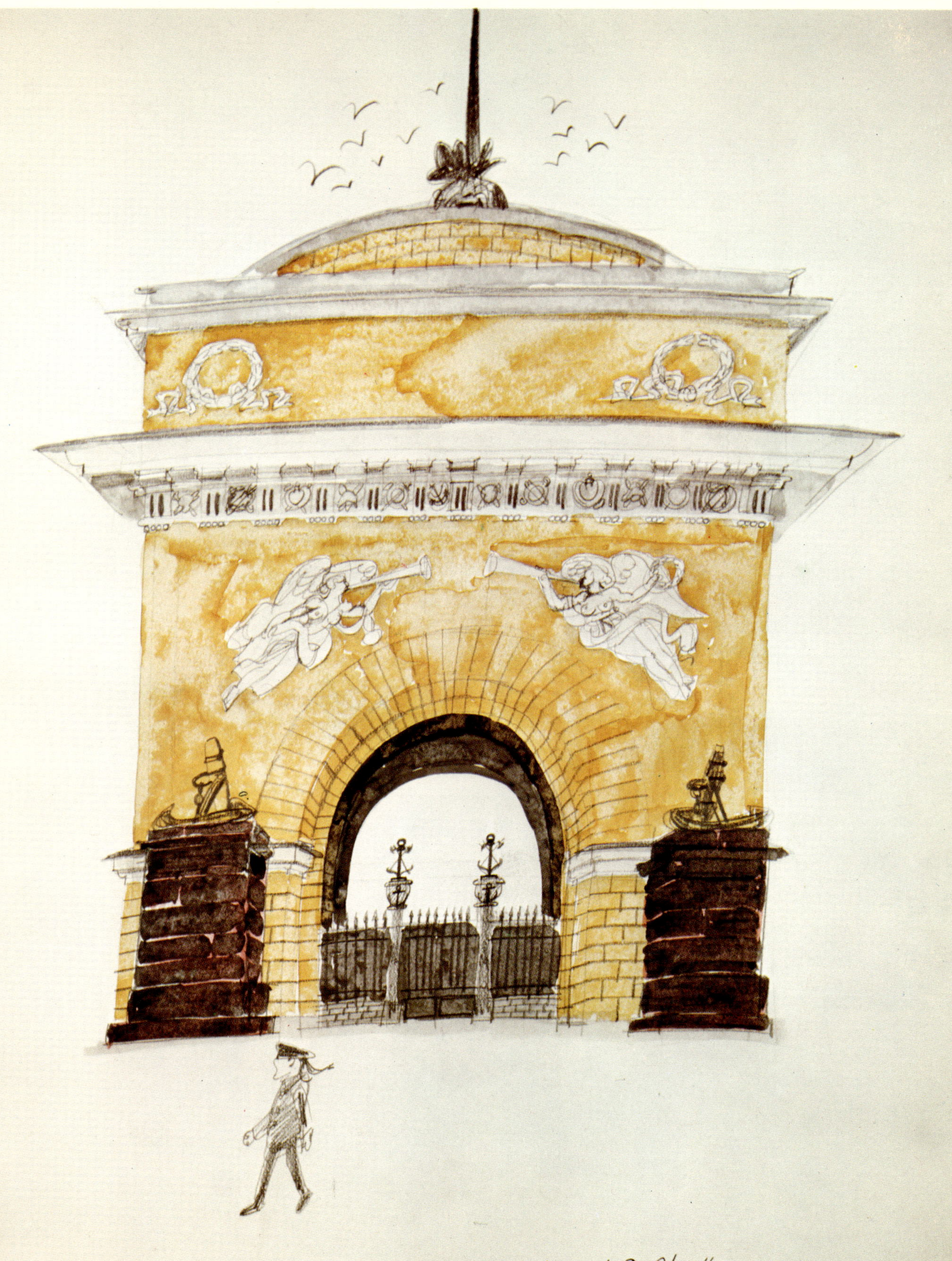
Leningrad: The Admiralty

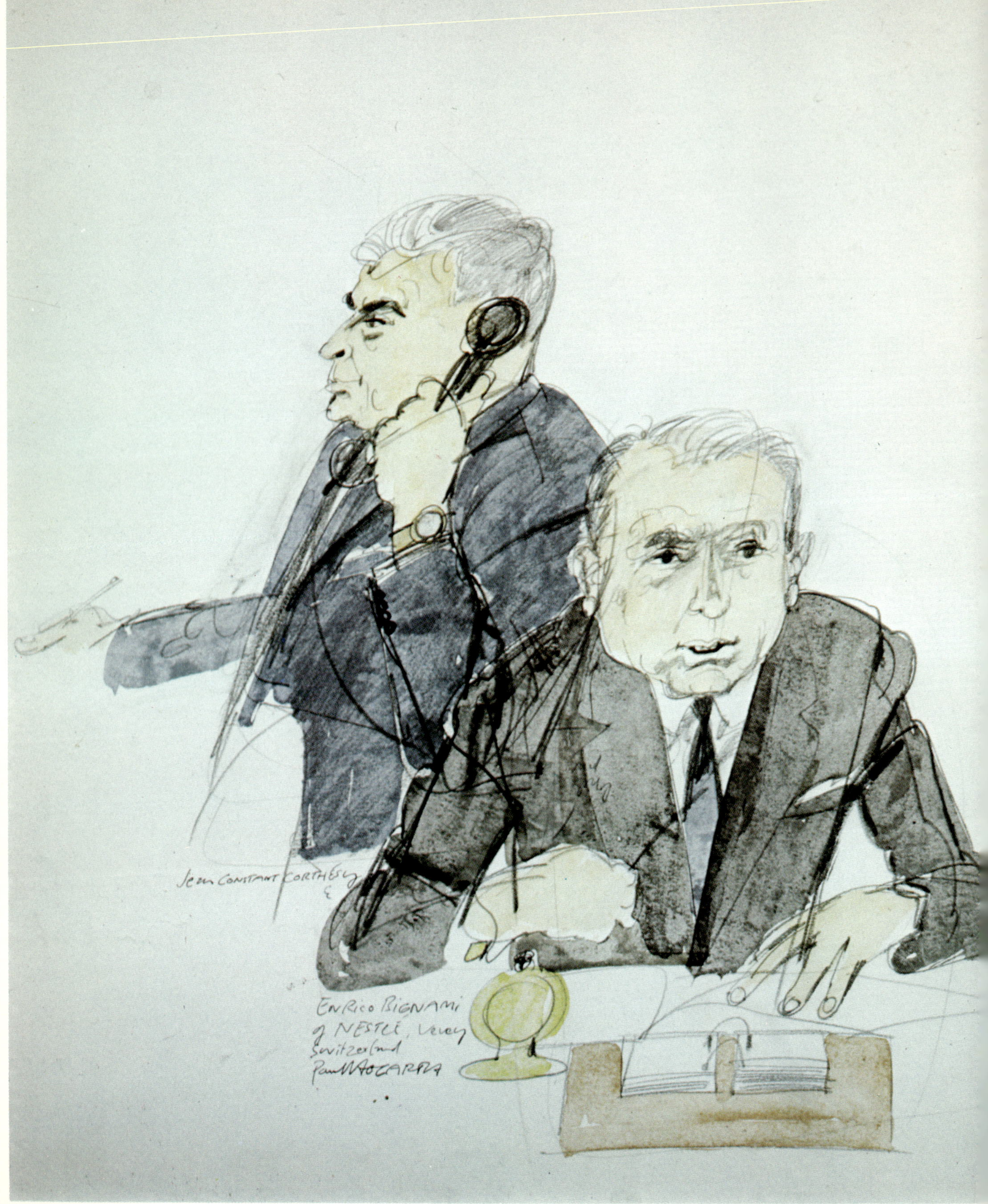
Jean CONSTANT CORTHESY
&
EnRico BIGNAMI
of NESTLÉ, Vevey
Switzerland
Paul MOZARRA

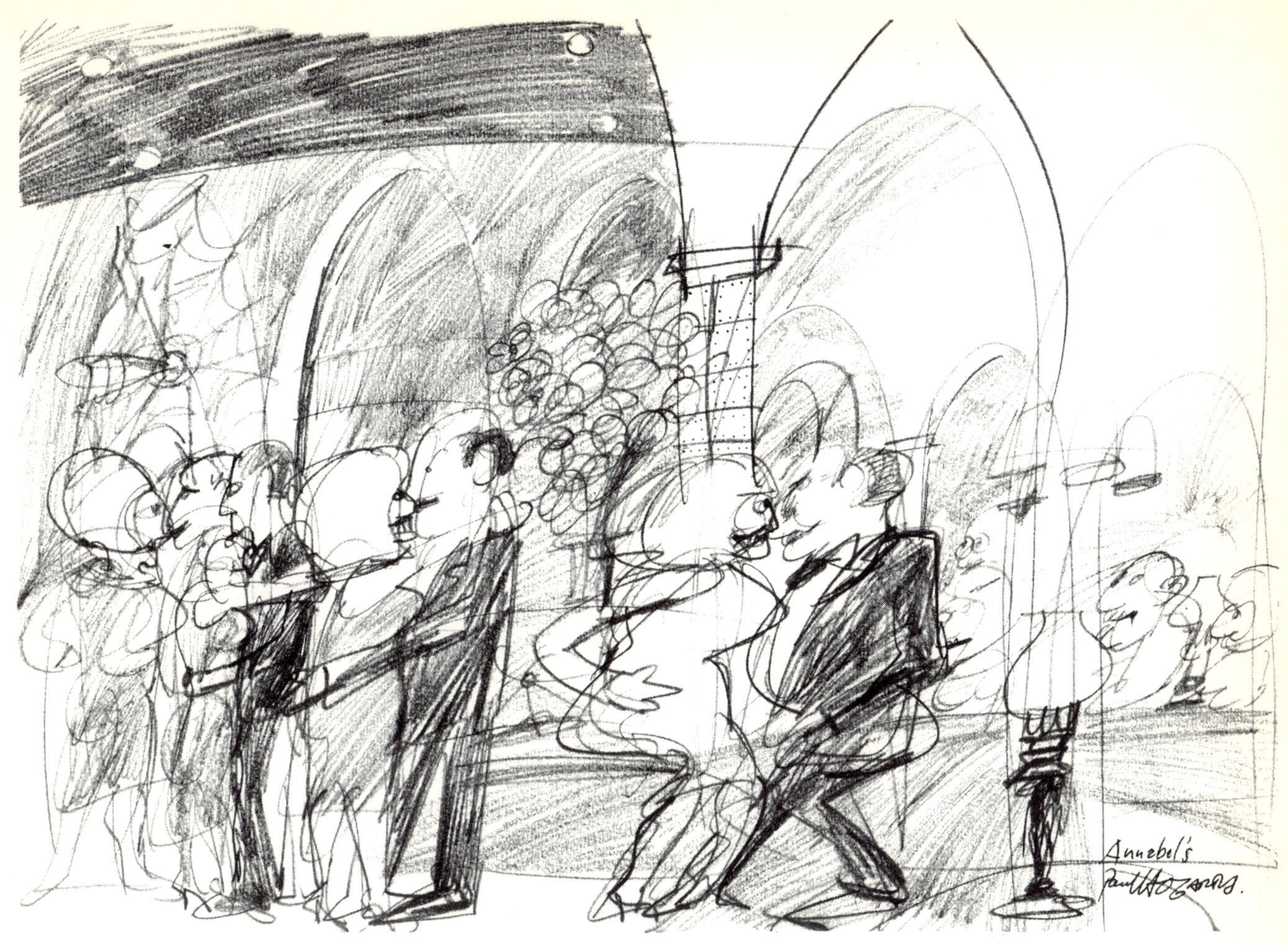

Jean Corthésy and Enrico Bignami of Nestlé Alimentara, S.A., Switzerland, 1967

This world-wide food company, whose graceful modern offices overlook Lake Geneva at Vevey, splits its high command between two managing directors, Jean Corthésy (left) and Enrico Bignami (right). They divide the responsibilities, with one running day-to-day operations and the other concentrating on long-range planning. This interdependence on one another prompted the idea of a Siamese twins type of composition, in which personal characteristics of both men could be emphasized. The problem of drawing each as an individual in a double portrait was resolved after requesting that they continue their normal office routine. Corthésy, for example, although a dynamic extrovert, looked livelier in profile, carrying on a long-distance telephone call. Bignami, on the other hand, was an introvert whose keen intelligence revealed itself more openly whenever he talked. Drawn in little more than an hour on Strathmore Script paper in 3B and 6B Venus graphite pencil and Grumbacher watercolor with a No. 6 Winsor & Newton sable brush. Courtesy Fortune *magazine, September 15, 1967. Copyright by Time, Inc. (Left)*

Annabel's, Mayfair, London, 1966

Any top brass discothéque usually protects regular customers from what might be unwelcome publicity by posting watchful waiters. So, to avoid the embarrassment of being asked to leave in the middle of making a drawing, I took along a couple of friends; I worked while they talked from each side of the table, covering me. Drawn in a 10¾" x 14½" English Planet sketchbook of smooth drawing paper with a push-action Hardtmuth Koh-i-noor soft pencil lead. From London à la Mode, *1966. Courtesy Studio Vista Ltd., London; and Hill & Wang, Inc., New York. (Above)*

Sketchbook study, London, 1968

This rapidly drawn study was made in semidarkness at a London strip club. But because I was several rows back, I could not see enough detail to make a drawing. I used a push-button Koh-i-noor medium soft lead pencil in a 7" x 10½" English Planet sketchbook of smooth drawing paper.

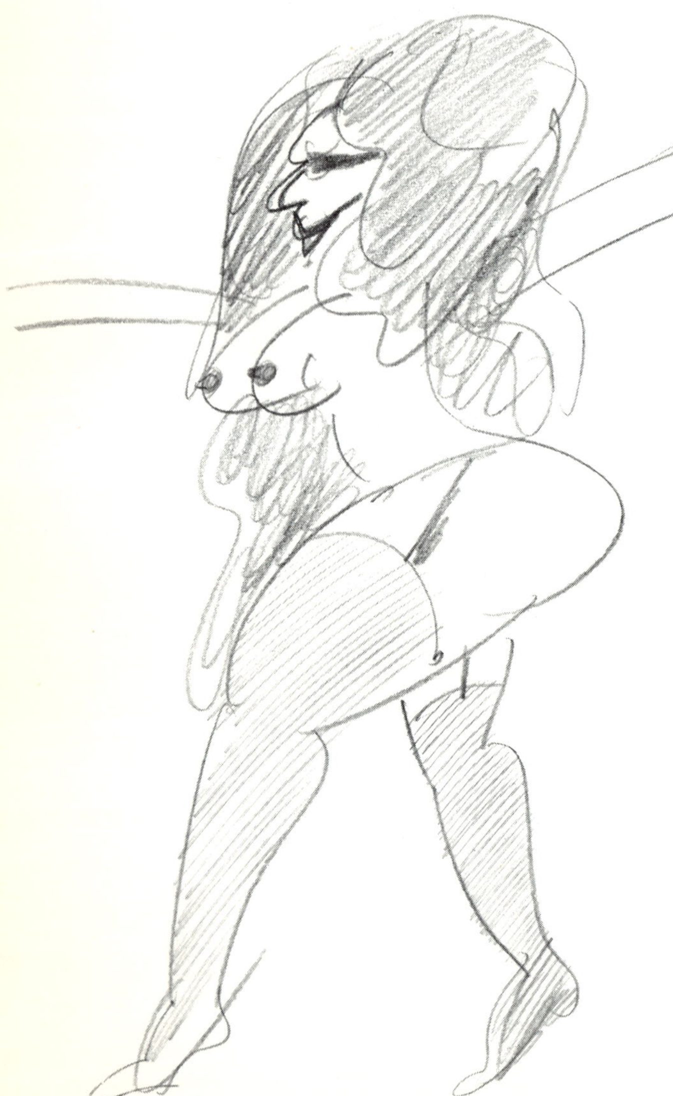

nature of your reaction, it will help you select not only *what* to draw, but also *how* to express your feelings about your subject.

My own feelings vary. For example, I almost always react negatively to "clip joints." Other places, like the first strip club I entered, I tend to see in comic terms. This initiation, which occurred in London, turned out to be completely different than what I had expected. Instead of an audience of hungry-eyed, bald satyrs, fashionably dressed young bachelors casually watched the grotesque enactments of everyman's fantasies. One long silence followed another until an impeccable Oxford English accent impatiently reminded everyone for the third and last time that, "Our uncensored and uninhibited film show is about to begin in the Red Room." My sketchbook was knocked to the floor in the rush!

Those who live in a big city will have a wide selection of spots to work in. Besides striptease clubs, these may include gambling casinos, topless restaurants, homosexual dives, and hippy havens. So much the better. You can draw people with a degree of insight and understanding only if you are also involved with them as a participant. (If he is to keep his cool to create, however, an artist must keep at least a part of himself aloof.)

METHODS OF WORKING

When you work in night spots, tools and materials naturally have to be kept to an absolute minimum. I usually carry two pocket sized sketchbooks (3½" x 5") for making thumbnail sketches of faces, figures, and miscellaneous notes; and a 5" x 7" for larger drawings. I use an 11" x 14" pad only in more informal places.

After I've determined when the action begins, I make sure to arrive early so that I can pick out a good vantage point. Usually, I try to get as close as I possibly can to the focus of attention without getting so close that I attract the attention myself.

To avoid this, I often sit at either side of a room, using whatever cover—such as plants, pillars, screens, or recesses—is available. Thus, I am at least partially concealed from the average onlooker—a particular advantage in a restaurant when I wish to draw completely unnoticed.

DRAWING IN DISCOTHEQUES AND NIGHTCLUBS

Conditions for drawing people dancing vary according to the kind of customers that the owners wish to attract. Certainly, the easiest discothéques or clubs to work in are those with no lights worth mentioning, and nothing else but the compulsive sound created by pop groups who play for hours on end. In any large city these are crowded with devotees of pop, rock,

"The French Maid," Soho strip club, London, 1966
London strip clubs are usually crowded; they play to every pocket. I went early to get a good seat—essential if I wanted to catch rapid movement with any quality of line. Drawn in a 14" x 17" Reeves sketchbook of Ingres paper with a Faber 702 sketching pencil. From London à la Mode, *1966. Courtesy Studio Vista Ltd., London; and Hill & Wang, Inc., New York.*

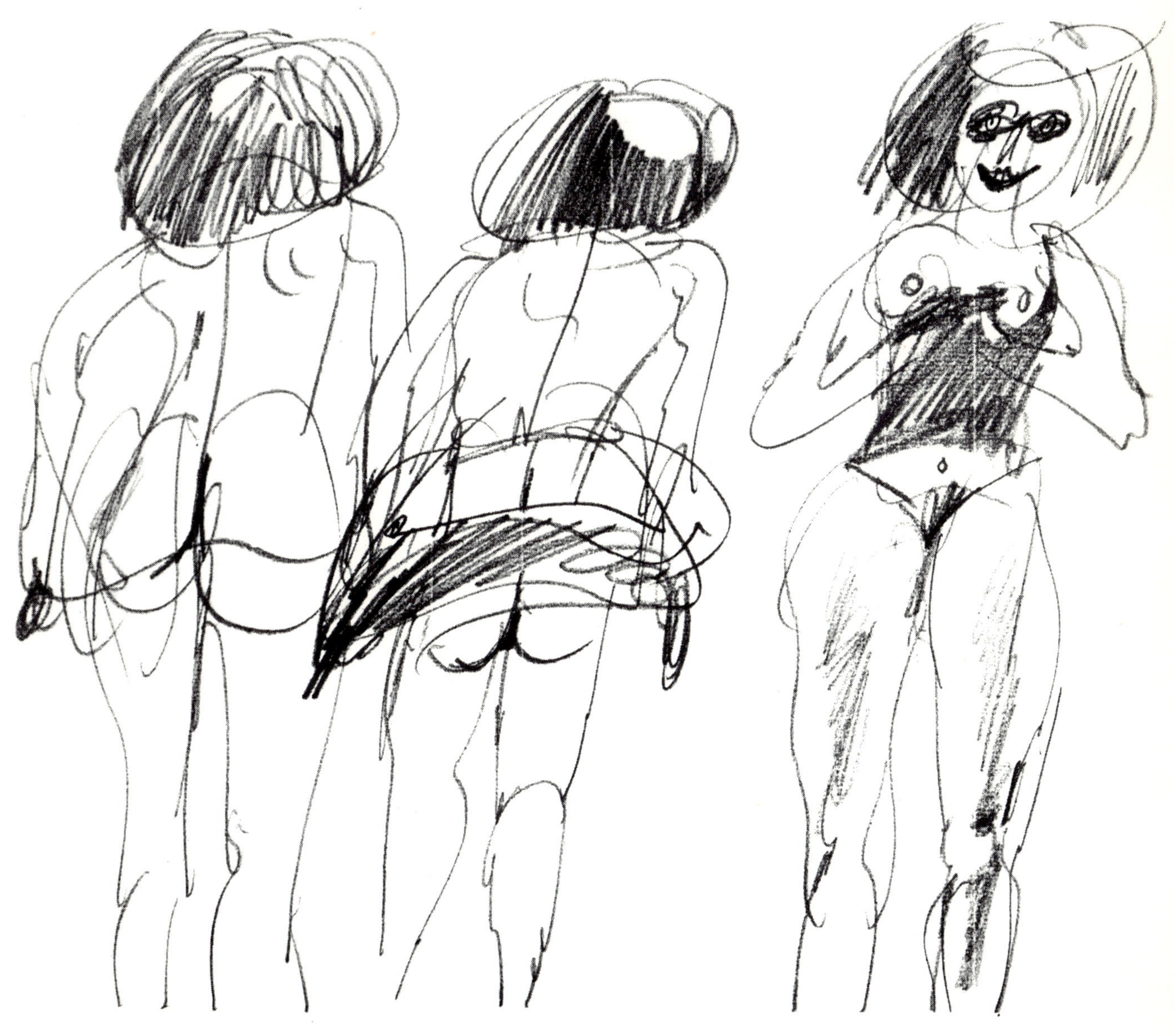

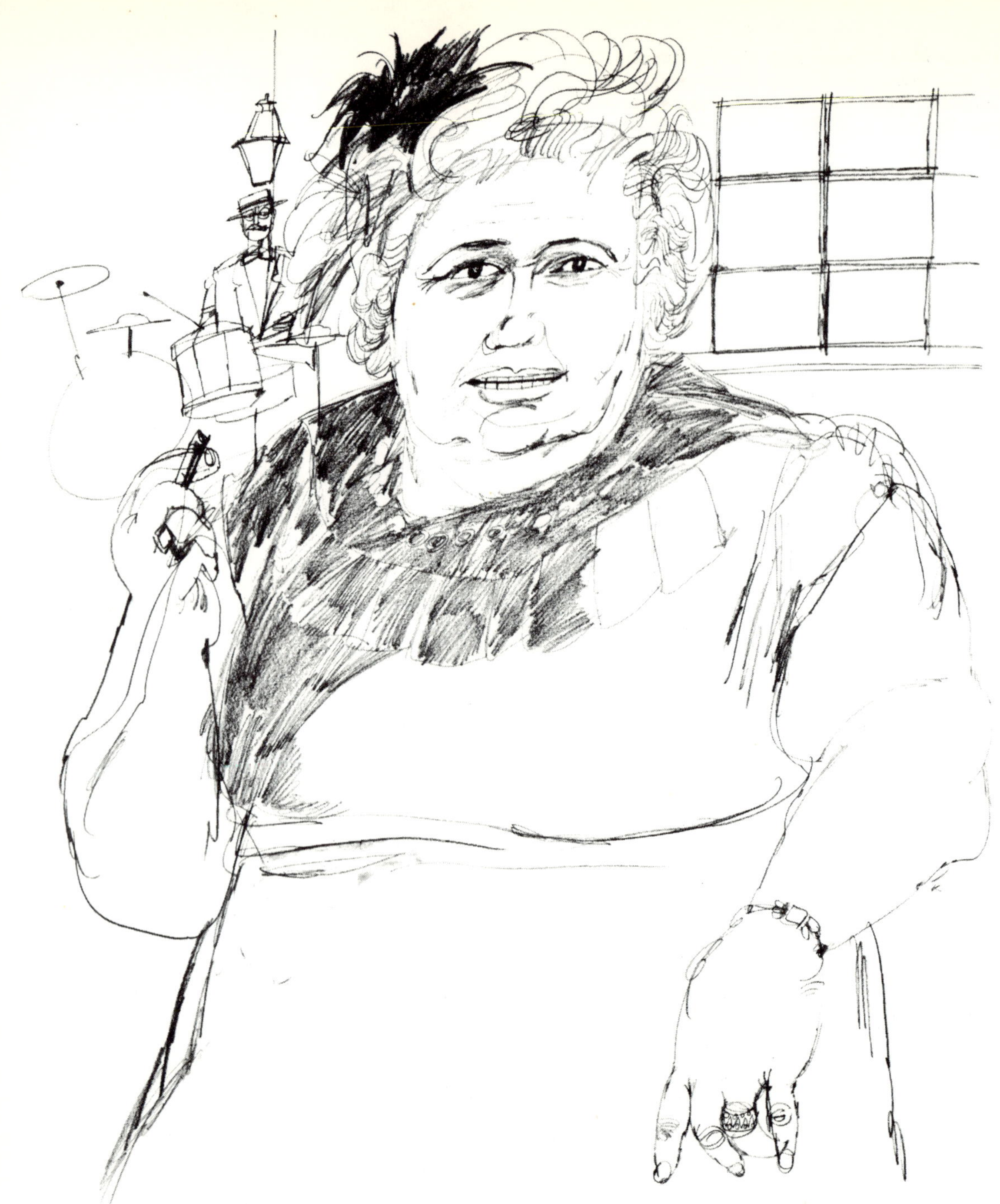

"Baby" Sandra, New York, 1963

Show business personalities, actors, and musicians are best drawn in the convivial atmosphere where they are playing. This gives everyone a chance to get acquainted, and if we like each other, the session usually goes well. Baby Sandra and I hit it off at once. Once a star, she was singing hits of the 1930s at Sammy's Bowery Follies. Between acts, she enjoyed a double whisky and a smoke. As I drew her, a hand slowly edged towards her cigarettes, which lay on the table. Several seconds later, without moving or batting an eyelid, her great right arm slammed down on the impertinence. "You must be a greenhorn," she growled to a cringing bum nursing his fingers. I made the portrait (at the cost of four double whiskies) in a 14" x 17" sketchbook of Daler drawing paper with 4B and 6B graphite pencils. From Brendan Behan's New York, *1964. Courtesy The Hutchinson Publishing Group, London; and Bernard Geis Associates, New York.*

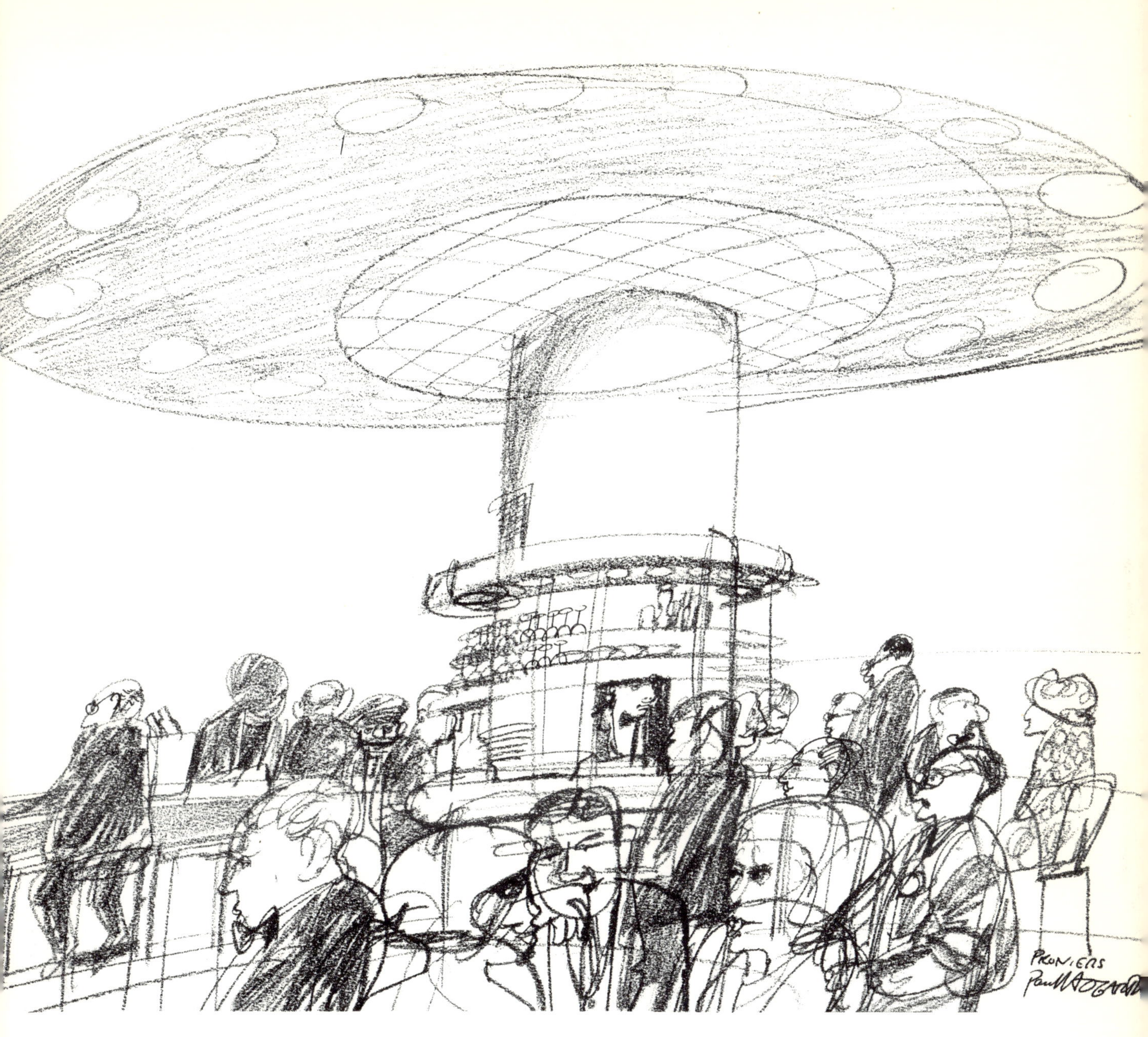

Prunier's, St. James's, London, 1966
In the chromium elegance of this gourmet restaurant, life aboard some obscure avant-garde liner of yesteryear is brought to mind. Time appears to have little significance, as customers wage a sustained attack on the formidable menu. Drawn in an 11" x 14" sketchbook of Strathmore drawing paper with a Faber 702 sketching pencil. From London à la Mode, *1966. Courtesy Studio Vista Ltd., London; and Hill & Wang, Inc., New York.*

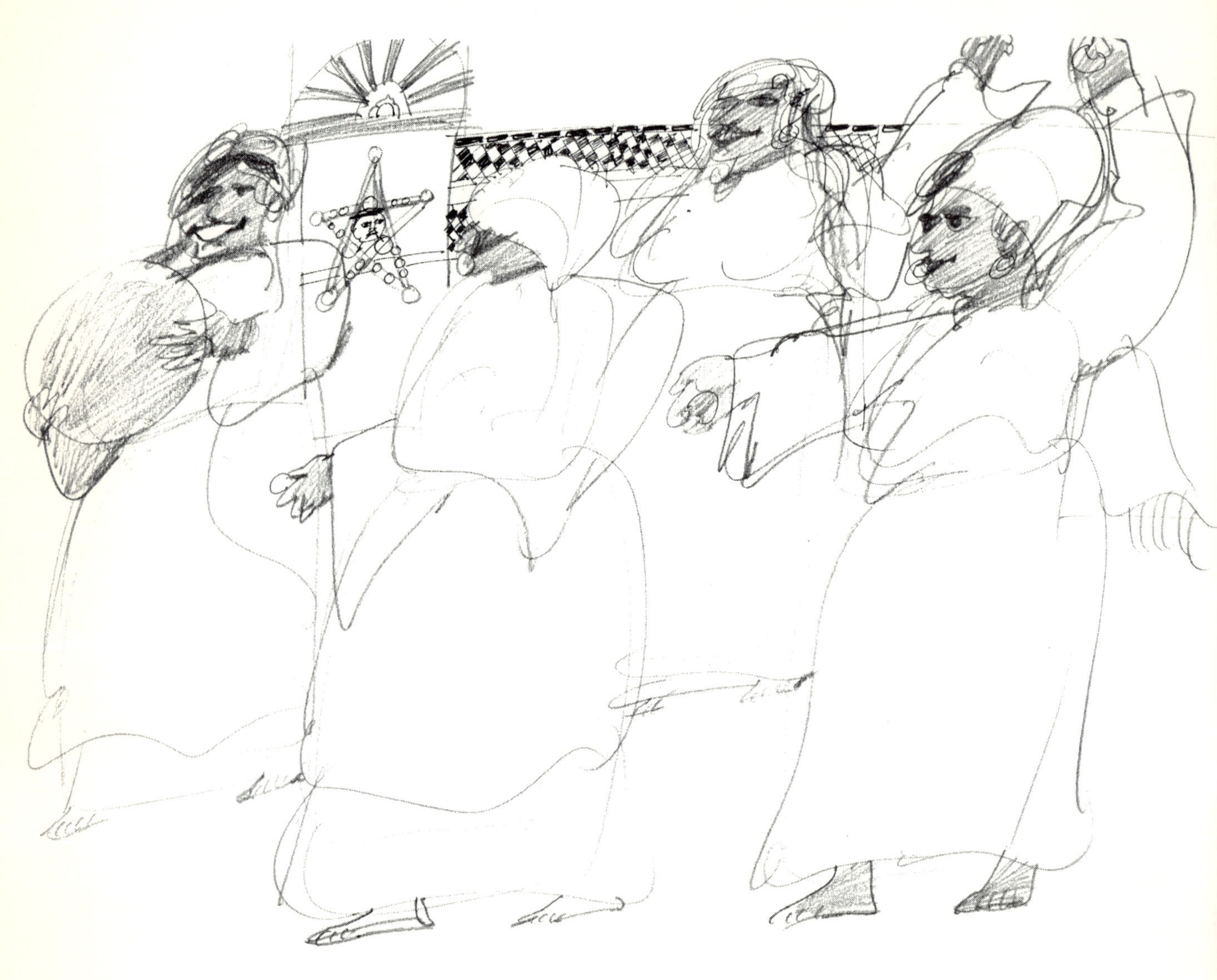

Berber dancing girls, Marrakesh, Morocco, 1966
Alas, the fabled beauty of Morocco's dancing girls is mostly fable; the "girls" are often oversize and gold-toothed. Yet they move with good-natured grace and rhythm to the whining bleat of Berber folk music. A Faber 702 sketching pencil was used in a 10¾" x 14½" Planet sketchbook. Courtesy Weekend Telegraph, *London.*

soul, country and western, folk, or traditional jazz who like to do their own thing to their preferred type of music—with or without a partner. No one is unduly curious, and usually you can work from the sidelines, unnoticed and untroubled.

Although much the same relaxed atmosphere prevails at the larger commercial nightclubs, you should take care not to get on the wrong side of the management. Remember that a sometimes formidable staff of henchmen is employed for the purpose of bundling those who misbehave into the unfriendly night!

Discretion is most essential when you visit the fashionable and more expensive discothéques, where waiters and bartenders invariably keep an eye on any situation which may embarrass their more publicity-shy customers. Whenever I visit such spots to make drawings, I take a friend along to avoid being too conspicuous a figure, and I casually make my sketches as we sit with our drinks.

STRIP CLUBS AND GAMBLING CASINOS

I have always found the most interesting strip shows to be those that attract the not-so-well-to-do, places where the men are content to study the gyrations of well-upholstered, but no longer young girls that are rounding off an arduous life in show business. Usually, these popular places pack their audiences into old theaters like sardines, so you have to try and get as close as you can to the stage.

The so-called "art" strip clubs are also worth a visit. The problem with these clubs is that the closer you get to the action, the more expensive the evening becomes. Sometimes, however, it is possible to have a modestly priced beer at the bar and still get a good enough veiwpoint, rather than be forced to drink overpriced champagne at a ringside table.

Gambling casinos, on the other hand, are the most difficult places to work in. Unless you accompany a regular customer or have the approval of the management, it is wiser to commit what you see to memory. Most casinos have strict rules about photography and drawing. At various times I have circumvented these restrictions by pretending to make calculations, as some gamblers do, while actually I was drawing in a 3½" x 5" sketchbook. Such sketches have to be made rapidly. Never forget that, whatever their ostensible business, some nightclubs may have one foot on the other side of the law. Therefore, it is essential for you to proceed cautiously in pursuit of your material. Check beforehand with the proprietors when you are in doubt in order to avoid misunderstanding and trouble!

RESTAURANTS AND CAFES

Frankly, I have only begun to explore the nightlife which centers on exclusive and fashionable restaurants since I took out my first credit card! Somehow, the card has given me the impetus to explore one great restaurant after another, penciling their respective ambiances with great enjoyment. London is a particularly rich hunting ground. Places like the Grill Room of the Café Royal, for example, with its Victorian caryatids supporting a hugely ornate ceiling, provide a magnificently flamboyant setting for observing the witty and the wealthy. The proprietors of another favorite spot of mine, the chromium-plated Prunier's in St. James's, surprised me one evening in 1966 by announcing their pleasure in taking care of a formidable bill in exchange for my original drawing. I was more than delighted to make the swap!

Naturally, you must make reservations at such restaurants. Before you do, find out from a bartender or a friendly waiter when the best side tables (the most concealed) are usually available. It is better to be seated discreetly, at an hour when the place is only a quarter full, than to find yourself out in the open and completely exposed! Fashionable London restaurants are at their best and most typical when they're filled with the after-theater crowd. At whatever hour the elegant congregate, settle in before they arrive and use the time to complete a background or two. By the time *they* are about to begin their dinner, *you* will be prepared to draw them (in between mouthfuls of your dessert) and can still beat the reproachful glances of the headwaiter anxiously waiting for you to vacate your table.

By contrast, the best roadhouses to work in, I find, are those which are used as stopping off places by the motorcycle boys (rockers or leather-boys, as they are called in England). Usually as grim on the inside as on the outside, these places become offbeat "niteries" on weekends, packed with the boys and their girls, alongside truckdrivers and bewildered strangers. No one stays very long and I cannot say I blame them! A fast Coke, then off on the bikes to roar up and down the luridly-lit highway outside.

As my suspicious mother used to tell me, "There's now't [nothing] as funny as folk." Until I began to stay up late, I never did believe her!

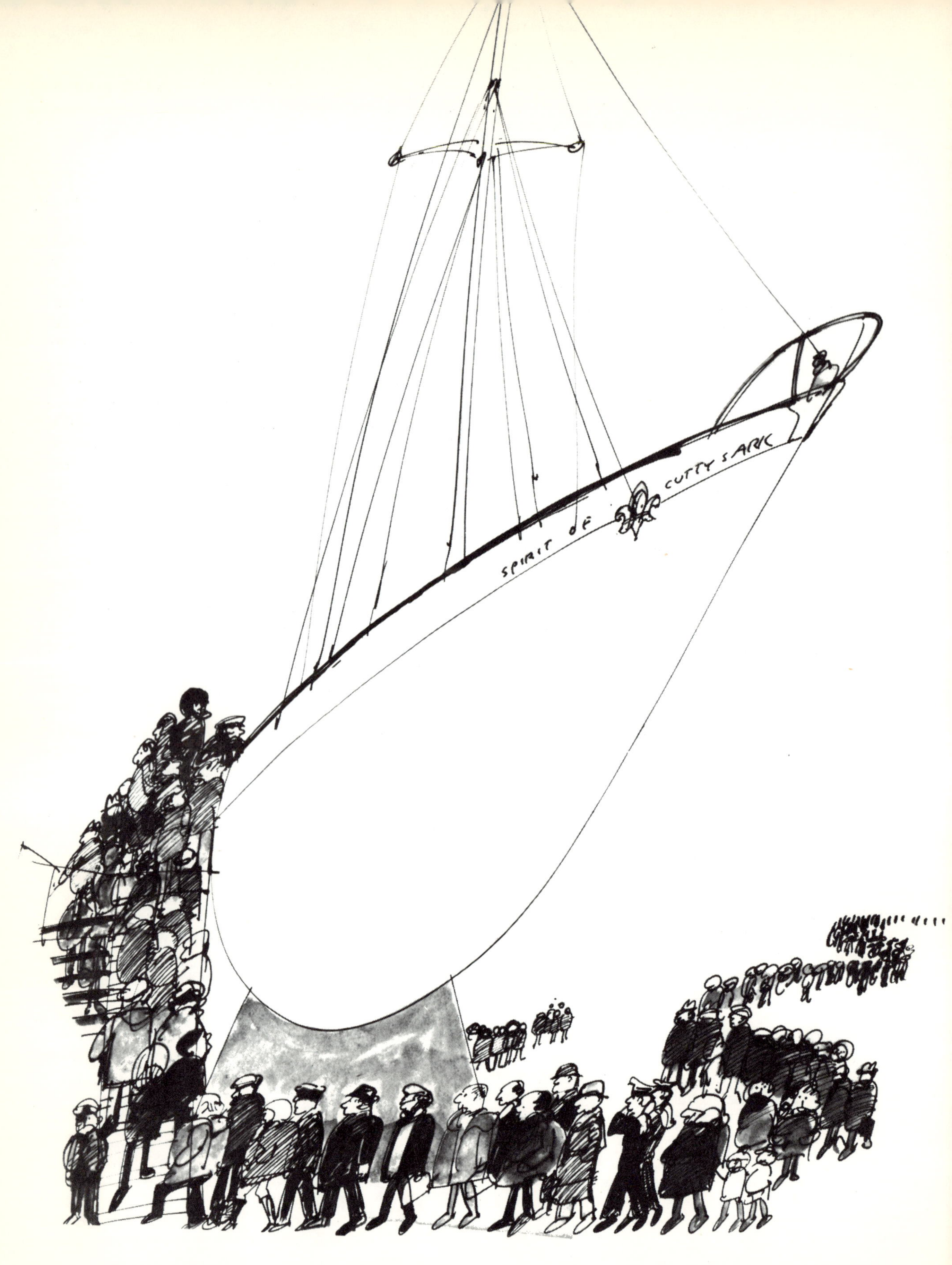
SPIRIT OF
CUTTY SARK

CHAPTER 10

Drawing Crowds

CROWDS HAVE ALWAYS held the greatest fascination for artists. I am thinking, at random, of the sinister pageantry of Jacques Callot, the turbulent mobs of William Hogarth, and the genial multitudes of Victorian artists like William Powell Frith. In our own time, consider the gray crowds of people on their way to work by Steinlen and Kathe Kollwitz; and, of course, the zany throngs of Steinberg.

ANGRY MOBS

No spectacle presents such extremes of human behavior as crowds do. The look of a mob on the rampage, consumed with hatred, looting and burning without regard for life or property is one few can forget. Such outbursts have become an almost common occurrence on both sides of the Atlantic. If you happen to be an eyewitness, I would be the last to discourage you from making drawings—it is therefore unnecessary for me to add that you should proceed cautiously!

DEMONSTRATIONS

Crowds demonstrating for a principled cause can be just as awesome as mobs. In the spring of 1956, I was en route to England from Bulgaria via Poland, and I found myself in Warsaw for a few days. Khrushchev's sensational revelations of the excesses of the Stalin regime had finally brought the long-suffering Poles into the streets and squares of their capital to express their solidarity with the embattled Hungarians. Against the monumental façade of the Josef Stalin Palace of Science and Culture, a vast slogan-shouting multitude of one hundred and fifty thousand swept down the city's biggest thoroughfare, the Marzalkowska. Trucks, crowded with men and women of all ages, waving Polish and Hungarian flags and demanding an end to tyranny, raced past the crowds. It was an inspiring spectacle.

The London Boat Show, England, 1968
The Spirit of Cutty Sark, *veteran of 1968's single-handed transatlantic race, becomes the center of attraction for this mixed crowd of Londoners. This drawing was made in Higgins India ink with a Spencerian school nib for stronger lines and a Gillot 303 for the finer in an 11" x 14" sketchbook of two-ply, high surface Strathmore drawing paper. Courtesy* Sports Illustrated. *Copyright January 6, 1969 by Time, Inc.*

PLEASURE SEEKERS

Crowds after a movie or a sports event, on the other hand, behave very differently—particularly on weekends. They move along in a relaxed, carefree way which is a pleasure to watch. Making drawings of such pleasure-seeking crowds, as I did in Greenwich Village, New York, in 1965, makes you feel glad to be alive. Even a cop will tend to growl, "Who'd be me on a Saturday night!"

IDENTIFYING THE NATURE OF THE CROWD

First, I discover what motivates a crowd. Then I try to relate the people as imaginatively as possible to the object of their interest. To accomplish this, I look for individual figures or characters who can help give a crowd identity and establish a sense of time, movement, and place.

FOCAL POINTS

I almost always think in terms of a focal point, which, if I work outside, may be a building, a detail such as an arch, or even the shape of a street. If I work inside, the focal point may be some ornate device, a clock, or a window. I can choose any interesting or significant shape that acts as a foil for my figures. I also think about *movement*; it is important to describe *what* a crowd is doing. Time and weather are other

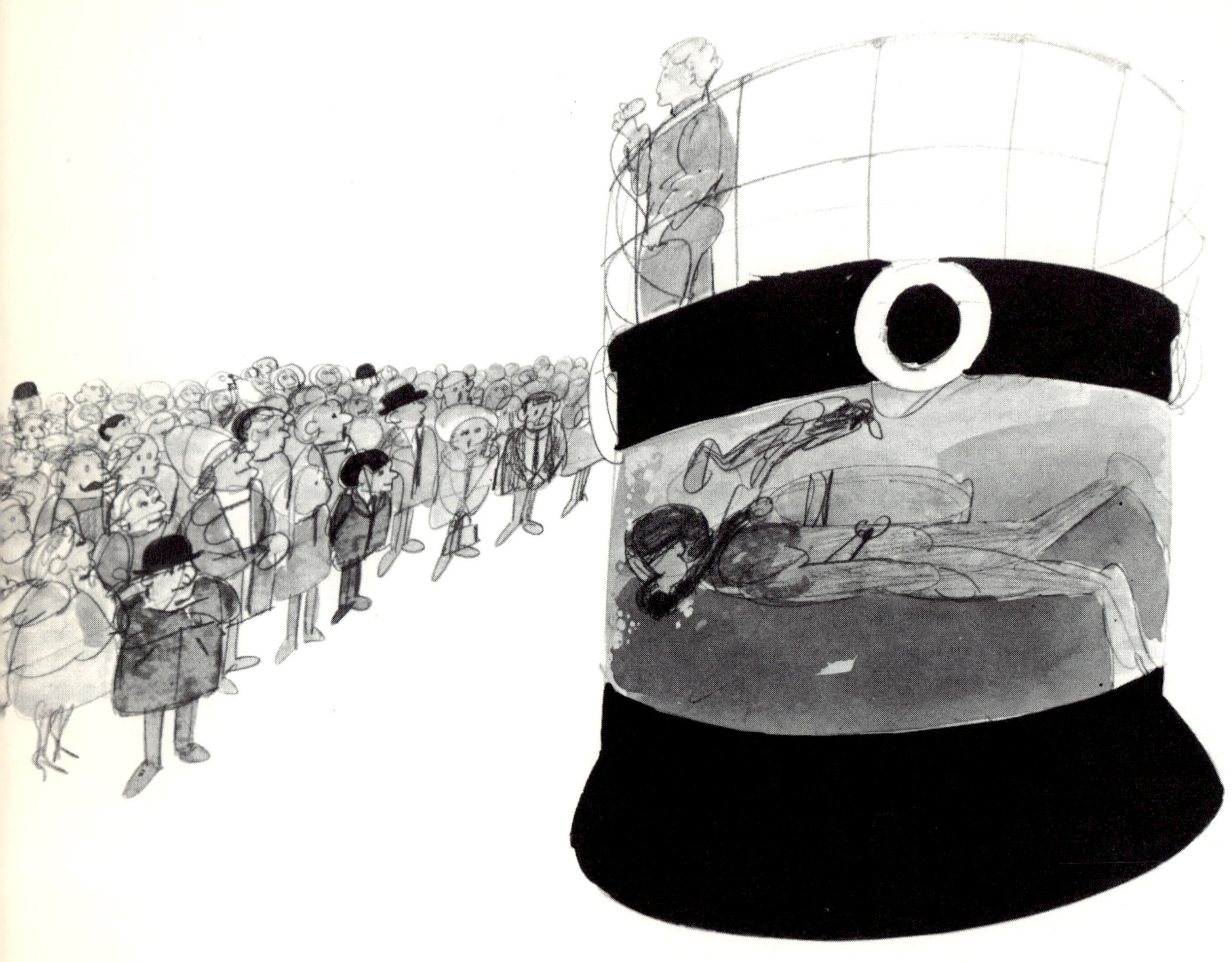

The London Boat Show, England, 1968
While they watched a demonstration of diving gear, a yearning for the far-away summer was expressed on the faces of this mid-winter crowd. Drawn with a Faber 702 sketching pencil, augmented with blotted washes of Higgins India ink and Grumbacher watercolor. Two brushes were used, a Japanese type for ink, and a Winsor & Newton No. 6 sable for watercolor. In an 11" x 14" sketchbook of Strathmore Alexis drawing paper. Courtesy Sports Illustrated. *Copyright January 6, 1969 by Time, Inc. (Above)*

The Borne, Palma, Majorca, 1963
I feel a crowd should possess its own identity, plus a comment of one's own. This drawing of tourists under the shaded avenue off the Paseo Generalissimo Franco, also expresses my own relaxed feelings about being abroad in the summertime. Drawn on a 16" x 20½" sheet of Saunders mold-made, cream wove writing paper with 3B and 7B Venus graphite pencils. From Majorca Observed, *1965. Courtesy Cassell and Company, London; and Doubleday and Company, New York. (Right)*

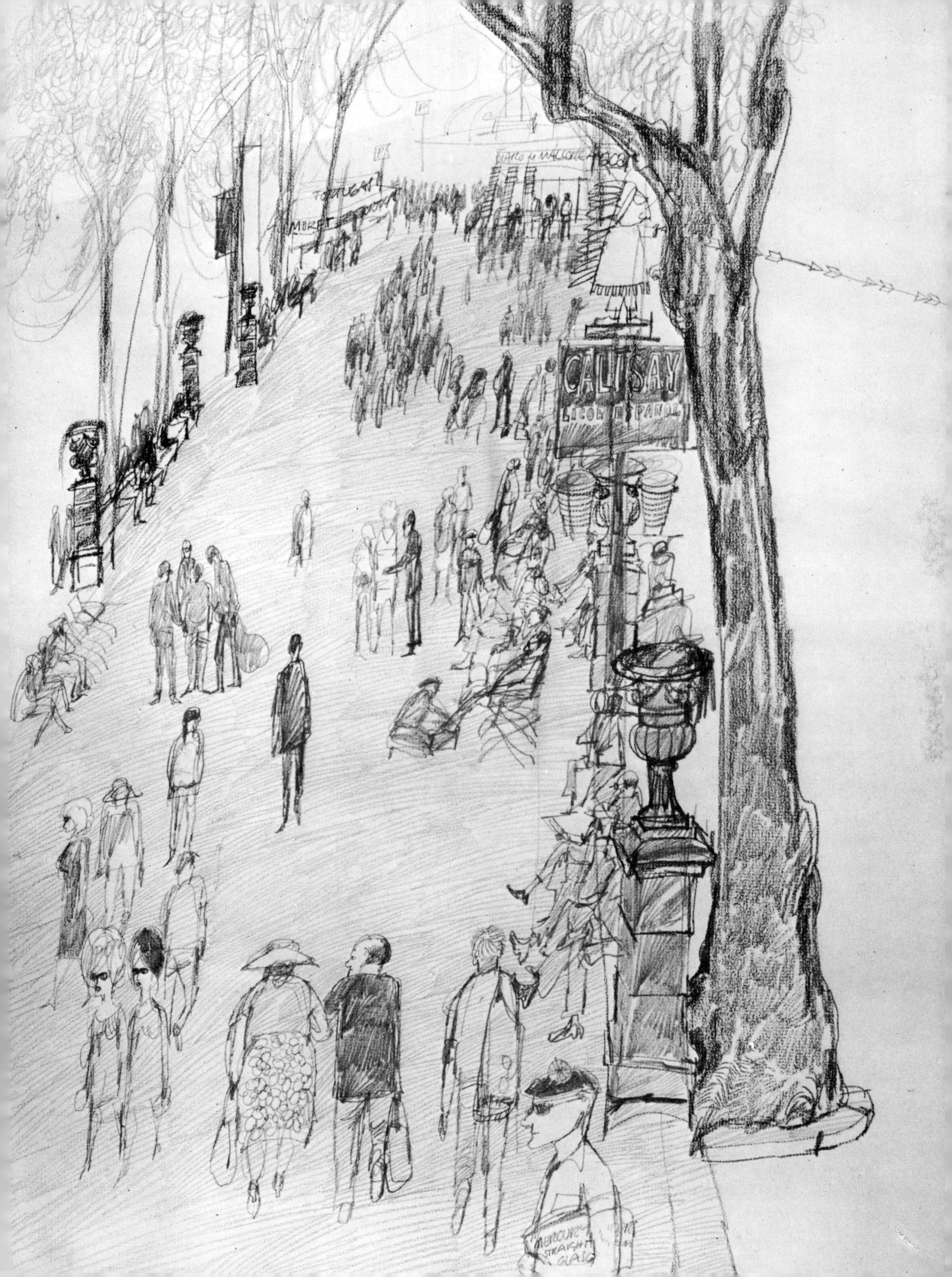
CALISAY
LICOR

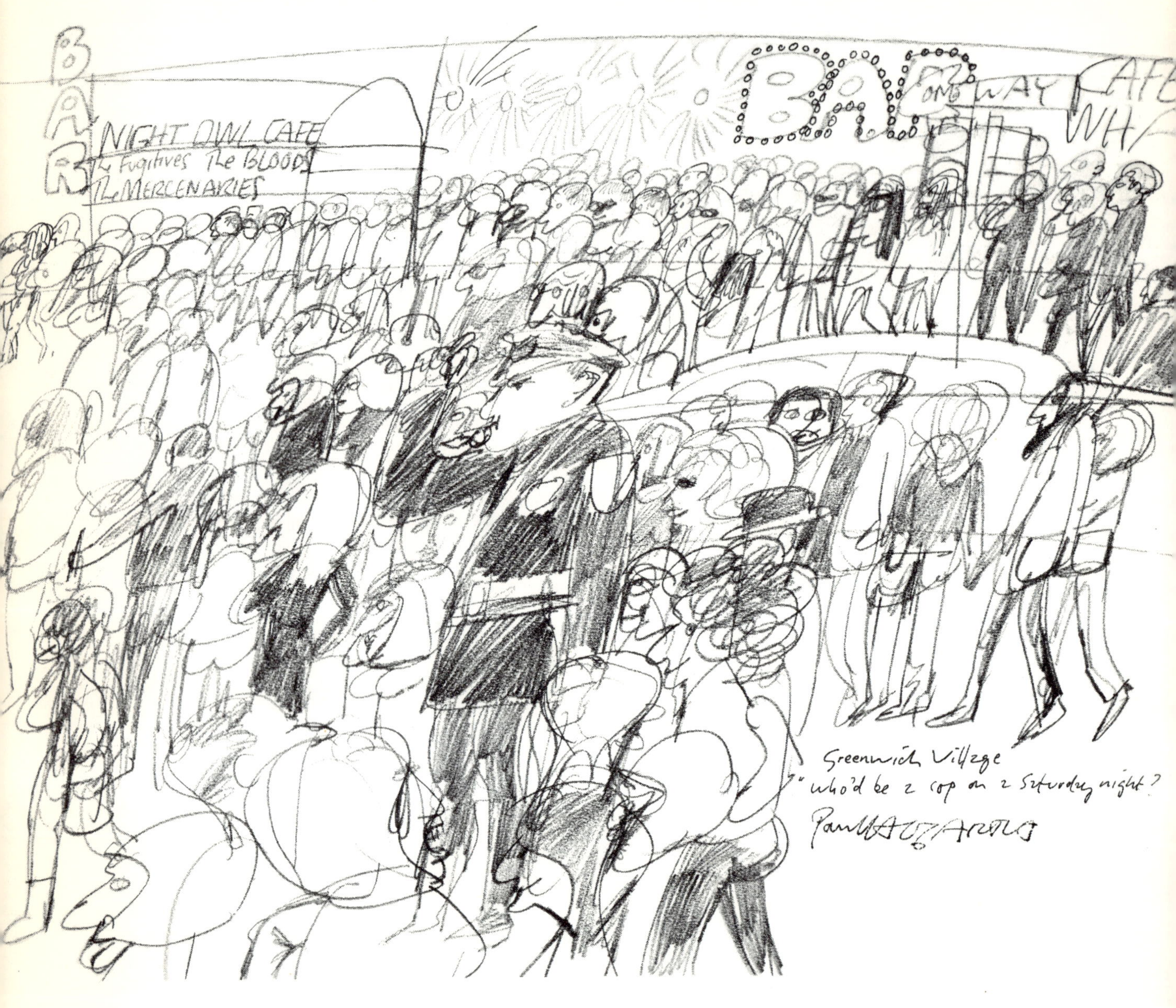

Saturday night, Greenwich Village, New York, 1965
The light-heartedness of a teen-age crowd, and the isolation of a lone cop, made me stop to draw this one in an 11" x 14" sketchbook of Strathmore Alexis drawing paper with a Faber 702 sketching pencil. Touches of ink were added with an Esterbrook fountain pen filled with Pelikan Fount India ink. Courtesy The Strathmore Paper Company, West Springfield, Mass.

important considerations. Whether it is morning, noon, or night, as well as whether it is raining, snowing, or sunny, noticeably affects *how* people look, move, and behave.

HOW TO BEGIN

Before you actually try to draw crowds, study them first on every possible occasion—at football games, stock-car races, political demonstrations, and in department stores. Watch people as they go to and from work. Try to identify your own reactions to what you see.

By far the easiest places to begin drawing crowds are neighborhood locations—outside a local movie theater, for example; the choice, of course, is yours. Wherever you begin, observe the general movements of the crowd a day or a week beforehand. Make notes on how long a crowd takes to disperse and jot down ideas of how you might draw it. You should also note where you can work without being exposed to the unbridled curiosity of passers-by. By a tree or inside a doorway of a store are my favorite positions. Remember that *nothing* interests people more than being drawn in the context of what they doing!

HOW TO PROCEED

Having discovered that a particular crowd will take about half an hour to leave a movie, I make sure to position myself at least fifteen minutes before the action starts. During that time, I draw in a background shape of some kind. Then, when people start to come out, I am ready to work fast. I draw swiftly, but not in detail. Since I always assume that a crowd will vanish before I am even half done, I work not only on the main drawing, but also scribble down (in a 3½" x 5" sketchbook) as many details of faces, movements, and clothing as I possibly can. Such details enable me to complete the drawing in my studio. This I invariably do as soon as I can.

You may find, as I once did, a certain resistance in yourself to drawing so many figures. If so, you are probably trying to adapt the practice of life drawing to a situation that requires a different approach. It is vital, in drawing crowds, to supplement what you *see* with what you *feel,* and to invent as freely as possible. I shall return to this point in greater detail in Chapter 16.

WORK OUT YOUR COMPOSITION IN ADVANCE

Although I often evolve an image without previous thought, I advise you to acquire the habit of working out your ideas in advance. This will help you summarize your reaction to the subject. Once you have gotten in touch with this response, you can then aim at putting it into pictorial form. Also, drawing crowds can be just about the most confusing kind of drawing any artist can attempt, and this can simplify matters, as a composition often acts as a means to keep you on a steady course.

Once you have an idea for a composition—however rough—at the back of your mind, you can weave almost any assembly of types and characters, no matter how diverse, into an organized drawing. Be as flexible as you can; let such an image take a variety of forms. For example, you can draw your people in equal sizes or in different sizes. Or you can focus on a single figure or on a group of figures, leaving the others to be drawn on a much smaller scale.

I find that characters on the fringe of a crowd may sometimes give me an idea for an image. This often happens as I wander about different cities looking for material. In London during the spring of 1966, for example, I saw a pair of cockney roustabouts entertaining a crowd of tourists who were waiting for the Tower of London to open. Their act consisted of Bill Jones bundling his partner, Max, into a sheet of canvas and tying him up securely in chains. Swathed from head to foot, Max looked as sinister as a mummy about to rejoin the living. After telling us all to stand well back, Bill cracked an enormous stock-whip. The chains miraculously fell apart and Max threw off the canvas.

Since Max's appearance really made the drawing, I decided on a T-shaped composition which placed him as the dominant vertical element. A crowd of tourists, watching open-mouthed from behind, was drawn as the horizontal top bar, on a smaller scale. I rendered the figure of Bill, cracking the whip, in a size between the two.

WORKING AT CLOSE QUARTERS

Although drawing crowds at close quarters is difficult, it can be done. At the famous Chelsea annual Flower Show in London, I fought my way around the congested interior of an enormous tent. There seemed little hope of finding a place to stand—let alone to open a stool and sit down. Overwhelmed by close contact with the dense crowd, I almost gave up. To make matters worse, *everybody*—as far as I could tell—looked exactly alike! The differences revealed themselves to me only upon closer acquaintance.

Somewhat frantically, I looked around for a focal point that I could use as a place to begin. A massive display of flowers caught my eye. After noting that it held everyone else's attention for at least several minutes—long enough for me to draw complete figures—I found space by a tentpole to open my stool. There was not much room, but at least people passed *by* me and not *into* me.

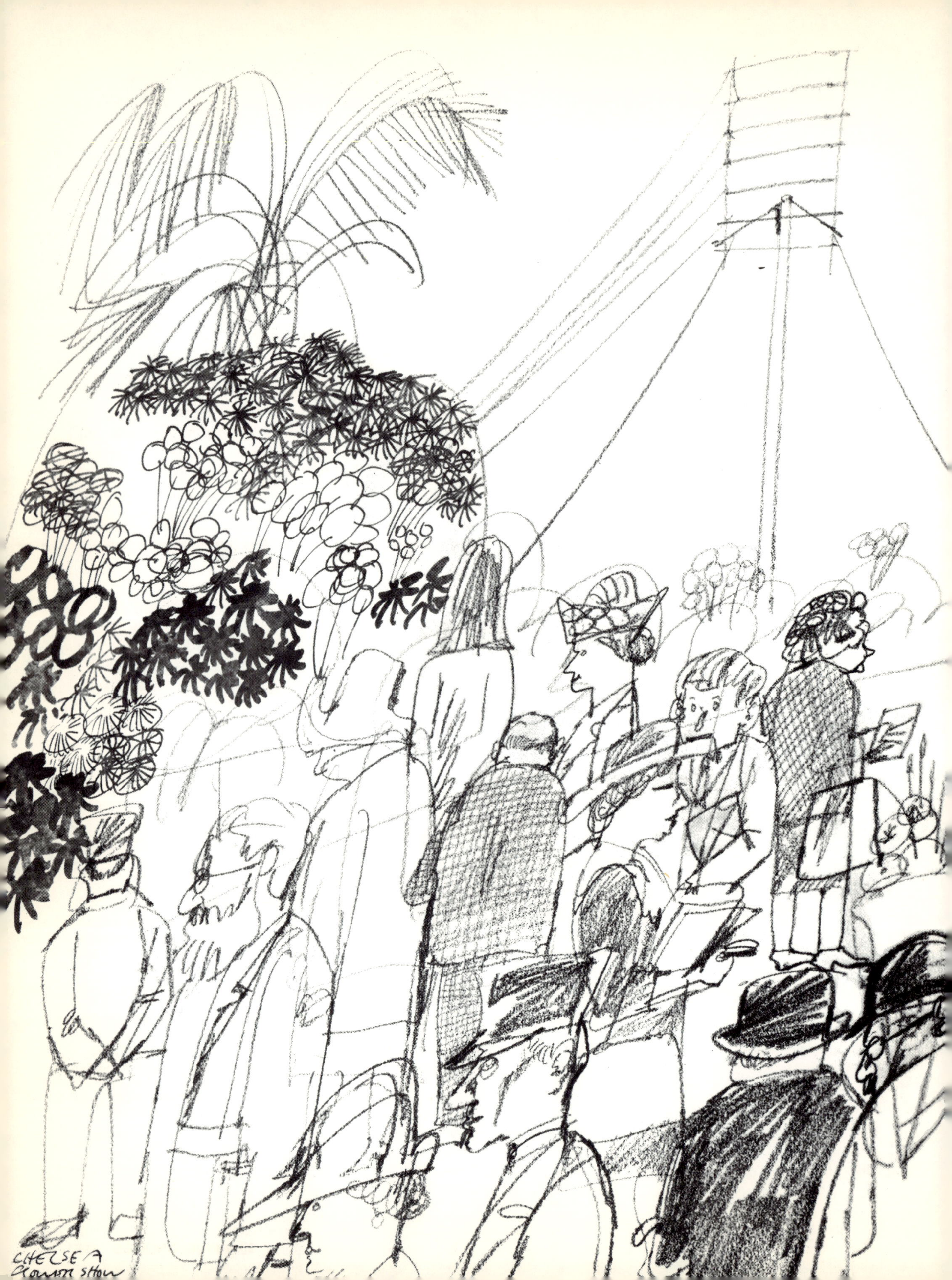
CHELSEA
Flower Show

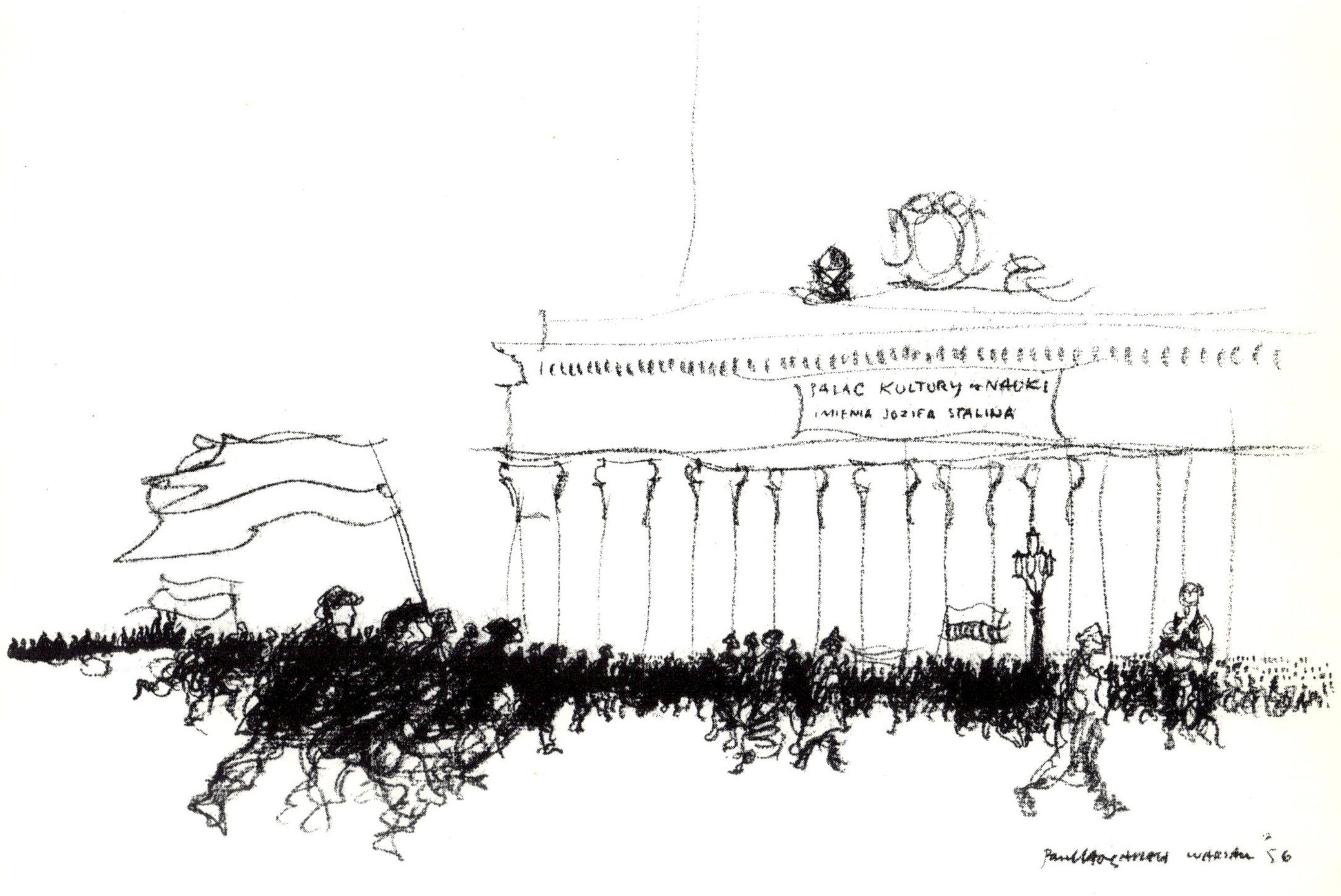

Chelsea Flower Show, London, 1965
Not an easy drawing to do—there was hardly room enough to take out a sketchbook, let alone draw in one. I began by following the movements of the crowd; then built up the drawing by selecting one figure of each type of visitor to give maximum variety and show the social character of the show. Drawn with a Faber 702 sketching pencil in an 11" x 14" sketchbook of Strathmore drawing paper. From London à la Mode, *1966. Courtesy Studio Vista Ltd., London; and Hill & Wang, Inc., New York. (Left)*

Warsaw, Poland, 1956
The heroic days of the Hungarian uprising created many crowds throughout the world in support of a struggle for freedom. I was a fortuitous eyewitness to this one in Warsaw, where I happened to be at the time. Rapidly drawn in a 14" x 17" Reeves sketchbook of Ingres paper with a Hardtmuth medium charcoal lead. (Above)

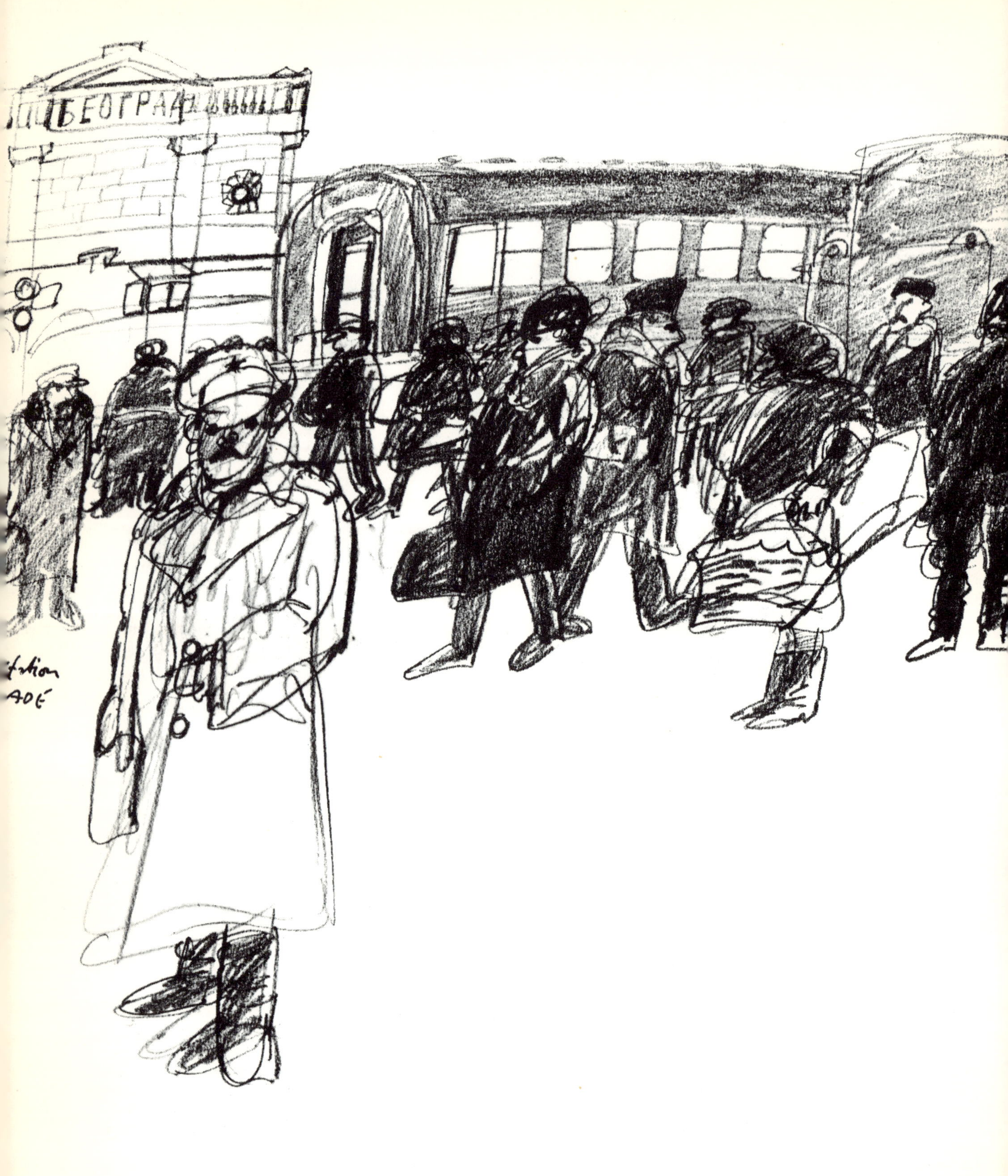
БЕОГРАД

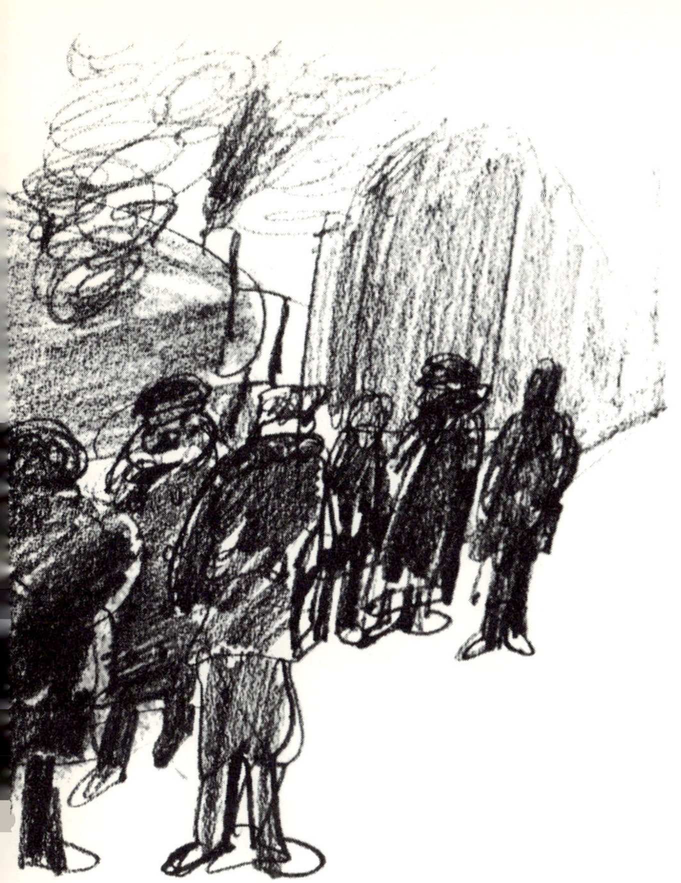

I sketched in the floral display, then went on to catch a wide collection of upper middle class characters who looked as if they had just stepped out of a John Galsworthy novel. Stockbrokers from the City of London jostled against Norfolk-jacketed country squires and retired army officers in tweeds; gimlet-eyed country women in out-sized hats towered above Chelsea pensioners in vivid crimson uniforms. To insure variety, I was careful not to have more than a single example of each type of character. I fitted them all together like the interlocking pieces of a jigsaw puzzle. Because they were so absorbed in the colorful spectacle, no one—surprisingly enough—even noticed I was drawing!

Even when they actually see me sketching, members of a crowd are the *last* to realize that they could possibly be the object of an artist's interest. This reaction, alas, applies only to the United States, Britain, and the countries of the Western world. Elsewhere, particularly in eastern Europe, Africa, and Asia, crowds are *never* so naïve or blasé!

Central Railroad Station, Belgrade, Yugoslavia, 1967
In mountainous Yugoslavia, railroads are still the most important means of carrying everything from live chickens to people. I massed the small waiting crowd to heighten both the hint of the mysterious Balkans and the similarity to a scene from a nineteenth-century novel. Drawn in a 10¾" x 14½" Planet sketchbook of smooth drawing paper with a Faber 702 sketching pencil. Courtesy Fortune *magazine. Copyright December, 1967 by Time, Inc.*

The Launching of Apollo 9, Florida, March 1969

I was so engrossed in getting this colorful vignette of Cape Kennedy absolutely right that I forgot to include passing figures at the time; I drew them in later, from memory. An 11" x 14" sketchbook of Strathmore Alexis drawing paper was used. After a light outline drawn with a Venus 3B pencil, a wash of diluted Pelikan Fount India ink was laid over the billboard. While this was drying, I used a yellow Faber Design Markette for the trees and shrubs, changing to a green Markette for greater decorative effect. The billboard was now dry, so I drew in the lettering with an orange Markette. Lastly, the figures were drawn in with Higgins India ink and a Spencerian school nib. Courtesy Daily Telegraph Magazine, *London. Copyright April, 1969.*

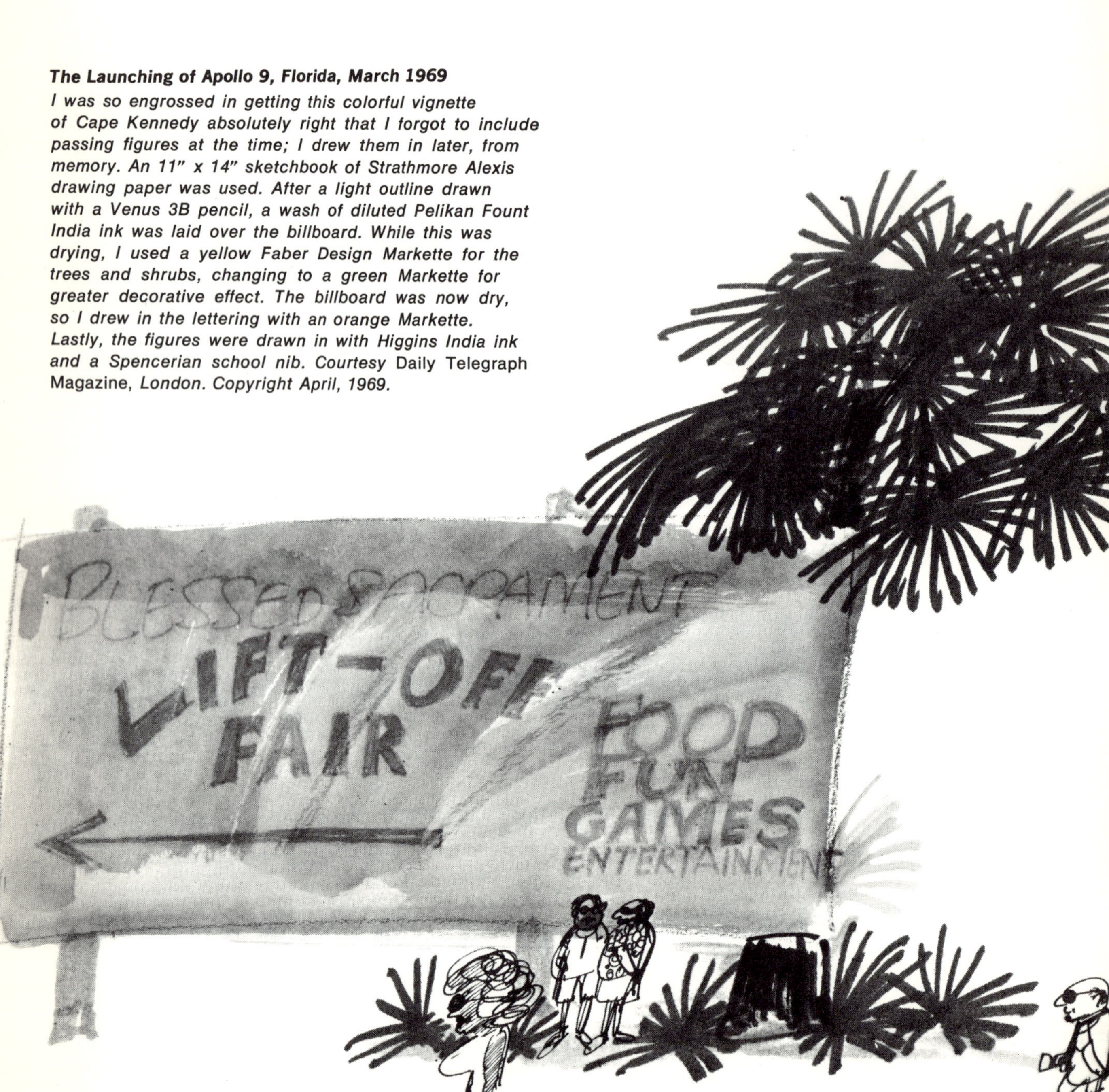

CHAPTER 11

Drawing People from Memory and Imagination

IT IS a big temptation to play it safe by drawing only those people who stand still long enough. Certainly no harm is done as long as you feel there is still a lot you can learn by working this way. On the other hand, you may lose interest in the whole idea of drawing people if you look at them as if they were models in a life class.

INTERPRETATION

Working on location does not necessarily mean that you have to literally represent appearances at the expense of looking beneath the surface. Never forget that drawing people is not just drawing how people look—it is also your own personal interpretation!

In order to effectively make such an interpretation, it is essential to break away from the directly made drawing from life, and make the kind of drawing which knits observation with threads of fantasy.

COMBINING MEMORY AND IMAGINATION

Usually, drawing from memory or imagination implies two separate exercises: you draw a figure or a face from memory more or less exactly as you remember it; you save your imagination for more offbeat drawing. I like to use a third method. I look at people, then draw them from memory *with* my imagination.

In this way, I flex the muscles of memory to derive ideas from what I see. Then I use my imagination to express my reaction, with a sense of humor and commitment, to things seen. I look closely at people as they pass by, remembering as much as I can about them in the same way as I would remember a fine looking girl, glimpsed in a busy city street. Wherever possible, I get these down with a soft pencil in a pocket sketchbook, using whatever license may spontaneously suggest itself to me as I think about their various individual characteristics. These notes help me give pictorial significance to my impressions, even though I may freely improvise on them afterwards.

CAPTURING THE FIRST IMPRESSION

I always assume that whoever interests me will soon wander off. So I work fast. I look hard at them to fix *character* and *movement* firmly in my mind. Quickly and lightly, I then make an outline sketch of a head or of how they walk or hold themselves. They may already have gone, but I still add my impressions of their character, freely increasing the size of their arms or legs, possibly emphasizing outstanding features of expression or clothing.

Later, in my studio or hotel room, or on location if I have the time or the inclination, I transcribe the sketch and make another drawing. If I have already made a large background drawing, I transfer the sketches either directly or by means of a light box. I take every opportunity to add a note of fantasy or humor. More often than not, this may have been sparked off by what I have seen or overheard.

COMBINING FANTASY WITH REALITY

Take the morning I saw crowds of commuters at Liverpool Street, one of London's biggest railway stations. I was really drawing its cavernous Victorian interior, with perhaps a few figures moving or standing around. But then the trains arrived and presented me with such a lively spectacle that I felt compelled to draw it all. I decided to work from the window of a nearby snackbar, which looked out on the tracks. I was only just in time. The trains pulled in, disgorging hordes of black-bowlered, pipe-smoking commuters, each clutching an identical briefcase and tightly rolled umbrella. I looked on what seemed like a genial invasion of remote control puppets. When a military march opened up on Musak, I decided then and there that I had to draw them as an offbeat, mindless army marching in step.

Movement was far too rapid to attempt careful drawings, so I selected my targets and rapidly sketched a handful of characters, noting their features in particular. I then returned home to fill in the back-

Gerd Siemoneit's Wild Animals, Bertram Mills' Circus, London, 1966

Here, I quickly re-composed the action, moving the three principals around to create a more effective design; referring only to what was going on for general details. I worked from memory of a movement rather than attempting to copy what I saw. Drawn with a Faber 702 sketching pencil in a 10¾" x 14½" English Planet sketchbook of smooth drawing paper. From London à la Mode, *1966. Courtesy Studio Vista Ltd., London; and Hill & Wang, Inc., New York.*

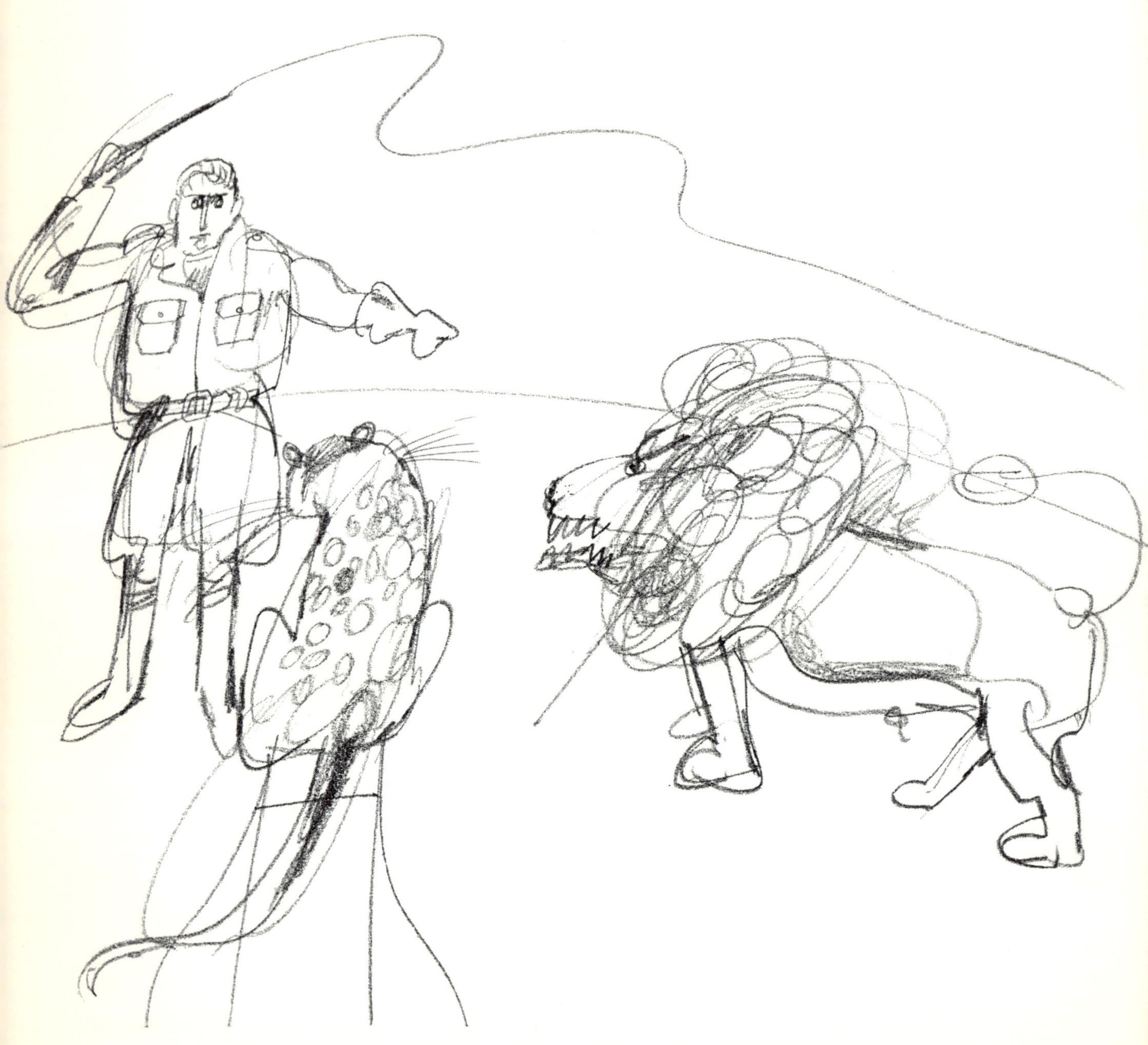

ground of my uncompleted drawing of the interior with hundreds of marching figures, all freely improvised to express my amused reaction to the whole experience.

KEEP A PICTORIAL RECORD

The practice of memory drawing can extend your graphic vocabulary to such a remarkable extent that I highly recommend it for drawing people.

I found by far the most effective way of achieving this enviable facility was to keep a sort of pictorial journal of the little incidents I felt I had missed out on by not having enough time.

So, try keeping a pictorial diary in a small pocket sketchbook (3½" x 5"), in which daily or weekly experiences are remembered and drawn. Not only the trivial incidents such as waiting for a movie or bus, but your own actual personal experiences with other people, whatever these may be.

If you are on vacation, fill in some of the traveling time by keeping a daily pictorial record. Not only will it help remove a sense of frustration and loss at not being able to absorb what you see, it will rapidly increase your facility to conjure up characters and situations at will. But this will not work if you take a camera with you!

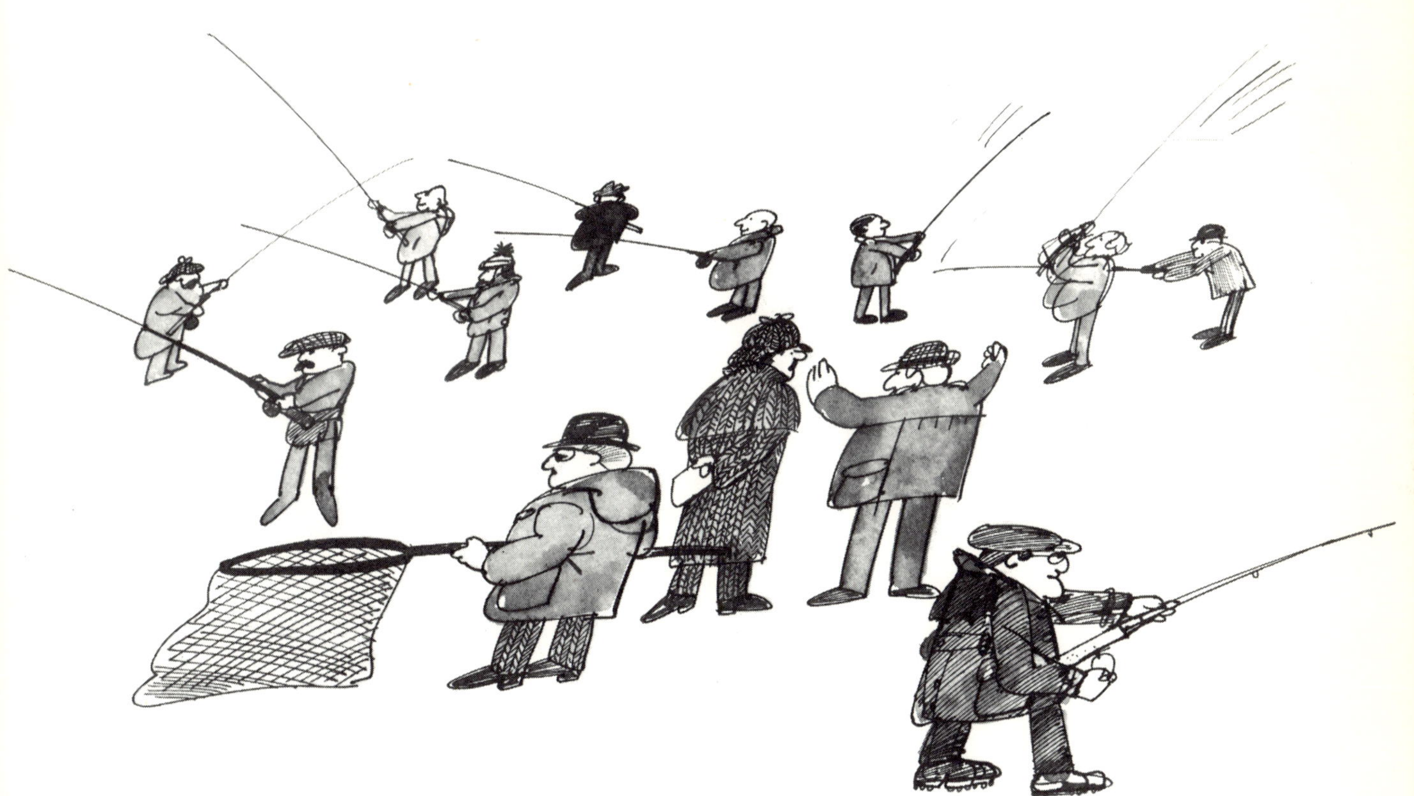

The London Boat Show, England, 1968
Most of the figures in this drawing were largely motivated by the four very British types in the foreground. More were needed, so I included imaginary caricatures of artist friends, as well as the local postman. Drawn in Higgins India ink with a Spencerian school nib and a Japanese brush in an 11" x 14" sketchbook of two-ply, high surface Strathmore drawing paper. Courtesy Sports Illustrated. *Copyright January 6, 1969 by Time, Inc.*

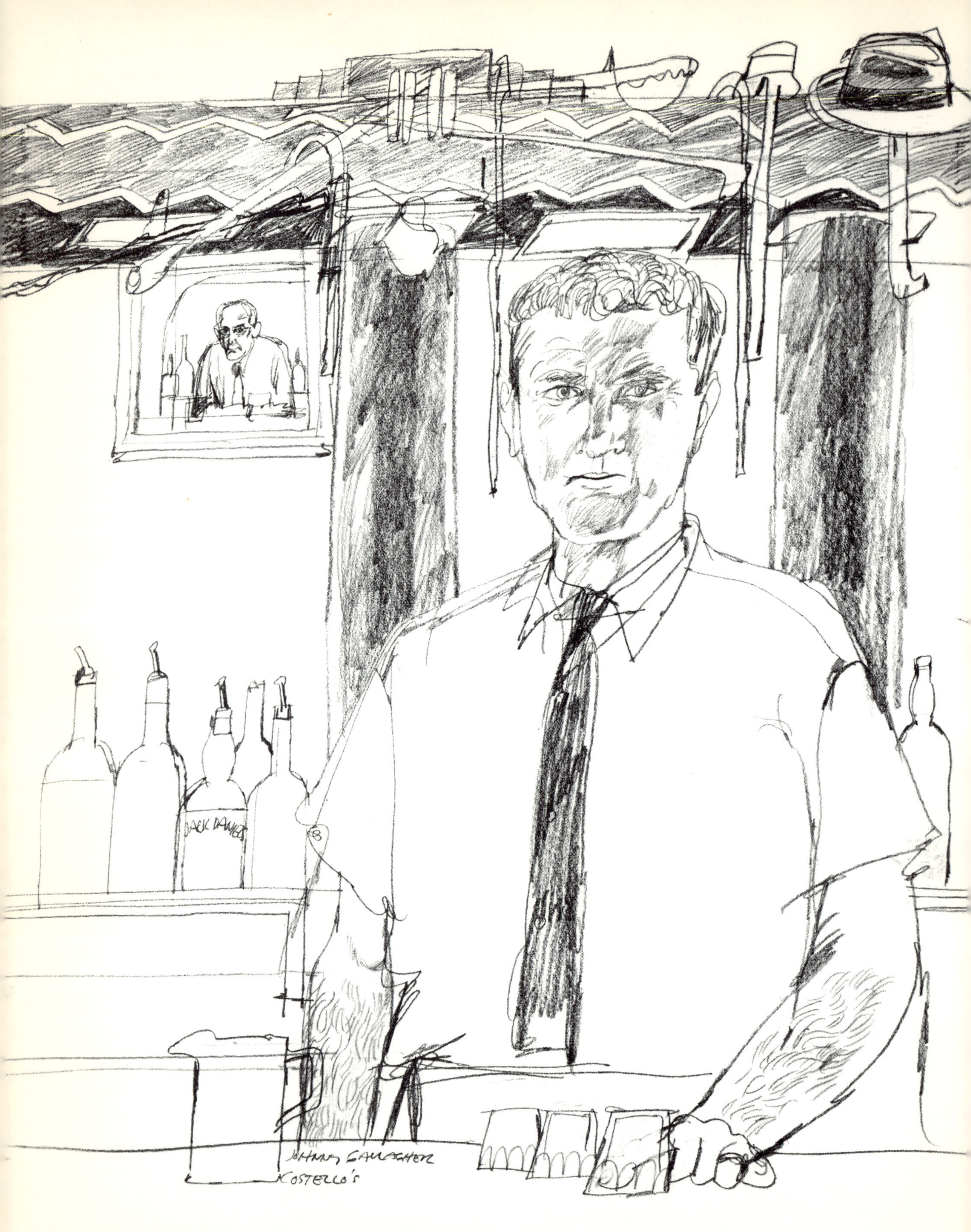
JOHNNY GALLAGHER
COSTELLO'S

CHAPTER 12

Drawing Portraits: Getting to Know Your Sitter

EVERY TIME I agree to make a portrait drawing I feel as if I had an appointment with the dentist. Why does it seem such a formidable undertaking? It is not of course, but the *idea* of having to grapple with a stranger, to be face to face with him even for an hour or so, certainly appears to be. The answer is simply that art is thought to be an essentially private affair, and that the practice of it before others makes us feel that we may make fools of ourselves.

Because of this, there is a great temptation to compromise and make a likeness instead of a portrait. It is far from easy to bring off the synthesis of character revelation (what the artist should seek) and a sympathetic likeness (what the sitter hopes for). And so we make the mistake of trying to please. There is much more to portraiture than merely reproducing a face, and drawing a portrait the way a creative artist *should* is a matter of establishing a human relationship.

PLANNING IS NECESSARY

The greatest satisfaction to be derived from portraiture is to have sufficiently strong reasons for wanting to make a portrait drawing in the first place. It is equally important to consider how best you can effectively execute it. Do not assume that you can bring off a portrait drawing without some prior thought; if you do, your efforts can easily bring disappointment.

Drawing people as individuals in private *is* different from drawing them in public. In a bar, for instance, the barriers usually come down enough to permit free and easy conversation. In private, however, this informality may not be so readily forthcoming if your sitter is nervous or inhibited.

Johnny Gallagher, barman at Costello's, Third Avenue, New York, 1963
The unpredictable can frequently determine the course of a portrait sitting. Johnny Gallagher, for example, was restless and uncertain about having his portrait drawn at all, until he heard that it might be reproduced in a book. (I had taken along the editor, Rae Jeffs.) No trouble then at all. Memorabilia, including Hemingway's hat and H. L. Mencken's walking stick, hanging from an elaborate thirties Aztec bar-screen, made a perfect setting. Drawn in about an hour and a half on a sheet of 16" x 20½" Saunders mold-made, cream wove writing paper with a 7B Venus graphite pencil. From Brendan Behan's New York, *1964. Courtesy The Hutchinson Publishing Group, London; and Bernard Geis Associates, New York.*

ENVIRONMENT

A great deal also depends on *where* the portrait is drawn. I usually prefer to work where I am able to see the sitter in his own environment, as this frequently gives me an idea of how I might actually draw him. The sitter, too, is much less nervous and is inclined to play host or patron, and therefore relax you at the same time! If, on the other hand, the sitter comes to my studio, I find myself having to play the part of the portrait artist somewhat self-consciously, and, frankly, I find this a burden as well as far too formal a procedure for my particular kind of drawing.

HANDLING THE SITTER

The social art of handling different types of private sitters should be practiced as much as possible before undertaking a portrait assignment. You may prefer to rehearse with a friend, or better still, as I do, with people you draw in public. Try always to establish a human relationship. Put your sitter at ease by being totally relaxed yourself. Make requests to pose in an easy, natural manner. Be prepared to change your approach or qualify any such requests when dealing with more volatile and sophisticated people. Never forget that although the majority will react to a well-tried formula of putting them at ease, there will also be the minority who will not! So be intelligent or witty when you wish to make the odd remark.

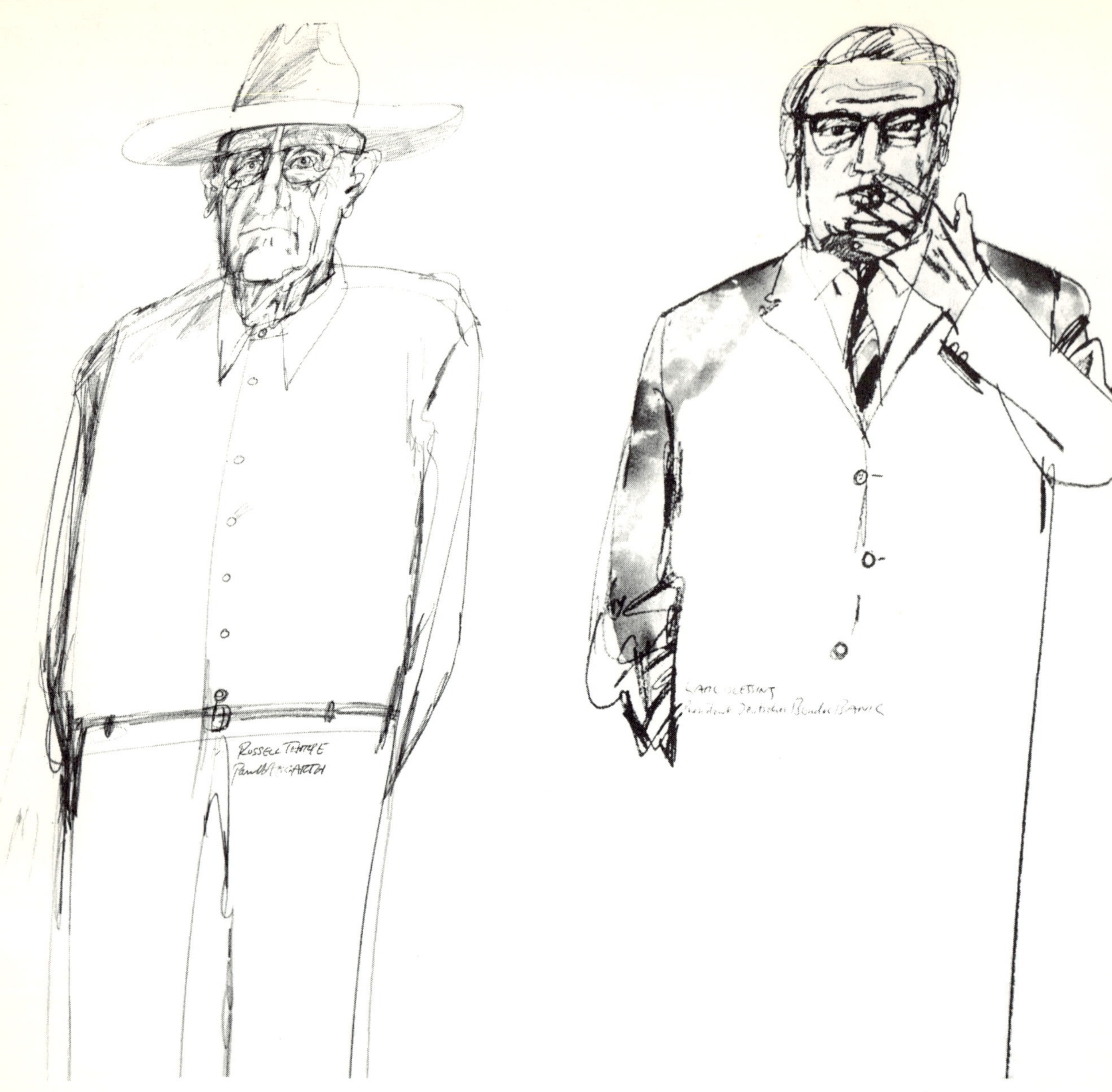

Russell Thorpe Jr., Cheyenne, Wyoming, 1965
An eighty-eight-year-old ex-rancher, whose father had owned the celebrated Cheyenne-Deadwood stageline, Russell Thorpe was an unconventional subject for any artist, and that includes Remington! Faded photographs of stagecoaches, cowpunchers, prize cattle, and frontier marshals lined a simply furnished room. We got on extraordinarily well and talked through an afternoon and most of an evening before I drew him in his Stetson. For some unaccountable reason, he wore only long-johns, although when I drew him, I put him in trousers. Seeing this, he said to me, "Those settlers who headed out here had a helluva lot of nerve—and so have you, for putting my pants on without asking!" Drawn on a 22" x 25" sheet of three-ply, medium surface Strathmore drawing paper with a 7B Venus graphite pencil. Courtesy The Strathmore Paper Company, West Springfield, Mass.

Karl Blessing, President of the Deutsche Bundersbank, Frankfurt/Main, Germany, 1965
There are times when the assured sitter will take the initiative and establish a human relationship. Karl Blessing, for example, asked me to sit down, pushing a box of Havana cigars across to me; he then helped himself and stood up to light one. I asked him to remain standing. We talked about cigars while I went on working. In a matter of thirty-five minutes I had finished the portrait! Drawn in a 14" x 17" sketchbook of Strathmore drawing paper with a 7B Venus graphite pencil. Watercolor washes of Grumbacher color were added later from notes made during the sitting. Courtesy Fortune *magazine. Copyright August, 1965 by Time, Inc.*

TALKING TO THE SITTER

How much you wish to talk to a sitter before beginning work will be determined largely by how you react yourself, and by how he reacts to you. Any conversation should be easy and natural. Listen attentively to everything a sitter may wish to tell you about himself. This not only gives you valuable time to appraise his personality, but will also enliven facial expression. If you do not wish to carry on a continuous conversation while working, make a leading remark that will make your sitter talk. Such a remark can refer to the sitter's profession or business, his preference to being drawn by an artist rather than being photographed, etc.

THE FIDGETY SITTER

One of the biggest headaches is to draw a sitter who cannot remain still in any position. Ignore such restlessness when it occurs. Try to be totally relaxed yourself. I tell such sitters that the sitting may not have to be a long one and involve them with doing something. For example, reading, writing, or using a telephone. If, however, it is essential that I draw them straight, without any props, I ask them to give me ten minutes. By this I usually mean fifteen or twenty minutes, which gives me enough time to get the essential lines of a drawing in. Completing the rest—even if they move—is not, therefore, so difficult.

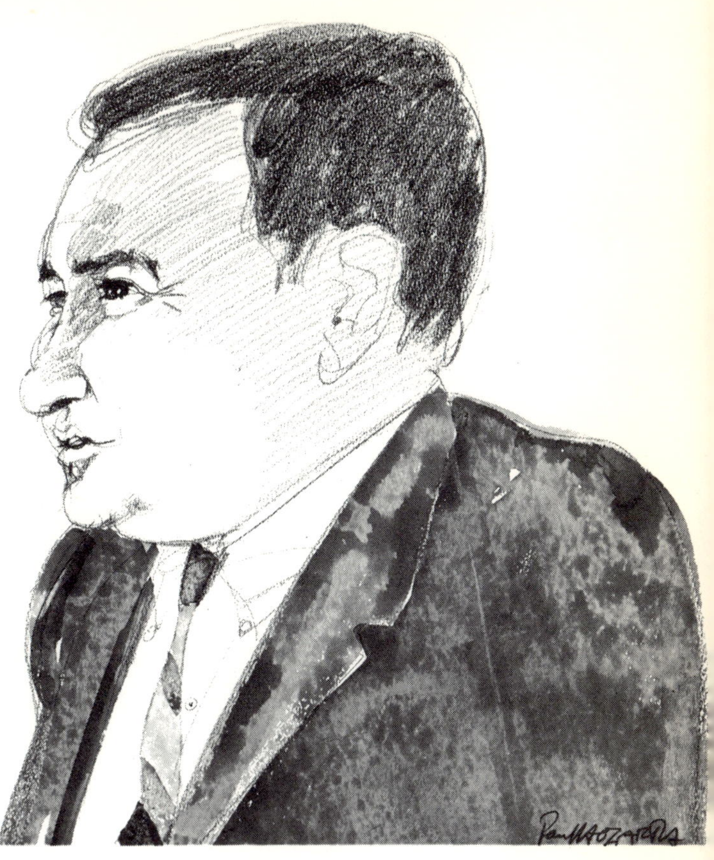

Dr. Louis Castor, Philadelphia, 1969
Louis Castor was an elusive spirit, sharply intelligent, hiding behind the bonhomie *of the wise neighborhood doctor which he is for part of his crowded life. Making an exact analysis of his true character and temperament took almost all of a most enjoyable afternoon. Drawn in a 14" x 17" sketchbook of Strathmore Alexis drawing paper with a Faber 702 sketching pencil. The jacket was painted in with washes of Pelikan Fount India ink applied with a Japanese brush; the tie (an important characteristic detail) was done in Grumbacher watercolors with a Winsor & Newton No. 6 sable brush. Courtesy Dr. Louis Castor, Philadelphia. Reproduced by his special permission.*

USING PSYCHOLOGY ON THE SITTER

You will also find that the more people think of themselves, the more they will cooperate with you. Such sitters will probably need a remark that implies a sincerely made but flattering analogy. I remember this was the case when I made a portrait of L. E. J. Brouwer, the Chairman of the giant Royal Dutch Shell Corporation. This was one of a series for *Fortune* of Europe's top tycoons, all completely different from each other, and only a few projecting the fullest extent of their power.

Brouwer, who was tall and tanned, played into my hands by asking how I saw him. "As a Western marshal," I replied. This remark was right on target and gave him so much pleasure that he literally did not budge an inch for the agreed forty minutes of the sitting. He even volunteered a further half-hour, in spite of a crowded work schedule.

PRACTICE FIRST

Tycoons and Very Important People, unlike celebrities, are not unlike ordinary people. They even share our sense of humor. But before you take them on, *do* get plenty of practice on the ground floor! Unless, of course, your father is Chairman of the Board of Directors, in which case the reverse will be true!

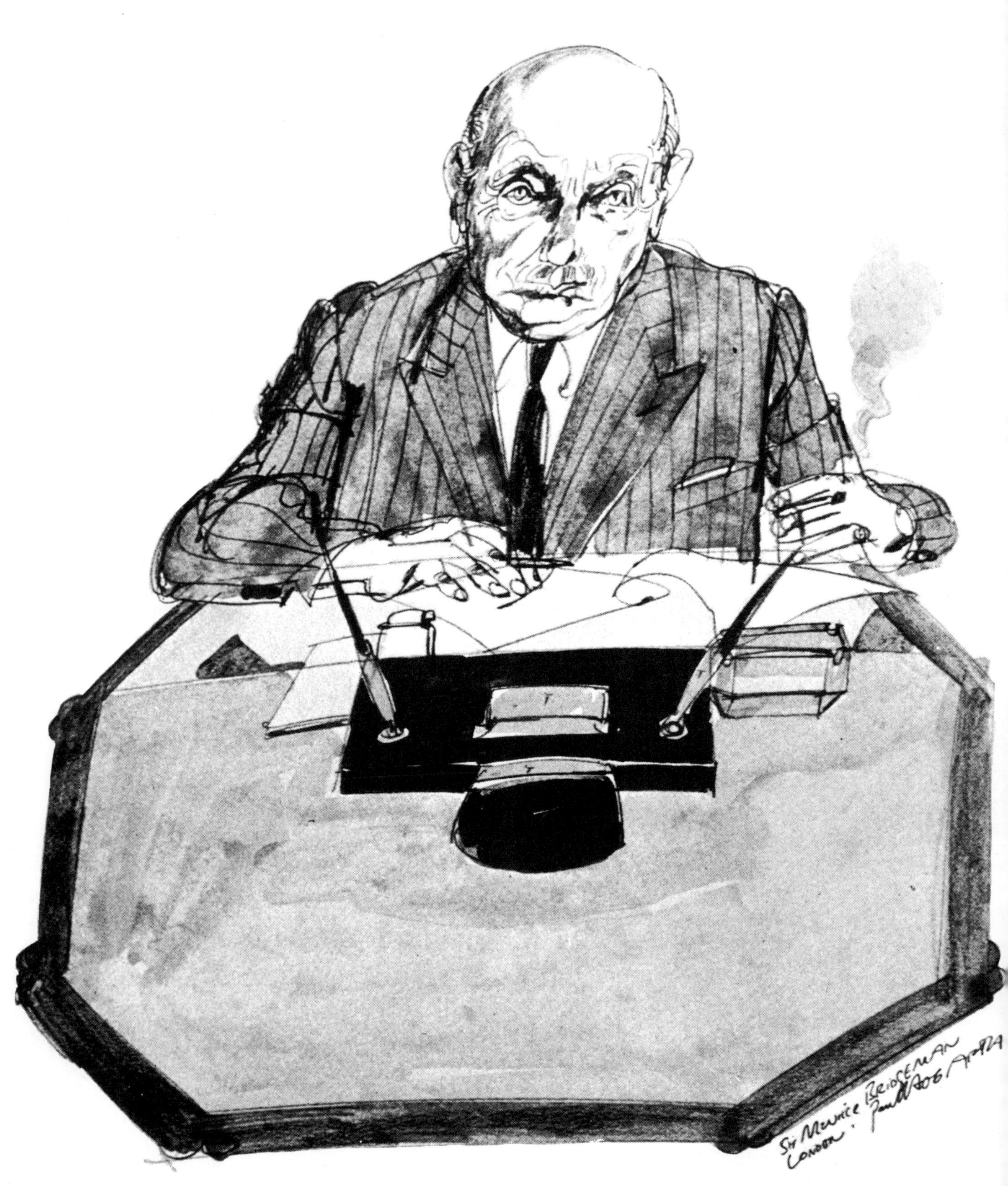
Sir Maurice Bridgeman
London

CHAPTER 13

Planning a Portrait

I USUALLY START by deciding how much I should draw of the person before me. This might be the head only, head and shoulders, three-quarter figure, or full figure; facing left, right, or full face in each case. It will depend on the visual appeal of the head, the general deportment of the sitter, and even on the background in which he or she can be placed.

THE HEAD

If a head is striking, of great character interest, I will probably just draw the head, concentrating on the personality and temperament of the sitter. If the head is only moderately interesting, I might take in more of the figure, emphasizing more than a facial trait—the hands perhaps—and possibly introducing the background as an integral part of the picture. Thus, the effect may owe as much to atmosphere as it does to the personality of the sitter. All these elements often exist in one subject and I will sometimes combine them in a single full-length drawing.

Sir Maurice Bridgeman, London, 1967
A table or desk, and what may be on it, can often suggest a clue to portraying the more elusive and sophisticated personality. "By their books ye shall know them" also applies to personal possessions and memorabilia. This tough urbane tycoon, a product of Eton and Trinity College, Cambridge, works like a diplomat at an antique Chinese card table. A gallery of signed and framed photographs of successfully outwitted oil sheiks of Araby lines the walls of his chambers. There was only one way to draw him—as a master poker player! Drawn in a 16" x 20" sketchbook of high surface Daler drawing paper with a Faber 702 sketching pencil and a 3B Venus pencil. Notes were lightly penciled on the drawing at the end of the sitting, before washes of Winsor & Newton artists' watercolor were later painted in with Nos. 3 and 6 Winsor & Newton sable brushes. Courtesy Fortune *magazine. Copyright September 15, 1967 by Time, Inc.*

POSING THE SITTER

More often than not, I will have to pose a sitter in such a way that the sum of whatever individual qualities he may or may not possess can be seen to maximum advantage. I may find, for example, that a profile may show certain qualities of character more graphically than if viewed from the front.

THUMBNAIL SKETCH

Using a small pocket sketchbook, I now scribble a thumbnail pen or pencil sketch of a possible pose or composition. This helps me in several ways. Such a sketch, however hasty, is really a plan of action which pins me down to making a definite move to begin the portrait. At the same time, I jot down written impressions of the sitter: *physique* (fat or thin, short or tall); *character* (personality, traits, habits); and *temperament* (vivacious or phlegmatic, optimistic or pessimistic, impulsive or cautious). I also note the colors of clothing, including accessories, such as cufflinks or jewelry, and furniture which may be used as props.

PROPS

Props—if I may digress—such as a particular type of table, desk, or clock, can suggest a key to unlock the role or personality of the more sophisticated sitter. Another tycoon I enjoyed tackling for *Fortune* in his skyscraper lair was the tough, urbane head of British Petroleum, Sir Maurice Bridgeman, who worked at an antique Chinese card table not much bigger than a child's desk, on which lay a gold-faced clock and a cut-glass bowl. When I realized that it was a *card* table however, I drew him full face, over the table, looking every inch the Klondike gambler he actually is.

FINAL PLACEMENT

I now estimate what distance I must put between myself and the sitter, how to place the subject in relation

Walter Allner, New York, 1969

Walter Allner—painter, wit, and art director of Fortune*—has the eagle-like vitality I associate with German flying aces of World War One. Intensely blue eyes twinkle with alert brilliance, occasionally expanding into a prolonged chortle at some memory of an extraordinary escapade involving a colleague or contributor. Obviously, these qualities would not be so easy to catch! Yet, no portrait of him could possibly be without at least a hint that they existed. But this was one of those days when my pencil seemed to be guided by an unseen friendly spirit; the sitting went off without a single hitch. Color was added later—notes of hair, face, shirt, and tie were taken during the sitting at the Time-Life Building. Drawn in a 14" x 17" sketchbook of Strathmore Alexis drawing paper with a Faber 702 sketching pencil. Face and hands were painted in flesh-colored tints of Grumbacher watercolor; tie and the stripes of a very characteristic shirt in mixtures of red, orange and green with Winsor & Newton's Nos. 0, 5, and 8 sable brushes. Courtesy Walter Allner, New York. Reproduced by special permission.*

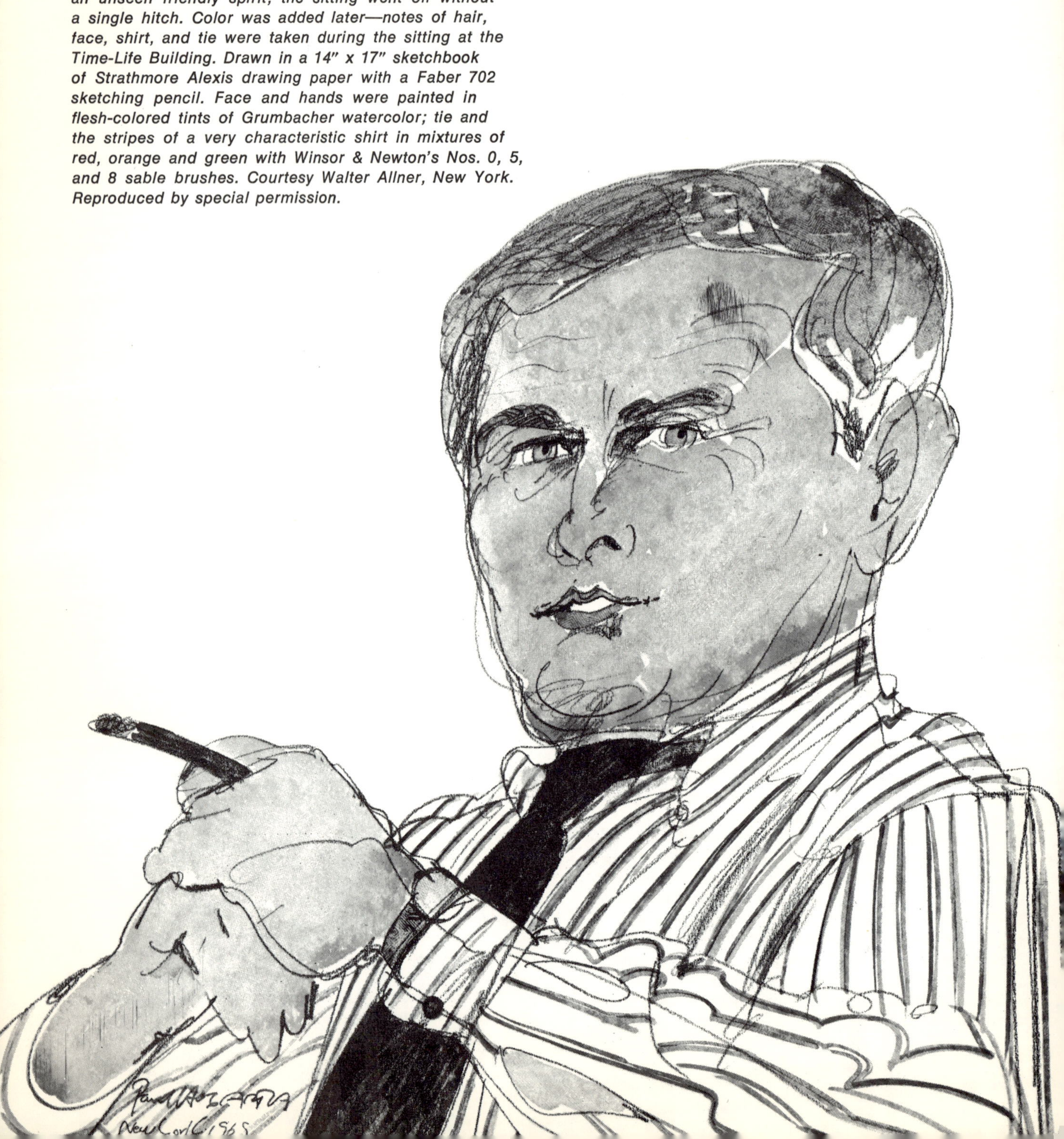

to the light, facing or against a window or an article of furniture. All these preparations may take ten minutes or so, but they save a great deal of effort later if I am working against time and with a self-conscious sitter, as the average person is. Such preliminaries help soothe them. For when you know what *you* want, your self-confidence is readily communicated to your sitter and helps to establish the right atmosphere.

HOW YOU SEE THE SITTER IS IMPORTANT

There can, however, be few rules after you have gotten used to drawing people. Your personal reaction will very largely determine your whole approach, even what size you will want to draw your subject. Moreover, no artist sees the same individual as another artist does. At times, I have been bored stiff grappling with a face that, for me, was undrawable; but on other occasions when drawing unprepossessing sitters after having reconciled myself to making the best of it, I have eventually made successful drawings.

What really makes for the creative practice of portrait drawing is your ability to courageously appraise the potentialities of a situation from which a good portrait might conceivably emerge. Sometimes this will have nothing to do with drawing at all, and more to do with the art of relaxing and drawing out a person with a few well-chosen words!

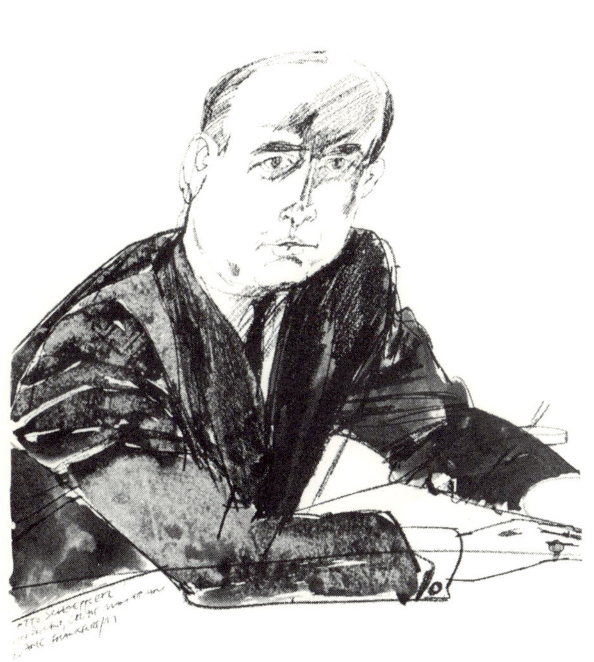

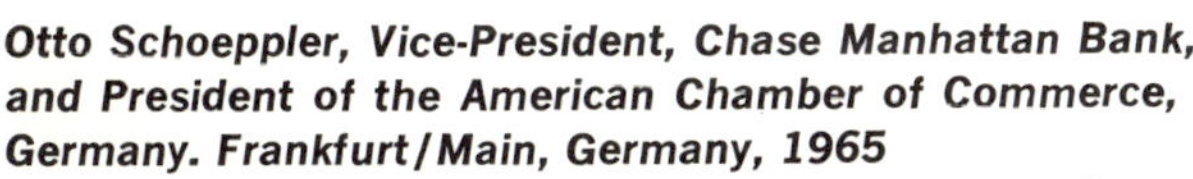

Otto Schoeppler, Vice-President, Chase Manhattan Bank, and President of the American Chamber of Commerce, Germany. Frankfurt/Main, Germany, 1965
I posed Schoeppler against a large window to make a livelier and more interesting movement and shape of head and shoulders. This also threw his somewhat sensitive, expressive face into greater relief. Drawn in a 16" x 20" sketchbook of high surface Daler drawing paper with a 7B Venus pencil. Touches of color were added later with Winsor & Newton artists' watercolor and a No. 6 Winsor & Newton sable brush. Courtesy Fortune *magazine. Copyright August, 1965 by Time, Inc.*

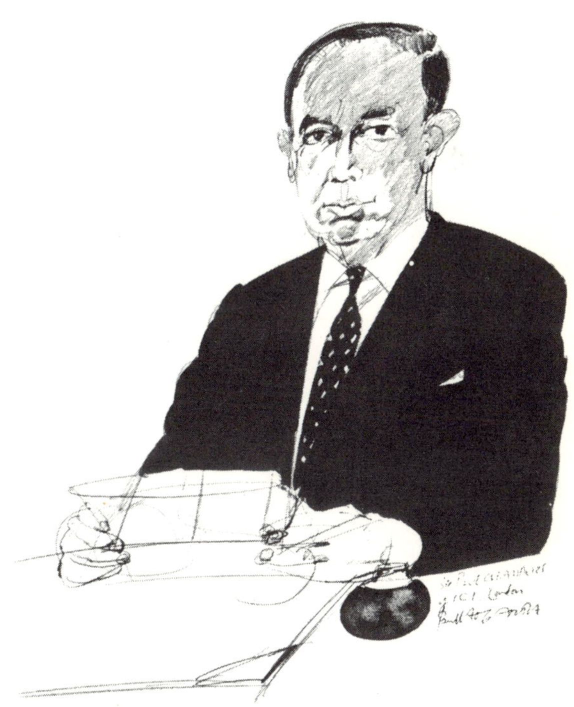

Sir Paul Chambers, Chairman of Imperial Chemical Industries, London, 1967
Sir Paul had been a government civil servant before he became ICI's financial wizard in 1947. Yet his clever face and correct manners created an unfriendly atmosphere. I was faced with the problem I most dread in portrait drawing: the necessity of somehow having to make an interesting drawing out of a personality one way or another I somehow could not bring myself to react to. All I could do was work out a relationship between his well-cut clothes and his suave personality. Drawn in a 16" x 20" sketchbook of high surface Daler drawing paper with Faber 702 sketching and 6B Venus pencils. Color was added later with Faber Design Markettes and Winsor & Newton artists' watercolor. Courtesy Fortune *magazine. Copyright September 15, 1967 by Time, Inc.*

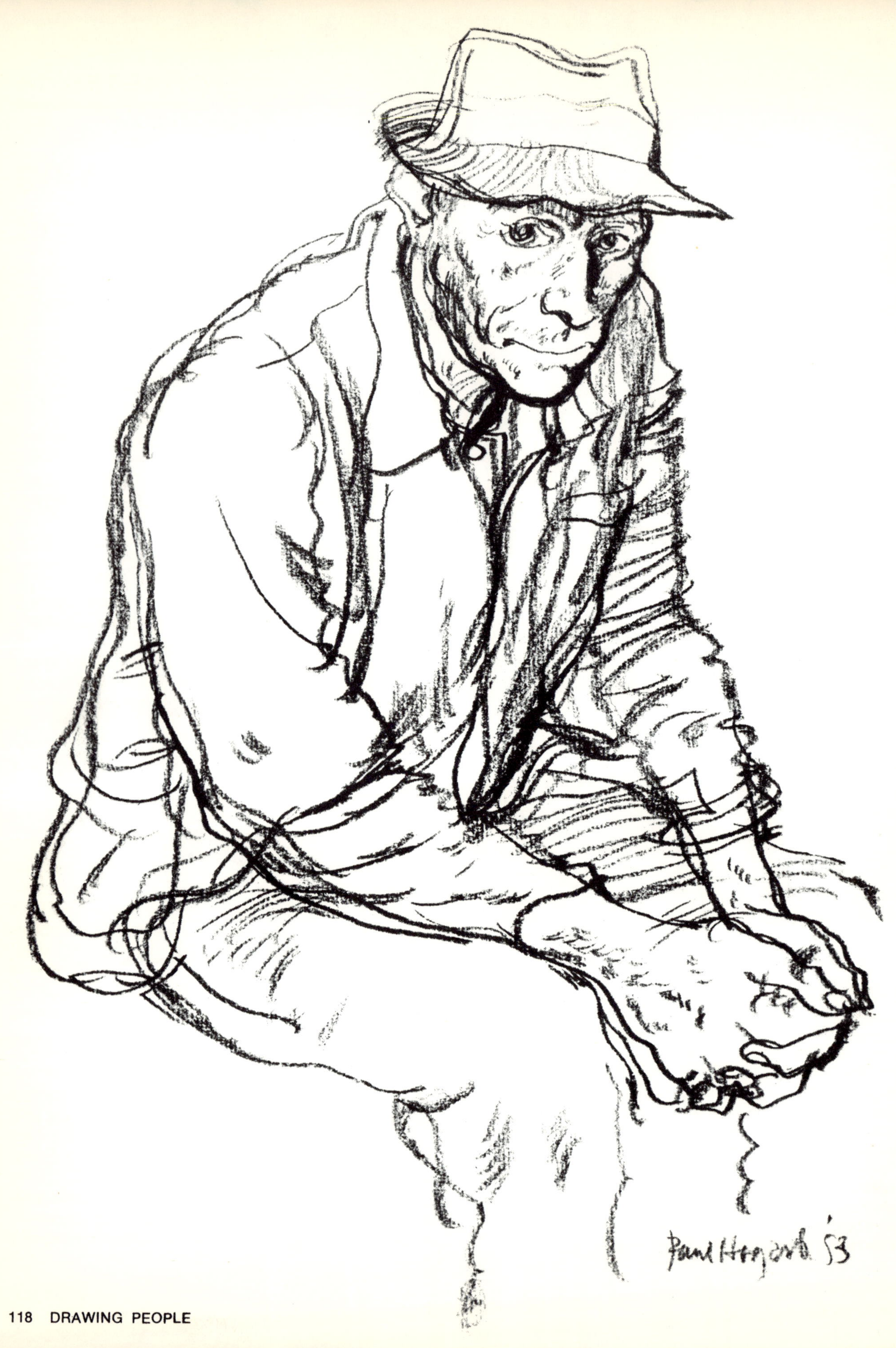
Paul Hogarth '53

CHAPTER 14

Drawing the Portrait

MY OWN portrait drawings are made in one sitting, which usually lasts for at least an hour. Out of this, I estimate that I need five to ten minutes for decision-making and note-taking, with a further five for a break, leaving a minimum working period of between thirty and forty minutes to begin and complete the portrait.

SIZING UP THE SITUATION

During the first moments of becoming acquainted with my sitter, I have to make several decisions: I must hit on an idea of how best I can reveal character; I must analyze and summarize the proportions of face, figure, features (nose, ears, eyes, hair), and facial expression; I must estimate proportion—that is, the length and width of a head compared to its height. I may not wish these to be over-literal but I need to note them in case I may wish to emphasize or distort. I must also note sources of light—both natural and artificial—as these can be used most effectively to dramatize a face. Shadows can give solidity and strength to a head in the presence or absence of other marked characteristics.

PRELIMINARY SKETCHES

I pause to recap my decisions before I actually begin, by rapidly sketching a possible pose or composition in my small pocket sketchbook. I keep these notes beside me and use them as a general guide to help me make the drawing. But frequently, I have drawn right away without such preliminaries. I make myself comfortable, with my pencils, fixative, and eraser at hand.

WORK FROM TOP TO BOTTOM

Now that I am able to take refuge behind my pencil, I work swiftly and surely, working from top to bottom. First, I use an HB pencil to make a light, rough outline, then a softer pencil to develop the drawing. After I have about a third of the drawing in, I usually apply a first spray of fixative to prevent smudging. I then begin to evolve the detail, concentrating on the features in particular. If time is short, this takes priority. Notes can always be made of clothing but not of a face.

CORRECTING A FALSE START

Very often, I get off to a false start. What seemed like a good idea does not work out. Sometimes, this may be because I have used a new kind of paper or an unfamiliar pen or pencil, or simply because I have used the wrong paper for the kind of drawing I originally had in mind. Under these circumstances, I revert to a completely different idea, which may bring me to tackle a different angle or view of the sitter.

KEEPING THE SITTER INTERESTED

Half way through the sitting it frequently happens that a sitter may show signs of losing interest and assume a bored or tired expression. Few people can, in fact, relax for even half-an-hour without showing some restlessness. As I place great importance on vitality of facial expression, I suggest the sitter take a short break of five minutes or so. If he is bored, I may start a conversation to do with his interests

Feliks Krolik, Polish stonemason, Gdansk, Poland, 1953
This portrait, one of my earliest, was made spontaneously after Krolik had watched me complete a large drawing of the reconstruction of the city ravaged by World War Two. There was an extraordinary feeling of mutual understanding as I made this drawing of a simple working man. A soft Hardtmuth charcoal lead was used on Abbey Mill paper. From Drawings from Poland, *1954. Courtesy Wydawnictwo Artystczno-Graficzne, Warsaw.*

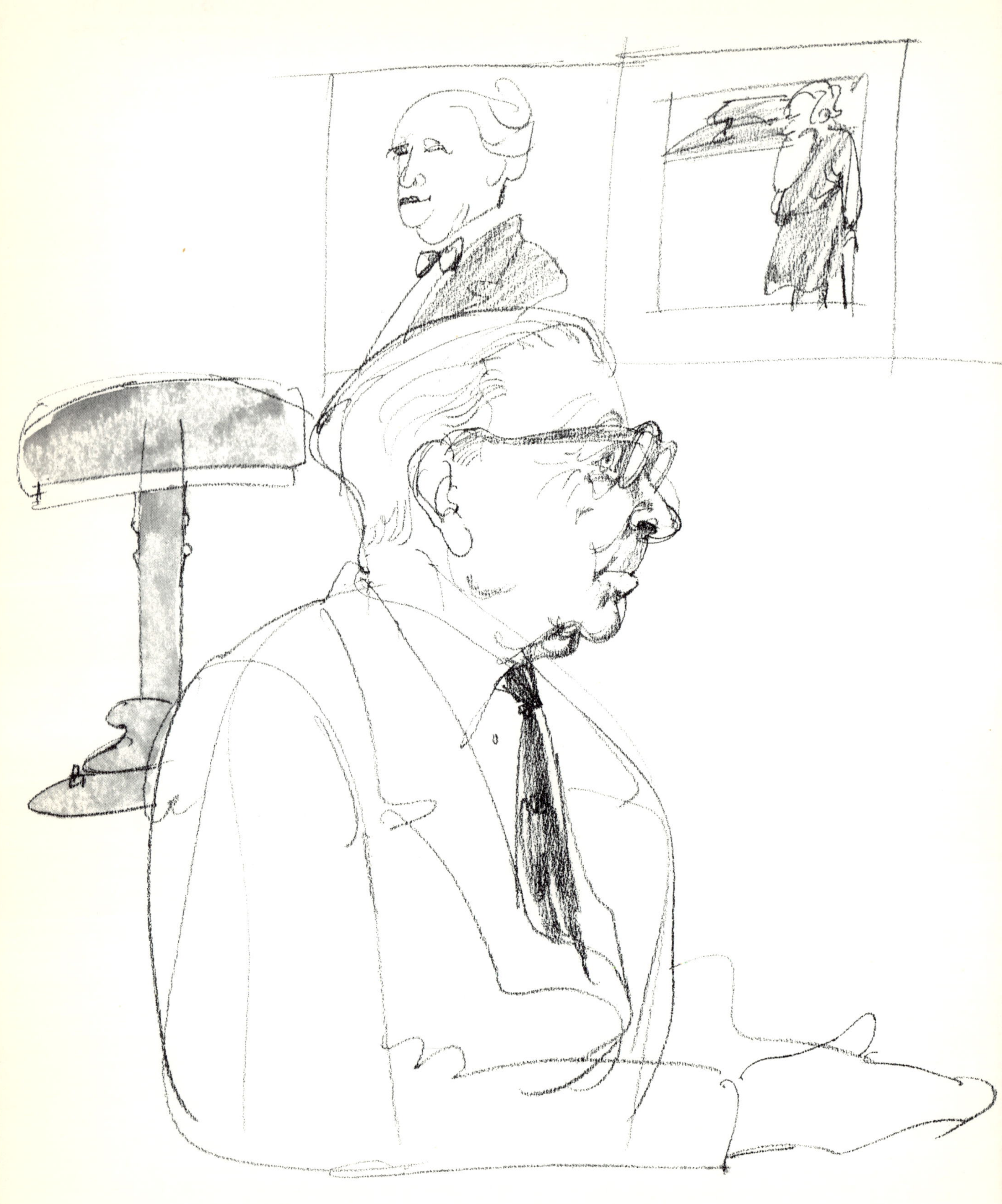

In the House of Veterans of the Stage, U.S.S.R., 1967 *In old age, actors and dancers possess an indefinable pathos which makes them most sympathetic subjects. Both these portraits were drawn during my visit to the U.S.S.R. in a newly opened home for retired stalwarts of the boards in southeastern Moscow.* Vladimir Gardenin *(left), aged eighty-five, was trained by the great Stanislavsky at the Moscow Arts Theatre and played Romeo there. Signed photographs of the* maestro *and Tolstoy held places of honor in his otherwise austere apartment.* Lydia Nelidova *(right), widow of Feveisky, conductor to Chaliapin's Opera Company, which flourished in America during the 1920s, had been a dancer with Fokine in New York in 1940 and ran a ballet school there. Her apartment resembled the dressing room of a star during a long run. The fashionable face in the cloche hat was a photograph taken in the days of the Charleston. Both drawings were made with a Faber 702 sketching pencil in an 11" x 14" sketchbook of one-ply, medium surface Strathmore drawing paper. From* A Russian Journey: from Suzdal to Samarkand, *1969. Courtesy Cassell and Company, London; and Hill & Wang, Inc., New York.*

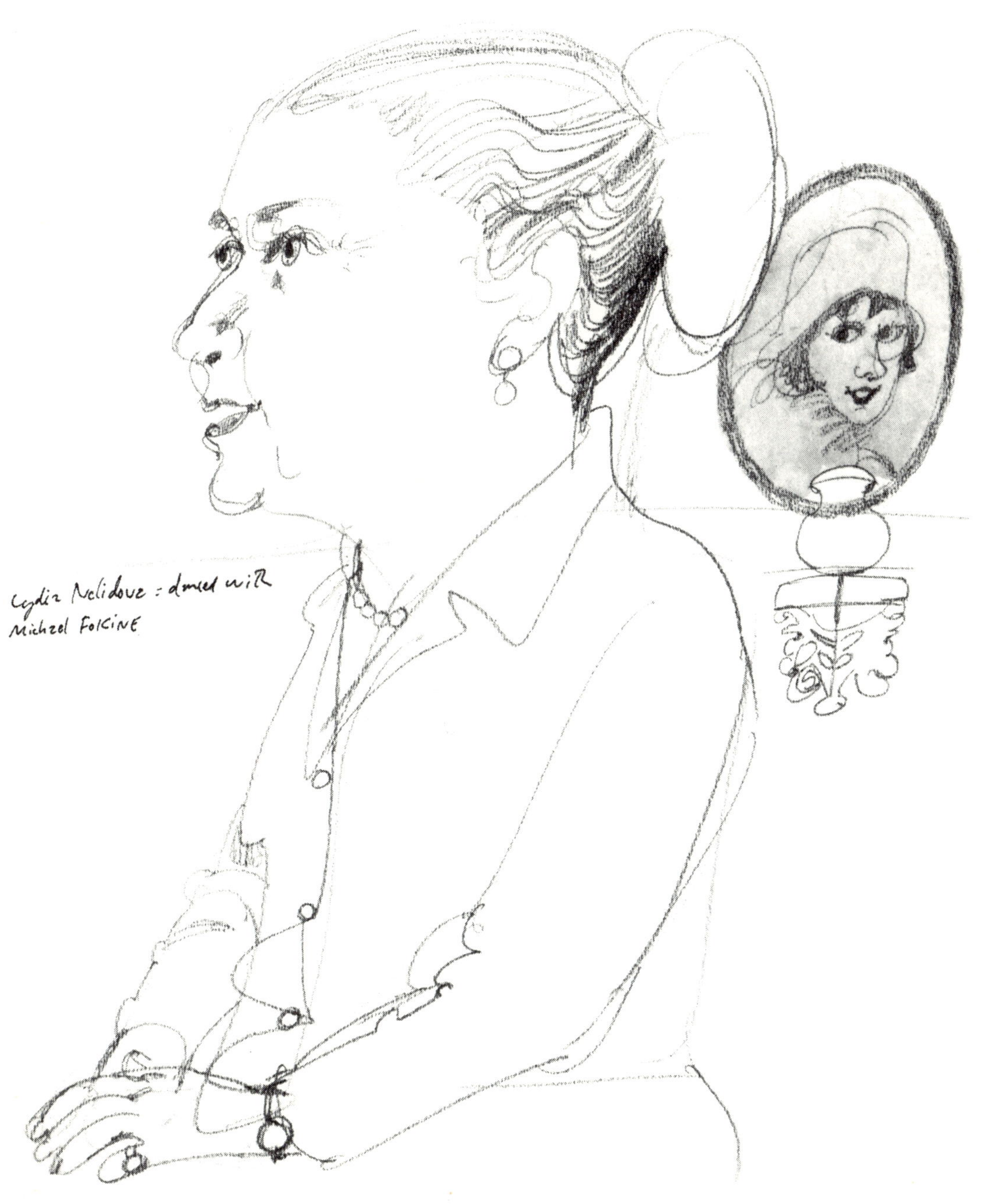

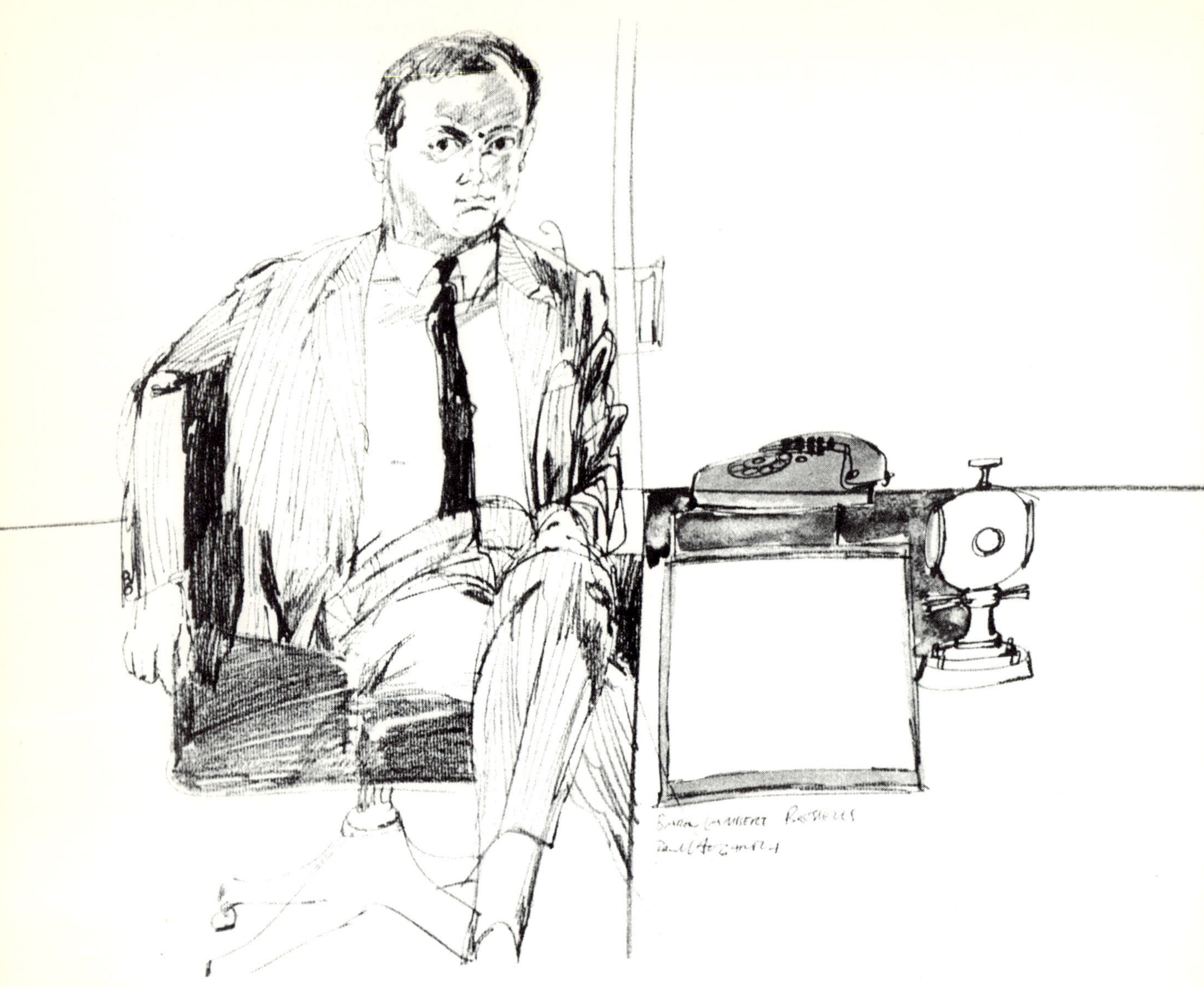

Baron Léon Lambert, Brussels, 1965
The Baron's sharply intelligent and handsome face reminded me of the boulevardiers *of Degas. His was an elusive personality who would not suffer fools gladly. Fortunately, I hit on an appropriate formula to draw him. Using the compositional device of a cross, I filled the left half with foreshortened seated figure and the right with a selection of objects on his desk. Keenly interested in the drawing, he stepped over and made an appreciative comment, requesting only that I slightly reduce the size of his well-fleshed chin. Both his taste and tact had contributed to a successful sitting. Drawn with a Venus 6B pencil in a 16" x 20" sketchbook of high surface Daler drawing paper. As time on this occasion seemed no object, I completed the drawing on the spot by adding touches of Winsor & Newton artists' watercolor with a No. 6 Winsor & Newton sable brush. Courtesy* Fortune *magazine. Copyright August, 1965 by Time, Inc. Reproduced by permission of the owner, Edward Booth-Clibborn, London, England.*

or activities, or recount anecdotes about art and other artists. But this can be highly diverting, so I only do it if I am making good progress. Boredom can also be dissipated by satisfying the sitter's natural curiosity by showing him how the drawing is going.

DRAWING PORTRAITS ON LOCATION

If I am able to make a portrait at the sitter's place of work, boredom is seldom a problem. I usually request such people—usually executives of industrial corporations or business enterprises, or engineers on the job—that they just continue their daily routine and forget all about me. I select a particular posture that seems to me in character and is good to draw. Most settle down to a set of basic postures enlivened by a series of typical movements, such as pressing the buzzer of an office intercom system, using a dictaphone or a telephone, briefing a secretary, or persuading a colleague. All of these help reveal the character and personality of this particular kind of sitter, as well as ensuring continuous facial vitality.

DRAWING EMOTIONS

Although your sitter will naturally seek to show the best side of himself, do not be afraid to probe beneath the surface. Facial expression should, therefore, be studied carefully. It is both an index of the emotions and of character. Thoughts are conveyed by looks as well as by words, and both affect the appearance of a face to a remarkable extent. Every expression has its own movement of each feature. Eyes are the most expressive of all, because they reflect the emotions, but mouth and eyebrows also play an important role.

Practice rendering such over-all facial expressions as anger, despair, determination, fear, scorn, jealousy, and joy, as well as strength, pride, lust, greed, envy, and laziness by drawing yourself in a mirror. Make pencil studies of the eyes to express amusement, surprise, fear, and hatred. Familiarize yourself with the four basic human temperaments: the vivacious, the phlegmatic, the optimistic, and the pessimistic. You will discover that you will be much better equipped to cope with the problem of identifying and depicting traits, emotions, and temperament in a face.

SUPPOSE YOUR EFFORTS ARE NOT APPRECIATED?

One of the problems in creative portraiture, if not *the* problem, is the final acceptance and approval of the completed drawing. You will find, as I have found, that a well-drawn appraisal which may be highly satisfactory in your eyes, may not please your sitter one bit! The esthetic qualities your portrait possesses may be completely ignored by the indignant sitter, disappointed or outraged by what he or she may feel to be an unsympathetic portrayal.

This is a difficult problem to give advice about in a general sense. The majority of *commissioned* portraits as opposed to spontaneously made portraits of friends or acquaintances, should be done with a tacit understanding that an artist differs from a photographer in his approach to the subject. Nevertheless, even if this is understood, the artist has relatively little ground in which to maneuver. Generally speaking, the artist is expected to produce a viable likeness. I seldom neglect, therefore, an opportunity to tell a sitter beforehand that my drawing will be essentially more of an *interpretation* of character than a superficial likeness.

So much depends on the taste and understanding of the individual sitter, as well as one of the skill and standing of the artist. If these qualities exist in your sitter you will be fortunate. Such sitters will accept what you do, and be the first to appreciate a lively and imaginative portrayal of their personalities. If they do not, you should—but only if you believe in your drawing—be prepared to defend it. When placed in this predicament, I judge both the taste and the experience of the sitter to ascertain whether I am the best judge or not! On principle, I will not concede, but I am always prepared to discuss a valid objection and discuss my reasons for drawing a sitter in a particular way. While not prepared to change my basic approach—without making another drawing—I do sometimes agree to make minor changes, such as relaxing the line of the mouth which may have been drawn in too tightly. Usually, I like to be given the opportunity to think over any changes, and I prefer *not* to make them at a sitting, as I sometimes find the next day that the drawing could be as easily ruined as it could be improved.

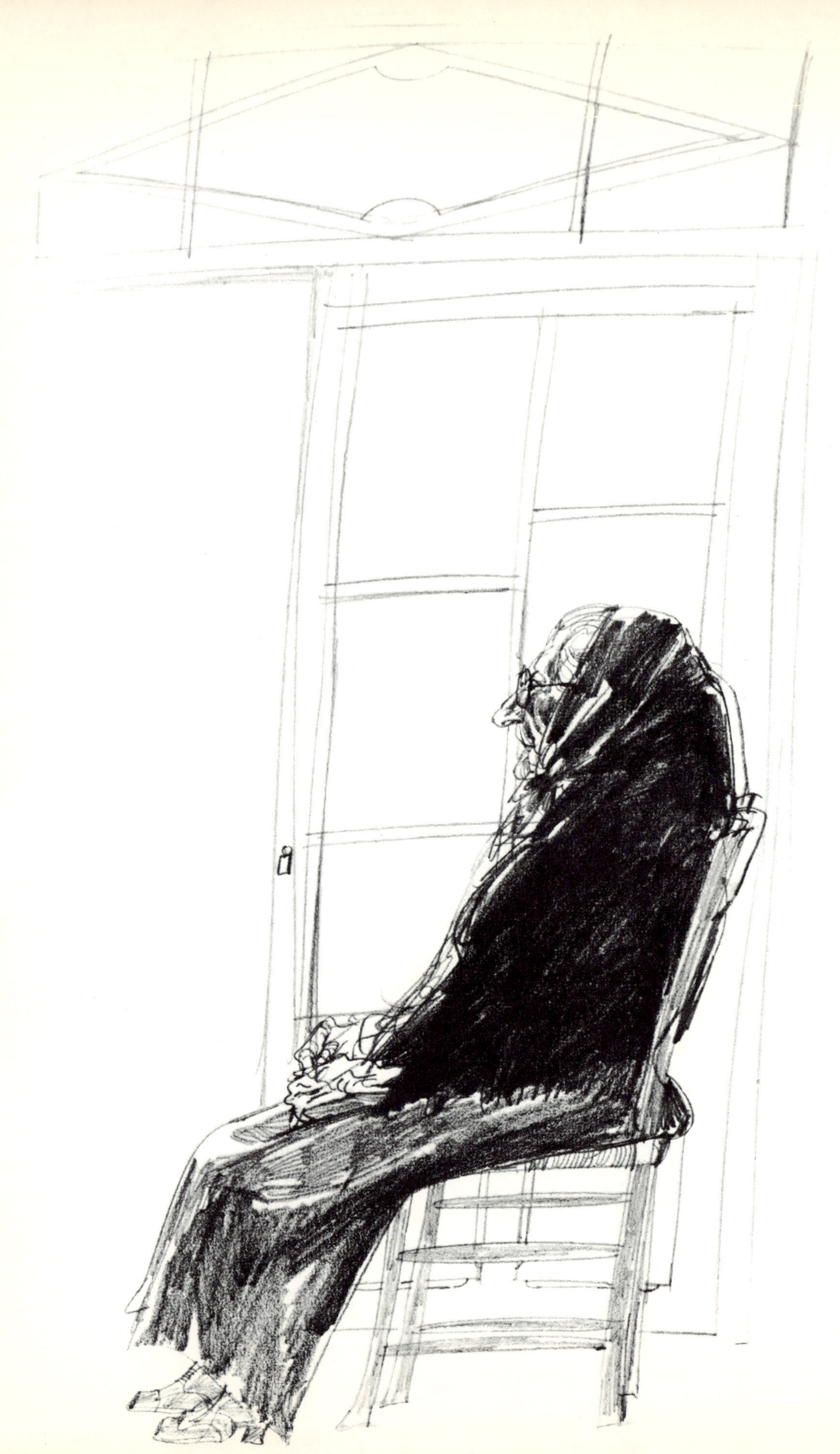

CHAPTER 15

Men, Women, and Children

THERE ARE PEOPLE who are not so much interested in an acceptable likeness as they are in providing you with a memorable experience. To draw such people is as much a privilege as it is a pleasure, because they do not particularly care whether they show the best side of themselves or not. Such people accept the most candid portrayal of themselves as the prerogative of the artist with a stoicism and dignity which produces a totally relaxed, and at times an enchanted, atmosphere. They can, therefore, be drawn with much greater ease than other people. Such people—men, women, and children—I call "naturals."

DRAWING "NATURALS"

I sometimes despair of ever meeting another "natural" again, then suddenly one comes along. More often than not, they are encountered by chance. One of my earliest "naturals" was a Szechwan stonemason. I was traveling in southwest China during the summer of 1954, and had been drawing the terraced fields near Chungking until a rainstorm forced me to take shelter. Under a bamboo awning, a group of stonemasons chipped away, dressing slabs of stone. A strongly featured man wearing a red towel twisted pirate style around his shaven head caught my attention. Hooded eyes gazed out over a long, finely chiseled nose. Without even asking him, I drew his portrait. With an intuitive understanding of my interest, he remained relaxed and motionless for a full three-quarters of an hour. Yet he did not show the slightest interest in seeing what I had drawn until one of his mates gestured that it looked good.

Another "natural" was a young Louisiana welder who went by the name of Greville Mander, whom I met in the back country of Mississippi while making drawings for a *Fortune* portfolio on the construction of the Colonial Oil pipeline during the summer of 1962. There could not have been more of a contrast between the muscle and brawn of the Chinese stonemason and the nimble, almost balletic grace of the boy from Baton Rouge, but what they had in common was the rare quality of a "natural"—of being themselves, while accepting a completely unorthodox situation, then being tickled to death that you saw enough in them to actually enjoy drawing them.

The Irish, of course, provide an inexhaustible supply of "naturals" in every size, shape, and age group. Their innate gregariousness gives them a very special personal quality I have not found anywhere else. Every man, woman, and child among them is an actor, a conversationalist who loves to get involved with people. On so many occasions during my various travels in Ireland, they have good-naturedly abandoned themselves to the mercy of my pencil just to extend the pleasure of their company. All of which confirms my belief that portraiture is but the pictorial part of a communication with people simply because each enjoys the other's personality.

Maria Bauza, Deya, Majorca, 1963
Peasant women in the frail splendor of old age, are often "naturals." I drew this one silhouetted against the Mondrian-like tracery of the front door of her house. Drawn in about an hour with a 7B Venus graphite pencil on a 16" x 20½" sheet of Saunders mold-made cream wove writing paper. From Majorca Observed, *1966. Courtesy Cassell and Company, London; and Hill & Wang, Inc., New York.*

DRAWING WOMEN

"Naturals" are less frequently found among women. As a rule, any Western woman over thirty is less philosophical and much more conscious of her looks than a man. And, of course, the older she is, the more self-conscious she usually becomes. I am reminded of the Dublin "shawlie" who, when I had finished drawing her portrait, sat by my side to watch me make the finishing touches. I was adding a line or two to

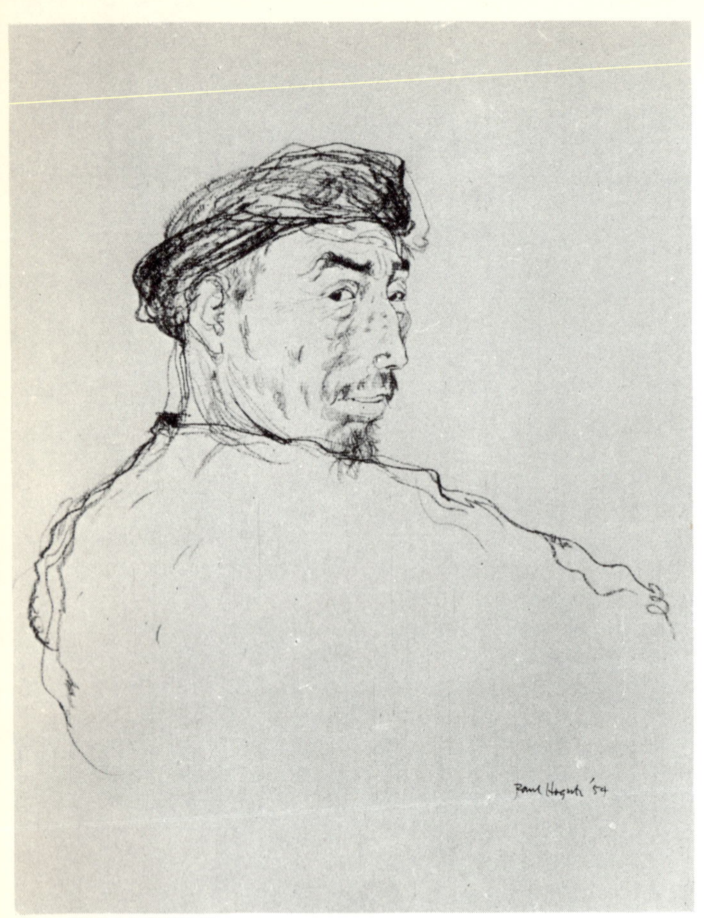

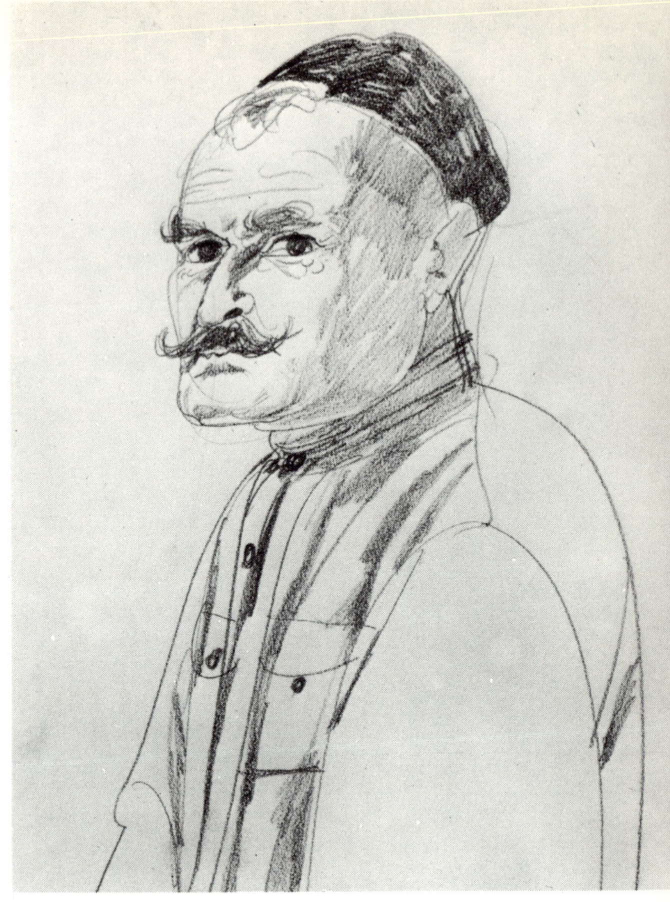

Two "naturals," China
There are people who accept the most candid portrayal of themselves as the prerogative of the itinerant artist with stoical dignity. Such people I call "naturals." More often than not, one meets them by chance. Like, for example, the Szechwan stonemason, China, 1954 *(left) who, without being even asked to pose, remained relaxed and motionless for the entire forty-five minutes it took me to make the drawing. I used a Hardtmuth medium charcoal lead on Chinese bamboo paper. From* Looking at China, *1955. Courtesy Lawrence and Wishart, London. In the collection of the Whitworth Art Institute, University of Manchester, England. Reproduced by permission. The* Georgian farmer, U.S.S.R., 1967 *(right) was drawn before a dinner party in his house to honor the visit of our party to his village of Signachi, a village in the Georgian highlands. The party included officials from the American Embassy in Moscow as well as local bigwigs and the poet Stanley Kunitz. Although bewildered by the influx of foreigners, the old farmer took this additional experience in his stride, confiding that there hadn't been a day like it since his son got married. From* A Russian Journey: from Suzdal to Samarkand, *1969. Courtesy Cassell and Company, London; and Hill & Wang, Inc., New York.*

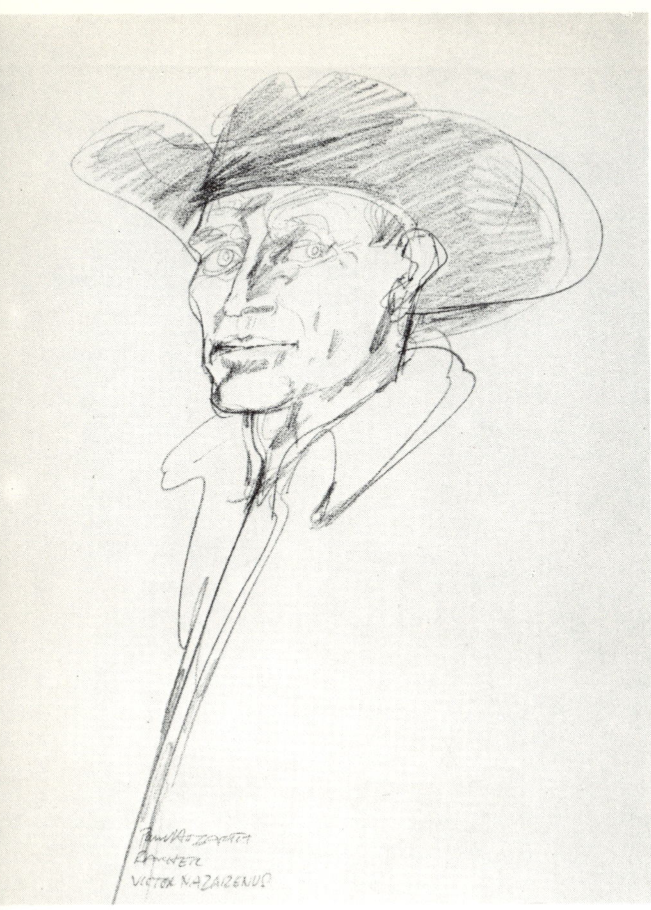

Victor Nazarenus, Ak-Sar-Ben Rodeo, Omaha, 1965
Victor is a rancher with one of those good-to-draw outdoor faces. He breeds horses, and I made this rapidly drawn portrait sketch in twenty minutes over a drink. Drawn in an 11" x 14" sketchbook of two-ply Strathmore drawing paper with a Faber 702 sketching pencil. Courtesy the Strathmore Paper Company, West Springfield, Mass.

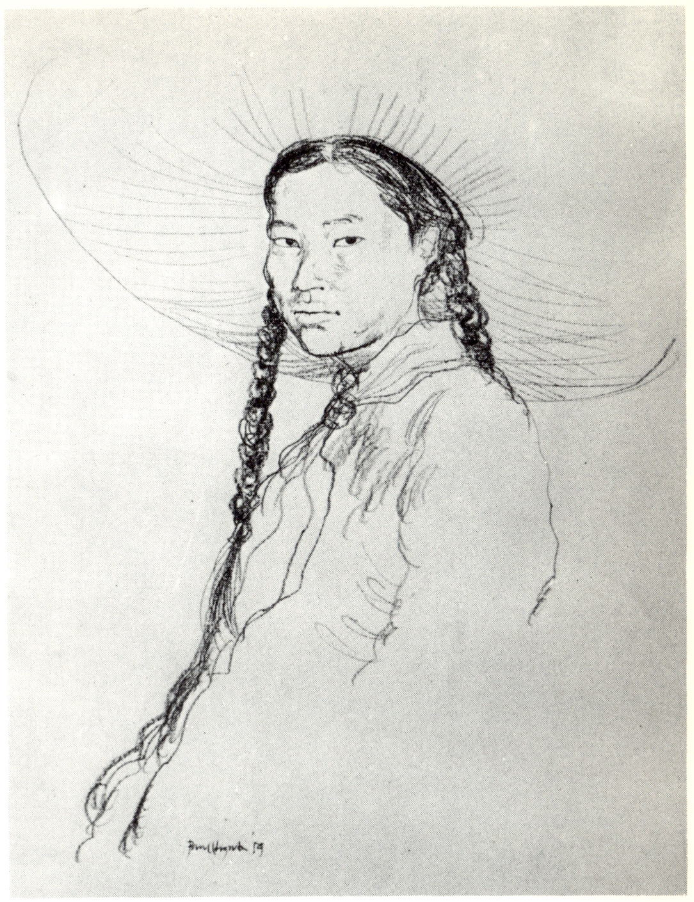

Canton schoolgirl, China, 1954
This twelve-year-old girl pioneer was brought to my hotel room for the portrait sitting. Quiet and self-controlled, of strong character, she was an ideal, if inscrutable, model—providing an excellent opportunity to study the Chinese face. The drawing was made in about an hour, on Chinese bamboo paper, using Hardtmuth medium charcoal leads. From Looking at China, *1955. Courtesy Lawrence and Wishart, London. Reproduced by permission of the owner, Mr. Jack Silver, Manchester, England.*

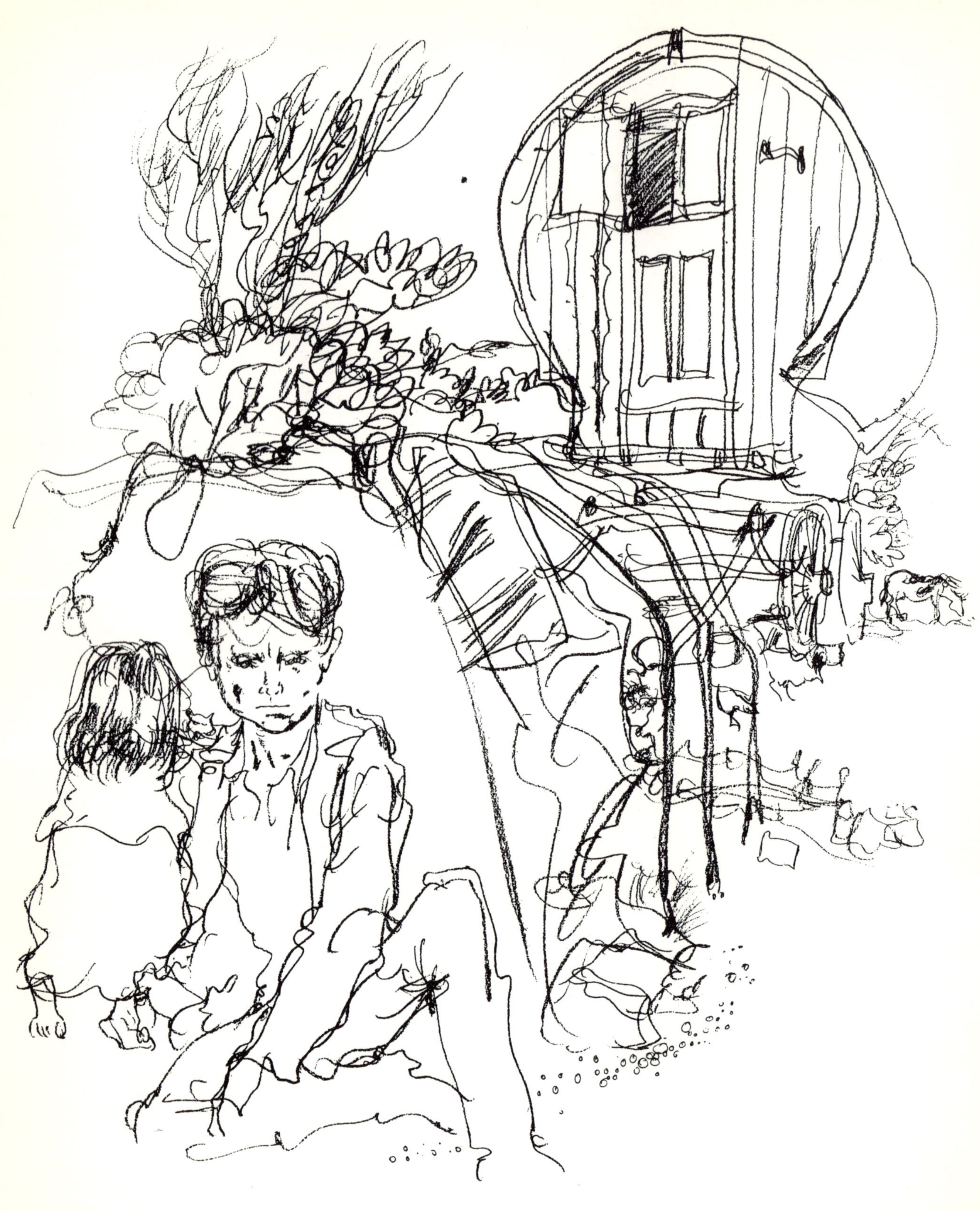

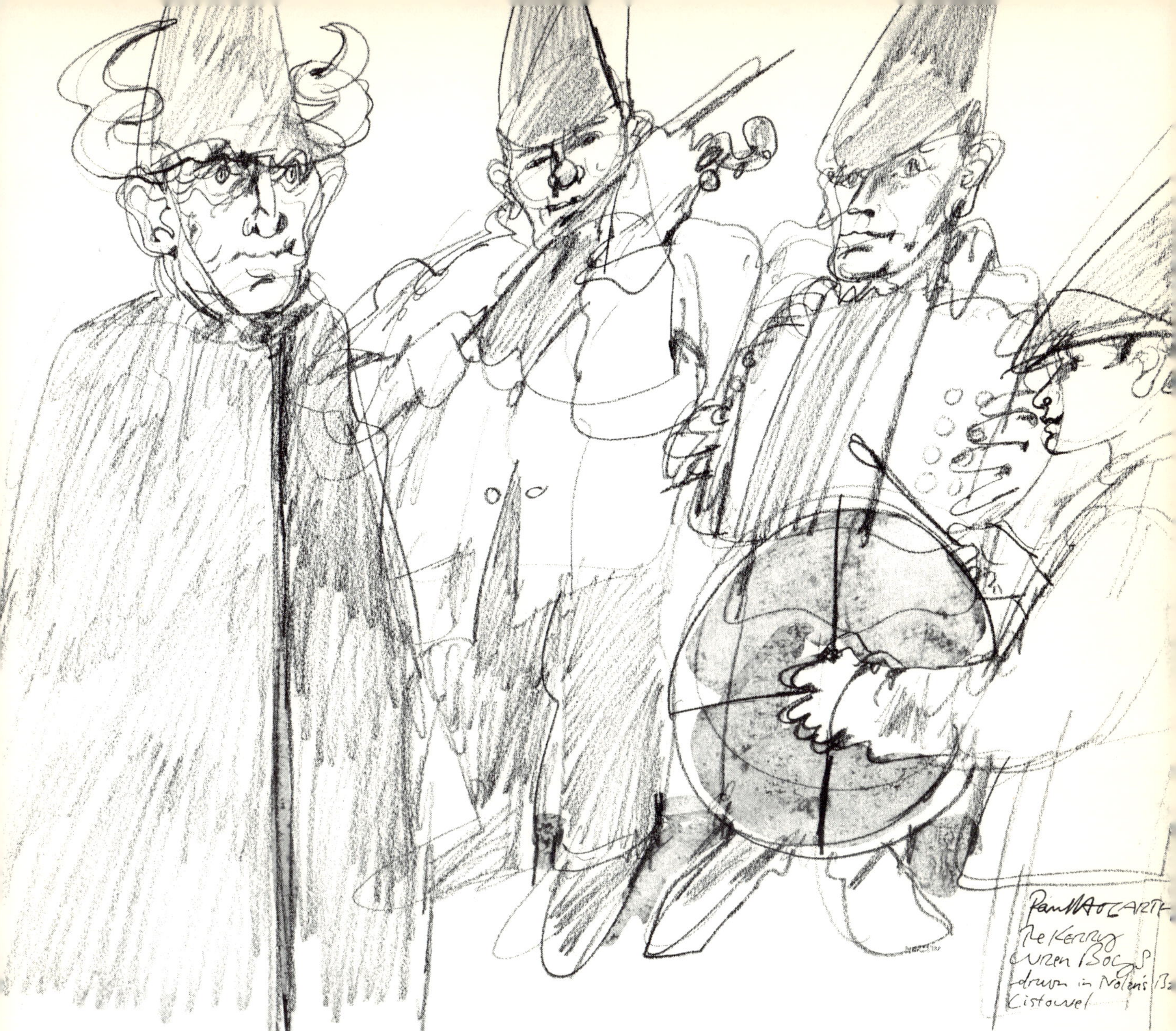

Tinker children, Connemara, Ireland, 1959
Children are sometimes easy, occasionally difficult, to draw. The main thing is to capture their interest in what you are doing; then you can make all the drawings you want. You may have to go about this in a roundabout way. I made a landscape drawing to gain the interest of these tinker children, but they were tough nuts, and I was only able to make this drawing if I promised to ask my wife if she would like to buy a horse; I also had to present the eldest with a coveted picture book. Drawn with a Number 3 Conté Pierre Noir *charcoal lead on Abbey Mill pastel paper. From* Brendan Behan's Island, *1962. Courtesy The Hutchinson Publishing Group, London; and Bernard Geis Associates, New York. Reproduced by permission of the owner, Edna O'Brien, London. (Left)*

The Kerry "Wren Boys," Listowel, Ireland, 1969
Drawn at Nolan's Bar on a Saturday night with whisky flowing like water. All part of the scene at the Listowel Races, the oldest in Ireland. Left to right: the "King" of the All-Ireland "Wren Boys," sixty-eight-year-old laborer Sonny Canaem; fiddler Jeremiah O'Connell, farmer; Tommy Doran, farmer; and fourteen-year-old Martin Scanlon. The "King" is elected each year and has to be the best singer, dancer, and musician. Here, the main problem was to capture the movement of the fiddler and the accordionist; once I had done this, I turned to the "King," making him an overlapping dominant personality with features drawn in greater detail. Finally, the boy was brought in from the right to key the composition. Courtesy Lithopinion, *Winter 1969. Copyright by Amalgamated Lithographers of America, Local One, New York. (Above)*

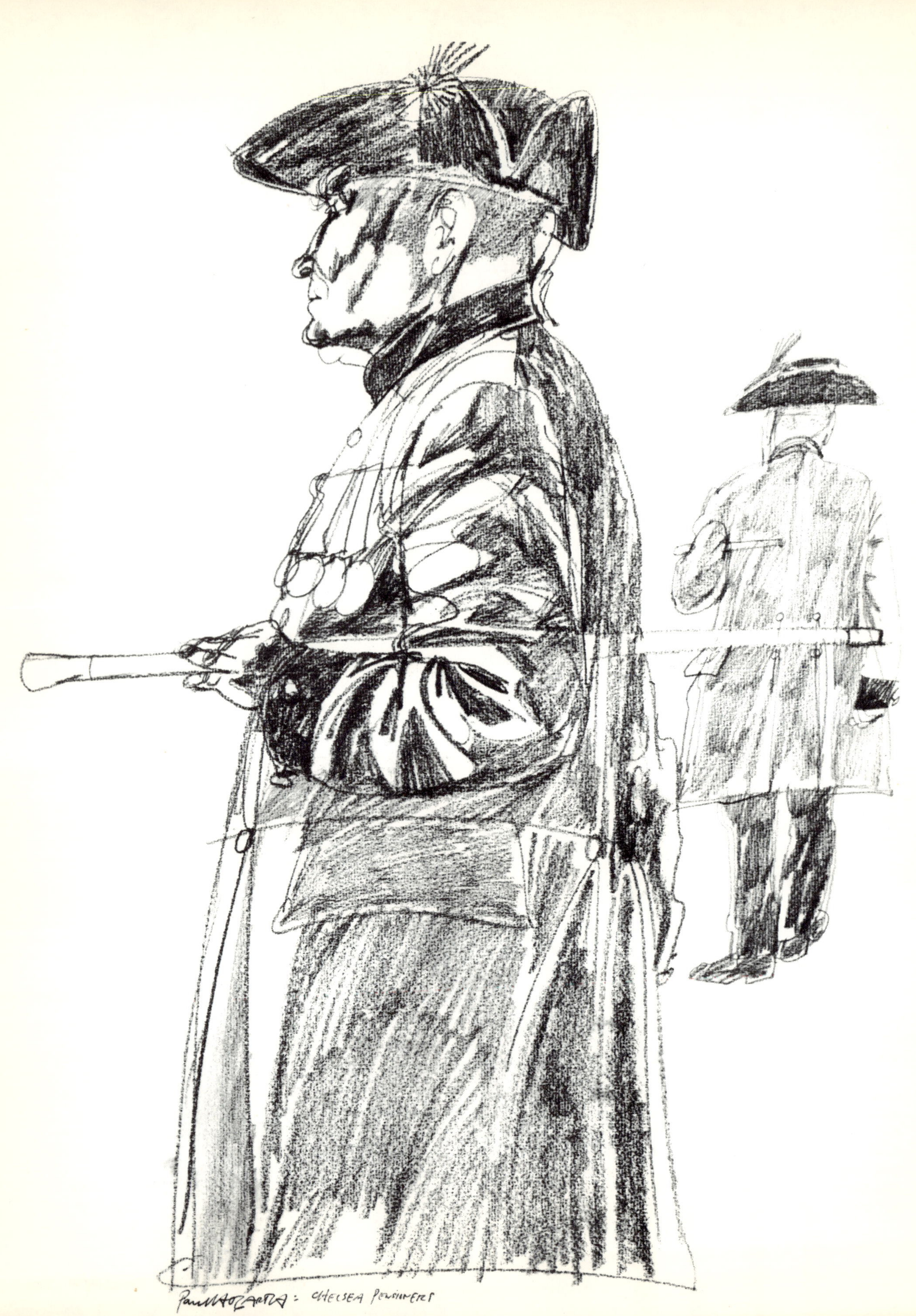
Chelsea Pensioners

her face when she gently placed a warm, calloused hand on my wrist and whispered, "Spare the hand, yer honor, I'm not yit in the grave!" The raucous laughter that followed shook the foundations of the bar, but there was no doubt that she meant every word!

Most of my women "naturals" have been discovered among country people who relax more easily and are nearly always a delight to draw because they pose with little or no embarrassment. In the country districts of South and Central Africa; of India, Japan, and China, women are not so obsessed with the passage of time. Moreover, they act with grace and dignity, disdaining payment or reward of any kind. More than can be said of some Western girls I have drawn!

DRAWING YOUNG CHILDREN

Children are sometimes easy, occasionally difficult, to draw. It can only be easy if you talk to the child and involve him in what you are doing. It can be difficult, even impossible, if you shut the child out and treat him like an inanimate puppet. Because they so seldom relax, children have to be drawn much more rapidly than adults. I therefore work in a slightly different way. Sometimes I keep two, even three, drawings going at the same time, besides making more notes on how I will actually complete the drawings in my studio.

Up to the age of ten, children can be very restless human material indeed. So I try to capture their interest in various ways. For example, I may give them a sheet of paper and pencil and ask that they make a drawing of me while I am drawing them. I may also encourage whatever play fantasies they respond to by telling them to go ahead and be a gun-fighter and blaze away with a toy revolver, or be a nurse and put a doll to bed.

DRAWING OLDER CHILDREN

Over the age of ten, children are much less likely to move the whole time. They will relax because they are more likely to be interested in the whole experience of watching a professional artist at work. As most children like drawing, they are intrigued with the difference between their own imagery and that of a grown-up. For older children and young adults, the artist is also a symbol of freedom, of a life based on personal choice.

So much of an artist's life is like that of a child—a restless quest for self-identity and self-expression—that I, for one, often feel very close to them.

Chelsea pensioners, London, 1966
Here, the figures were drawn in different sizes in order to heighten the military effect and character. Drawn with a Faber 702 sketching pencil on a 20" x 25" sheet of Strathmore medium surface drawing paper. From London à la Mode, *1966. Courtesy Studio Vista Ltd., London; and Hill & Wang, Inc., New York.*

CHAPTER 16

Drawing Portrait Groups

THE GROUP PORTRAIT, or conversation piece as it is sometimes called, usually consists of two, three, or more small portraits of people represented in the context of the appropriate surroundings, domestic or otherwise. Such portraits, therefore, are usually informal and depict friends, colleagues, or members of the same family.

IMPORTANCE OF COMPOSITION

Because it is a multiple portrait, with different or conflicting elements, a group portrait has a far greater chance of going wrong if you do not make the extra effort to plan your moves with care. I therefore try to spend at least fifteen minutes, even longer whenever possible, observing the characteristics of each sitter and working out ideas and a sketch for a composition which will enable me to organize the group into an effective pictorial image.

Placing such importance on composition invariably leads me to collect all kinds of arrangements which I hope I will be able to use one day. After watching people sit or talk in the street or at the movies, I scribble these down on the backs of old envelopes and odd scrapes of paper. Although this does help extend my compositional expertise, I find that I am rarely able to use them. The structure of the group itself, in the context of its particular setting, invariably determines an on-the-spot original solution, which may be born out of a surprise analogy or similarities.

A typical example was the time I was enjoying a "jar" of beer in Slattery's Bar on the quays of Dublin during the summer of 1960. Over the rim of my glass, I caught sight of a remarkable trio of battered Irishwomen. All were dockworkers' wives, known as "shawlies" because of the black shawls they wear. The biggest, Mary Dignam, was a huge, genial soul, while her two cronies could not have been more different. One was tall and of mournful countenance; the other, small and bird-like. I was at once reminded of the three fates of classical myth, quenching their thirst with a glass of Guinness stout before spinning the threads of destiny. I had struck on such an apt compositional idea that drawing them seemed to be much less difficult a problem than it might otherwise have been.

TWO PEOPLE

Important as a parallel idea or analogy can be, a good group portrait cannot stand on its own without the support of *scale* and *movement.* After noting physical and psychological characteristics, the next step is to relate people to one another and work out the size I should draw them. This may involve using a different scale for each figure. Two people, always a tricky number, can be drawn very effectively in this way. For example, one can be drawn in the foreground as a seated figure (full-face or profile), the other in the background as a standing full figure.

It may be necessary for two figures to be of equal size and importance. In this case, I will probably emphasize whatever character differences exist by using movement (in face and figure) to achieve contrast. This was the case with a *Fortune* portrait assignment in 1966, a group portrait of Jean Corthésy and Enrico Bignami, who run Nestlé, the giant Swiss food and chocolate empire. Happily, I at once thought of their resemblance to Siamese twins, talking and gesturing as a single administrative brain while possessing strikingly different personalities. Bignami (whom I drew first), for example, was an introvert of great charm. He had a tormented face which instantly assumed an expression of imaginative intelligence whenever he grappled with a problem in conversation. After watching him, I decided to draw him facing me as if he were talking to a colleague or secretary. Corthésy, on the other hand, was a dynamic, bluff extrovert. He was a bulky man who carried on forceful telephone conversations with aides stationed in various capitals of far-off lands. I drew him behind his partner, facing left in profile, making such a call.

THREE OR MORE SITTERS

Although the problem of drawing a larger group can be tackled in a greater variety of ways, the forms these take will depend on how long the group can actually remain together. If time is short, I usually go for a simple composition, selecting a big and impressive personality, like Mary Dignam, around whom two or more companions can be placed "out-of-focus." I also use a more flexible, strip-like composition with, say, three figures drawn in a row and one figure seated or standing on the left, on the right, or in the center. I found this very useful for my group portrait, *Farmers in a Samarkand teahouse, U.S.S.R., 1967,* because it enabled me to add other people who joined the group without disturbing the balance of the composition. As I did not know exactly how long the group would remain seated, I could only hope they would stay long enough for me to fit them all in. I quickly decided who was essential and who was not, before sketching in a rough outline of the entire group with an HB pencil. The first, a hawk-eyed elder with a turbaned head of great character interest, was the most important figure, and I placed him in the center. Next was a companion to his right, then another seated in front reading a newspaper. In each case, I concentrated mainly on the head, because I could, if necessary, complete the rest from notes and memory. As they got up to leave, I was left one figure short, so I brought in another from the right to balance the group.

If a large group can be drawn at leisure in my studio, or the home or office of the sitters, I may use a more elaborate type of composition which depends on a much more closely knit and compact grouping.

Whatever type of composition I choose, and wherever I may actually draw the group portrait, I aim at a lively and expressive portrayal. In order to make this possible, I will use whatever may be going on off the paper—a sports event, a family discussion, a business deal, or a rendezvous in a bar—to help give my drawing the vitality of involvement with experience.

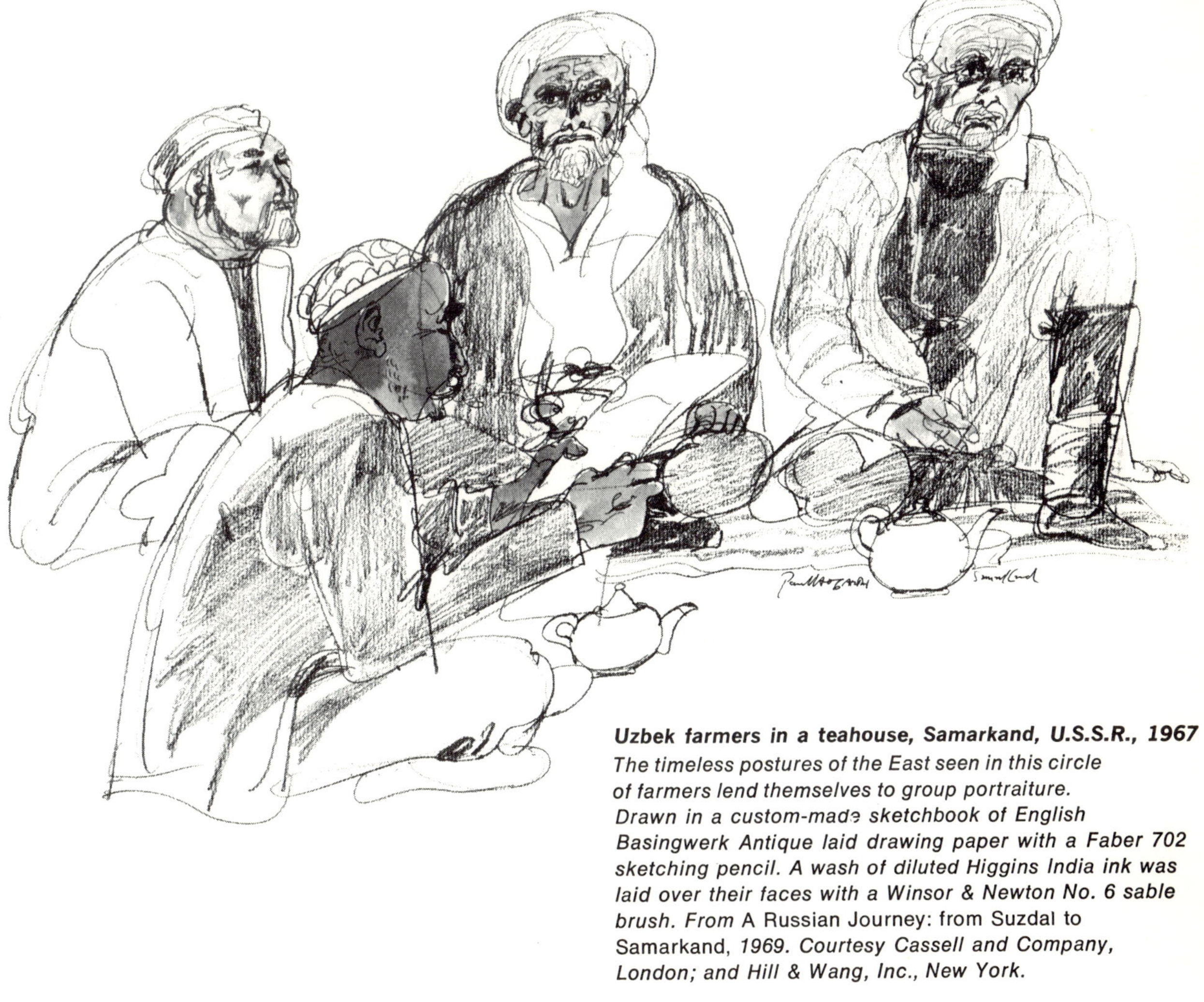

Uzbek farmers in a teahouse, Samarkand, U.S.S.R., 1967
The timeless postures of the East seen in this circle of farmers lend themselves to group portraiture. Drawn in a custom-made sketchbook of English Basingwerk Antique laid drawing paper with a Faber 702 sketching pencil. A wash of diluted Higgins India ink was laid over their faces with a Winsor & Newton No. 6 sable brush. From A Russian Journey: from Suzdal to Samarkand, *1969. Courtesy Cassell and Company, London; and Hill & Wang, Inc., New York.*

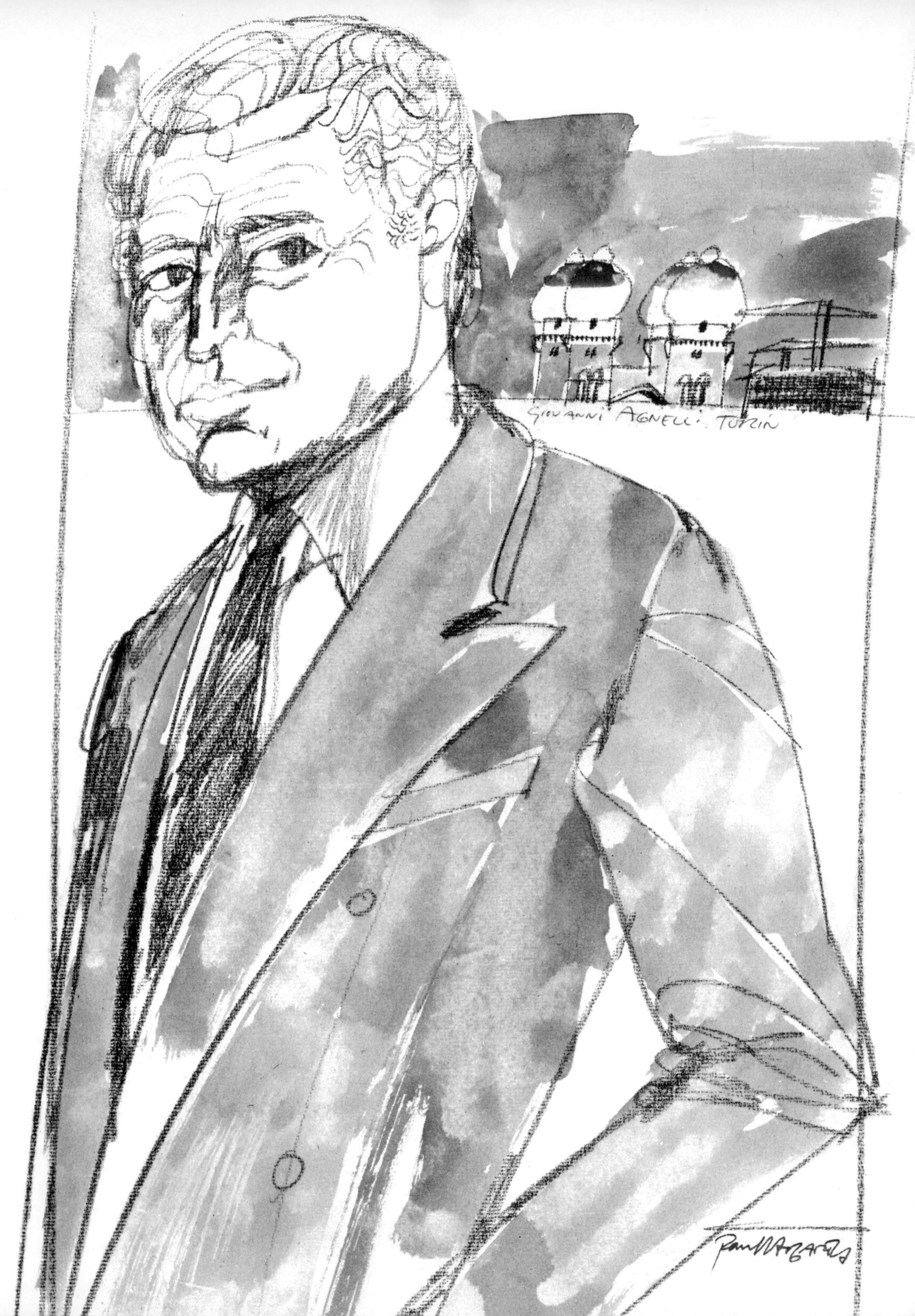
GIOVANNI AGNELLI · TURIN

CHAPTER 17

Drawing the Famous

DRAWING THE famous or distinguished is rather like speaking in public after being used to conversing quietly with friends. You may, therefore, run the risk of being heckled or unexpectedly put off your stroke at the very moment your portrait is going well.

APPROACH WITH CAUTION

I have never forgotten the experience of drawing my earliest celebrities at a prestigious cultural gathering I covered in Vienna some years ago. Among the many famous figures was the Russian composer Shostakovitch. I felt compelled to draw his portrait; he had such a fine introverted face, with bird-like features half concealed by thick eyeglasses. As I had taken him by surprise, he vaguely agreed to sit for me. After a few minutes, however, he twisted in his seat like a captured butterfly. When he could stand it no longer, he leaped up and disappeared into the crowded conference!

Giovanni Agnelli, President of Fiat, Turin, Italy, 1965
A playboy in his younger days, but a brainy one, Agnelli at fifty is head of the huge auto company founded by his grandfather in 1899. Handsome, sophisticated, with a great zest for life, he is Italy's richest man. Drawing him was a tough and tricky assignment. I flew in from London for the sitting, but a big deal made Agnelli late by several hours. When he finally arrived, he could only give me thirty minutes; and in addition to this limitation, I found that he was unable to relax for more than a few moments at a time. Total disaster was narrowly averted by my introduction of a topic of mutual interest, the art of the English painter Francis Bacon. We talked, and the portrait was finished on time. Drawn on an 18½" x 22½" sheet of Strathmore Script drawing paper with 3B and 6B Eagle Charco pencils. Grumbacher watercolors were used with a Number 6 Winsor & Newton sable brush to paint in the suit and the Turin skyline. Courtesy Fortune *magazine. Copyright August, 1965 by Time, Inc.*

Shostakovitch's sudden exit was a big blow to my self-confidence, and the unfortunate incident rankled in my memory for quite some time before I eventually realized that my approach had been totally wrong. A news photographer may presume on a brief encounter with the famous. An artist cannot and should not. Since that time, therefore, my drawings of the famous have been made because they are either friends or acquaintances I have worked with on a book or an article, or because a magazine or a publisher has actually commissioned me to do so.

TRY TO BECOME ACQUAINTED FIRST

I find it much easier to draw a celebrity if we know each other—at least casually—or if he knows of me. And, of course, celebrities are much more likely to unbend and accept the ordeal more easily if we can get acquainted with each other socially. There have been times when further acquaintance has created tension, making things even more difficult, but usually, because celebrities are, paradoxically, isolated by their fame, they relish the experience—particularly if they are being drawn for a famous magazine, and by an artist whose work they like, or at least are familiar with.

Celebrities are always interesting to draw, and as a rule present fewer problems than most less exalted mortals, although I might qualify this by adding that it does depend on what they are famous for! A famous man of letters or science, for example, is likely to be a very different person than a top tycoon or a political leader.

WRITERS

On the whole, I have found writers to be the most congenial group of people to do portraits of. They are nearest to artists and meet us halfway. Invariably, the task of drawing them is a relatively relaxed and mutually enjoyable experience. I can think of at least

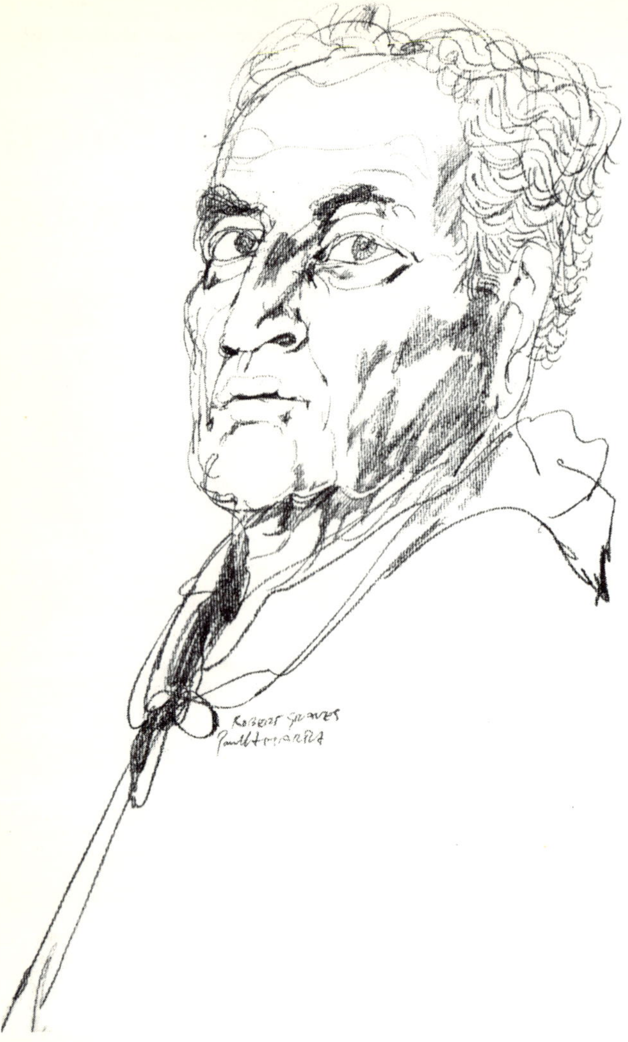

Robert Graves, Deya, Majorca, 1963
The famous poet and essayist gave me a bad time drawing his portrait. The sitting took place during the afternoon, and only that morning a hawk had swooped down and carried off the last of a cherished brood of Abyssinian cats. He was morose and did not respond to requests that he should try on his wide selection of exotic headgear. "Draw me like this, or not at all!" he commanded. The first attempt failed, and what was worse, he noticed that I was getting flustered. I kept on, determined to succeed because he had such a splendid head. Eventually, a second attempt began to materialize into a strongly expressive drawing. But then he did not like it! After our book had appeared, he told me that he did not really mind the portrait but that I should have remembered that some people have a favorite age. "Mine," he said with a twinkle in his eye, "is thirty-five!" Drawn on a 16" x 20½" sheet of Saunders mold-made, cream wove writing paper with a 7B Venus graphite pencil. From Majorca Observed, *1965. Courtesy Cassell and Company, London; and Doubleday and Company, New York. Reproduced by permission of the owner, Desmond Flower, London.*

two of the famous writers I have known—the late Brendan Behan and Robert Graves—who got as much out of the occasion as I did, although it did take a little time for the opportune moment to materialize.

Literary men, as the once famous English book illustrator Edmund Sullivan said, have strange notions of the functions of an artist. A famous writer reaches a mass audience, an audience no longer so readily available to a graphic artist. This, Sullivan added, often makes for an attitude of superiority.

Brendan Behan, on the other hand, was surprisingly modest; the only thing he would have against an artist, he once said, would be if he were illiterate or teetotal. He did not care if an artist were abstract or realist! I qualified as an imbibing realist on both our books, on Ireland and New York. I did not, however, draw his portrait until we had worked together for some weeks. During this time, it was rather like living backstage Victorian vaudeville in the company of an Irish revolutionary who had turned public relations man for the Emerald Isle. Fierce brows and a shaggy mane gave him a combative charm which demanded that whatever else was attempted, a striking profile study should also be drawn. Finding the time to get it done was, of course, another matter!

As we rushed around Ireland, there were few moments to spare. One day the great man and I *had* to relax and really get to know each other. The day came when our wives—Beatrice Behan and Pat Douthwaite—insisted on a break of a week at the Behans' seaside cottage in Connemara.

Early one morning, the local fishermen delivered two huge lobsters—which we spent the rest of the afternoon eating. During this glorious feast, washed down with champagne, the moments to act presented themselves like time signals on the radio. I started a full-face portrait, but somehow it was not quite right. Again, I watched the mobility and humor of his face while we all sat waiting for another breathless line. Brendan stood up and gazed pensively at the turbulent Atlantic through a French window. I had already begun my profile, when he gasped, "Jesus, I love most things, except wimmen wid rotten teeth!"

After I had finished, Brendan walked over and stood behind my back for a few moments and solemnly viewed the portrait. "Time marches on," he chortled, "but I suppose I must bloody well look like this!"

The poet Robert Graves was no less friendly. I found him ideal to work with on our book, *Majorca Observed,* because he always knew what would interest me about the life and architecture of the island and advised me where to go and what to draw. But he gave me a bad time drawing his portrait. We had been working together on and off for two years, but I still found him an awe-inspiring figure, difficult to feel at ease with. His extraordinary erudition was used without mercy to trip me up on all sorts of assumptions and generalizations I made on various topics—from George Sand to the British artists he had known during World War One. Even if he did have a magnificent head, reminiscent of the emperors of Imperial Rome, facing this oracle of knowledge became a task I put off to the last possible moment!

When I finally did pull myself together, Graves was morose because a hawk had, that very morning, swooped down on the patio of his house in the mountains of Majorca, and killed the last of a cherished brood of Abyssinian cats.

The portrait sitting was so like drawing a lion in his den that I snapped pencil after pencil through stage fright. The first attempt failed miserably. A second attempt materialized into a strong three-quarter view of the great poet's leonine head. I thought it good, but he at once disagreed! A year later, however, when the book had appeared, I met him at a party in Deya. After talking about other things, he said, with a twinkle in his eye, "I really didn't mind the portrait at all, but you should have remembered my favorite age is thirty-five!"

POLITICAL LEADERS

Political leaders are not so sympathetic, for they seldom let their hair down enough to permit a long close look at their real personalities. Even politicians of principle assume pompous facial expressions which they imagine to be impressive. And those who are without principles are perhaps best caricatured.

DOCTORS AND SCIENTISTS

Doctors and surgeons are the worst sitters. I find them unaccustomed to relaxing naturally. They are too disturbingly aware of the passage of time. I suppose they are not egotistical enough to indulge themselves. Scientists, on the other hand, usually offer a glimpse of human personality in its lowest possible key. By this, I mean they are usually colorless characters. I almost invariably set them as figures in an appropriate background, such as a laboratory or study. They rarely emerge as strongly marked individuals.

PUBLIC FIGURES

Public personalities, because they may be anxious to present a favorable image of themselves, are generally easier to draw. They may be in show business, they may be sports stars or captains of industry, but they all like to relax and show off a little. They are usually best drawn in the convivial atmosphere of a typical haunt—a favorite restaurant or club, or in the inner sanctum of a palatial office.

Not all of them are easy prey. One of the most

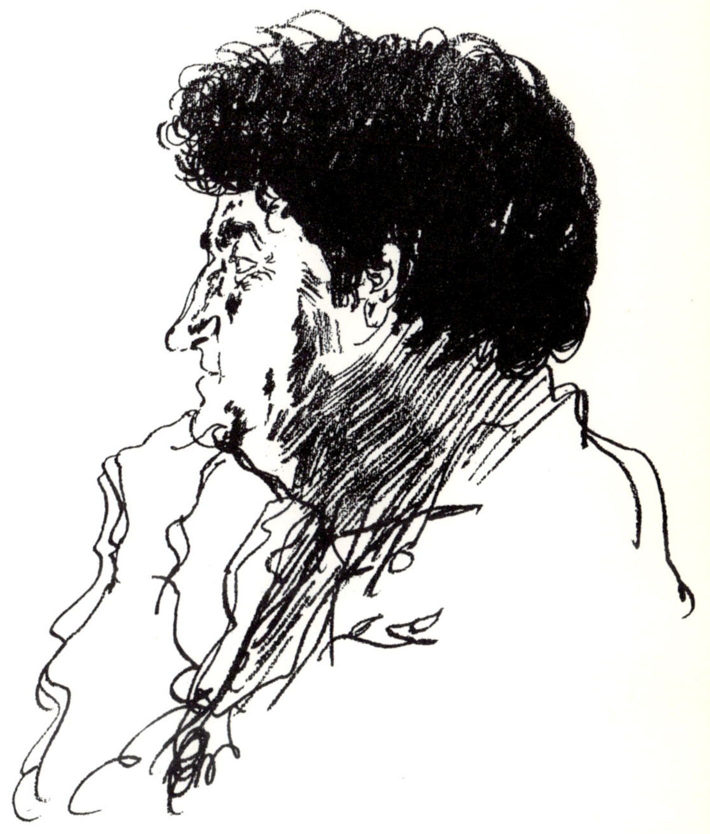

Brendan Behan, Ireland, 1959
My best portrait of the famous Irish playwright was drawn as he gazed pensively at the turbulent Atlantic through the window of his cottage in Connemara. Brendan was not the best of sitters, but the after-effects of our feast of lobsters and champagne calmed his restless spirit—at least for an hour or so. I used a Number 3 Conté Pierre Noir *on a 20" x 25" sheet of Abbey Mill pastel paper. From* Brendan Behan's Island, *1962. Courtesy The Hutchinson Publishing Group, London; and Bernard Geis Associates, New York. Reproduced by special permission of the owner, Professor Donald Egbert, Princeton, N.J.*

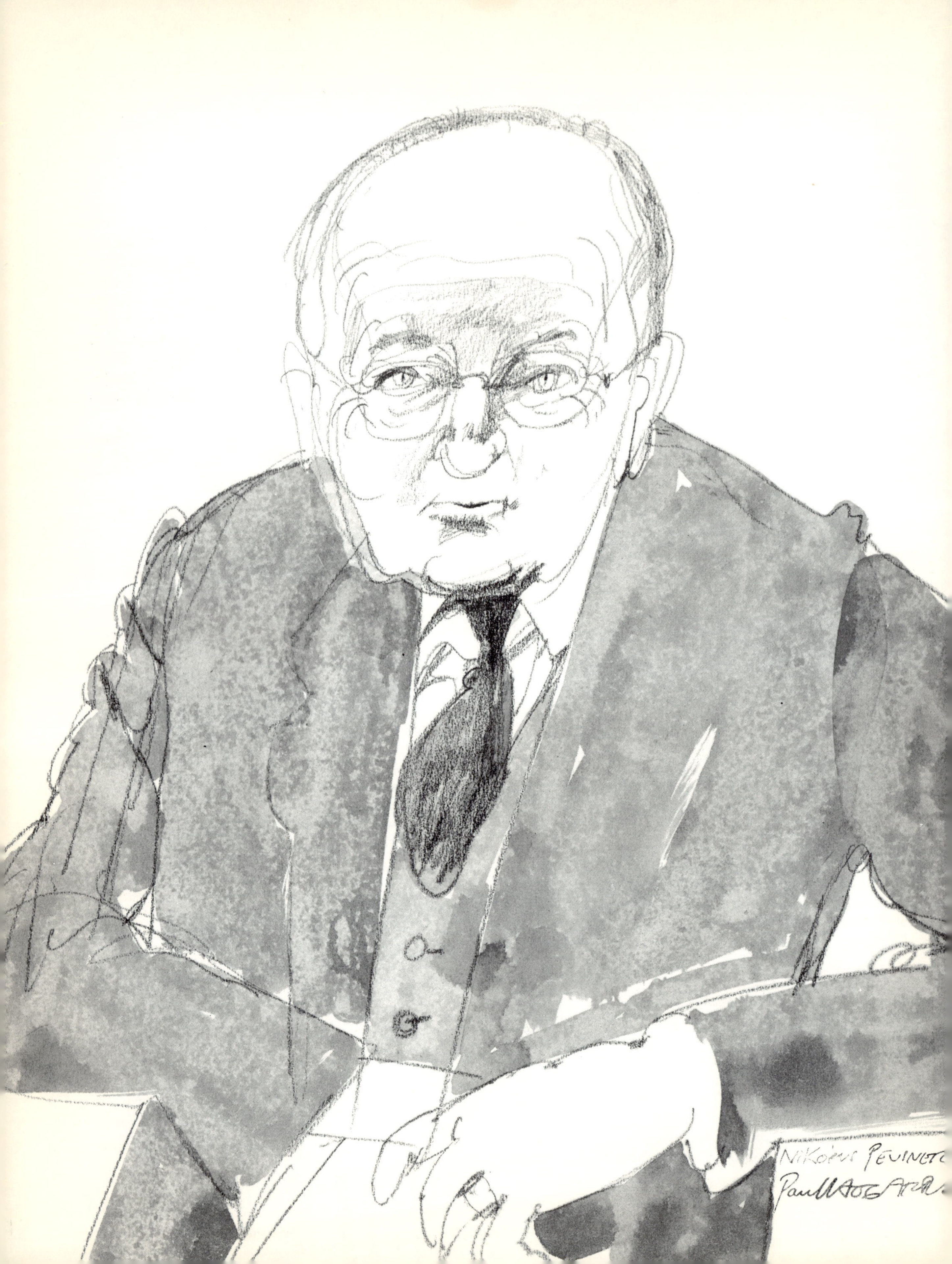
Nikolaus Pevsner
Paul Hogarth

elusive portrait drawings I ever made was a *Fortune* portrait of Giovanni Agnelli, the multi-millionaire chief of Fiat, the biggest automobile maker in Europe. Not yet fifty, Agnelli is Italy's richest man and lives in the style of a Florentine prince of the High Renaissance. He is handsome, urbane, articulate, and has a healthy zest for life. As such, he was a restless and dynamic personality the like of which I had not, until then, encountered. As I looked at him, the portrait rapidly took shape in my head, but getting it drawn was a tough and tricky assignment.

The longest period he remained relaxed was never more than a few minutes, then he would change his posture completely! Face to face with privilege, wealth, and power, I sought frantically in my head for a conversational gambit to save the day from total disaster. Just when all seemed lost, I remembered his interest in modern art, particularly in the British painter Francis Bacon, with whom he frequently played roulette in the big casinos of Europe. His response was so immediate that I realized that he, no less than I, was nervous and anxious to talk. After a discussion on Bacon and drawing portraits, he expressed disappointment that the painter had not turned up for their last appointment at Monte Carlo!

The sitting, which had begun so painfully, ended with Agnelli relaxing for a full half-hour, and I obtained what I feel to be one of my best portrait drawings of an extraordinary man, one of the top tycoons of the century.

KNOW ABOUT YOUR SITTER

Before you face your celebrity, do bear in mind three things. First, know about your sitter. Before you enter his presence, familiarize yourself with his achievements, even if you may not necessarily have an affinity with them. This will help you see him for what he is, and for what he has become. Moreover, if the worst comes to the worst, you can discuss his attitudes!

For the *Fortune* portraits of tycoons, Time-Life's indefatigable researchers thoughtfully provided a run-down, photographs, and biography of each "victim." But as this was usually superficial, I frequently supplemented it with my own material, such as newspaper or magazine profiles, from my own files.

PUTTING YOUR SITTER AT EASE

Second, think of several topics for possible conversations. You do not have to be a conversationalist, but if an opportunity *does* present itself, for example, an awkward silence or a nervous condition on the part of your sitter, introduce your topic to ease such tension. Be short and to the point. Brevity is the soul of wit. Ask intelligent questions only if you are curious. If questioned by your subject, answer in a few words. The object of this exercise is to make him feel relaxed and well respected for what he has done. So cultivate the habit of listening.

Finally, if you do feel like rising to the occasion and paying your sitter a compliment, be sure that such compliments are sincere. *Nothing* sounds more pathetic than insincere flattery.

DRAWING IS COMMUNICATION

Drawing the famous continues to be the biggest challenge to my skill, ingenuity, and imagination. And looking at my portraits of various celebrities—famous writers, actors, bankers, and industrialists—I recall emotions of failure, success, or partial success. Rarely have I felt that I had conveyed more than one aspect of their complex characters. The only thing which comforted me was if someone who knew the sitter made an intelligent comment suggesting that I had indeed caught *something* after all. Failing, perhaps, in the whole-hearted approach to the portrait, I am buoyed by my own conviction that not only have I made an expressive and honest drawing, but also that both the sitter and myself have achieved a measure of articulate personal communication.

Dr. Nikolaus Pevsner, Cambridge, 1968
This portrait of the charming and erudite art historian was drawn before he delivered one of his celebrated Cambridge lectures in the Faculty of Fine Arts. I reacted warmly to the occasion and created—or so I thought—a sympathetic interpretation of his analytical humanism. But the portrait proved to be unacceptable to his friends and family who were, perhaps, looking for something entirely different. It was not, therefore, used for the purpose it was commissioned for: the frontispiece of a Penguin Press library edition of his lectures. Drawn with a Faber 702 sketching and 3B Venus pencils in an 11" x 14" sketchbook of Strathmore Alexis drawing paper. Commissioned by Penguin Books, London. Copyright 1968 by Paul Hogarth.

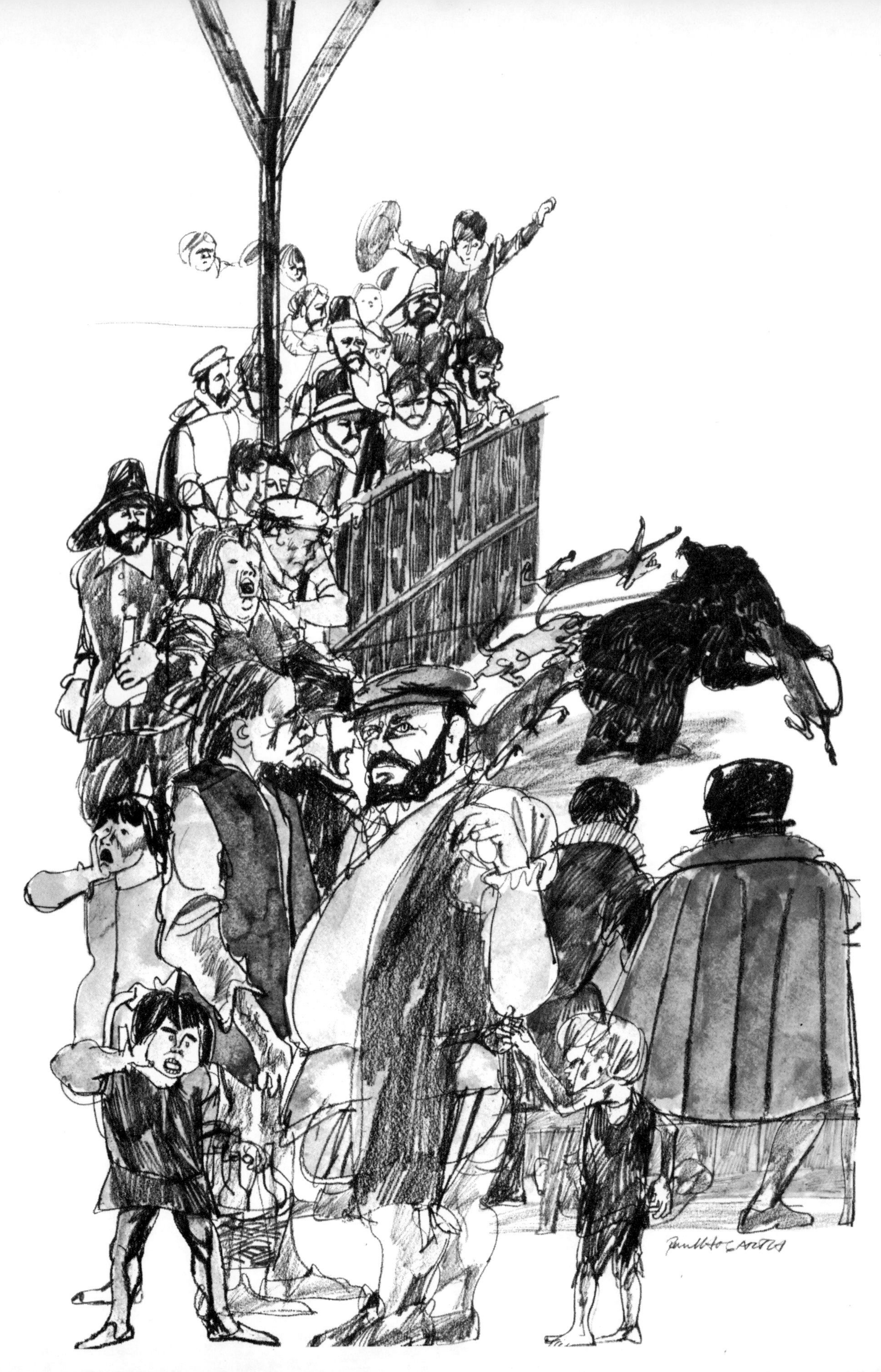

CHAPTER 18

People in Illustration

HAVING TALKED at such length about drawing people from life and on location, it seems important that I should also discuss drawing people in illustration. Although, as far as my own work is concerned, they are frequently one and the same thing.

DRAWING FROM MEMORY AND IMAGINATION

From time to time, I find it a pleasure to retreat inside my studio to create people from memory and imagination rather than from life. I look forward with eagerness to such occasions, because all sorts of new discoveries become possible; not only in relation to the drawing of a face, or the composition of a group of figures, but also in the handling of lines, shapes, and colors. My powers of *characterizing* people, of surrounding them with a particular ambiance or atmosphere, also takes a further step forward.

PEOPLE IN HISTORY

Evoking an episode of history for a magazine or educational publication, a human situation for a children's book, even a modest thumbnail drawing for the jacket of a paperback novel, has to have a personal sense of pictorial narrative woven around a single character or group of characters. People seem to me, therefore, to emerge as much from an understanding of a given historical episode or event as much as by how they may really have looked.

Whenever I am given such assignments, I increasingly feel like a translator, amplifying and interpreting famous as well as ordinary people as protagonists in the *social* context of their time. Yet I also see them in as personal and intimate a way as possible.

As an illustrator, my strong sense of history ran a somewhat uneven course until 1964. In that year, I undertook an eight-page portfolio of paintings for a special Shakespeare number of *Life*. This was followed by an extended trip to Istanbul in 1966 to evoke the past glories of twelfth-century Constantinople for *Byzantium* (a volume in the Great Ages of Man series published by Time-Life Books). A more recent example occurred in 1969, when Art Director Germano Facetti, of the British Publishing Corporation, asked me to represent what he defined as the "irrational component"—namely, those vital episodes in the history of mankind which are not covered by the logical artifacts of archaeology.

I was asked to make a large double-page illustration in color for the Carolingian volume of a projected part-work encyclopedia on the history of the world and was given a formidable-looking synopsis prepared by a historian, which informed me that Charlemagne, Emperor of the Holy Roman Empire, was a zealous, reforming spirit who reintroduced writing as a means of recording orders issued by a central authority, and imposed literacy on his noblemen and administrators. Charlemagne, it seems, broke the monopoly of the Church on literacy and established a civil service to administer and render effective imperial power across disorganized territories. My problem was to find an image to summarize this achievement—an "irrational component."

RESEARCHING YOUR SUBJECT

As I read about the period (A.D. 790–890) I became increasingly aware of *who* was trying to do *what,* and *why,* and *who* tried to put a brake on such progress.

Carousing crowds at the bearbaiting, 1964
A magazine illustration in graphite pencil, Caran d'Ache charcoal lead, and soft Hardtmuth charcoal lead, augmented with passages of gouache color and washes of diluted drawing ink. Done on Hollingworth Kent Mill drawing paper. Originally reproduced in Life *by letterpress in color. From the special Shakespeare number of* Life, *April 23, 1964. Copyright by Time, Inc.*

I made a short list of possible subjects, but none seemed to lend themselves to my approach as some everyday aspect covering the introduction of writing. I decided to depict a discussion of an affair of state being recorded by scribes in the palatial context of Charlemagne's palace, which once stood at Aachen (Aix-la-Chapelle), Germany.

Research material was sent to me, photographs of empty, ruined buildings of the period and of costumes and furniture. I supplemented this with a little research of my own, soaking up a drama of momentous decision-making in old Victorian encyclopedias. I set to work, making my preliminary sketches in thumbnail scribbles in a pad of tracing paper with a 6B Venus graphite pencil. Then, with the general idea of the composition in mind, I scaled up the working area to about half up on the reproduced size of 5½" x 16". Using a sheet of tracing paper cut from a 36" roll, I sketched in the composition, starting with the architectural features and the furnishings of the court-chamber, which were, of necessity, based on the few Carolingian examples that exist.

VISUALIZING THE CHARACTERS

Once the setting was complete, the action began increasingly to suggest itself, and it was a short move from the dominating figure of Charlemagne himself, surrounded by his court, to hit upon the idea of having them react in various ways to the discussion. Courtiers of different types were then worked out as individual characters on separate sheets of paper before incorporating them in my working drawing. These ranged from "magnates," or nobles, on whose strong arms Charlemagne's power depended, to cardinals, bishops, and abbots, wary of a king whose reforms might challenge their privileges. There were also officials and bodyguards watchfully concerned with procedure and security. Finally, there were the scribes who dutifully recorded.

My portrayal of Charlemagne himself was based on contemporary records which only described him in general detail. This left me with enough freedom to add some personal touches. He was, apparently, bearded, heavily built, "seven times the length of his own foot," with light-colored hair, and of good bearing. With the help of a mirror to reflect my own bearded face, I made him a forceful and intelligent personality, seated vigorously on his throne with one leg swung over the other, frowning with the effort of listening to a nobleman making a speech.

THE FINAL DRAWING

With the idea and the composition fully worked out, and after having had Facetti's approval to go ahead, it took about six hours to complete the final art. I

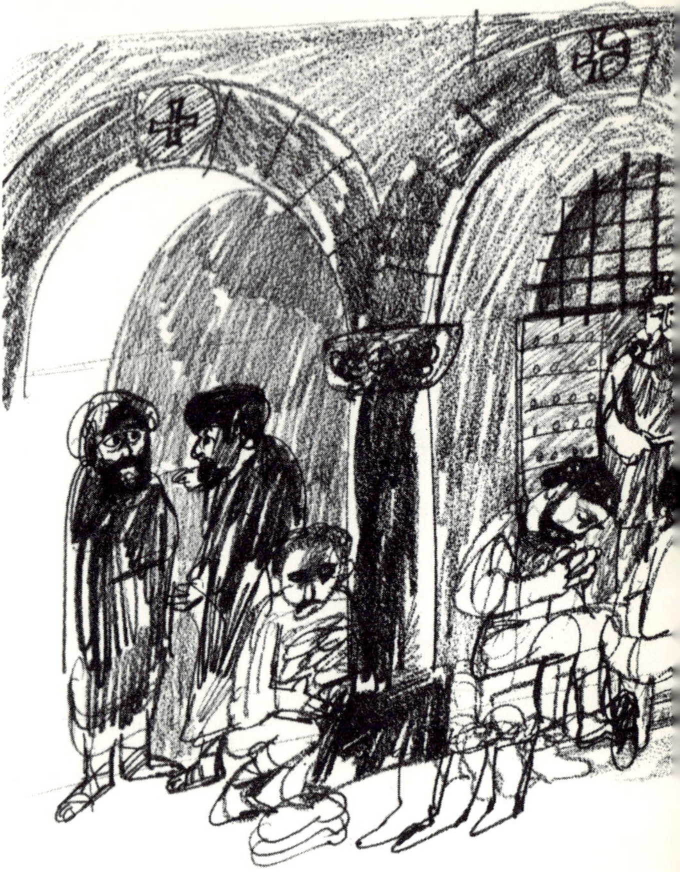

Shoemakers and leatherworkers, 1966
One of a series of historical illustrations depicting everyday life in twelfth-century Constantinople, the capital of Byzantium, for Time-Life Books. These were developed from sketches and drawings made on location, in order to reveal what lay half buried beneath later Turkish and modern buildings. Amazingly enough, a few of Constantinople's ancient streets and arcades assigned to craftsmen still exist, and are in many instances inhabited by members of the same trades. After a morning in the Byzantine Studies Library, to obtain greater authenticity, I decided to draw the whole subject on location, changing only such details as beards and costumes. From Byzantium, *a volume in* The Great Ages of Man *series, Time-Life Books. Courtesy Time, Inc. Copyright 1966 by Time, Inc.*

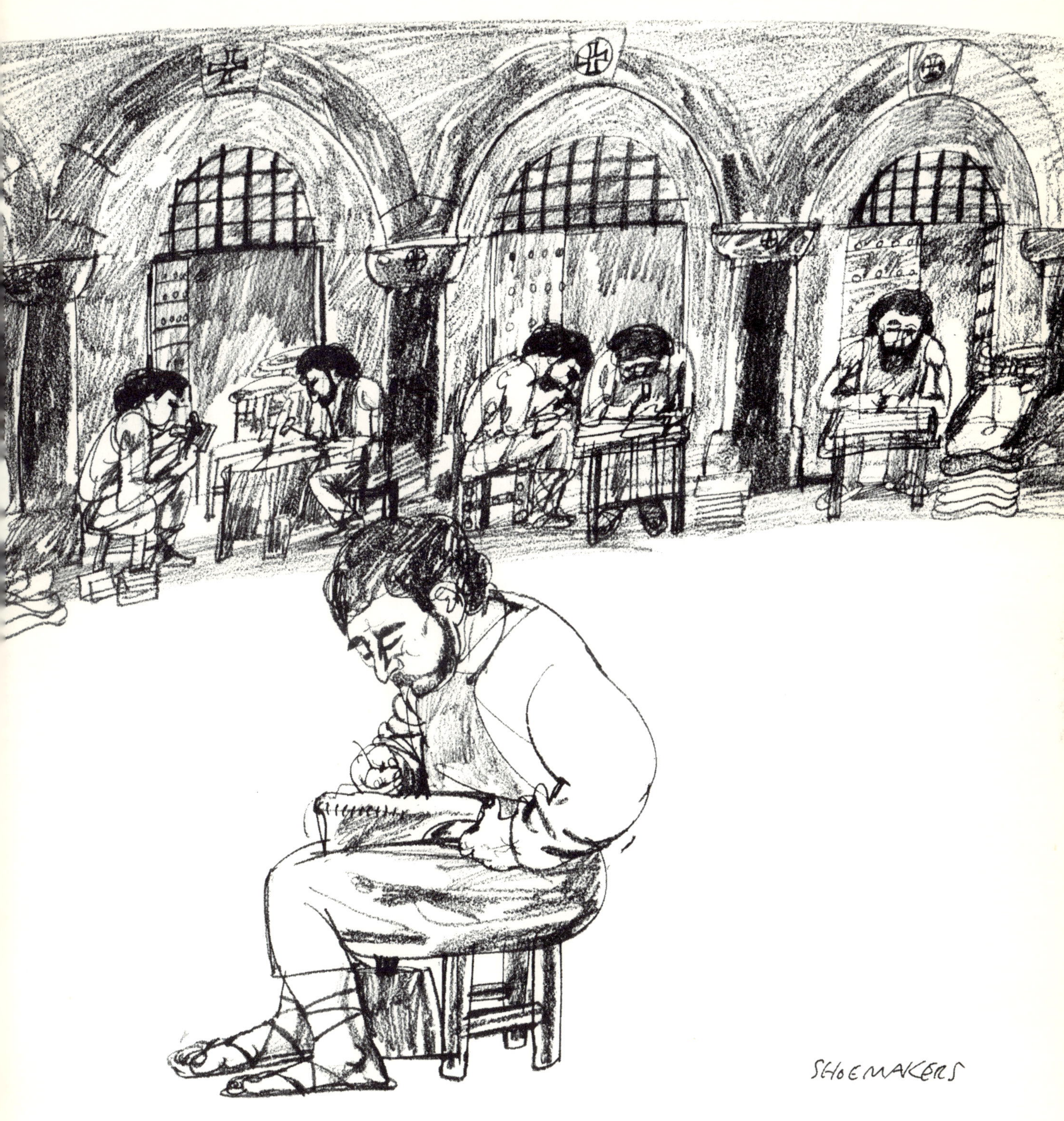
SHOEMAKERS

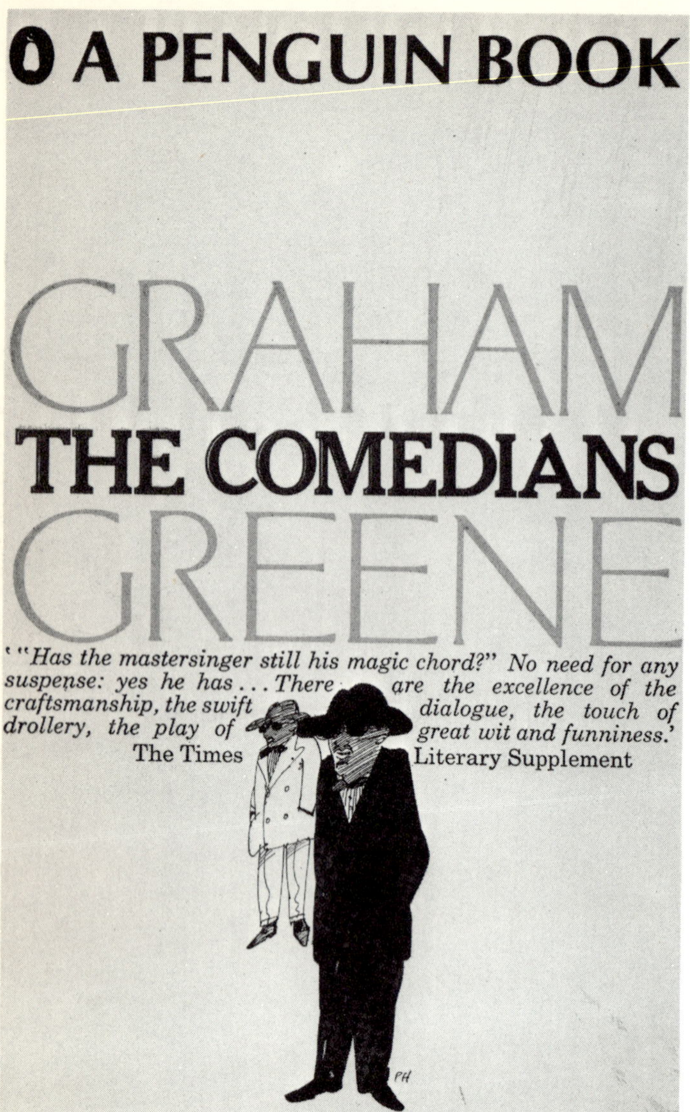

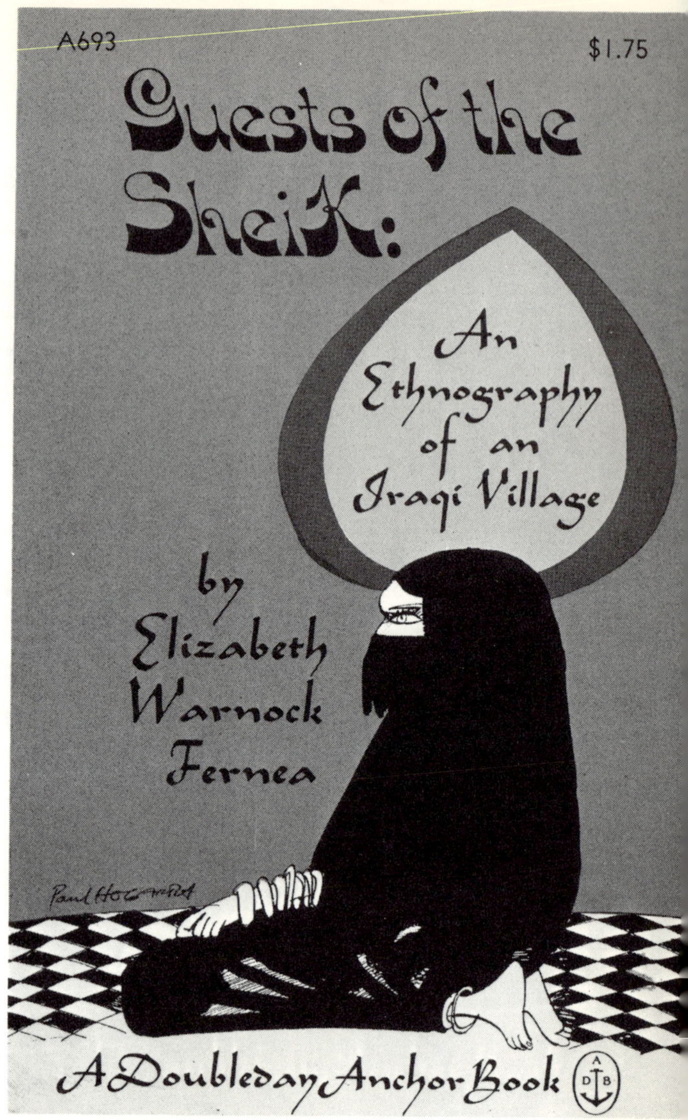

Book jacket illustration, 1967
I have been creating illustrations for various Penguin paperback editions of Graham Greene's bestselling novels since the early 1960's. But this new edition, which gives greater emphasis to author and title, presents a problem of making a small illustration (2½" high when reproduced) bold enough to give the potential reader a flavor of its contents. In this case, I did so by evolving a counterchange of black and white suggested by a pair of Tontons Macoute *(Dictator Duvalier's secret police) who play such a sinister role in the novel. The original, four times up in size, was drawn in Higgins India ink with a Gillot 303 and a Japanese brush. Courtesy Penguin Books, England.*

Another book jacket illustration, 1968
To assist her anthropologist husband in his researches, the author agreed to lead her daily life much as the women of a town in southern Iraq did. This gave me the image of a sharp-eyed don's wife disguised in the black veils and yashmak of a Moslem woman. Drawn in Higgins India ink with a Japanese brush and a Gillot 303 nib. Courtesy Doubleday and Company, New York.

placed the working drawing on a light box, and traced in the main outlines with a B pencil, switching to a heavier Faber 702 sketching pencil to develop the drawing. Washes of watercolor were then laid on to enliven and emphasize the drama of the scene, but kept away from faces and essential lines that might be weakened by tone.

When the washes were dry, more pencil work was added with a Venus 3B. After completing the architectural background, the drawing progressed from Charlemagne, outward to his bodyguard, and then to the group of clerics, officials, and nobles. Finally, after drawing in the two scribes, I worked over the color washes once more, strengthening tone wherever necessary.

If, at this stage, the final illustration somehow lacks the immediacy of the original working sketch, then I scrap the whole thing and re-draw. If I ever have the slightest uneasiness about the finished work, I always re-draw rather than scratch or paint out. The moment an illustration appears labored and tight, it loses both flow and quality.

THE DEMANDS OF LITERARY ILLUSTRATION

Literary illustration in its classical sense was handed down to us by the nineteenth century. Suitable for a different age, it enjoyed a different attitude, when the public accepted the artist's interpretation. The characters of Charles Dickens, and their situations, lent themselves readily to a visual accompaniment, but the problems of the characters in, say, James Joyce's *Ulysses* have to be taken in more by the mind than by the eye.

If the novelist of today cannot create three-dimensional characters which establish themselves visually in the reader's mind, he is bound to fail, even with the help of the best illustrator; if he can, no illustrator is needed.

Yet, while this may be true in an absolute sense, publishers of children's books and adult fiction increasingly make use of the artist as an illustrator, largely because new audiences are being created by the side effects of a visual revolution created by television. Again, as in the nineteenth century, the public responds to the artist's interpretation.

LITERARY STANDARDS AND EDITORIAL TASTES

Situations involving people in the literature of the recent past and the living present invariably compel me to reach out for what amounts to a regiment of characters and personalities who have settled in my subconscious over the years. The difficulty is to relate them in my own way to the author's conception.

Although literary standards and editorial tastes vary enormously from publisher to publisher, few authors, and even fewer art directors, expect over-literal representations of people. Generally speaking, if I am asked to illustrate a children's book, I am expected to give the author's characters the touch of inspired or enchanted reality that will make them irresistible to the reader. Whether this is, in fact, possible depends very much on the book itself. Be advised, therefore, to read the manuscript of a book before committing yourself to accepting an assignment to illustrate it. Otherwise you may find, as I have, that you may experience a mental block in translating someone else's characters into flesh and blood.

PEOPLE IN CHILDREN'S BOOKS

After accepting an assignment to illustrate a book for children, on the basis of an affinity either with the characters or the subject, I carefully re-read the manuscript, visualizing the people concerned from the viewpoint of a child. At the same time, I make notes of what I feel the character may look like. I also scribble thumbnail sketches, which I afterward develop and incorporate into half-up working sketches. Children adore plenty of action and well-defined characterization, so I make sure that plenty does go on, with *movement* and *expression* playing an important part.

PEOPLE IN FICTION

My illustrations of adult fiction—past and present—on the other hand, permit me to depict a much wider range of humanity in heightened yet recognizable settings of crime, intrigue, and war.

Once only to be seen in avant-garde reviews and highbrow magazines, this particular type of literary illustration now flourishes on the jackets of quality paperback editions of every type of modern or classical fiction (and non-fiction). I must add that it has enabled me to make some of my best graphic comments on both people and literature. For if I feel an affinity toward a writer, I evolve characterizations of people without effort. One such writer I have particularly had such a feeling for is Graham Greene, whose novels have stimulated me to make a gallery of imaginative re-creations of his memorable misfits since the early 1960s.

In evolving such characters, I almost experience a catharsis, a purification. At last, I think, after completing such a drawing, I have brought another one of my own repertoire of unfortunates out into the broad light of day!

ORGANIZING A "MORGUE"

Illustration assignments do not always permit me to go out and make location studies, nor may they

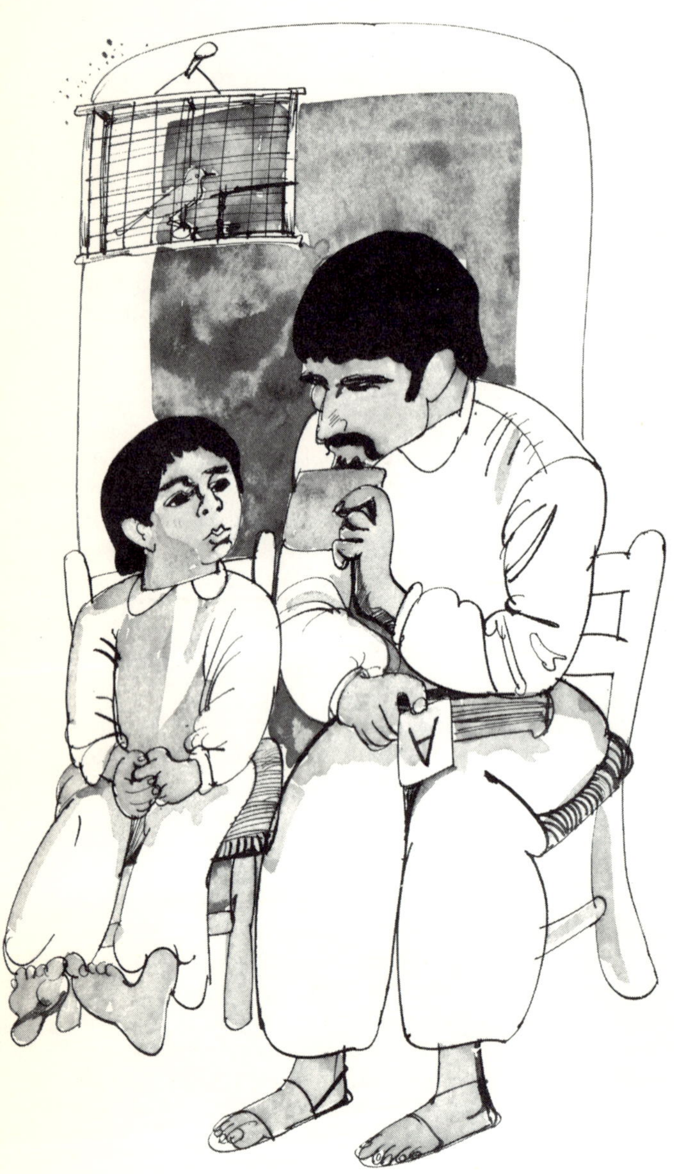

Benito Juarez, as a boy, learns to read, 1969
A drawing in pen and ink wash for a children's book on Mexico's struggle for independence. In this illustration, I focussed on the serious character of the child Juarez, and his close relationship with his guardian, Uncle Bernardino, who taught him to read. Originally reproduced with a second background color. From Out from Under, *by James D. Atwater and Ramon E. Ruiz, 1969. Courtesy Zenith Books, Doubleday and Company, New York.*

justify the services of a professional model. To develop rough memory sketches into working drawings, then final art, I usually go to reproductions and photographs clipped from newspapers and magazines, or to my working library devoted to such essential subjects as historical costume, town and village life, and creatures of the sea, land, and air. On these occasions my "morgue," or library of reference files and reference books, can be indispensable.

Such personal files can be as extensive as you want them to be. Artists are such natural collectors, however, that there is a danger of overdoing it. Once you start, it may be difficult to stop! I used to cut out everything I thought might be useful. Boxes and folders overflowed with an avalanche of clippings, cut weekly from a mounting pile of newspapers and magazines donated by eager friends. My career as an illustrator was in front of me, so I felt sure all would be needed. But when an assignment did come along, I never seemed to have the particular clipping I wanted! I discovered, too, that the more I worked on location, the more I developed the habit of filling notebooks and sketchbooks with sketches and studies of poeple. I seldom found the need to dip into my now enormous collection of clippings.

Nevertheless, a "morgue" often gets me started in that it sparks off an idea. And even when I do not actually use this material, brooding over old paintings and pictorial memorabilia gives me the atmosphere of a given period of history. You may find, as I did, that to restrict your "morgue" to basic material is not only the best solution to a pressing storage problem but also the preservation of your creative independence!

My own "morgue," therefore, is confined to clippings of men, women, and children of every race, color, and creed. Their legs, eyes, hands, and feet; their way of life (past and present); historical figures (political and cultural); and ceremonial and social events. My clippings start with prehistory and continue through each century to the present. They include military uniforms and regalia connected with various religious faiths and professions. I also have a collection of bound volumes of Victorian picture weeklies such as *Illustrated London News, The Graphic,* and *Harpers Weekly,* a good illustrated dictionary like the *Oxford Illustrated Dictionary,* and old popular encyclopedias. All of which are in constant use whenever I am asked to produce illustrations of a historical character.

OTHER REFERENCE SOURCES

If my own sources are insufficient, and they sometimes are, I obtain more detailed references from a commercial picture archive, although I only use these

The Battle of the Alamo, 1969
Here, in this pen and ink wash drawing, emphasis was placed on action. The "baddies" in this case are the Americans! Originally reproduced with a second background color. From Out from Under, *by James D. Atwater and Ramon E. Ruiz, 1969. Courtesy Zenith Books, Doubleday and Company, New York.*

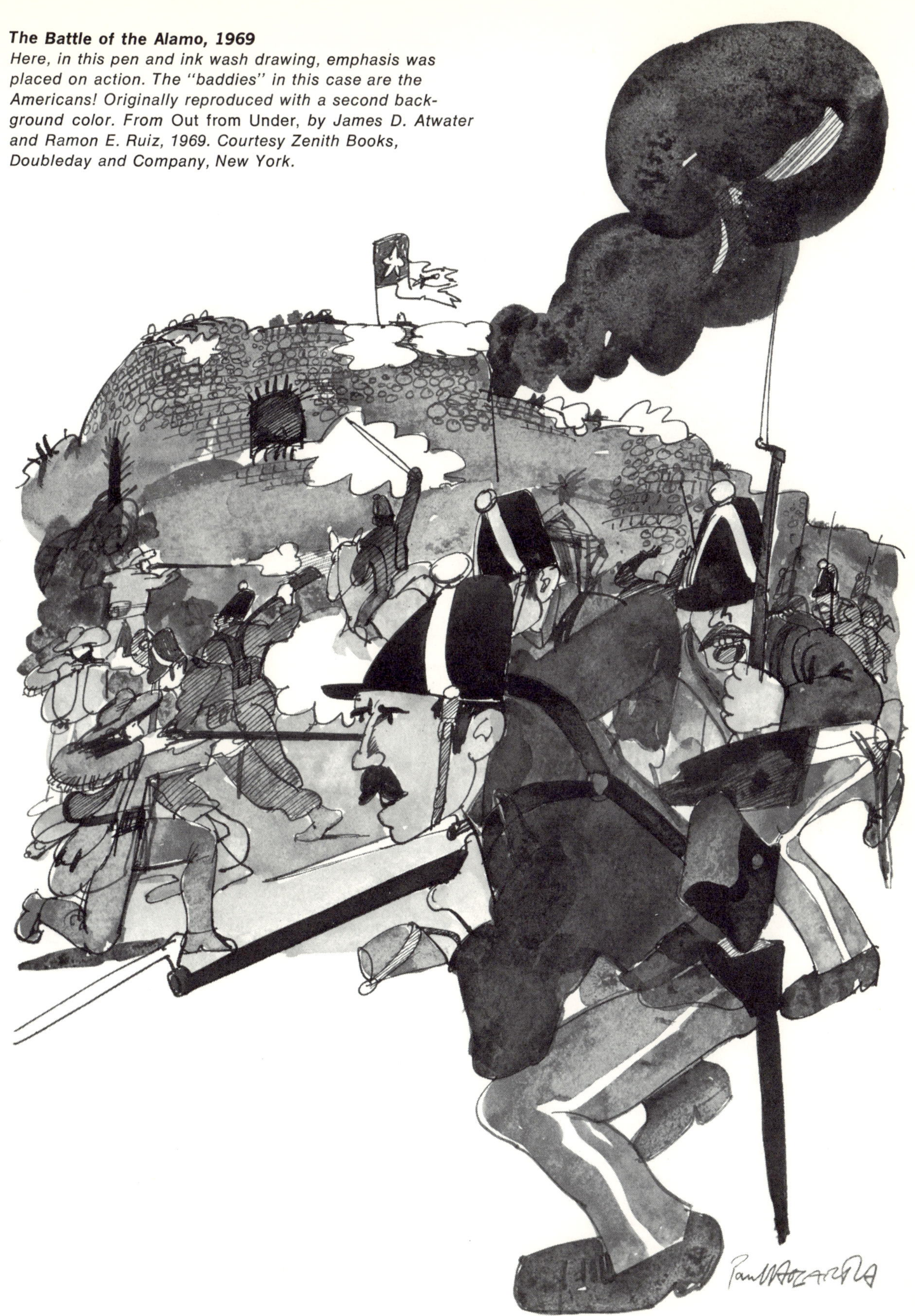

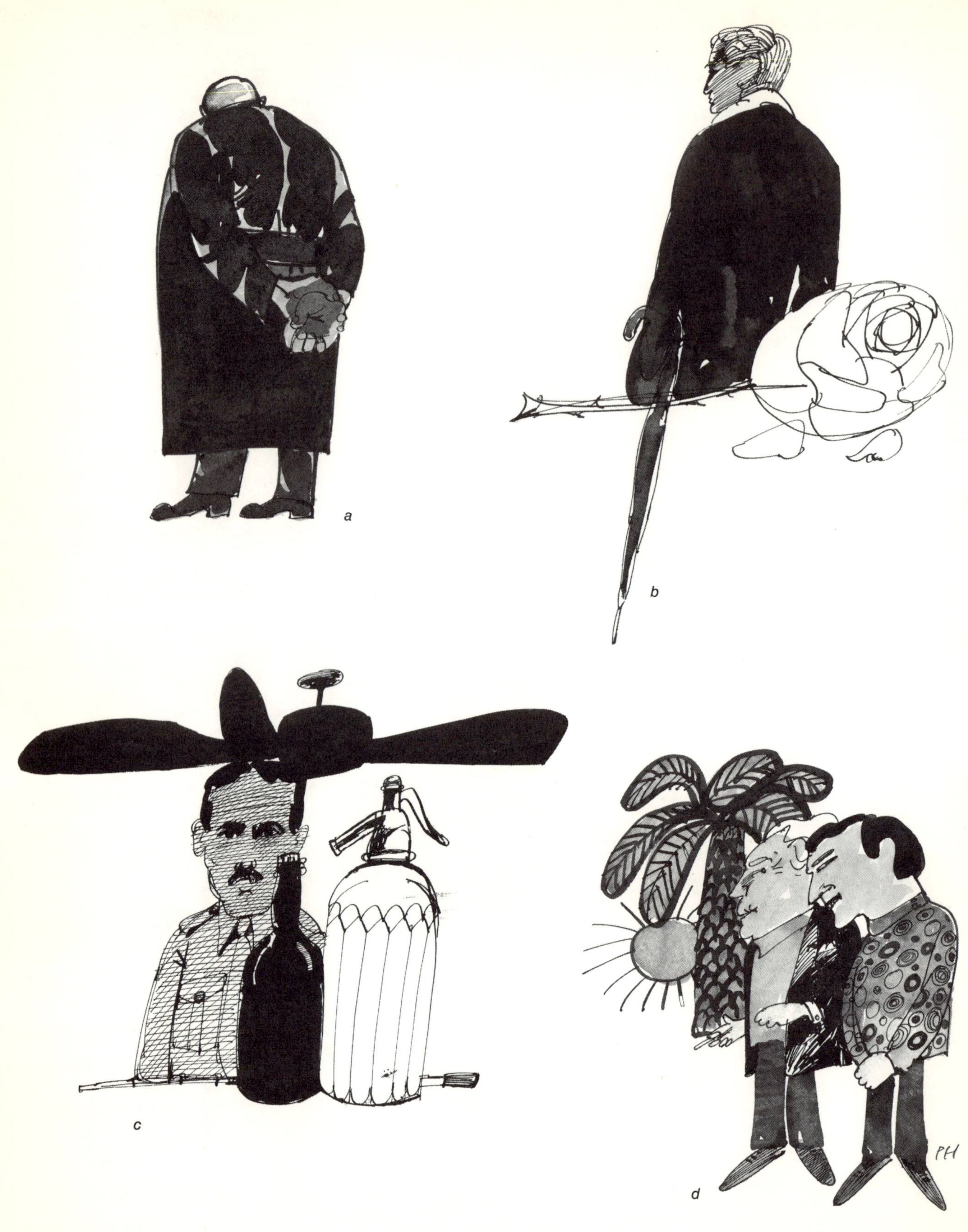
a
b
c
PH
d

if I have to, as their fees can be high. On exceptional occasions, my client may be good enough to provide reference material without charge. Time-Life, in the United States, and the British Publishing Corporation, in Britain, for example, like to make sure that illustrations are accurate in their historical books and partwork encyclopedias. They therefore have a research staff to provide such information for writers and artists working on their behalf. The task of clothing my people in the garb of both past and present is thereby made much less lugubrious and time-consuming.

To sum up. People in illustration demand much more reliance on the memory and the imagination. The characters of a historical essay, a children's story, or a novel for adults, whose acts, features, and gestures are already described in words, require much more than the equivalent in drawing. Here, your imagination must be set to work—on the basis of your own knowledge or of reference material—in order to *heighten* the effect of literature. People in illustration, therefore, should be very much larger than life.

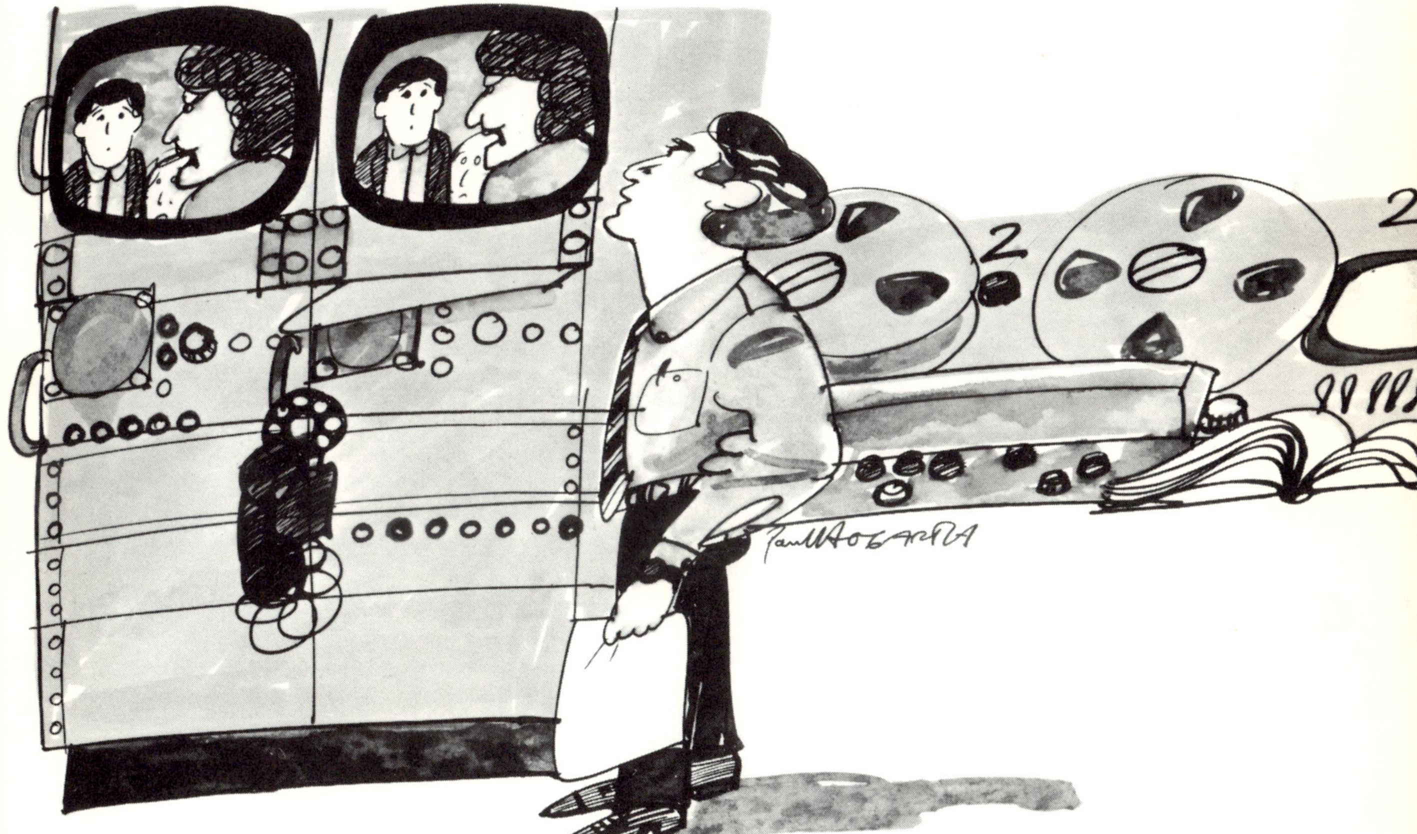

Characters from the novels of Graham Greene, 1966–69
These rough pen and wash ink drawings—except for minor changes—formed the basis for the final versions. They characterize, respectively: (a) the sinister Dr. Forester from the phantasmagoric Ministry of Fear*; (b) Bendrix, the romantic hero-victim of an obsessive love from* The End of the Affair*; (c) Scobie, police officer in a flyblown African colony and fallen angel from* The Heart of the Matter*; (d) Stefan and Tony, two inseparable and amiable social butterflies, from* May We Borrow Your Husband? *Courtesy Penguin Books, England. (Left)*

Magazine illustration, 1968
This illustration was made for an article on closed circuit television in the service of mental health. A technician is pictured recognizing his particular problem in the monitors which show an improvised play about the dictatorial mother opposing her son's wishes to have a girlfriend. Drawn with a vermilion Faber Design Markette and in Higgins India ink with a Spencerian nib and a Japanese brush. From Psychiatric Reporter, *January-February, 1969. Courtesy Smith, Kline and French Laboratories, Philadelphia. (Above)*

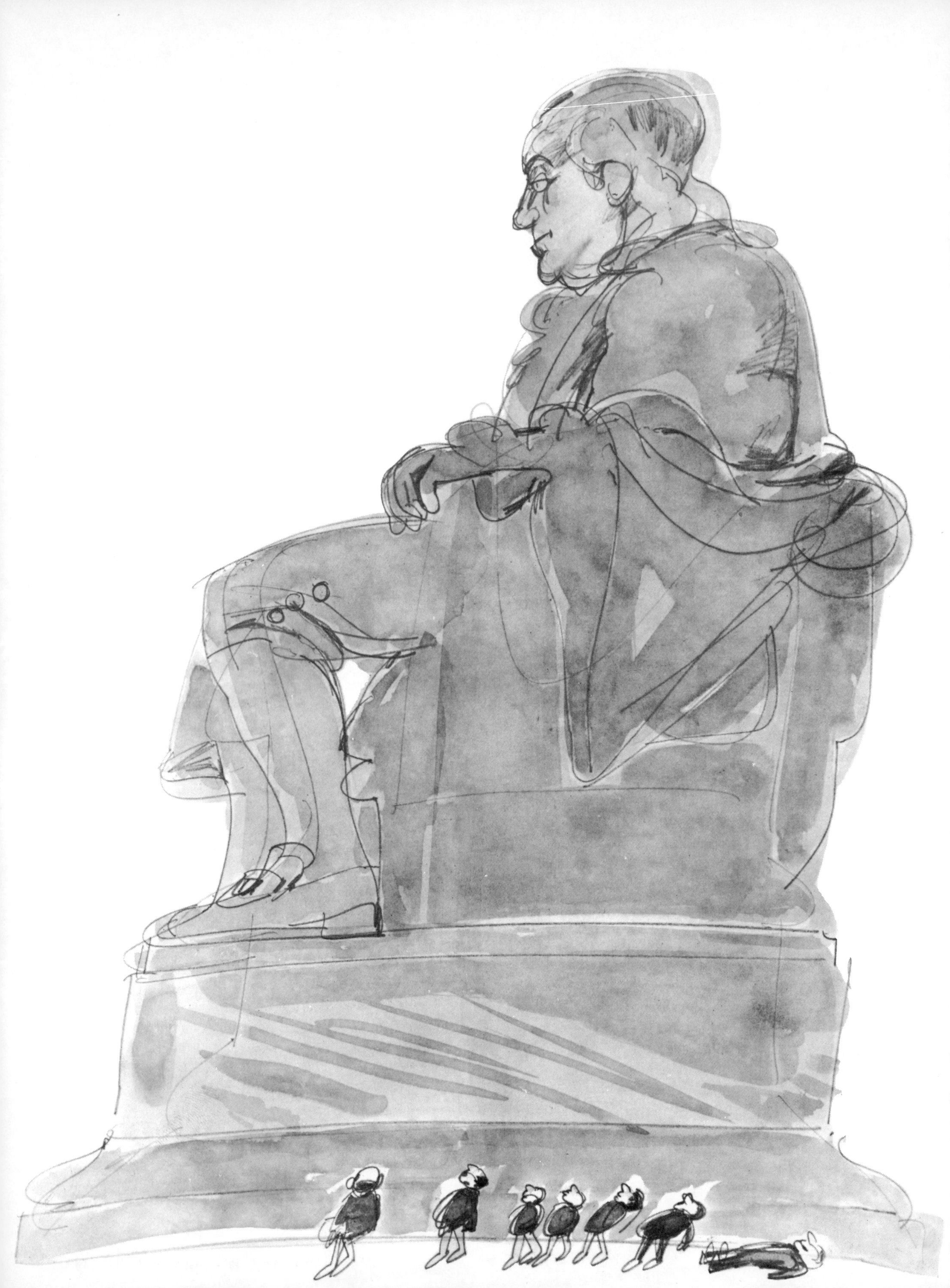

CHAPTER 19

Caricature and Social Comment

IF DRAWING PEOPLE makes you feel like dipping your pen or pencil in the acid of ridicule; if you suddenly feel an urge to castigate the establishment with the biting edge of your wit or to indulge yourself by making humorous comments on life's absurdities, then caricature and other forms of social comment are fields you should certainly turn to.

CARICATURE: WIT OR HUMOR?

Wit and a spirit of fun, or sense of humor, are equally important in caricature. They are often so intimately related that they are found in one and the same artist. The great Daumier, for example, whose political wit made him a force to be reckoned with before censorship stayed his hand, was equally a wit and a humorist, turning to the unconscious theater of everyday life with gregarious enthusiasm.

Wit is largely a matter of words, a caption, a play of the mind, conscious and not involving the emotions. "Nothing succeeds like excess," said Oscar Wilde. This is wit. But for the play on words, the thought could never have been expressed in such a funny way. Wit in art, however, has a more serious purpose. Allied to satire in the form of caricature, or even to "straight" drawing, it can be a formidable weapon.

While wit can be biting and spiteful, orientation and quality shift from one generation to another—particularly in our century, because life has become so increasingly complex. Political idealism, which once gave an immensely crusading edge to political caricature of the 1920s and 1930s, survives only to find the same weapon turned back against itself. Targets are as plentiful as they are varied, as the establishment invariably defends itself against the challenge of new ideas. The older generation ridicules the young; the young, in turn, attack the attitudes of the old; in-groups ridicule out-groups, etc.

Humor, on the other hand, is generally more human and sympathetic. The phrase "to have a sense of humor" means to be able to see one's own absurdities, as well as those in other people. Humor, or seeing the funny side of life, therefore, implies an attitude toward life and ourselves: we can be ridiculous as well as sublime. But again, however hilarious or free-wheeling, humor, like wit, changes with time. A different sense of humor usually appeals to various different social or age groups. The life-style of a suburban housewife or professional man produces a more sophisticated reaction to life's ups and downs and is considerably different from that of a farmer or a miner, for example, who may prefer the broader humor of slapstick or burlesque.

At the Franklin Institute, Philadelphia, 1968
Museums invariably stimulate my sense of fun. Here, there seemed only one image that would sum up my long day in this vast, sedate pile. Appropriately enough, an idea came at the end of my tour around the Institute, which was to have me and everybody else around happily collapse! Drawn with a Faber 702 sketching pencil in an 11" x 14" sketchbook of two-ply, high surface Strathmore drawing paper. Washes of diluted Higgins India ink were added later with a Japanese brush.

HUMOROUS SITUATIONS

Circumstances that are usually guaranteed to make most of us laugh, or at least grin, might be said to include the following: a departure from conventional ways of doing everyday things (like eating with a huge spoon instead of a fork); forbidden breaches of social etiquette or behavior (like belching in public); a placing of a situation in a location in which it does not belong (being drunk in church); the strange, or almost anything, masquerading as something it is not (a man dressed up as a bear, asking for cookies); nonsense (Edward Lear's limericks and rhymes); ridiculous misfortune (someone slipping on a banana skin); ignorance or lack of skill (the stockbroker who gets tangled up in his own ticker-tape); veiled insults (*Wife*: "To you, marriage is just a word." *Husband*: "It's more than a word, it's a sentence.").

Security Guard, J. F. Kennedy Space Center, Cape Kennedy, Florida, 1969
The operatic uniforms of the more specialized "fuzz," or police, make good subjects for both the heavy and the light-hearted brands of caricature. This one was drawn with a 6B Venus pencil and later painted with watercolor, markers, and washes of drawing ink. Courtesy Daily Telegraph Magazine, *London.*

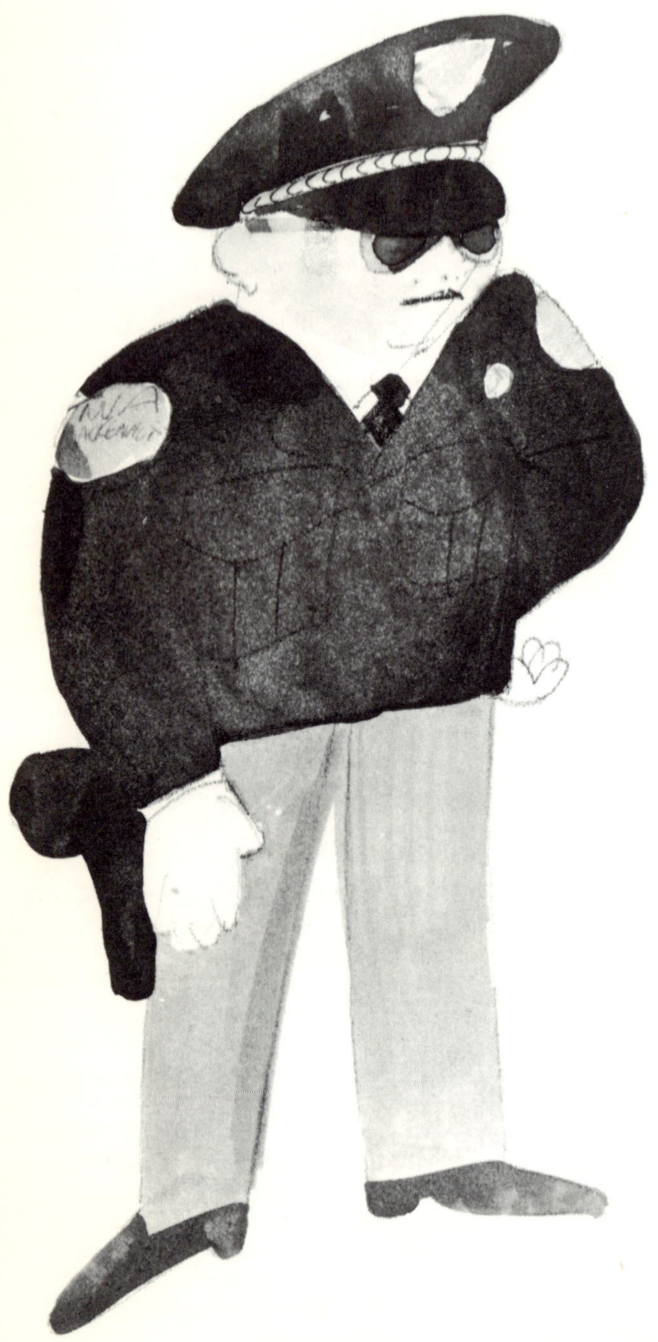

LOOK AT SATIRICAL PUBLICATIONS

I strongly recommend a study of the satirical press of any period, particularly periods to which you yourself may feel oriented. I favor the 1900s because in many ways they resemble the complexity and vitality of today. As today, many young painters and draftsmen were involved, thus reviving a medium that had become dominated by the purely commercial newspaper cartoon.

These are listed in Chapter 9, but it is well worth making special mention of what is perhaps the most unusual—the little known Paris *L'Assiette au Beurre* (1901–14), because it is so full of extraordinary comment on people by a generation of celebrated artists whose careers were afterward to take on a totally different direction. It also illustrates the vital role a great editor can play in caricature.

L'Assiette au Beurre, or, literally, "the butterdish" (graft), is a French term for the source of livelihood of all who seek to further themselves by mainly foul means. It was edited by one Gustave Blanchot, or "Gus Bofa," an indifferent caricaturist but one of the most able editors in the history of pictorial journalism. He made sure that all matters of concern were covered, come what may in the shape of fines, official pressures, or imprisonment.

Bofa recruited his artists on an international scale and classed them as "good" and "not so good." Sometimes a group of three or four artists would be sent out to make a scathing report on the dangers of using the newly opened Paris Métro, while a single artist would be asked to illustrate an entire number devoted to Peeping Toms or men-with-wooden-legs. Special numbers were devoted to what he liked to call "character assassination," in which the lives of monarchs, presidents, generals, and admirals were mercilessly pilloried. Entire numbers were devoted to the exposure of every trade, vice, and racket known to man. These included: alcoholics, esthetes, burglars, bosses, con-men, dressmakers, firemen, fat men, lawyers, lesbians, landlords, men-of-letters, men-with-one-eye, marriage brokers, orphans, priests, pederasts, pickpockets, prostitutes, royalists, republicans, socialists, soldiers, satyrs, tourists, trade-union leaders, widows, widowers, and undertakers.

Many of the artists were strangers to Paris, a fact which seems to support the theory that caricature is essentially the art of the outsider. All observed the city with an insight which only the outsider seems to possess. Many came from less liberal climes of central and eastern Europe and included: Kupka, a pioneer of abstract painting; Van Dongen, the painter of fashionable women of the 1920s; Jacques Villon, Juan Gris; and that lesser known but important satirical draftsman, Miklos Vadasz.

A REVIVAL OF SATIRE

In America today, as in Britain, the *L'Assiette au Beurre* tradition can be seen in the pages of the regular or "above ground" press as well as in those of the "underground." *Esquire, New York, Ramparts,* and *Avant Garde* are of course the leading examples in the United States, as is *Private Eye,* a re-vitalized *Punch, Black Dwarf,* and *Oz* in Britain. But the latest upsurge of satire appearing in West Coast hippy magazines and newspapers promises an even greater display of comic caricature and grotesque satire.

These new journals come and go—but there's one in particular, called *Yellow Dog,* which, although sometimes bad, occasionally offers one or two things in each issue which are extraordinary. For example, R. Crumb's motorcycle maniacs and their girls, drawn with incredible detail. More impressive still are the fantastic drawings by Andy Martin, creator of characters which have to be seen to be believed. His "Hop-Frog, the Lunatic Genius Dwarf" reaches beyond satire to a nightmare world of pure terror.

SOCIAL COMMENT

No matter *how* an artist may draw, or in *what* style, any judgment of people an artist may make can be defined as comment. And if these judgments concern such issues as injustice, poverty, or discrimination, they can be fairly said to be critical of the flaws and abuses of human society.

A desire to see things put right exists in most of us, but particularly among artists. It was the American painter Ben Shahn who rightly said that art can arise from something stronger than stimulation or even inspiration. It can, he added, take fire from something closer to provocation. And as well we know, whatever our personal opinions may be, these provocations are particularly plentiful today. Anyone who is at all thoughtful, and uses his eyes, cannot help but become aware of what is right or wrong in his particular city or country, or even in the world at large.

One of my early drawing trips took me to South Africa in 1956. I became curious about African life, as well as moved by the haunting beauty of the landscape. Out of the experience of drawing people on the farms and in shantytowns, where I unexpectedly came face to face with glaring contrasts between rich whites and poor blacks, came a natural desire to make known my own feelings about such inequalities—and in the sharpest graphic terms I could muster at the time.

Even when I do not make a comment out of such direct experience, a recollection of an event in recent history which may have happened before I was even born will intervene to arouse my feelings and so compel me to make a drawing.

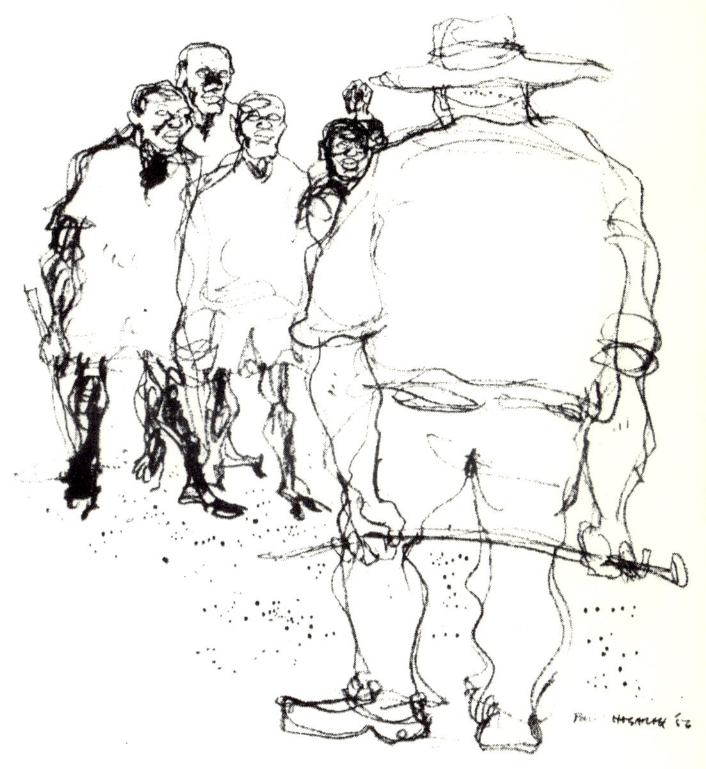

Down on the farm, South Africa, 1956
This sketchbook vignette depicting a white Afrikaans plantation foreman confronting a group of poor Negro laborers was intended as a comment on the potentially explosive state of affairs at the time of my visit. Drawn in a 7" x 10½" English Planet sketchbook of smooth drawing paper with a Number 3 Conté Pierre Noir *charcoal lead. From* Sons of Adam, *1958. Courtesy Thomas Nelson and Company, New York.*

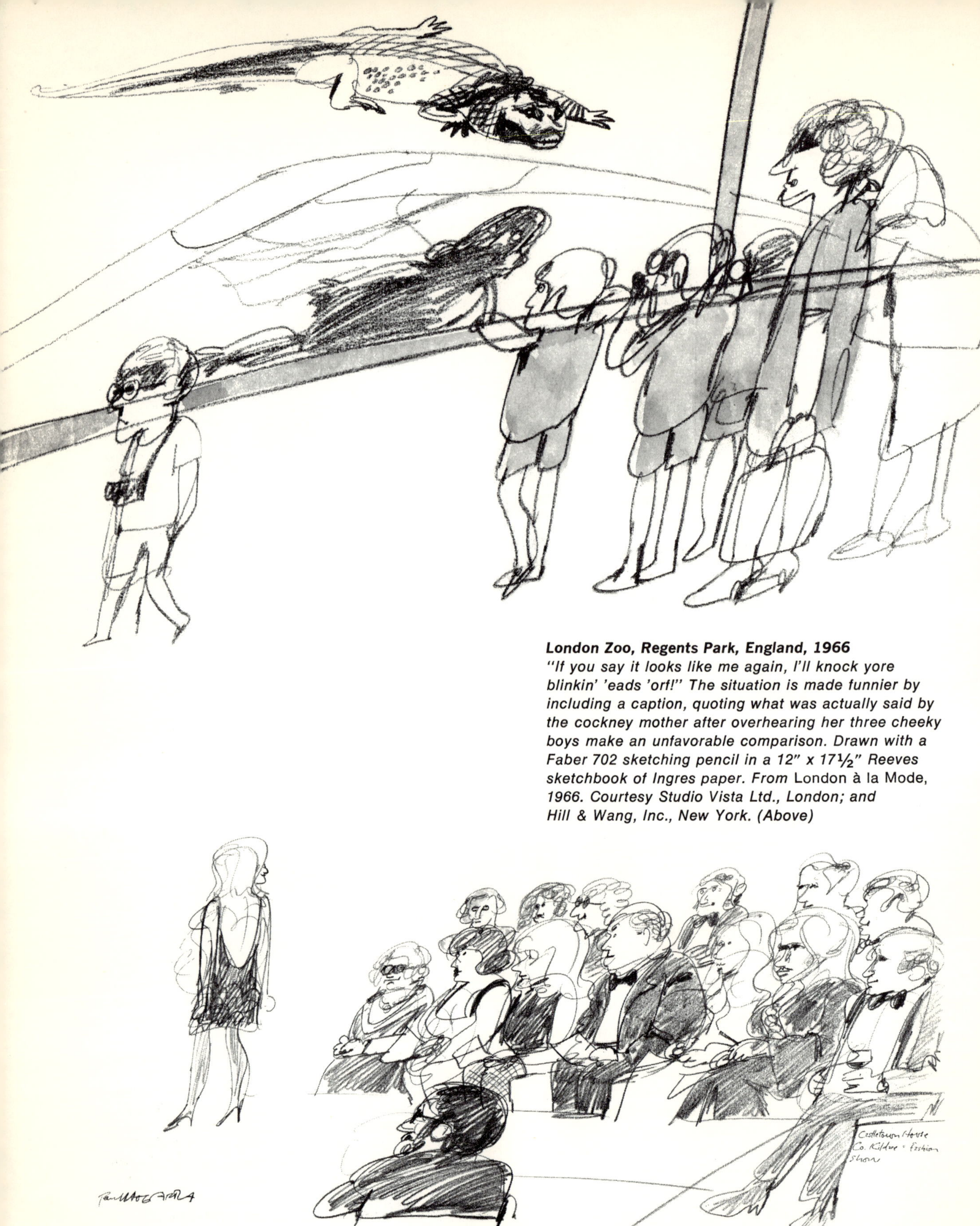

London Zoo, Regents Park, England, 1966
"If you say it looks like me again, I'll knock yore blinkin' 'eads 'orf!" The situation is made funnier by including a caption, quoting what was actually said by the cockney mother after overhearing her three cheeky boys make an unfavorable comparison. Drawn with a Faber 702 sketching pencil in a 12" x 17½" Reeves sketchbook of Ingres paper. From London à la Mode, *1966. Courtesy Studio Vista Ltd., London; and Hill & Wang, Inc., New York. (Above)*

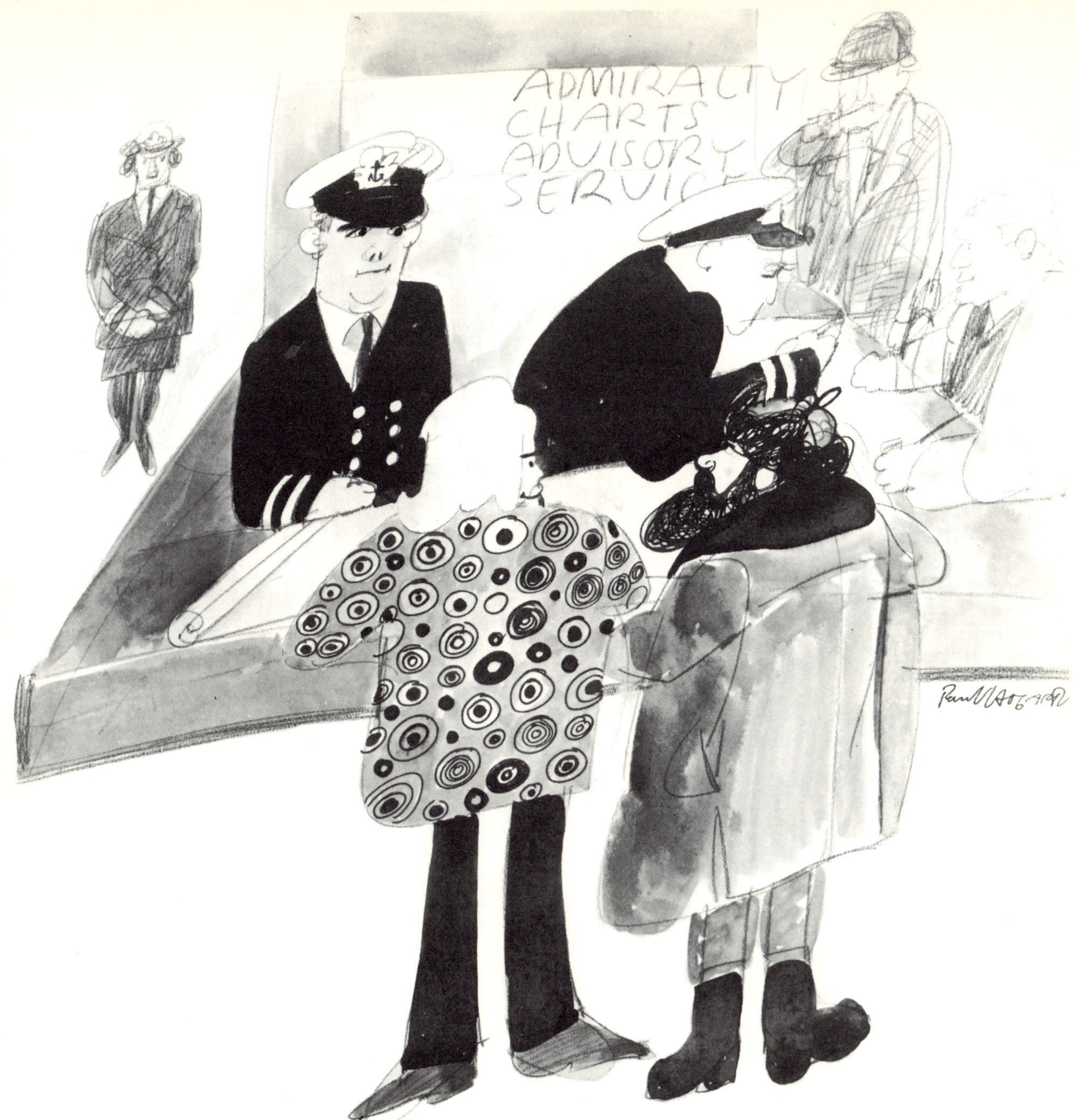

Fashion show at Castletown House, Celbridge, Ireland, 1969
Awareness of the spectrum of humanity is a must for caricature and social satire. This fashion show presented a gallery of characters largely drawn from Irish county society; selected and exaggerated to heighten their individual personalities. From left to right (on the front row) these include: a wealthy widow; the wife and the unmarried daughter of a Dublin businessman; two debutante friends; an aristocrat; and the local bearded doctor. Drawn with a Faber 702 sketching pencil on a double spread of $10\frac{3}{4}$*" x* $14\frac{1}{2}$*" Planet sketchbook of smooth drawing paper. Courtesy* Lithopinion, *Winter 1969. Copyright by Local One, Amalgamated Lithographers of America, New York. (Left)*

The London Boat Show, England, 1968
Watching the impeccable conservatism of the Admiralty Charts Advisory Service and their dignified handling of all kinds of people requesting charts of England's waterways, I was tempted to wonder what their reaction might be if a lone Russian yachtsman asked that he be given 1000 sailing charts of the Thames River for the use of the Moscow Pioneer Sailing Club! Drawn in an 11" x 14" sketchbook of two-ply, high surface Strathmore drawing paper with a 6B Venus pencil, a Gillot 303 pen, and a Japanese brush using Pelikan Fount India ink. Courtesy Sports Illustrated. *(Above)*

Crime in the cities, New York, 1965
The growth of crime in the big cities of America has created a crisis of law enforcement with too few police chasing too much crime. Fortune *asked me to enter the nightmare world of the unfortunate, the misguided, and the corrupt in New York City. For a crowded week in October, 1965, I rode in patrol-cars and with crime-squads, with the somewhat naive hope that perhaps I might be an eye-witness to some spectacular incident. This never happened, but I did fill a sketchbook with many scenes of human pathos which may be fairly described as social comment.*

My drawings were made in the street and in squad-rooms, precinct stations, and night courts. I only took an 11" x 14" Strathmore sketchbook (of Alexis drawing paper), several Faber 702 sketching pencils, and an Esterbrook fountain pen. I had never continuously drawn such subject matter before at first-hand. Yet, doing so, pushed still further the boundaries of my ability to understand as well as to draw people.

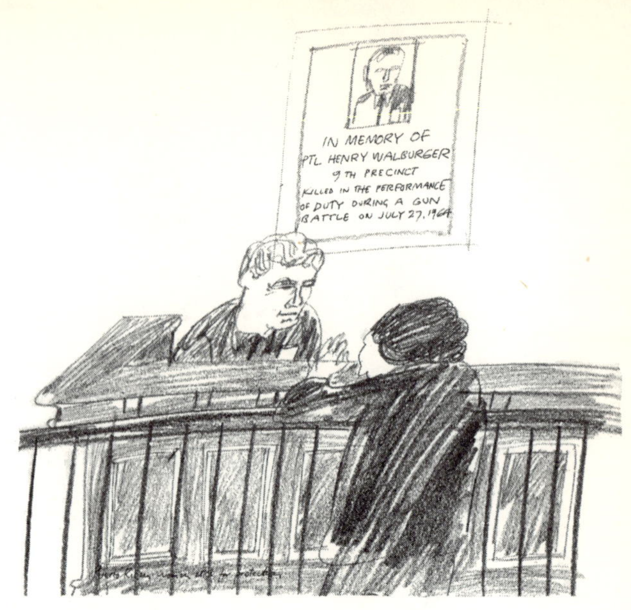

Lower East Side, 9 October
Perhaps the most pathetic scene I saw, which also illustrated the main point of Fortune's *investigation, occurred at the 9th Precinct Station where a terribly distraught Puerto Rican widow, whose apartment had been being broken into, had run to ask the protection of a solitary overworked station officer. "There's no one here to protect you, lady!" he told her. Courtesy* Fortune *magazine. Copyright December, 1965 by Time, Inc.*

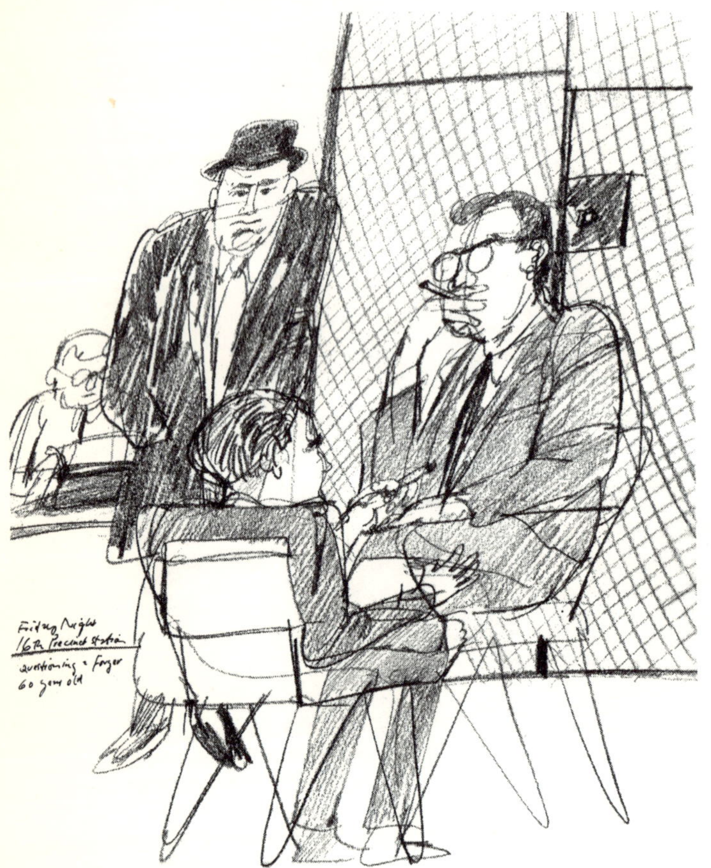

Questioning a sixty-year-old forger
On other days and nights I sat around waiting for subjects such as this one at the 16th Precinct Station. Detectives had just brought in an elderly ex-con with a face like George Raft. He had been arrested for signing stolen travelers' checks and would now spend the rest of his life in jail. Courtesy Fortune *magazine. Copyright December, 1965 by Time, Inc.*

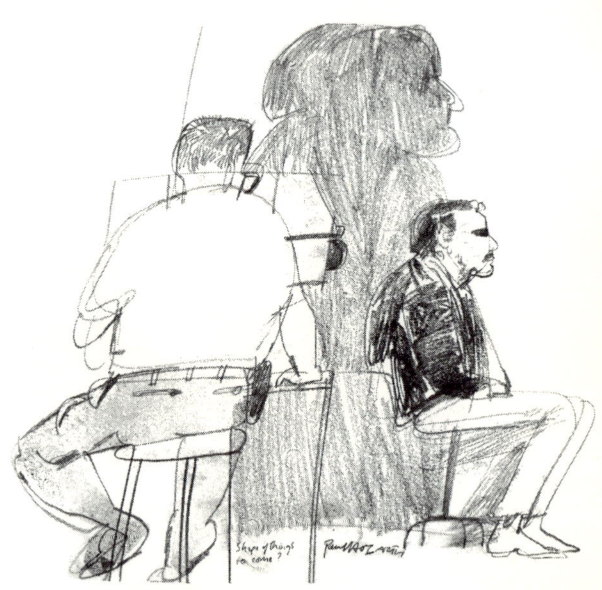

"Mugging" a junkie
I watched overworked specialists grapple with pugnacious Puerto Ricans, white junkies, and deliquent Negro teenagers. I was told that it was "a slow day"—only fifty waiting to be fingerprinted and photographed. Courtesy Fortune *magazine. Copyright December, 1965 by Time, Inc.*

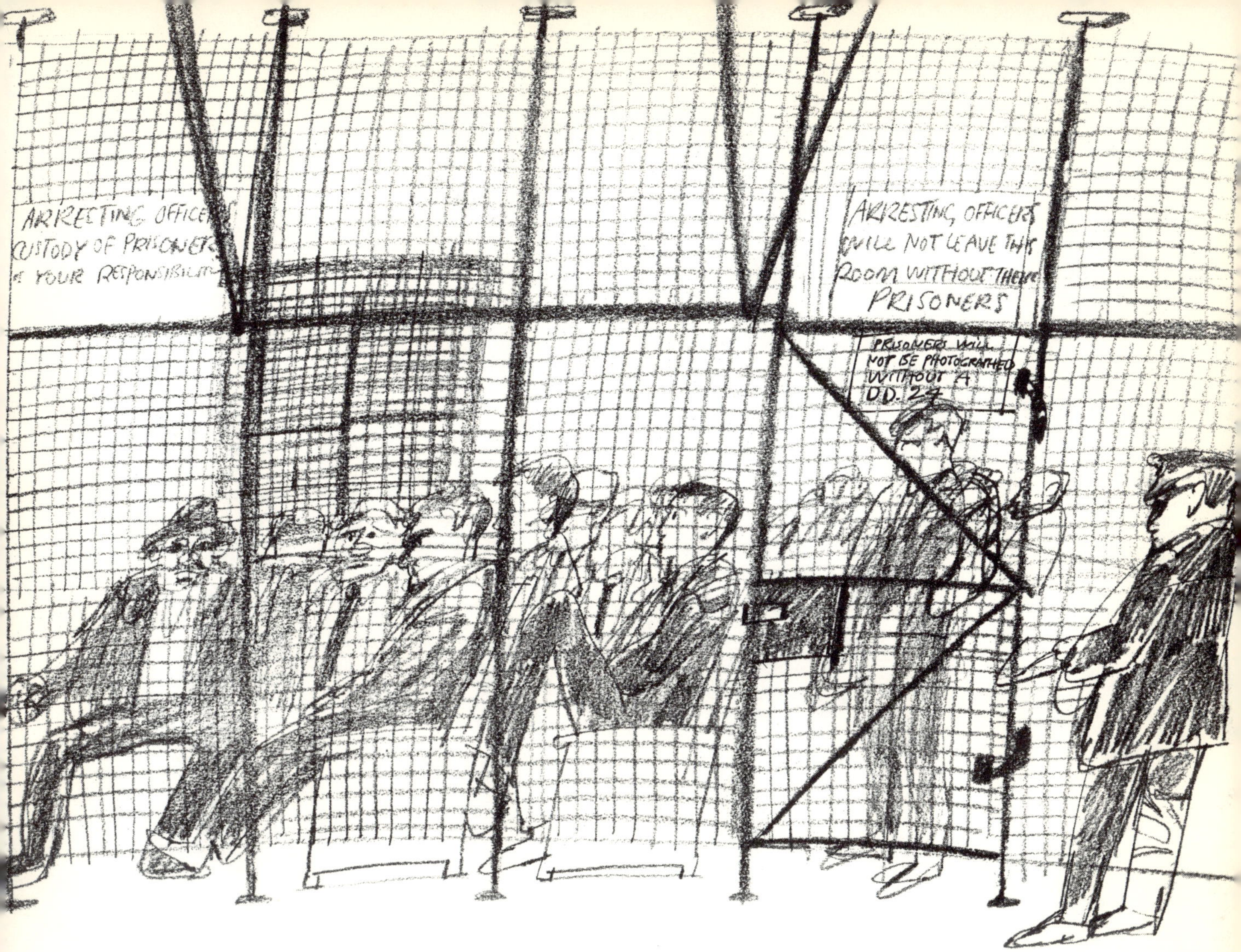

Slow day at Center Street
I started from inside police headquarters at Center Street. Here, every dawn, the "fishnet" is emptied. Courtesy Fortune *magazine. Copyright December, 1965 by Time, Inc. (Above)*

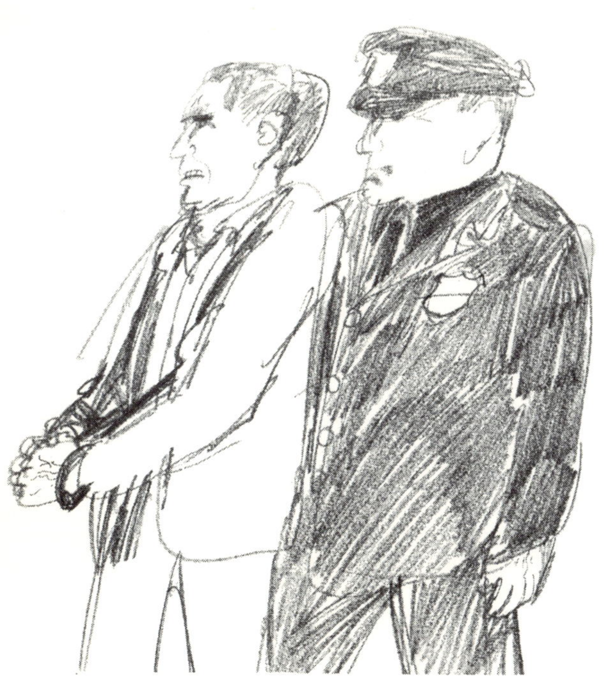

Drunk and disorderly
As I was going downstairs a handcuffed aggressive truck driver was being steered toward a cell. He was booked for being drunk and disorderly in a nearby bar. Courtesy Fortune *magazine. Copyright December, 1965 by Time, Inc. (Left)*

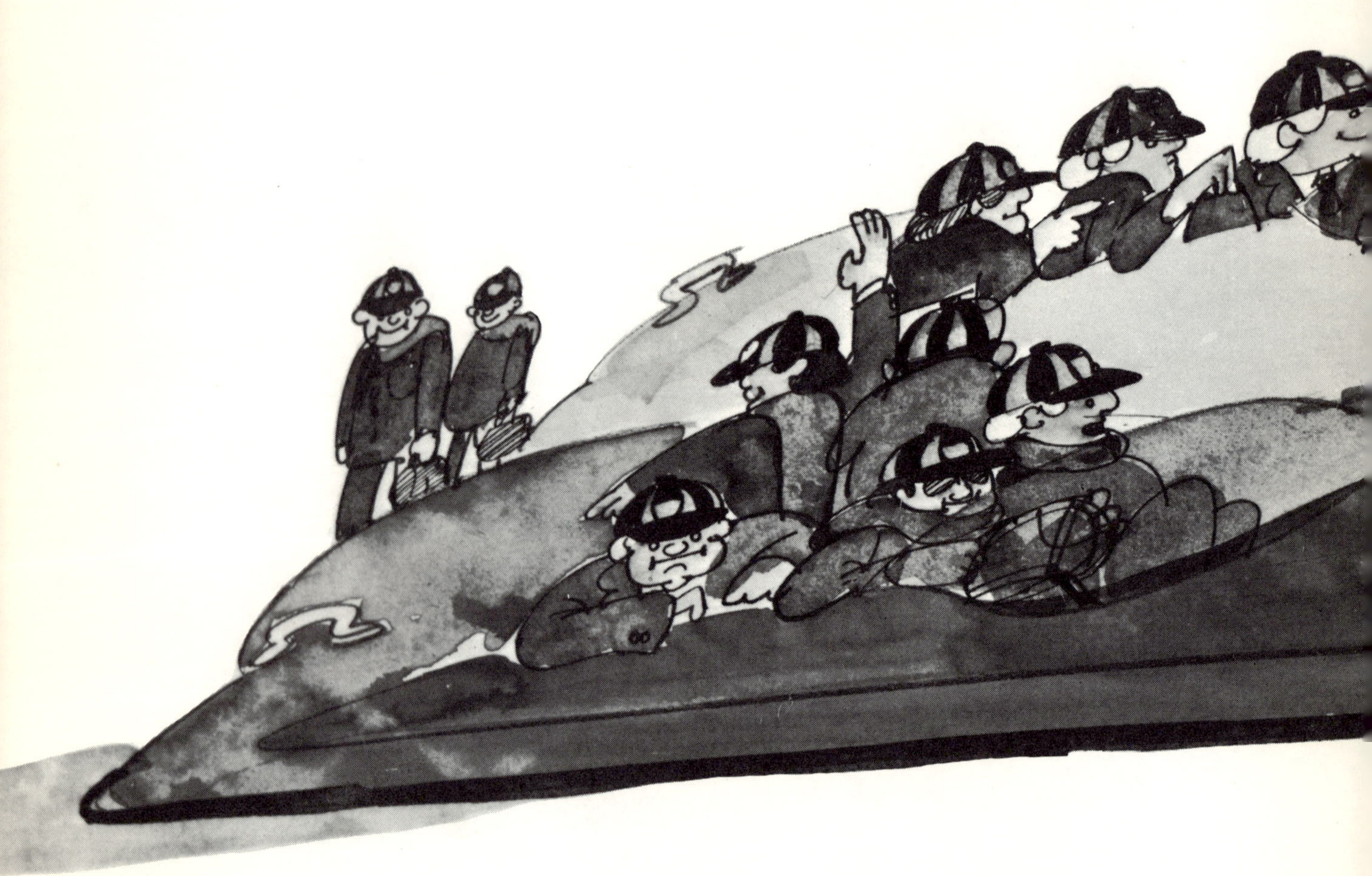

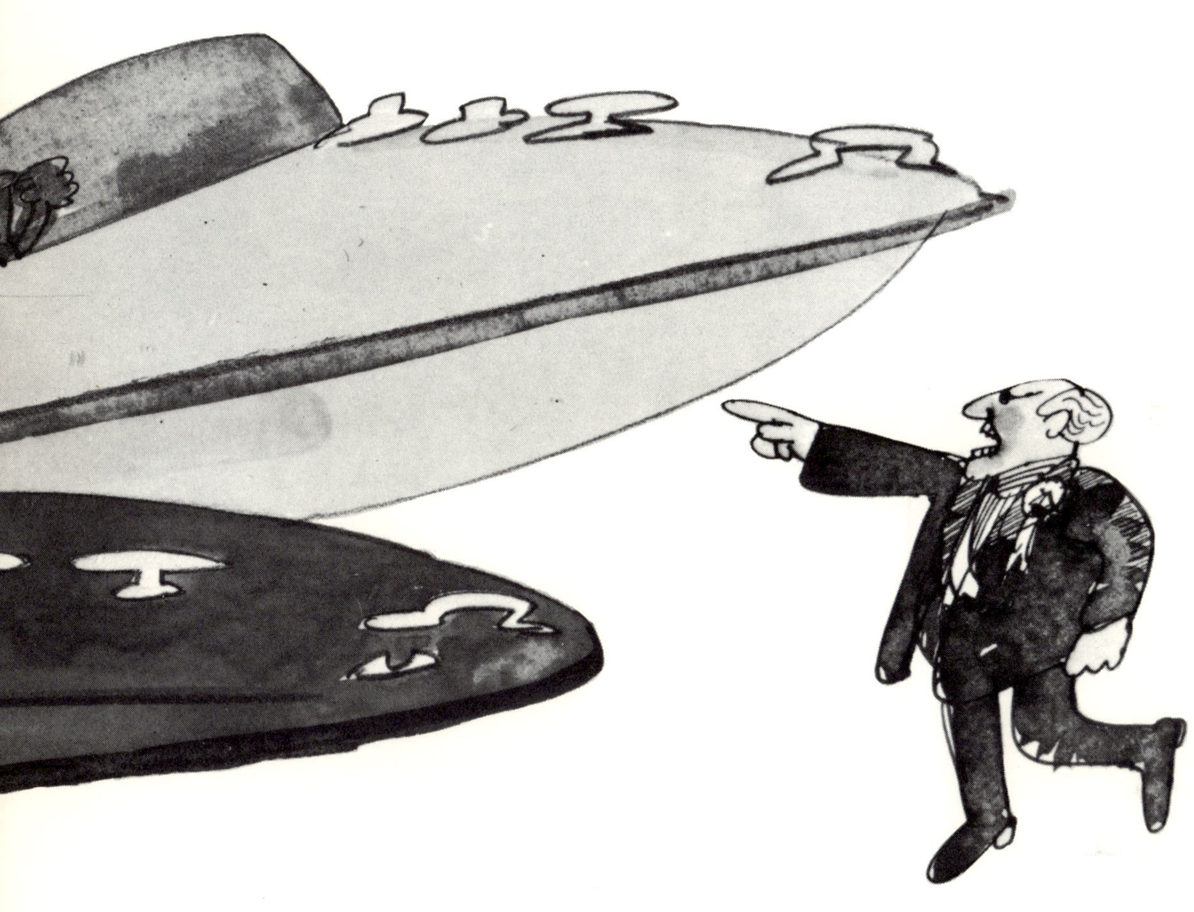

The London Boat Show, England, 1968
Here, a comic scene has been created by exaggerating the gleeful delight of the schoolboys and the reaction of the sales manager. Drawn in pen and wash and markers on Hollingworth Kent Mill drawing paper. Courtesy Sports Illustrated. *Copyright January 6, 1969 by Time, Inc.*

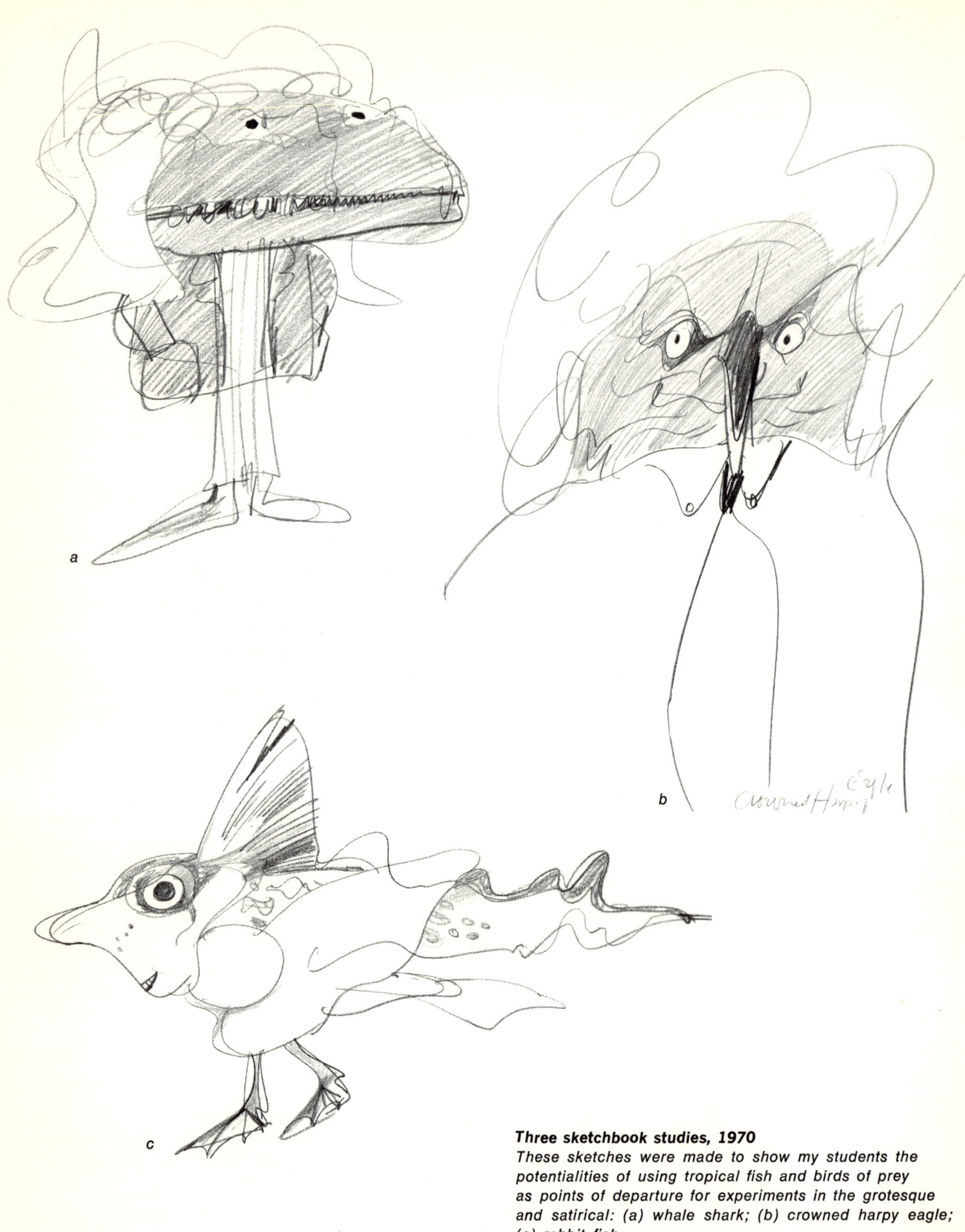

Three sketchbook studies, 1970
These sketches were made to show my students the potentialities of using tropical fish and birds of prey as points of departure for experiments in the grotesque and satirical: (a) whale shark; (b) crowned harpy eagle; (c) rabbit fish.

For example, in 1959 I found myself in the Falls Road district of Belfast in Northern Ireland—the locale of the riots of 1969—and while looking for a likely street scene to draw, I read the slogan "Honor Ireland's Dead—Remember 1916" on the wall of a battered house. Old sympathies for the struggle for Ireland's independence were aroused, and when a sad old widow-like woman in a black shawl tottered by, I thought how like an Irish play of the 1920s it was. On the sidewalk stood the ominous figure of an armed officer of the Royal Ulster Constabulary, eyeing me with mounting suspicion as I took out my sketching pad. A cluster of children sang, and as a solitary nun walked by, I was reminded that here Catholics were a vulnerable minority.

THE IMPORTANCE OF HAVING A SENSE OF HUMOR

Between 1965 and 1966, the humorous side of my temperament began to assert itself. I began to experiment more with making a social comment that was sometimes wit and sometimes humor, that had elements of both the grotesque and the absurd.

Increasingly, I found that my sense of humor helped me find subjects to draw, and that this, in turn, helped relieve my anxieties and tensions, enabling me to tolerate the ups and downs of my own life. And as my own particular sense of humor inclines towards slapstick and the comic, I found myself laughing at plump ladies with large floppy hats, wearing tweeds and clumpy shoes.

Sympathy for people and their absurdities of behavior must have been at the back of my mind when I spent a whole week of mornings wandering around Madame Tussaud's in 1966. The celebrated London Waxwork Museum provided me with some highly entertaining scenes, based mostly on the fear and laughter induced by the distorting mirrors and lifelike effigies of the famous and the infamous. It must have been no common injury which prompted Madame Tussaud to take such terrible revenge!

Starting with the Hall of Mirrors, visitors, in an atmosphere of suppressed giggling, are startled to discover that they are instantly converted into every kind of monster. Downstairs in the darkness of the Chamber of Horrors, open-mouthed lovers, incorrigible schoolboys, and questing girls laugh helplessly at the ghastly crimes of history.

The outcome of these visits resulted in a series of drawings which may be seen in my book, *London à la Mode.* They were good, bad, and indifferent, but I had started a process of converting my own sense of humor into a form of caricature. By distorting figure, movement, and faces to express and heighten the incongruity of such scenes, I discovered that I had given my people a heightened sense of comic character, which in turn communicated itself to others and made them laugh.

Comic and grotesque elements can, therefore, play such an important part that a lively sense of humor (gay, black, or whimsical) becomes the key factor. I would even go as far as to place it ahead of sheer drawing ability, which, after all, *can* be acquired. On the other hand, a sense of humor can often be inhibited merely because you may never have been sparked off to develop a pictorial technique to express it. The following exercise may be a good way to help you find out about your own sense of humor.

LEARNING TO SEE IN TERMS OF CARICATURE

Shortly after my memorable visits to Madame Tussaud's, I decided to devise a series of exercises at the Royal College of Art, with the object of "turning" my students "on" to the potentialities of caricature. I might add that, in doing so, I "turned" myself "on" as well.

One of these exercises has already been described in Chapter 2, but another, based on museum studies as a point of departure, turned out to be even more popular!

I gave the project the title of "The Monsters of the Deep," and we duly assembled in the vast marine life rooms of the British Museum of Natural History, South Kensington. There, surrounded by thousands of stuffed tropical fish of every type, size, and shape, we made sketches as material for a set of five different 16" x 23" image-type figure drawings in full color.

It was left entirely up to each student to see the possibilities and to develop them as he wished. Such extraordinary specimens as angling-fish, giant squids, rabbit-fish, and basking sharks, if seen full-face from the front, could be equated with certain prominent political figures (political satire). More ordinary types on the other hand, such as bookies, barbers, gangsters, and mothers-in-law, would qualify as comic figures (social satire).

Denizens of the tropical deep, therefore, became points of departure for a vast collection of free-wheeling caricatures. But there is no reason why birds, insects, and animals in your local zoo or museum might not also be utilized. My students discovered that the exercise not only tapped their subconscious sense of humor but that they were able to use it to develop a whole new area of fantasy and satire in relation to drawing people. In this way, their ability to draw was related to attitudes they had never, or seldom, brought to the surface. Try it sometime!

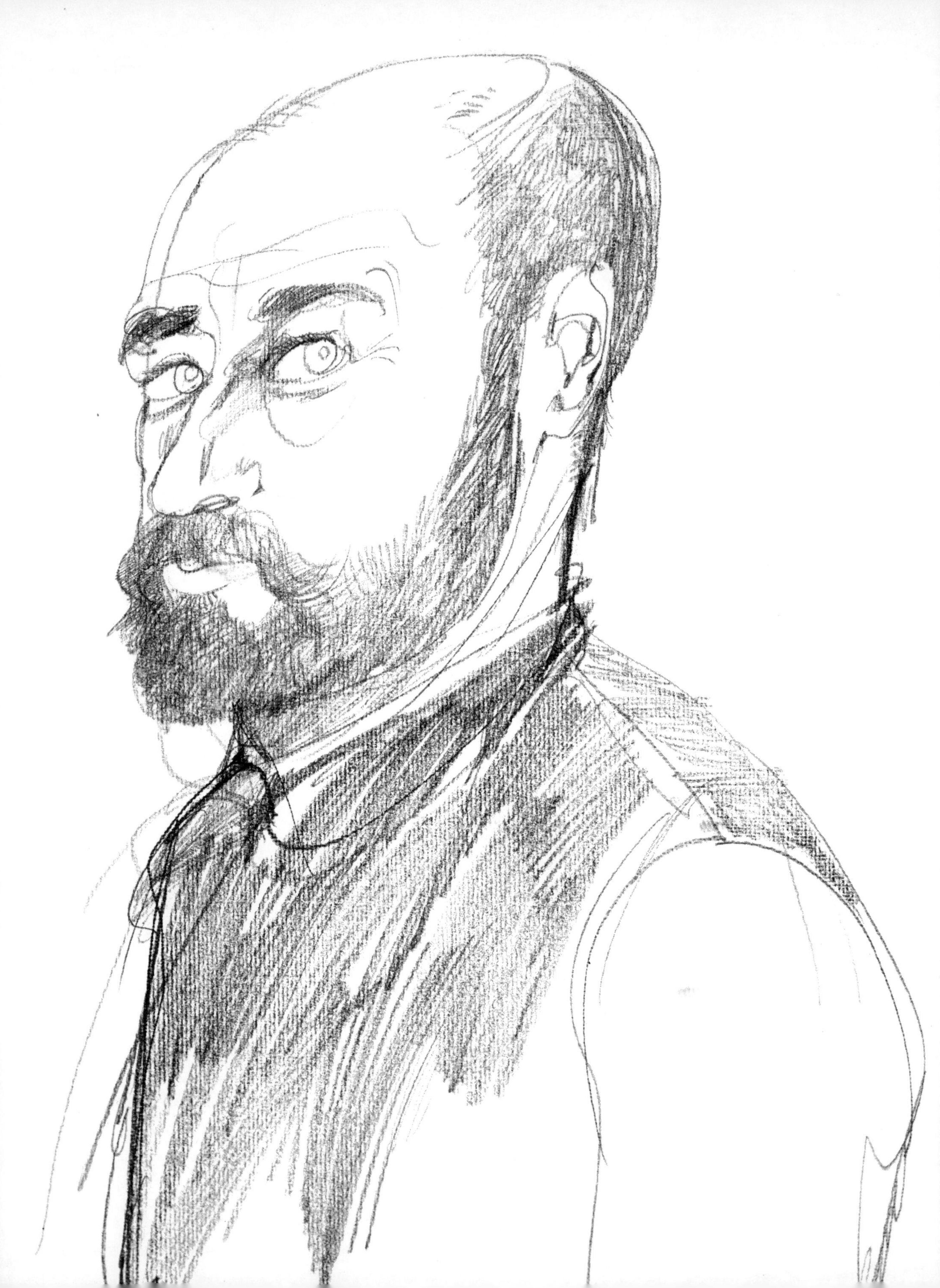

CHAPTER 20

Random Notes

SOME POINTS or techniques which have a useful bearing on drawing people have not been discussed in detail or have been overlooked completely. So they are put together in one convenient place—my final chapter.

KEEP YOURSELF UP TO DATE

Drawing people with *any* degree of sensibility at all depends on a ceaseless quest for ideas and stimuli in the most unlikely places.

Whatever your interest may be—reportage, portraiture, illustration, or caricature—the process of becoming a more *creative* artist largely depends on exercising your own ability to devise ways of feeding your intelligence as well as your imagination. Once you can begin to do so, your awareness of life and people will show a continuing improvement.

Push this awareness forward by cultivating these everyday habits of acquainting yourself with what goes on in the world: read an authoritative daily paper or weekly magazine with a beaver-like curiosity; select television programs, particularly those which involve the interviewing of people or report the life-styles of peoples in far-off foreign lands; when you go to movies, watch the interplay of emotion as registered on the faces of actors; widen both your social and your geographical horizons by getting around to theaters, bars, clubs, and restaurants—and, if you feel so inclined, by travel to places you have never seen before.

You will soon discover that this will not only help you place your understanding of people on a much higher level, but will inevitably give your work a quality of increased authority and style. All you have to decide is how much you really want to be an artist of this type. Motivation, or your ambition, can be the difference between success and failure.

USING A MIRROR

The one model you can absolutely depend on in any emergency is yourself! You will be able to draw and use yourself for every kind of study. I have often used myself in the mirror for figures in a drawing or illustration when working to a deadline on a rush magazine assignment. And, if it is possible, get another mirror of smaller size in addition, so that you can draw three-quarters side and back views by using the mirrors at an angle.

SELF-PORTRAITS

Many of the problems I have discussed in relation to portraiture can be effectively rehearsed by drawing yourself in a mirror. Practice drawing your own head in as many positions and with as many different expressions as possible. Aim at posture and expression, using different sources of both natural and artificial light. Think in large, bold terms to avoid falling into a cramped, self-conscious style.

PORTRAITS FROM PHOTOGRAPHS

Because I personally feel the result can never have the quality of my personal reaction to the sitter, I generally avoid using photographs to draw portraits. Illustration or portrait assignments intended for publication are sometimes the exception, however, because they may be records of actual people, long since gone, and of particular gestures; or, possibly,

Self-portrait, New York, 1964
I often use a mirror to simulate facial expression for use in various illustration assignments. Honesty is essential, although on this occasion, I was drawing myself for the back flap of the jacket for Majorca Observed. *So, naturally, I gave way to temptation and cheated a little! Drawn with 3B Eagle Charco pencil and 3B Venus graphite pencil on a 17″ x 22″ sheet of Strathmore Script drawing paper. From* Majorca Observed, *1965. Courtesy Cassell and Company, London; and Hill & Wang, Inc., New York.*

a last-minute hitch may make a sitter unavailable.

In fact, the latter did happen once on a hastily briefed *Fortune* portrait assignment in the summer of 1966, when it was discovered that at least four out of fourteen important tycoons, whose portraits were essential for an important article, were either on vacation or in the hospital. As I had journeyed from one European capital to another over a period of ten hectic days and had completed most of the assignment, I was reluctant to let my art director down by refusing to work from photographs. I got around the problem in the following way.

After careful study and assessment of the sort of people I imagined they might be, I simulated the actual experience of drawing them by tacking various photographs of the same person—full-face, profile, and three-quarter shots—all over the wall. I then made the drawing directly, just as if the person were actually sitting in front of me. Such significant details as eyes, mouth, and hair were heightened and intensified to produce a new, yet recognizable, image.

One vital point: make sure your client supplies as many *different* shots, revealing various angles, as possible so that you are, as I was, able to use the photograph as a point of departure and not to copy from.

PEOPLE AND BUILDINGS

Often a streetscape or a single building can be a perfect foil and dramatic backdrop for small, yet well-observed drawings of various characters which seem a part of the place. Avoid including anybody and everybody just because they happen to pass by. Select *only* those who will contribute to your picture by either looking pictorially interesting or significant in some comic or mysterious way.

For example, in a large watercolor drawing I once made of the English village of Lavenham, Suffolk, I included several enigmatic Margaret Rutherford-type figures striding along in floppy hats and tweeds with either dogs pulling, or cats following, them. Although I had only seen three such typically English characters, they were much too good to leave out, as they *are* so significantly a feature of English country life. Besides, they also provided a welcome relief to the vast number of medieval buildings I had been drawing.

Avoid drawing such figures in directly, as you may place them in the wrong position; or worse still, spoil an otherwise successful picture! You can always transcribe a sketch made rapidly in a pocket sketchbook into a more detailed drawing and then place it where it looks most effective.

Index

Edited by Margit Malmstrom
Designed by James Craig and Robert Fillie
Set in Nine Point Helvetica by Atlantic Linotype Company, Inc.